HISTO

OF TE

PROTESTANT REFORMATION

IN

ENGLAND AND IRELAND;

SHOWING HOW THAT EVENT HAS IMPOVERISHED THE MAIN BODY OF THE PEOPLE IN THOSE COUNTRIES

IN A SERIES OF LETTERS
ADDRESSED TO ALL SENSIBLE AND JUST ENGLISHMEN

BY WILLIAM COBBETT

Published by the Ex-classics Project, 2009
http://www.exclassics.com
Public Domain

TABLE OF CONTENTS

TREASONS OF CRANMER AND HIS ASSOCIATES,
DEATH OF THE KING.

MARY'S ACCESSION TO THE THRONE.
HER MILD AND BENEVOLENT LAWS.
THE NATION RECONCILED TO THE CHURCH.
THE QUEEN'S GREAT GENEROSITY AND PIETY.
HER MARRIAGE WITH PHILIP.
FOX'S "MARTYRS,"

MARY AT WAR WITH FRANCE.
THE CAPTURE OF CALAIS BY THE FRENCH.
THE DEATH OF QUEEN MARY.
ACCESSION OF QUEEN ELIZABETH.
HER CRUEL AND BLOODY LAWS RELATIVE TO RELIGION.
HER PERFIDY WITH REGARD TO FRANCE.
THE DISGRACE SHE BROUGHT UPON HER GOVERNMENT AND THE
COUNTRY BY THIS PERFIDY.
HER BASE AND PERPETUAL SURRENDER OF CALAIS.

MASSACRE OF SAINT BARTHOLOMEW.
TAIL-PIECE TO IT.
A MAN'S HAND CUT OFF FOR THWARTING BESS IN HER LOVE-SICK FIT.
HER FAVOURITES AND MINISTERS.
HISTORY AND MURDER OF MARY, QUEEN OF SCOTLAND.

BESS'S HYPOCRISY AS TO THE DEATH OF MARY STUART.
SPANISH ARMADA.
POOR-LAWS .
BARBAROUS TREATMENT OF IRELAND.
BESS'S INQUISITION.
HORRID PERSECUTION OF THE CATHOLICS.
THE RACKS AND TORTURES SHE EMPLOYED.
HER DEATH.

ACCESSION OF JAMES I.
HORRID PERSECUTION OF THE CATHOLICS.
GUNPOWDER PLOT.
CHARLES I. QUALIFIED FOR THE RANK OF MARTYR.
"REFORMATION" THE SECOND, OR "THOROUGH GODLY REFORMATION."
CHARLES II. THE PLOTS AND INGRATITUDE OF HIS REIGN.
JAMES II.. HIS ENDEAVOURS TO INTRODUCE GENERAL TOLERATION.
DAWN OF "GLORIOUS" REVOLUTION.

"GLORIOUS" REVOLUTION, OR REFORMATION THE THIRD.
THE DUTCH KING AND HIS DELIVERING ARMY.
THE "CRIMES" OF JAMES II., WITH ELUCIDATIONS.

INTRODUCTION TO THE EX-CLASSICS EDITION.

William Cobbett (1763-1835) had a long and adventurous life as soldier, fugitive, political prisoner, journalist, farmer on Long Island, N.Y., and finally MP. In the course of his life as a writer he started as a Tory supporter (in America) and became a Radical supporter (in England). He was always against the status quo and railed against its many injustices; but though he was regarded as an ally by many who also opposed it he held constant to his own ideas. He never expressed these as a coherent philosophy for to him they were just common sense -- "the politics of every natural man", according to the historian A. J. P. Taylor. Nowadays he would be called a libertarian. Observing the corruption, widespread poverty and institutionalised injustice of England in the early 19th century he advanced his own solution:

- Default on the National Debt (owed to *"swarms of Jews, Quakers, usurers of every description, feeding and fattening on the vitals of the country"*)

- Abolish the Army and the Civil Service (*"placemen and pensioners"*)

- Abolish taxation and run the greatly reduced Government from the personal resources of the King.

- Abolish paper money and substitute gold; abolish the Bank of England, the Stock Exchange and most forms of commercial finance.

And thus the prosperity and happiness of the people would be assured.

In support of these taxi-driver's ideas he set up a newspaper called the *Political Register* in which to publish his articles. His most famous work, *Rural Rides,* was published in it as a series of articles, as also was this book.

The *History of the Protestant Reformation* was published in instalments from 1824 to 1826. At the time the cause of Catholic Emancipation was being hotly debated. Some of the more atrocious parts of the Penal Laws had been repealed, and enforcement of the rest was sporadic and rare, but Catholics were still prevented from being Members of Parliament, owning land, or practising certain professions, and it was still a crime to say or hear Mass or build a Catholic Church. Cobbett threw himself into this cause with characteristic gusto and this book was the result. His take on history is that

> The Reformation was engendered in beastly lust, brought forth in hypocrisy and perfidy, and cherished and fed by plunder, devastation, and by rivers of innocent English and Irish blood.
> (Introduction, Par. 4)

All the current woes of England derived from these events. He contrasts a largely imaginary pre-Reformation land of peace and plenty with the all too real squalor and destitution of the rural poor in the 1820s and declares that Protestantism is the cause of the difference.

The book is written in a most lively and vehement style and is very entertaining; the buzzing of the bees in Cobbett's bonnet is quite wonderful. For example, his belief that the population of England was higher in the Middle Ages than in 1825 was an article of faith with him, and he reserves some of his best abuse for those historians who disagree. He also takes, or pretends to take, at face value the religious motives offered for the Anglo-French wars of the 18th century, which no-one with any sense believed even at the time.

Catholic Emancipation was achieved in 1829. It is unlikely that Cobbett had much influence on the Whig grandees such as Grey and Melbourne who brought it about, but his ideas must have contributed to popular acceptance of the reforms. In 1780 a relaxation of the Penal Laws provoked the Gordon riots in which hundreds were killed and there was huge destruction of property. Nothing of the sort happened in 1829.

Cobbett's ideas found little favour with "respectable" historians then or for long afterwards, though popular with Catholic writers of the Chesterbelloc variety. In fact, Chesterton was a great admirer and wrote a biography of Cobbett. *The Secret People,* one of Chesterton's best-known poems, is very obviously derived from Cobbett. It is interesting, however, to note that one of Cobbett's theses -- that the Reformation in England had little popular support and was the product of a handful of fanatics backed by the awesome power of the Tudor Monarchy and supported by the greed of those who looted the monasteries and Churches -- is now increasingly being accepted by historians. See for example the TV series and book *A History of Britain* by Simon Schama, or the more specialised and detailed account *The Stripping of The Altars* by Eamon Duffy.

INTRODUCTION.

Kensington, 29th November, 1824

MY FRIENDS,

1. WE have recently seen a rescript from the King to the Bishops, the object of which was, to cause them to call upon their Clergy to cause collections of money to be made in the several parishes throughout England, for the purpose of promoting what is called the "*religious education*" of the people. The Bishops, in conveying their instructions, on this subject, to their Clergy, direct them to send the money thus collected to a Mr. JOSHUA WATSON, in London, who, it seems, is the Treasurer of this religious education concern, and who is, or lately was, a wine and spirit dealer, in Mincing-lane, Fenchurch-street. This same Mr. WATSON is also the head man of a society, called the "Society for Promoting *Christian Knowledge.*" The present Bishop of Winchester, in his first charge to the Clergy of his diocese, says, that this society is the "*correct expounder of evangelical truth, and firm supporter of the established Church;*" and he accordingly strongly recommends that the publications put forth by this society be put into the hands of the scholars of those schools, to promote which, the above-mentioned collections were made by royal authority.

2. We shall, further on, have an opportunity of asking what sort of a Clergy this must be, who, while they swallow, in England and Ireland, about eight millions a year, call upon their parishioners for money to be sent to a wine and spirit merchant, that he may cause the children of the country to have a "religious education." But not to stop, at present, for this purpose, pray observe, my friends, that this society for "promoting Christian knowledge" is continually putting forth publications, the object of which is to make the people of England believe that the *Catholic* religion is "*idolatrous* and *damnable*;" and that, of course, the one-third part of the whole of our fellow subjects are idolaters, and are destined to eternal perdition, and that they, of course, ought not to enjoy the same rights that we Protestants enjoy. These calumniators know well, that this same Catholic religion was, for nine hundred years, the only Christian religion known to our forefathers. This is a fact which they cannot disguise from intelligent persons; and, therefore, they, like the Protestant Clergy, are constantly applauding the change which took place about two hundred years ago, and which change goes by the name of the REFORMATION.

3. Before we proceed further, let us clearly understand the meaning of these words: CATHOLIC, PROTESTANT, and REFORMATION. CATHOLIC means universal, and the religion, which takes this epithet, was called *universal*, because all Christian people of every nation acknowledged it to be the only true religion, and because they all acknowledged one and the same head of the Church, and this was the POPE, who, though he generally resided at Rome, was the *head* of the Church in England, in France, in Spain, and, in short, in every part of the world where the Christian religion was professed. But, there came a time, when some nations, or, rather, parts of some nations, cast off the authority of the POPE, and, of course, no longer acknowledged him as the head of the Christian Church. These nations or parts of nations, declared, or protested, against the authority of their former head, and also against the doctrines of that Church, which, until now, had been the only Christian Church. They, therefore, called themselves *Protestors*, or PROTESTANTS; and this is now the appellation

given to all who are not Catholics. As to the word REFORMATION, it means, an alteration for the better; and it would have been hard indeed if the makers of this great alteration could not have contrived to give it a good name,

4. Now, my friends, a fair and honest inquiry will teach us, that this was an alteration greatly for the worse; that the "REFORMATION," as it is called, was engendered in beastly lust, brought forth in hypocrisy and perfidy, and cherished and fed by plunder, devastation, and by rivers of innocent English and Irish blood; and that, as to its more remote consequences, they are, some of them, now before as in that misery, that beggary, that nakedness, that hunger, that everlasting wrangling and spite, which now stare us in the face and stun our ears at every turn, and which the "Reformation" has given us in exchange for the ease and happiness and harmony and Christian charity, enjoyed so abundantly, and for so many ages, by our Catholic forefathers.

5. Were there, for the entering on this inquiry, no motive other than that of a bare love of justice, that motive alone would, I hope, be sufficient with the far greater part of Englishmen. But, besides this abstract motive, there is another of great and pressing practical importance. A full third part of our fellow-subjects are still Catholics; and when we consider, that the principles of the "Reformation" are put forward as the ground for excluding them from their civil rights, and also as the ground for treating them in a manner the most scornful, despiteful and cruel; when we consider, that it is not in human nature for men to endure such treatment, without wishing for, and without seeking, opportunities for taking vengeance; when we consider the present formidable attitude of foreign nations, naturally our foes, and how necessary it is that we should all be cordially united in order to preserve the independence of our country; when we consider, that such union is utterly impossible as long as one-third part of the people are treated as outcasts, because, and only because, they have in spite of two hundred years of persecutions unparalleled, adhered to the religion of their and of our fathers: when we consider these things, that fair and honest inquiry, on which a bare love of justice might well induce us to enter, presses itself upon us as a duty which we owe ourselves, our children, and our country.

6. If you will follow me in this inquiry, I will first show you how this thing called the "Reformation" began; what it arose out of; and then I will show you its progress, how it marched on, plundering, devastating, inflicting torments on the people, and shedding their innocent blood. I will trace it downward through all its stages, until I show you its natural result, in the schemes of Parson MALTHUS, in the OUNDLE PLAN of Lord John Russell's recommending, in the present misery indescribable of the labouring classes in England and Ireland, and in that odious and detestable system, which has made Jews and paper-money makers the real owners of a large part of the estates in this kingdom.

7. But, before I enter on this series of deeds and of consequences, it is necessary to offer you some observations of a more general nature, and calculated to make us doubt, at least, of the truth of what we have heard against the Catholic religion. Our minds have been so completely filled with the abuse of this religion. that, at first, we can hardly bring ourselves to listen to any thing said in defence of it, or, in apology for it. Those whom you will, by-and-by, find in possession of the spoils of the Catholic Church, and, indeed, of those of the Catholic nobles and gentlemen, not forgetting those of the poor; these persons have always had the strongest possible motive for causing the people to be brought up in the belief, that the Catholic religion was, and is, something to inspire us with horror. From our very infancy, on the knees

of our mothers, we have been taught to believe, that to be a Catholic was to be a false, cruel, and bloody wretch; and "popery and slavery" have been rung in our ears, till, whether we looked on the Catholics in their private or their public capacity, we have inevitably come to the conclusion, that they were every thing that was vicious and vile.

8. But you may say, *why* should any body, and particularly our countrymen, take such pains to deceive us? *Why* should they, for so many years take the trouble to write and publish books of all sizes, from big folios down to halfpenny tracts, in order to make us think ill of this Catholic religion? Now, my friends, take an instance in answer to this way. The immense property of the Catholic Church in Ireland, in which, mind, the *poor* had a share, was taken from the Catholics and given to the Protestant Bishops and Parsons. These have never been able to change the religion of the main body of the people of that country; and there these Bishops and Parsons are enjoying the immense revenues without having scarcely any *flocks*. This produces great discontents, makes the country continually in a state of ferment, causes enormous expenses to England, and exposes the whole kingdom to great danger in case of war. Now, if those who enjoy these revenues, and their close connections in this country, had not made us believe, that there was something very bad, wicked and hostile in the Catholic religion, should we not, long ago, have asked *why* they put us to all this expense for keeping that religion down? They never told us, and they never tell us, that this Catholic religion was the only religion known to our own forefathers for nine hundred years. If they had told us this, we should have said, that it could not possibly have been so very bad a religion, and that it would be better to leave the Irish people still to enjoy it; and that, since there were scarcely any Protestant folks, it would be better for us all, if the Church revenues were to go again to the original owners!

9. Ah! my friends! here we have the *real* motive for all the abuse, all the hideous calumnies that have been heaped upon the Catholic religion, and upon all that numerous body of our fellow-subjects who adhere to that ancient faith. When you think of the power of this motive, you will not be surprised at the great and incessant pains that have been taken to deceive us. Even the Scripture itself has been perverted in order to blacken the Catholics. In books of all sizes, and from the pulpit of every church, we have been taught from our infancy, that the "*beast*, the *man of sin*, and the *scarlet whore*," mentioned in the Revelations, were names which God himself had given to the POPE; and we have all been taught to believe of the Catholic Church, that her worship was "*idolatrous*," and that her doctrines were "*damnable*."

10. Now let us put a plain question or two to ourselves, and to these our teachers; and we shall quickly be able to form a just estimate of the *modesty, sincerity*, and *consistency* of these revilers of the Catholic religion. They will not, because they cannot, deny, that this religion was the ONLY CHRISTIAN religion in the world for fifteen hundred years after the death of Christ. They may say, indeed, that for the first three hundred years there was no POPE seated at Rome. But, then, for twelve hundred years there had been; and, during that period, all the nations of Europe, and some part of America, had become Christian, and all acknowledged the POPE as their head in religious matters; and, in short, there was no other Christian Church known in the world, nor had any other ever been thought of. Can we believe, then, that Christ, who died to save sinners, who sent forth his gospel as the means of their salvation, would have suffered a false Christian religion, and no other than a false Christian religion. to be known amongst men all this while? Will these modest assailants of the faith of their and our ancestors assert to our faces, that, for twelve hundred years at least, there

were no true Christians in the world? Will they tell us, that Christ, who promised to be with the teachers of his word to the end of the world, wholly left them, and gave up hundreds upon hundreds of millions of people to be led in darkness to their eternal perdition by one whom his inspired followers had denominated the "*man of sin* and the *scarlet whore*"? Will they, indeed, dare to tell us, that Christ gave up the world wholly to "Antichrist" for twelve hundred years? Yet this they must do; they must thus stand forward with bold and unblushing blasphemy; or they must confess themselves guilty of the most atrocious calumny against the Catholic religion.

11. Then, coming nearer home, and closer to our own bosoms; our ancestors became Christians about six hundred years after the death of Christ. And how did they become Christians? *Who* first pronounced the name of Christ to this land? *Who* converted the English from Paganism to Christianity? Some Protestant saint, doubtless, warm from a victory like that of SKIBBEREEN. Oh, no! The work was begun, continued, and ended by the POPES, one of whom sent over some *Monks*, (of whom we shall see more by-and-by), who settled at CANTERBURY, and from whose beginnings the Christian religion spread, like the grain of mustard seed, rapidly over the land. Whatever, therefore, any other part of the world might have known of Christianity before the POPE became the settled and acknowledged head of the Church, England, at any rate, never had known of any Christian religion other than that at the head of which was the POPE; and in this religion with the POPE at its head, England continued to be firmly fixed for nine hundred years.

12. What, then: will our kind teachers tell us, that it was the "scarlet whore" and "Antichrist" who brought the glad tidings of the gospel into England? Will they tell us, too, that all the millions and hundreds of millions of English people, who died during those nine hundred years, expired without the smallest chance of salvation? Will they tell us, that all our fathers, who first built our churches, and whose flesh and bones form the earth for many feet deep in all the church-yards; will they tell us, that all these are now howling in the regions of the damned? Nature beats at our bosom, and bids us shudder at the impious, the horrid thought! Yet, this, even this, these presumptuous men must tell us; or they must confess their base calumny, in calling the POPE "Antichrist." and the Catholic worship "idolatrous" and its doctrines "damnable."

13. But. coming to the present time, the days in which we ourselves live; if we look round the world, we shall find that now, even now, about nine-tenths of all those who profess to be Christians are *Catholics*. What, then: has Christ suffered "Antichrist" to reign almost wholly uninterrupted even unto this day? Has Christ made the *Protestant* Church? Did he suggest the "Reformation?" And does he, after all, then, suffer the followers of "Antichrist" to outnumber his own followers nine to one? But, in this view of the matter, how lucky have been the Clergy of our Protestant Church, established by *law!* Her flock does not, if fairly counted, contain one-five-hundredth part of the number of those who are Catholics; while, observe, her Clergy receive more, not only than all the Clergy of all the Catholic nations, but more than all the Clergy of all the Christian people in the world, Catholics and Protestants all put together! She calls herself a Church "by *law* established." She never omits this part of her title. She calls herself "*holy*," "*godly*," and a good deal besides. She calls her ministers "*reverend*," and her worship and doctrines "*evangelical*." She talks very much about her reliance for support upon her "*founder*" (as she calls him) Christ; but, in stating her claims and her qualities, she never fails to conclude with, "by LAW established." This "law," however, sometimes wants the bayonet to enforce it; and her

tithes are not unfrequently collected by the help of soldiers, under the command of her ministers, whom the *law* has made Justices of the Peace!

14. To return; are we to believe, then, that Christ has, even unto this day, abandoned nine-tenths of the people of Europe to "Antichrist?" Are we to believe, that, if this "*law*-established" religion had been the religion of Christ, and the Catholic religion that of "Antichrist:" if this had been the case, are we to believe, that the "law-established" religion, that our "*holy* religion," as George Rose used to call it, while his grasping paw was deep in our purses; if this had been the case, are we to believe that the "law-established" religion, that the "*holy*" religion" of John Bowles, the Dutch Commissioner; are we to believe, that that "holy religion" (the fruits of which we behold in those worthy sons of the church, VITAL CHRISTIANITY and JOCELYN RODEN) would, at the end of two hundred years, have been able to count only one member for about every five hundred members (taking all Christendom together) of that Church against which the "*law*" Church protested and still protests?

15. Away, then, my friends, with this foul abuse of the Catholic religion, which, after all, is the religion of about nine-tenths of all the Christians in the world! Away with this shameful calumny, the sole object of which is, and always has been, to secure a quiet possession of the spoils of the Catholic Church, and of the poor; for, we shall, by-and-by, clearly see how the poor were despoiled at the same time that the Church was.

16. But, there remains to be noticed, in this place, an instance or two of the consistency of these revilers of the Catholic Church and faith. We shall, in due time, see how the Protestants, the moment they began their "Reformation," were split up into dozens and scores of *sects*, each condemning the other to eternal flames. But, I will here speak only of the "Church of England," as it is called, "by *law* established." Now, we know very well, that we, who belong to this Protestant Church, believe, or profess to believe, that the NEW TESTAMENT, as printed and distributed amongst us, contains the true and genuine "*word of God:*" that it contains the "*words of eternal life;*" that it points out to us the means, and the only means, by which we can possibly be saved from everlasting fire. This is what we believe. Now, *how did we come* by this New Testament? Who gave us this real and genuine "word of God?" From *whom* did we receive these "*words of eternal life?*" Come, JOSHUA WATSON, wine and spirit merchant, and teacher of religion to the people of England: come, JOSHUA, answer these questions! They are questions of great importance; because, if this be the book, and the only book, which contains instructions relative to the means of saving our souls, it is manifest, that it is a matter of deep interest to us, *who* it was that this book came from to us, through *what channel* we received it, and *what proof* we have of its authenticity.

17. Oh! JOSHUA WATSON! Alas! wine and spirit merchant, who art at the head of a Society "for promoting Christian Knowledge," which Society the Bishop of Winchester calls the "*correct expounder of evangelical truth*, and the firm supporter" of the *law*-established Church: oh! JOSHUA, teacher of religion to the people of England, who pay six or eight millions a-year to the Parsons who employ thee to do this teaching; oh! JOSHUA, what a shocking thing it is, that we Protestants should have received the NEW TESTAMENT; this real and genuine "*word of God;*" these "*words of eternal life;*" this book that points out to us the means, and the only means, of salvation: what a shocking fact, that we should have received this book from that POPE and that CATHOLIC CHURCH, to make us believe that the first of whom is

the whore of Babylon, and that the worship of the last is idolatrous and her doctrines damnable, you, JOSHUA, and your Society "for promoting *Christian* Knowledge," are now, at this very moment, publishing and pushing into circulation no less than seventeen different books and tracts!

18. After the death of Christ, there was a long space of time before the gospel was put into any thing like its present shape. It was preached in several countries, and churches were established in these countries, long before the written gospel was known much of, or, at least, long before it was made use of as a guide to the Christian churches. At the end of about four hundred years, the written gospels were laid before a council of the *Catholic Church*, of which the POPE was the head. But there were several gospels *besides* those of MATTHEW, MARK, LUKE and JOHN! Several other of the apostles, or early disciples, had written gospels . All these, long after the death of the authors, were, as I have just said, laid before a council of the Catholic Church; and that council determined which of the gospels were genuine and which not. It retained the four gospels of MATTHEW, MARK, LUKE and JOHN; it determined that these four should be received and believed in, and that all the rest should be rejected.

19. So that here JOSHUA WATSON's Society is without any other gospel; without any other word of God; without any guide to eternal life; without any other than that which that Society, well all the rest of us, have received from a church which that Society calls "idolatrous," and the head of which it calls "the *beast*, the *man* of *sin*, the *scarlet whore*, and *Antichrist*"! To a pretty state, then, do we reduce ourselves by giving in to this foul-mouthed calumny against the Catholic Church: to a pretty state do we reduce ourselves by our tame and stupid listening to those who calumniate the Catholic Church, because they live on the spoils of it. To a pretty state do we come, when we, if we still listen to these calumniators, proclaim to the world, that our only hope of salvation rests on promises contained in a book, which we have received from the Scarlet Whores and of the authenticity of which we have no voucher other than that Scarlet Whore and that Church, whose worship is "idolatrous" and whose doctrines are "damnable."

20. This is pretty complete; but still this, which applies to all Protestants, is not enough of inconsistency to satisfy the *law*-Church of Enzland. That Church has a Liturgy in great part made up of the Catholic service; but, there are the two creeds, the Nicene and Athanasian. The first was composed and promulgated by a Council of the Catholic Church and the POPE; and, the second was adopted, and ordered to be used, by another Council of that Church, with the POPE at its head. Must not a Parson of this *law*-Church be pretty impudent, then, to call the POPE "Antichrist," and to call the Catholic Church "idolatrous?" Pretty impudent, indeed; but we do not, even yet, see the grossest inconsistency of all.

21 . To our *law*-Church PRAYER-BOOK there is a CALENDAR prefixed, and, in this Calendar there are, under different days of the year, certain names of holy men and women. Their names are put here in order that their anniversaries may be attended to, and religiously attended to, by the people. Now, who are those holy persons? Some Protestant Saints to be sure? Not one! What, not saint Luther, nor saint Cranmer, nor saint Edward the Sixth, nor the "VIRGIN" saint Elizabeth? Not a soul of them; but, a whole list of POPES, Catholic BISHOPS, and Catholic holy persons, female as well as male. Several virgins; but not the "VIRGIN Queen;" nor any one of the Protestant race. At first sight, this seems odd; for, this CALENDAR was made by Act of

Parliament. But, the truth is, it was necessary to preserve some of the names, so long revered by the people, in order to keep them in better humour, and to lead them by degrees into the new religion. At any rate, here is the Prayer-Book, holding up for our respect and reverence a whole list of POPES and of other persons belonging to the Catholic Church, while those who teach us to read and to repeat the conntents of this same Prayer-Book, are incessantly dinning in our ears, that the POPES have all been "*Antichrists*," and that their Church was, and is, idolatrous in its worship and damnable in its doctrines!

22. JUDGE BAYLEY (one of the present twelve Judges) has, I have heard, written a Commentary on the Common Prayer-Book. I should like to know what the Judge says about these Catholic Saints (and no others) being placed in this Protestant Calendar. We shall, in due time, see the curious way in which this Prayer-Book was first made, and how it was new-modelled from time to time. But, here it is now, even to this day, with the Catholic Saints in the Calendar, whence it seems, that, even down to the reign of Charles II., when the last "improvement" was made in it, there had not appeared any Protestant Saint to supply the place of the old Catholic ones.

23. But there is still a dilemma for these revilers of the Catholic religion. We *swear* on the four Evangelists! And these, mind, we get from the POPE and a Council of the Catholic Church. So that, if the POPE be "Antichrist," that is to say, if those who have taught us to abuse and abhor the Catholics; if those be not the falsest and most malignant wretches that ever breathed, here are we *swearing* upon a book handed down to us by "Antichrist"? And, as if the inconsistencies and absurdities springing out of this Protestant calumny were to have no end, that "*Christianity*," which the judges say, "*is part and parcel of the law of the land;*" that Christianity is no other than what is taught in this same NEW TESTAMENT. Take the New Testament away, and there is not a particle of this "part and parcel" left. What is our situation; what a figure does this *part and parcel of the law of the land* make, with a dozen of persons in gaol for offending against it; what a figure does it make, if we adopt the abuse and falsehood of the revilers of the Catholic Church! What a figure does that "part and parcel" make, if we follow our teachers; if we follow JOSHUA WATSON's Society; if we follow every brawler from every tub in the country, and say that the POPE (from whom we got the "part and parcel") is "Antichrist" and the "scarlet whore"!

24. Enough! Ay, and much more than enough to make us sorely repent of having so long been the dupes of the crafty and selfish revilers of the religion of our fathers. Were there ever presumption, impudence, inconsistency and insincerity equal to those of which we have just taken a view? When we thus open our eyes and look into the matter, we are astonished at, and ashamed of, our credulity; and, this more especially when we reflect, that the far greater part of us have suffered ourselves to be misled by men not possessing a tenth part of our own capacity; by a set of low-minded greedy creatures; but indefatigable; never losing sight of the spoil; and, day after day, and year after year, close at the ears of the people from their very childhood, *din, din, din,* incessantly, until, from mere habit, the monstrous lie got sucked in for gospel-truth. Had the lie been attended with no consequences, it might have been merely laughed at, as all men of sense laugh at the old silly lie about the late King having "*made the Judges independent of the Crown.*" But, there have been consequences, and those most dreadful. By the means of the great Protestant lie, the Catholics and Protestants have been kept in a constant state of hostile feeling towards each other; and both, but particularly the former, have been, in one shape or another, oppressed and plundered for ages, with impunity to the oppressors and plunderers.

25. Having now shown, that the censure heaped on the religion of our forefathers is not only unjust, but absurd and monstrous; having shown that there could be no good reason for altering the religion of England from Catholic to Protestant; having exposed the vile and selfish calumniators, and duly prepared the mind of every just person for that fair and honest inquiry, of which I spoke in paragraph **4**; having done this, I should now enter on that inquiry, and show, in the first place, how this "Reforma tion," as it is called, *"was engendered by beastly lust;"* but, there is yet one topic to be touched on in this preliminary Number of my little Work.

26. Truth has, with regard to this subject, made great progress in the public mind, in England, within the last dozen years. Men are not now to be carried away by the cry of *"No-Popery,"* and the *"Church in danger."* Parson HAY, at Manchester, Parson DENT, at Northallerton, and their like all over the country, have greatly enlightened us. Parson MORRIT, at Skibbereen, has done great good in this work of enlightening. Nor must we forget a Right Reverend Protestant Father in God, who certainly did more in the opening of eyes than any Bishop that I ever before heard of. So that it is now by no means rare to hear Protestants allow, that, as to faith, as to morals, as to salvation, the Catholic religion is quite good enough; and, a very large part of the people of England are forward to declare, that the Catholics have been most barbarously treated, and that it is time that they had justice done them.

27. But, with all these just notions, there exists, amongst Protestants in general, an opinion that the Catholic religion is unfavourable to civil liberty, and also unfavourable to the producing and the exerting of genius and talent. As to the former, I shall, in the course of this work, find a suitable place for proving, by the melancholy experience of this country, that a total want of civil liberty was unknown in England, as long as its religion was Catholic; and, that the moment it lost the protection of the POPE, its kings and nobles became horrid tyrants, and its people the most abject and most ill-treated of slaves. This I shall prove in due time and place; and I beg you, my friends, to bear in mind, that I pledge myself to this proof.

28. And now to the other charge against the Catholic religion; namely, that it is unfavourable to the producing of genius and talent, and to the causing of them to be exerted. I am going, in a minute, to prove, that this charge is not only false, but ridiculously and most stupidly false; but, before I do this, let me observe, that this charge comes from the same source with all the other charges against the Catholics. *"Monkish ignorance and superstition"* is a phrase that you find in every Protestant historian, from the reign of the "VIRGIN" Elizabeth to the present hour. It has, with time, become a sort of magpie-saying, like *"glorious revolution," "happy constitution," "good old king," "envy of surrounding nations,"* and the like. But there has always, false as the notion will presently be proved to be, there has always been a very sufficient motive for inculcating it. BLACKSTONE, for instance, in his Commentaries on the Laws of England, never lets slip an opportunity to rail against "Monkish ignorance and superstition." BLACKSTONE was no fool. At the very time when he was writing these Commentaries, and reading them to the students at Oxford, he was, and he knew it, LIVING upon the spoils of the Catholic Church, and the spoils of the Catholic gentry, and also, of the poor! He knew that well. He knew that, if every one had had his due, he would not have been fattening where he was. He knew, besides, that all who heard his lectures were aware of the spoils that he was wallowing in. These considerations wae quite suffcient to induce him to abuse the Catholic Church, and to affect to look back with contempt to Catholic times.

29. For cool, placid, unruffled impudence, there has been no people in the world to equal the "Reformation" gentry; and BLACKSTONE seems to have inherited this quality in a direct line from some altar-robber of the reign of that sweet young Protestant saint, Edward the Sixth. If BLACKSTONE had not actually felt the spoils of the Catholics sticking to his ribs, he would have recollected, that all those things which he was eulogising, magna charta, trial by jury, the offices of sheriff, justice of the peace, constable, and all the rest of it, arose in days of *"monkish ignorance and superstition."* If his head had not been rendered muddy by his gormandizing on the spoils of the Catholic Church, he would have remembered, that FORTESCUE and that that greatest of all our lawyers, LITTLETON, were born, bred, lived and died in the days of "monkish ignorance and superstition." But, did not this BLACKSTONE know, that the very roof, under which he was abusing our Catholic forefathers, was made by these forefathers? Did he not, when he looked up to that roof, or, when he beheld any of those noble buildings, which, in defiance of time, still tell us what those forefathers were; did he not, when he beheld any of these, feel that he was a pigmy in mind, compared with those whom he had the impudence to abuse?

30. When we hear some Jew, or Orange-man, or parson-justice, or Jocelyn saint, talk about "monkish ignorance and superstition," we turn from him with silent contempt: but, BLACKSTONE is to be treated in another manner. It was at OXFORD where he wrote, and where he was reading, his Commentaries. He well knew, that the foundations for learning at Oxford were laid, and brought to perfection, not only in monkish times, but, in great part, by monks. He knew, "that the Abbeys were public schools for education, each of them having one or more persons set apart *to instruct the youth of the neighbourhood without any expense to the parents."* He knew, that "each of the greater monasteries had a peculiar residence *in the universities;* and, whereas there were, in those times, nearly THREE HUNDRED HALLS and PRIVATE SCHOOLS at Oxford, besides the colleges, there were not above EIGHT remaining towards the middle of the 17th century." [Phillips' Life of Cardinal Pole, Part I. p. 220.] That is to say, in about a hundred years after the enlightening "Reformation" began. At this time (1824) there are, I am informed, only FIVE halls remaining, and not a single school.

31. I shall, in another place, have to show more fully the folly, and, indeed, the baseness, of railing against the monastic institutions generally; but, I must here confine myself to this charge against the Catholic religion, of being unfavourable to genius, talent, and, in short, to the powers of the mind. It is a strange notion; and one can hardly hear it mentioned without suspecting, that, somehow or other, there is plunder at the bottom of the apparently nothing but stupid idea. Those who put forward this piece of rare impudence do not favour us with *reasons* for believing that the Catholic religion has any such tendency. They content themselves with the bare assertion, not supposing that it admits of anything like disproof. They look upon it as assertion against assertion; and, in a question which depends on mere hardness of mouth, they know that their triumph is secure. But, this is a question that does admit of proof, and a very good proof too. The "Reformation," in England, was pretty nearly completed by the year 1600. By that time all the "monkish ignorance and superstition" were swept away. The monasteries were all pretty nearly knocked down, young Saint Edward's people had robbed all the altars, and the "VIRGIN" Queen had put the finishing hand to the pillage. So that all was, in 1600, become as *Protestant* as heart could wish. Very well; the kingdom of France remained buried in "monkish ignorance and superstition" until the year 1787: that is to say, 187 years after *happy* England

stood in a blaze of Protestant light! Now, then, if we carefully examine into the number of men remarkable for great powers of mind, men famed for their knowledge or genius; if we carefully examine into the number of such men produced by France in these 187 years, and the number of such men produced by England, Scotland and Ireland, during the same period; if we do this, we shall get at a pretty good foundation for judging of the effects of the two religions with regard to their influence on knowledge, genius, and what is generally called learning.

32. "Oh, no!" exclaim the fire-shovels. "France is a great deal *bigger*, and contains more people, than these Islands; and this is *not fair play!*" Do not be frightened, good fire-shovels. According to your own account, these Islands contain twenty-one millions; and the French say, that they have thirty millions. Therefore, when we have got the numbers, we will make an allowance of one-third in our favour accordingly. If, for instance, the French have not three famous men to every two of ours, then I shall confess, that the law-established Church. and its family of Muggletonians, Cameronians, Jumpers, Unitarians, Shakers, Quakers, and the rest of the Protestant litter, are more favourable to knowledge and genius, than is the Catholic Church.

33. But how are we to ascertain these numbers? Very well. I shall refer to a work which has a place in every good library in the kingdom; I mean, the "UNIVERSAL, HISTORICAL, CRITICAL, AND BIBLIOGRAPHICAL DICTIONARY." This work, which is every where received as authority as to facts, contains lists of persons of all nations, celebrated for their published works. But, then, to have a place in these lists, the person must have been really distinguished; his or her works must have been considered as worthy of universal notice. From these lists I shall take my numbers, as before proposed. It will not be necessary to go into all the arts and sciences: eight or nine will be sufficient. It may be as well, perhaps, to take the ITALIANS as well as the French; for we all know that they were living in most shocking "monkish ignorance and superstition;" and that they, poor, unfortunate, and un plundered souls, are so living unto this very day!

34. Here, then, is the statement; and you have only to observe, that the figures represent the number of persons who were famous for the art or science opposite the name of which the figures are placed. The period is, from the year 1600 to 1787, during which period France was under what young GEORGE Ross calls the "*dark despotism* of the Catholic Church," and what BLACKSTONE calls "monkish ignorance and superstition;" and, during the same period, these Islands were in a blaze of light, set forth by LUTHER, CRANMER, KNOX, and their followers. Here, then, is the statement:

	England, Scotland and Ireland	France.	Italy.
Writers on Law	6	51	9
Mathematicians	17	52	15
Physicians and Surgeons	13	72	21
Writers on Natural History	6	33	11

Historians	21	139	22
Dramatic Writers	19	66	6
Grammarians	7	42	2
Poets	38	157	34
Painters	5	64	44
	132	676	164

35. Here is that very "SCALE," which a modest Scotch writer spoke of the other day, when he told the public, that, "Throughout Europe, Protestants rank *higher* in the *scale* of *intellect* than Catholics, and that Catholics in the *neighbourhood of Protestantants are more intellectual* than those at a distance from them." This is a fine specimen of upstart Protestant impudence. The above "scale" is, however, a complete answer to it. Allow one-third more to the French, on account of their superior populousness, and then there will remain to them 451 to our 132! So that they had, man for man, three and a half times as much intellect as we, though they are buried, all the while, in "monkish ignorance and superstition," and though they had no Protestant neighbours to catch the intellect from! Even the Italians surpass us in this rivalship for intellect; for, their population is not equal to that of which we boast, and their number of men of mind considerably exceeds that of ours. But, do I not, all this while, misunderstand the matter? And, by *intellect*, does not the Scotchman mean the capacity to make, not books and pictures, but checks, bills, bonds, exchequer-bills, inimitable notes, and the like? Does he not mean loan-jobbing and stock-jobbing, insurance-broking, annuities at ten per cent., kite-flying, and all the "intellectual" proceedings of Change Alley; not, by any means, forgetting works like those of ASLETT and FAUNTLEROY? Ah! in that case, I confess that he is right. On this scale Protestants do rank high indeed! And I should think it next to impossible for a Catholic to live in their neighbour hood without being much "more intellectual;" that is to say, much more of a Jewish knave, than if he lived at a distance from them.

36. Here, then, my friends, sensible and just Englishmen, I close this introductory Letter. I have shown you how grossly we have been deceived, even from our very infancy. I have shown you, not only the injustice, but the absurdity of the abuse heaped by our interested deluders on the religion of their and our fathers, I have shown you enough to convince you, that there was no obviously just cause for an alteration in the religion of our country. I have, I dare say, awakened in your minds, a strong desire to know how it came to pass, then, that this alteration was made; and, in the following Letters, it shall be my anxious endeavour fully to gratify this desire. But, observe, my chief object is to show, that this alteration made the main body of the people poor and miserable, compared with what they were before; that it impoverished and degraded them; that it banished, at once, that "Old English Hospitality," of which we have since known nothing but the name; and that, in lieu of that hospitality, it gave us pauperism, a thing, the very name of which was never before known in England.

LETTER II.

ORIGIN OF THE CATHOLIC CHURCH.
HISTORY OF THE CHURCH, IN ENGLAND, DOWN TO THE TIME OF THE
"REFORMATION."
BEGINNING OF THE "REFORMATION" BY KING HENRY VIII.

Kensington, 30th December, 1824.

My FRIENDS,

37. It was not a *reformation* but a *devastation*, of England, which was, at the time when this event took place, the happiest Country, perhaps, that the world had ever seen; and, it is my chief business to show, that this devastation impoverished and degraded the main body of the people. But, in order that you may see this devastation in its true light, and that you may feel a just portion of indignation against the devastators, and against their eulogists of the present day, it is necessary, first, that you take a correct view of the things on which their devastating powers were exercised.

38. The far greater part of those books, which are called "*Histories of England*," are little better than romances. They treat of battles, negotiations, intrigues of courts, amours of kings, queens and nobles: they contain the gossip and scandal of former times, and very little else, There are histories of England, like that of Dr. GOLDSMITH, for the use of young persons; but, no young person, who has read them through, knows any more, of any possible use, than he or she knew before. The great use of history, is, to teach us how laws, usages and institutions arose, what were their effects on the people, how they promoted public happiness, or otherwise; and these things are precisely what the greater part of historians, as they call themselves, seem to think of no consequence.

39. We never understand the nature and constituent parts of a thing so well as when we ourselves have made the thing: next to making it, is the seeing of it made: but, if we have neither of these advantages, we ought, at least, if possible, to get at a true description of the origin of the thing and of the manner in which it was put together. I have to speak to you of the Catholic Church generally; then of the Church in England, under which head I shall have to speak of the parish churches, the monasteries, the tithes, and other revenues of the Church. It is, therefore, necessary that I explain to you how the Catholic Church arose; and how churches, monasteries, tithes and other church revenues came to be in England. When you have this information, you will well understand what it was which was devastated by Henry VIII. and the "Reformation" people. And, I am satisfied, that, when you have read this one Number of my little work, you will know more about your country than you have learned, or ever will learn, from the reading of hundreds of those bulky volumes, called "Histories of England."

40. The Catholic Church *originated* with Jesus Christ himself. He selected PETER to be head of his Church. This Apostle's name was SIMON; but, his Master called him PETER, which means a *stone* or *rock*; and he said, "on this *rock* will I build my church." Look at the Gospel of Saint Matthew, xvi. 18, 19, and at that of Saint John,

xxi. 15, and onward; and you will see, that we must deny the truth of the Scriptures, or acknowledge, that here was a *head of the Church* promised for all generations.

41. Saint PETER died a martyr at Rome in about 60 years after the birth of Christ. But another supplied his place; and there is the most satisfactory evidence, that the chain of succession has remained unbroken from that day to this. When I said in paragraph **10**, that it might be said, that there was no POPE seated at Rome for the first three hundred years, I by no means meant to admit the fact; but to get rid of a pretence which, at any rate, could not apply to England, which was converted to Christianity by missionaries sent by a POPE, the successor of other Popes, who had been seated at Rome for hundreds of years. The truth is, that, from the persecutions which, for the first three hundred years, the Church underwent, the Chief Bishops, successors of Saint Peter, had not always the means of openly maintaining their supremacy; but they always existed; there was always a Chief Bishop, and his supremacy was always acknowledged by the Church; that is to say, by all the Christians then in the world.

42. Of later date, the Chief Bishop has been called, in our language, the POPE, and, in the French., PAPE. In the Latin he is called PAPA, which is an union and abbreviation of the two Latin words *Pater Patrum* which means *Father of Fathers*. Hence comes the appellation of *papa*, which children of all Christian nations give to their fathers; an appellation of the highest respect and most ardent and sincere affection. Thus, then, the POPE, each as he succeeded to his office, became the Chief or Head of the Church; and his supreme power and authority were acknowledged, as I have observed in paragraph **3**, by all the bishops, and all the teachers of Christianity, in all the nations where that religion existed. The POPE was, and is, assisted by a body of persons called CARDINALS, or Great Councillors: and at various and numerous times, COUNCILS of the Church have been held, in order to discuss and settle matters of deep interest to the unity and well-being of the Church. These Councils have been held in the countries of Christendom. Many were held in England. The POPES themselves have been taken promiscuously from men of all the Christian nations. POPE ADRIAN IV. was an Englishman, the son of a very poor labouring man; but having become a servant in a monastery, he was there taught, and became himself a monk. In time he grew famous for his learning, his talents and piety, and at last became the head of the Church.

43. The POPEDOM, or office of POPE, continued in existence through all the great and repeated revolutions of kingdoms and empires. The Roman Empire, which was at the height of its glory at the beginning of the Christian era, and which extended, indeed, nearly over the whole of Europe, and part of Africa and Asia, crumbled all to pieces; yet the Popedom remained; and at the time when the devastation, commonly called the "Reformation," of England began, there had been, during the fifteen hundred years, about two hundred and sixty Popes, following each other in due and unbroken succession.

44. The History of the Church in England, down to the time of the "Reformation," is a matter of deep interest to us. A mere look at it, a bare sketch of the principal facts, wil show how false, how unjust, how ungrateful those have been who have vilified the Catholic Church, its Popes, its Monks, and its Priests. It is supposed, by some, and, indeed, with good authorities on their side, that the Christian religion was partially introduced into England so early as the second century after Christ. But we know for a

certainty, that it was introduced effectually in the year 596; that is to say, 923 years before Henry VIII. began to destroy it.

45. England, at the time when this religion was introduced, was governed by seven kings, and that state was called the HEPTARCHY. The people of the whole country were PAGANS. Yes, my friends, our ancestors were PAGANS: they worshipped gods made with hands; and they sacrificed children on the altars of their idols. In this state England was, when the POPE of that day, GREGORY I., sent forty monks, with a monk of the name of AUSTIN (or AUGUSTIN) at their head, to preach the gospel to the English. Look into the Calendar of our Common Prayer Book, and you will find the name of GREGORY THE GREAT under the 12th of March, and that of AUGUSTIN under the 26th of May. It is probable that the POPE gave his order to Austin on the former day, and that Austin landed in Kent on the latter; or, perhaps, these may be the days of the year on which these great benefactors of England were born.

46. Now please to bear in mind, that this great event took place in the year 596. The Protestant writers have been strangely embarrassed in their endeavours to make it out, that up to this time, or thereabouts, the Catholic Church was pure, and trod in the steps of the Apostles; but that, after this time, that Church became corrupt. They applaud the character and acts of POPE GREGORY; they do the same with regard to AUSTIN: shame would not suffer them to leave their names out of the Calendar; but still, they want to make it out, that there was no pure Christian religion after the POPE came to be the visible and acknowledged head, and to have supreme authority. There are scarcely any two of them that agree upon this point. Some say that it was 300, some 400, some 500, and some 600 years before the Catholic Church ceased to be the true Church of Christ. But, none of them can deny, nor dare they attempt it, that it was the Christian religion as practised at Rome; that it was the Roman Catholic religion, that was introduced into England in the year 596, with all its dogmas, rites, ceremonies, and observances, just as they all continued to exist at the time of the "Reformation," and as they continue to exist in that Church even unto *this day*. Whence it clearly follows, that if the Catholic Church were corrupt at the time of the "Reformation," or be corrupt *now*, be radically bad *now*, it was so in 596; and then comes the impious and horrid inference!, mentioned in paragraph **12**, that "All our fathers who first built our churches, and whose bones and flesh form the earth for many feet deep in all the churchyards, are now howling in the regions of the damned!"

47. "The tree is known by its *fruit*." Bear in mind, that it was the Catholic faith as now held, that was introduced into England by POPE GREGORY THE GREAT; and bearing this in mind, let us see what were the effects of that introduction; let us see how that faith worked its way, in spite of wars, invasions, tyrannies, and political revolutions.

48. Saint AUSTIN, upon his arrival, applied to the Saxon king, within whose dominions the county of Kent lay. He obtained leave to preach to the people, and his success was great and immediate. He converted the king himself, who was very gracious to him and his brethren, and who provided dwellings and other necessaries for them at Canterbury. Saint AUSTIN and his brethren being monks, lived together in common, and from this common home, went forth over the country, preaching the gospel. As their community was diminished by death, new members were ordained to keep up the supply; and besides this, the number was in time greatly augmented. A church was built at Canterbury. Saint AUSTIN was, of course, the BISHOP, or Head

Priest. He was succeeded by other Bishops. As Christianity spread over the island, other communities, like that at Canterbury, were founded in other cities; as at London, Winchester, Exeter, Worcester, Norwich, York, and so of all the other places, where there are now Cathedrals, or Bishops' Churches. Hence, in process of time, arose those majestic and venerable edifices, of the possession of which we boast as the work of our forefathers, while we have the folly and injustice and inconsistency, to brand the memory of these very forefathers with the charge of grovelling ignorance, superstition, and idolatry; and while we show our own meanness of mind in disfiguring and dishonouring those noble buildings by plastering them about with our childish and gingerbread "monuments," nine times out of ten, the offspring of vanity, or corruption.

49. As to the mode of supporting the clergy in those times, it was by oblations or free gifts, and sometimes by tithes, which land-owners paid themselves, or ordered their tenants to pay, though there was no general obligation to yield tithes for many years after the arrival of Saint AUSTIN. In this collective, or collegiate state, the clergy remained for many years. But in time, as the land-owners became converted to Christianity, they were desirous of having priests settled near to them, and always upon the spot, ready to perform the offices of religion. The land was then owned by comparatively few persons. The rest of the people were vassals, or tenants, of the land-owners. The land-owners, therefore, built churches on their estates, and generally near their own houses, for the benefit of themselves, their vassals, and tenants. And to this day we see, in numerous instances, the country churches close by the gentleman's house. When they built the churches, they also built a house for the priest, which we now call the parsonage-house; and, in most cases, they attached some plough-land, or meadow-land, or both, to the priest's house, for his use; and this was called his *glebe*, which word, literally taken, means the top-earth, which is turned over by the plough. Besides these, the land-owners, in conformity with the custom then prevalent in other Christian countries, endowed the Churches with the tithe of the produce of their estates.

50. Hence parishes arose. Parish means a priestship, as the land on which a town stands is a township. So that the great man's estate now became a parish. He retained the right of appointing the priest, whenever a vacancy happened; but he could not displace a priest, when once appointed; and the whole of the endowment became the property of the Church independent of his control. It was a long while, even two centuries or more, before this became the settled law of the whole kingdom; but, at last, it did become such. But, to this possession of so much property by the Church, certain important conditions were attached; and to these conditions it behoves us, of the present day, to pay particular attention; for, we are, at this time, more than ever, feeling the want of the performance of those conditions.

51 . There never can have existed a state of society; that is to say, a state of things in which proprietorship in land was acknowledged, and in which it was maintained by law; there never can have existed such a state, without an obligation on the land-owners to take care of the necessitous, and to prevent them from perishing for want. The landowners in England took care of their vassals and dependants. But when Christianity, the very basis of which is *charity*, became established, the taking care of the necessitous was deposited in the hands of the clergy. Upon the very face of it, it appears monstrous, that a house, a small farm, and the tenth part of the produce of a large estate, should have been given to a priest, who could have no wife, and, of course, *no family*. But, the fact is, that the grants were for other purposes as well as for

the support of the priests. The produce of the benefice was to be employed thus: "Let the priests receive the tithes of the people, and keep a written account of all that have paid them; and divide them, in the presence of such as fear God, according to canonical authority. Let them set apart the first share for the repairs and ornaments of the church; let them distribute the second to the poor and the stranger with their own hands in mercy and humility; and reserve the third part for themselves." These were the orders contained in a canon, issued by a Bishop of York. At different times, and under different Bishops, regulations somewhat different were adopted; but there were always two-fourths, at the least, of the annual produce of the benefice to be given to the necessitous, and to be employed in the repairing or in the ornamenting of the church.

52. Thus the providing for the poor became one of the great duties and uses of the Church. This duty rested, before, on the land-owners. It must have rested on them; for, as BLACKSTONE observes, a right in the indigent "to *demand* a supply sufficient to all the necessities of life from the more opulent part of the community, *is dictated by the principles of society.*" This duty could be lodged in no hands so fitly as in those of the clergy; for thus the work of charity, the feeding of the hungry, the clothing of the naked, the administering to the sick, the comforting of the widow, the fostering of the fatherless, came always in company with the performance of services to God. For the uncertain disposition of the rich, for their occasional and sometimes capricious charity, was substituted the certain, the steady, the impartial hand of a constantly resident and unmarried administrator of bodily as well as of spiritual comfort to the poor, the unfortunate and the stranger.

53. We shall see, by-and-by, the condition that the poor were placed in, we shall see how all the labouring classes were impoverished and degraded, the moment the tithes and other revenues of the church were transferred to a Protestant and married clergy; and we shall have to take a full view of the unparalleled barbarity with which the Irish people were treated at that time; but, I have not yet noticed another great branch, or constituent part, of the Catholic Church; namely, the MONASTERIES, which form a subject full of interest and worthy of our best attention. The choicest and most highly empoisoned shafts in the quiver of the malice of Protestant writers, seem always to be selected when they have to rail against MONKS, FRIARS and NUNS. We have seen BLACKSTONE talking about "*monkish ignorance and superstition;*" and we hear, every day, Protestant bishops and parsons railing against what they call "*monkery,*" talking of the "*drones*" in monasteries, and, indeed, abusing the whole of those ancient institutions, as something degrading to human nature, in which work of abuse they are most heartily joined by the thirty or forty mongrel sects, whose bawling-tubs are erected in every corner of the country.

54. When I come to speak of the measures by which the monasteries were robbed, devastated and destroyed in England and Ireland, I shall show how unjust, base and ungrateful, this railing against them is; and how *foolish* it is besides. I shall show the various ways in which they were greatly useful to the community; and I shall especially show how they operated in behalf of the labouring and poorer classes of the people. But, in this place, I shall merely describe, in the shortest manner possible, the origin and nature of those institutions, and the extent to which they existed in England.

55. *Monastery* means a place of residence for monks, and the word monk comes from a Greek word, which means a lonely person, or a person in *solitude*. There were

monks, friars, and nuns. The word *friar* comes from the French word *frère*, which, in English, is brother; and the word *nun* comes from the French word *nonne*, which means a *sister in religion*, a virgin separated from the world. The persons, whether male or female, composing one of these religious communities, were called a *convent*, and that name was sometimes also given to the buildings and enclosures in which the community lived. The place where monks lived was called a monastery; that where friars lived, a friary; and that where nuns lived, a nunnery. As, however, we are not, in this case, inquiring into the differences in the the rules, orders, and habits of the persons belonging to these institutions, I shall speak of them all as monasteries.

56. Then, again, some of these were abbeys, and some priories; of the difference between which it will be sufficient to say, that the former were of a rank superior to the latter, and had various privileges of a higher value. An abbey had an ABBOT, or an *Abbess*; a priory, a *Prior*, or a *Prioress*. Then there were different ORDERS of monks, friars, and nuns; and these ORDERS had different rules for their government and mode of life, and were distinguished by different dresses. With these distinctions we have here, however, little to do; for we shall, by-and-by, see them all involved in one common devastation.

57. The persons belonging to a monastery lived in common; they lived in one and the same building; they could possess no property individually; when they entered the walls of the monastery, they left the world wholly behind them; they made a solemn vow of celibacy; they could devise nothing by will; each had a life-interest, but nothing more, in the revenues belonging to the community; some of the monks and friars were also priests, but this was not always the case; and the business of the whole was, to say masses and prayers, and to do deeds of hospitality and charity.

58. This mode of life began by single persons separating themselves from the world, and living in complete solitude, passing all their days in prayer, and dedicating themselves wholly to the serving of God. These were called hermits, and their conduct drew towards them great respect. In time, such men, or men having a similar propensity, formed themselves into societies, and agreed to live together in one house, and to possess things in common. Women did the same. And hence came those places called monasteries. The piety, the austerities, and, particularly, the works of kindness and of charity performed by those persons, made them objects of great veneration; and the rich made them, in time, the channels of their benevolence to the poor. Kings, queens, princes, princesses, nobles, and gentlemen founded monasteries; that is to say, erected the buildings, and endowed them with estates for their maintenance. Others, some in the way of atonement for their sins, and some from a pious disposition, gave, while alive, or bequeathed, at their death, lands, houses, or money, to monasteries already erected. So that, in time, the monasteries became the owners of great landed estates; they had the lordship over innumerable manors, and had a tenantry of prodigious extent, especially in England, where the monastic orders were always held in great esteem, in con sequence of Christianity having been introduced into the kingdom by a community of monks.

59. To give you as clear a notion as I can of what a monastery was, I will describe to you, with as much exactness as my memory will enable me, a monastery which I saw in France, in 1792, just after the monks had been turned out of it, and when it was about to be put up for sale. The whole of the space enclosed was about eight English acres, which was fenced in by a wall about twenty feet high. It was an oblong square, and at one end of one of the sides was a gate-way, with gates as high as the wall, and

with a little door in one of the great gates for the ingress and egress of foot-passengers. This gate opened into a spacious court-yard, very nicely paved. On one side, and at one end of this yard, were the kitchen, lodging-rooms for servants, a dining or eating place for them and for strangers and poor people; stables, coachhouses, and other out buildings. On the other side of the court-yard, we entered at a door-way to the place of residence of the monks. Here was about half an acre of ground of a square form, for a burying ground. On the four sides of this square there was a cloister, or piazza, the roof of which was, on the side of the burying ground, supported by pillars, and, at the back, supported by a low building which went round the four sides. This building contained the several dormitories, or sleeping-rooms of the monks, each of whom had two little rooms, one for his bed, and one for his books and to sit in. Out of the hinder room, a door opened into a little garden about thirty feet wide, and forty long. On one side of the cloister, there was a door opening into their dining-room, in one corner of which there was a pulpit for the monk who read, while the rest were eating in silence, which was according to the rules of the CARTHUSIANS, to which Order these monks belonged. On the other side of the cloister, a door opened into the kitchen garden, which was laid out in the nicest manner, and was well stocked with fruit trees of all sorts. On another side of the cloister, a door opened and led to the church, which, though not large, was one of the most beautiful that I had ever seen. I believe, that these monks were, by their rules, confined within their walls. The country people spoke of them with great reverence, and most grievously deplored the loss of them. They had large estates, were easy landlords, and they wholly provided for all the indigent within miles of their monastery.

60. England, more, perhaps, than any other country in Europe, abounded in such institutions, and these more richly endowed than any where else. In England, there was, on an average, more than twenty (we shall see the exact number by-and-by) of those establishments to a county! Here was a prize for an unjust and cruel tyrant to lay his lawless hands upon, and for "Reformation" gentry to share amongst them! Here was enough, indeed, to make robbers on a grand scale cry out against "monkish ignorance and superstition"! No wonder that the bowels of CRANMER, KNOX, and all their mongrel litter, yearned so piteously as they did, when they cast their pious eyes on all the farms and manors, and on all the silver and gold ornaments belonging to these communities! We shall see, by-and-by, with what alacrity they ousted, plundered, and pulled down: we shall see them robbing, under the basest pretences, even the altars of the country parish churches, down to the very smallest of those churches, and down to the value of five shillings. But, we must first take a view of the motives which led the tyrant, Henry VIII., to set their devastating and plundering faculties in motion.

61. This King succeeded his father, Henry VII., in the year 1509. He succeeded to a great and prosperous kingdom, a full treasury, and a happy and contented people, who expected in him the wisdom of his father without his avarice, which seems to have been that father's only fault. Henry VIII. was eighteen years old when his father died. He had had an elder brother, named ARTHUR, who, at the early age of twelve years, had been betrothed to CATHERINE, fourth daughter of Ferdinand, King of Castile and Arragon. When ARTHUR was fourteen years old, the Princess came to England, and the marriage ceremony was performed; but ARTHUR, who was a weak and sickly boy, died before the year was out, and the marriage never was consummated, and, indeed, who will believe that it could be? Henry wished to marry Catherine, and

the marriage was agreed to by the parents on both sides, but it did not take place until after the death of Henry VII. The moment the young King came to the throne, he took measures for his marriage. CATHERINE being, though only nominally, the widow of his deceased brother, it was necessary to have from the POPE, as supreme head of the Church, a dispensation, in order to render the marriage lawful in the eye of the canon law. The dispensation, to which there could be no valid objection, was obtained, and the marriage was, amidst the rejoicings of the whole nation, celebrated in June, 1509, in less than two months after the King's accession.

62. With this lady, who was beautiful in her youth, and whose virtues of all sorts seem scarcely ever to have been exceeded, he lived in the married state, seventeen years, before the end of which, he had had three sons and two daughters by her, one of whom only, a daughter, was still alive, who afterwards was Mary, Queen of England. But now at the end of seventeen years, he, being thirty-five years of age, and eight years younger than the Queen, and having cast his eyes on a young lady, an attendant on the Queen, named ANNE BOLEYN, he, all of a sudden, affected to believe that he was living in sin, because he was married to the widow of his brother, though, as we have seen, the marriage between Catherine and the brother had never been consummated, and though the parents of both the parties, together with his own Council, had unanimously and unhesitatingly approved of his marriage, which had, moreover, been sanctioned by the POPE, the head of the Church, of the faith and observances of which Henry himself had, as we shall hereafter see, been, long since his marriage, a zealous defender!

63. But the tyrant's passions were now in motion, and he resolved to gratify his beastly lust, cost what it might in reputation, in treasure, and in blood. He first applied to the POPE to divorce him from from his Queen. He was a great favourite of the POPE, he was very powerful, there were many strong motives for yielding to his request; but that request was so full of injustice, it would have been so cruel towards the virtuous Queen to accede to it, that the POPE could not, and did not grant it. He. however, in hopes that time might induce the tyrant to relent, ordered a court to be held by his Legate and Wolsey, in England. to hear and determine the case. Before this court the Queen disdained to plead, and the Legate, dissolving the court, referred the matter back to the POPE, who still refused to take any step towards the granting of the divorce. The tyrant now became furious, resolved upon overthrowing the power of the POPE in England, upon making himself the head of the Church in this country, and upon doing whatever else might be necessary to insure the gratification of his beastly desires and the glutting of his vengeance.

64. By making himself the supreme head of the Church, he made himself, he having the sword and the gibbet at his command, master of all the property of that Church, including that of the monasteries! His counsellors and courtiers knew this; and, as it was soon discovered that a sweeping confiscation would take place, the parliament was by no means backward in aiding his designs, every one hoping to share in the plunder. The first step was to pass acts taking from the POPE all authority and power over the Church in England, and giving to the King all authority whatever as to ecclesiastical matters. His chief adviser and abettor was THOMAS CRANMER, a name which deserves to be held in everlasting execration; a name which we could not pronounce without almost doubting of the justice of God, were it not for our knowledge of the fact, that the cold-blooded, most perfidious, most impious, most blasphemous caitiff expired, at last, amidst those flames which he himself had been the chief cause of kindling.

65. The tyrant, being now both POPE and King, made CRANMER ARCHBISHOP OF CANTERBURY, a dignity just then become vacant. Of course, this adviser and ready tool now became chief judge in all ecclesiastical matters. But, here was a difficulty; for the tyrant still professed to be a *Catholic*; so that his new Archbishop was to be consecrated according to the usual pontifical form, which required of him to swear obedience to the POPE. And here a transaction took place that will, at once, show us of what sort of stuff the "Reformation" gentry were made. CRANMER, before he went to the altar to be consecrated, went into a chapel, and there made a declaration on oath, that, by the oath that he was about to take, and which, for the sake of form, he was obliged to take, he did not intend to bind himself to anything that tended to prevent him from assisting the King in making any such "reforms" as he might think useful in the Church of England! I once knew a Corrupt Cornish knave, who having sworn to a direct falsehood (and that he, in private, acknowledged to be such) before an Election Committee of the House of Commons, being asked how he could possibly give such evidence, actually declared, in so many words, "that he had, before he left his lodging in the morning, taken an oath, that he would swear falsely that day." He, perhaps, imbibed his principles from this very Archbishop, who occupies the highest place in lying Fox's lying book of Protestant Martyrs.

66. Having provided himself with so famous a judge in ecclesiastical matters, the King lost, of course, no time in bringing his hard case before him, and demanding justice at his hands! Hard case, indeed; to be compelled to live with a wife of forty-three, when he could have, for next to nothing and only for asking for, a young one of eighteen or twenty! A really hard case; and he sought relief, now that he had got such an upright and impartial judge, with all imaginable dispatch. What I am now going to relate of the conduct of this Archbishop and of the other parties concerned in the transaction is calculated to make us shudder with horror, to make our very bowels heave with loathing, to make us turn our eyes from the paper and resolve to read no further. But, we must not give way to these feelings, if we have a mind to know the true history of the Protestant "Reformation." We must keep ourselves cool; we must reason ourselves out of our ordinary impulses; we must beseech nature to be quiet within us for awhile; for, from first to last, we have to contemplate nothing that is not of a kind to fill us with horror and disgust.

67. It was now four or five years since the King and CRANMER had begun to hatch the project of the divorce: but, in the meanwhile, the King had kept ANNE BOLEYN, or, in more modern phrase, she had been "under his protection," for about three years. And here let me state, that, in Dr. BAYLEY's life of Bishop FISHER, it is positively asserted, that ANNE BOLEYN was the King's daughter, and that Lady BOLEYN, her rnother said to the King, when he was abouut to marry ANNE, "Sir, for the reverence of God, take heed what you do in marrying my daughters for, if you record your own conscience well, she is your own daughter as well as mine." To which the King replied "Whose daughter soever she is, she shall be my wife." Now, though I believe this fact, I do not give it as a thing the truth of which is undeniable. I find it in the writings of a man, who was the eulogist (and justly) of the excellent Bishop FISHER, who suffered death because he stood firmly on the side of Queen CATHERINE. I believe it; but I do not give it, as I do the other facts that I state, as what is undeniably true. God knows, it is unnecessary to make the parties blacker than they are made by the Protestant historians themselves, in even a favourable record of their horrid deeds.

68. The King had had ANNE about three years "under his protection," when she became for the first time with child. There was now, therefore, no time to be lost in

order to "make an honest woman of her." A private marriage took place in January, 1533. As ANNE's pregnancy could not be long disguised it became necessary to avow her marriage; and, therefore, it was also necessary to press onward the trial for the divorce; for, it might have seemed rather awkward, even amongst "Reformation" people, for the King to have two wives at a time! Now, then, the famous ecclesiastical judge, CRANMER, had to play his part; and, if his hypocrisy did not make the devil blush, he could have no blushing faculties in him. CRANMER, in April 1533, wrote a letter to the King, begging him, for the good of the nation, and for the safety of his own soul, to grant his permission to try the question of the divorce, and beseeching him no longer to live in the peril attending an "incestuous intercourse "! Matchless, astonishing hypocrite! He knew, and the King knew that he knew, and he knew that the King knew that he knew it, that the King had been actually married to ANNE three months before, she being with child at the time when he married her!

69. The King graciously condescended to listen to this ghostly advice of his pious primates who was so anxious about the safety of his royal soul; and, without delay, he, as *Head of the Church*, granted the ghostly father, CRANMER, who, in violation of his clerical vows, had, in private, a woman of his own; to this ghostly father the King granted a licence to hold a spiritual court for the trial of the divorce. Queen CATHERINE, who had been ordered to retire from the court, resided at this time at AMPTHILL, in Bedfordshire, at a little distance from DUN5TABLE. At this latter place CaSYMER opened his court, and sent a citation to the Queen to appear before him, which citation she treated with the scorn that it deserved. When he had kept his "court" open the number of days required by the law, he pronounced sentence against the Queen, declaring her marriage with the King null from the beginning; and having done this, he closed his farcical court. We shall see him doing more jobs in the divorcing line; but thus he finished the first.

70. The result of this trial was, by this incomparable judge, made known to the King, whom this wonderful hypocrite gravely besought to submit himself with resignation to the will of God, as declared to him in this decision of the spiritual court, acting according to the laws of holy Church! The pious and resigned King yielded to the admonition; and then CRANMER held another court at LAMBETH, at which he declared, that the King had been lawfully married to ANNE BOLEYN; and that he now confirmed the marriage by his pastoral and judicial authority, which he derived from the successors of the Apostles! We shall see him, by-and-by, exercising the same authority to declare this new marriage null and void from the beginning, and see him assist in bastardizing the fruit of it: but we must now follow Mrs. ANNE BOLEYN (whom the Protestant writers strain hard to whitewash) till we have seen the end of her.

71 . She was delivered of a daughter (who was afterwards Queen Elizabeth) at the end of eight months from the date of her marriage. This did not please the King, who wanted a son, and who was quite monster enough to be displeased with her on this account. The couple jogged on apparently without quarrelling for about three years, a pretty long time, if we duly consider the many obstacles which vice opposes to peace and happiness. The husband, however, had plenty of occupation; for, being now "*Head of the Church,*" he had a deal to manage: he had, poor man, to labour hard at making a new religion, new articles of faith, new rules of discipline, and he had new things of all sorts to prepare. Besides which he had, as we shall see in the next Number, some of the best then in his kingdom, and that ever lived in any kingdom or country, to behead, hang, rip up, and cut into quarters. He had, moreover, as we shall

see, begun the grand work of confiscation, plunder and devastation. So that he could not have a great deal of time for family squabbles.

72. If, however, he had no time to jar with ANNE, he had no time to look after her, which is a thing to be thought of when a man marries a woman half his own age, and that this "great female reformer," as some of the Protestant writers call her, wanted a little of husband-like vigilance, we are now going to see. The freedom, or rather the looseness, of her manners, so very different from those of that virtuous Queen, whom the English court and nation had had before them, as an example for so many years, gave offence to the more sober, and excited the mirth and set a-going the chat of persons of another description. In January, 1536, Queen CATHERINE died. She had been banished from the court. She had seen her marriage annulled by CRANMER, and her daughter and only surviving child bastardized by act of parliament; and the husband had had five children by her, that "Reformation" husband had had the barbarity to keep her separated from, and never to suffer her, after her banishment, to set her eyes on that only child! She died, as she had lived, beloved and revered by every good man and woman in the kingdom, and was buried, amidst the sobbings and tears of a vast assemblage of the people, in the Abbey-church of Peterborough.

73. The King, whose iron heart seems to have been softened, for a moment, by a most affectionate letter, which she dictated to him from her death bed, ordered the persons about him to wear mourning on the day of her burial. But, our famous "great female reformer" not only did not wear mourning, but dressed herself out in the gayest and gaudiest attire; expressed her unbounded joy; and said, that she was now in reality a Queen! Alas, for our "great female reformer!" in just three months and sixteen days from this day of her exultation, she died herself; not, however, as the real Queen had died, in her bed, deeply lamented by all the good, and without a soul on earth to impute to her a single fault; but, on a scaffold, under a death-warrant signed by her husband, and charged with treason, adultery, and incest!

74. In the month of May, 1536, she was, along with the King, amongst the spectators at a tilting-match, at GREENWICH, when, being incautious, she gave to one of the combatants, who was also one of her paramours, a sign of her attachment, which seems only to have confirmed the King in suspicions which he before entertained. He instantly quitted the place, returned to Westminster, ordered her to be confined at Greenwich that night, and to be brought, by water, to Westminster the next day. But, she was met, by his order, on the river, and conveyed to the TOWER; and, as it were to remind her of the injustice which she had so mainly assisted in committing against the late virtuous Queen; as it were to say to her, "See, after all, God is just," she was imprisoned in the very room in which she had slept the night before her coronation!

75. From the moment of her imprisonment her behaviour indicated anything but conscious innocence. She was charged with adultery, committed with four gentlemen of the King's household, and with incest with her brother, Lord ROCHFORD, and she was, of course, charged with *treason*, those being acts of treason by law. They were all found guilty, and all put to death. But, before ANNE was executed, our friend, THOMAS CRANMER, had another tough job to perform. The King, who never did things by halves, ordered, as "*Head of the Church*," the Archbishop to hold his "spiritual court," and to *divorce* him from ANNE! One would think it impossible that a man, that any thing bearing the name of man, should have consented to do such a thing, should not have perished before a slow fire rather than do it. What! he had, we have seen in paragraph 70, pronounced the marriage with ANNE "to be *lawful*, and

had confirmed it by his authority, *judicial* and *pastoral*, which he derived from the successors of the Apostles." How was he now, then, to annul this marriage? How was he to declare it unlawful?

76. He cited the King and Queen to appear in his "court!" (Oh! that court! His citation stated, that their marriaze had been *unlawful*, that they were living in adultery, and that, for the "salvation of their souls," they should come and show cause why they should not be separated. They were just going to be separated most effectually; for this was on the 17th of March, and Anne, who had been condemned to death on the 15th, was to be, and was, executed on the 19th! They both obeyed his citation, and appeared before him by their proctors; and after having heard these, CRANMER, who, observe, afterwards drew up the Book of Common Prayer, wound up the blasphemous farce by pronouncing, "in the name of Christ, and for the honour of God," that the marriage "was, and always had been null and void!" Good God! But we must not give way to exclamations, or they will interrupt us at every step. Thus was the daughter, ELIZABETH, bastardized by the decision of the very man who had not only pronounced her mother's marriage lawful, but who had been the contriver of that marriage! And yet BURNET has the impudence to say, that CRANMER "appears to have done every thing with a good conscience"! Yes, with such another conscience as BURNET did the deeds by which he got into the Bishoprick of Salisbury, at the time of "Old glorious," which, as we shall see, was by no means disconnected with the "Reformation."

77. On the 19th, ANNE was beheaded in the Tower, put into an elm-coffin, and buried there. At the place of exe cution she did not pretend that she was innocent; and there appears to me to be very little doubt of her having done some, at least, of the things imputed to her: but, if her marriage with the King had "always been null and void;" that is to say, if she had never been married to him, how could she, by her commerce with other men, have been guilty of treason? On the 15th, she is condemned as the wife of the King, on the 17th she is pronounced never to have been his wife, and, on the 19th, she is executed for having been his unfaithful wife! However, as to the effect which this event has upon the character of the "REFORMATION," it signifies not a straw whether she were guilty or innocent of the crimes now laid to her charge; for, if she were innocent, how are we to describe the monsters who brought her to the block? How are we to describe that "Head of the Church" and that Archbishop, who had now the management of the religious affairs of England? It is said, that the evening before her execution, she begged the lady of the lieutenant of the Tower to go to the Princess MARY, and to beg her to pardon her for the many wrongs she had done her. There were others, to whom she had done wrongs. She had been the cause, and the guilty cause, of breaking the heart of the rightful Queen; she had caused the blood of MORE and of FISHER to he shed; and she had been the promoter of Cranmer, and his aider and abettor in all those crafty and pernicious councils, by acting upon which, an obstinate and hard-hearted King had plunged the kingdom into confusion and blood. The King, in order to show his total disregard for her, and, as it were, to repay her for her conduct on the day of the funeral of CATHERINE, dressed himself in white on the day of her execution; and, the very next day, was married to JANE SEYMOUR, at MAREVELL HALL, in Hampshire.

78. Thus, then, my friends, we have seen, that the thing called the "REFORMATION" "was engendered in beastly lust, and brought forth in hypocrisy and perfidy." How it proceeded in devastating and in shedding innocent blood we have yet to see.

LETTER III.

RESISTANCE TO THE KING'S MEASURES.
EFFECTS OF ABOLISHING THE POPE'S SUPREMACY.
DEATH OF SIR THOMAS MORE AND BISHOP FISHER.
HORRIBLE MURDERS OF CATHOLICS.
LUTHER AND THE NEW RELIGION.
BURNING OF CATHOLICS AND PROTESTANTS AT THE SAME FIRE.
EXECRABLE CONDUCT OF CRANMER.
TITLE OF DEFENDER OF THE FAITH.

Kensington, 31st January, 1825.

MY FRIENDS,

79. No Englishman, worthy of that name, worthy of a name which carries along with it sincerity and a love of justice; no real Englishman can have contemplated the foul deeds, the base hypocrisy, the flagrant injustice, ex posed in the foregoing Letter, without blushing for his country. What man, with an honourable sentiment in his mind, is there, who does not almost wish to be a foreigner, rather than be the countryman of CRANMER and of HENRY VIII.? If, then, such be our feelings already, what are they to be by the time that we have got through those scenes of tyranny, blood and robbery, to which the deeds, which we have already witnessed, were merely a prelude?

80. Sunk, however, as the country was by the members of the parliament hoping to share, as they finally did, in the plunder of the Church and the poor; selfish and servile as was the conduct of the courtiers, the King's councillors, and the people's representatives; still there were some men to raise their voices against the illegality and cruelty of the divorce of CATHERINE, as well as against that great preparatory measure of plunder, the taking of the spiritual supremacy from the POPE and giving it to the King. The Bishops, all but *one*, which one we shall presently see dying on the scaffold rather than abandon his integrity, were terrified into acquiesence, or, at least, into silence. But, there were many of the parochial clergy, and a large part of the monks and friars, who were not thus acquiescent, or silent. These, by their sermons, and by their conversations, made the truth pretty generally known to the people at large; and, though they did not succeed in preventing the calamities which they saw approaching, they rescued the character of their country from the infamy of silent submission.

81. Of all the duties of the historian, the most sacred is, that of recording the conduct of those, who have stood forward to defend helpless innocence against the attacks of powerful guilt. This duty calls on me to make particular mention of the conduct of the two friars, PEYTO and ELSTOW. The former, preaching before the King, at Greenwich, just previous to his marriage with ANNE, and, taking for his text the passage in the first book of Kings, where MICAIAH prophecies against AHAB, who was surrounded with flatterers and lying prophets, said, "I am that "MICAIAH whom you will hate, because I must tell you "ruly that this marriage is unlawful; and I know, that I shall eat the bread of affliction, and drink the water of sorrow; yet because our Lord hath put it in my mouth, I must speak it. Your flatterers are the four hundred prophets, who in the spirit of King, seek to deceive you. But take good heed, lest you, being seduced, find AHAB's punishment, which was to have his blood licked up by

dogs. It is one of the greatest miseries in princes to be daily abused by flatterers." The King took this reproof in silence; but, the next Sunday, a Dr. CURWIN preached in the same place before the King, and, having called PEYTO dog, slanderer, base beggarly friar, rebel, and traitor, and having said that he had fled for fear and shame;• ELSTOW, who was present and who was a fellow-friar of PEYTO, called out aloud to CURWIN, and said: "Good Sir, "you know that Father PEYTO is now gone to a provincial council at Canterbury, and not fled for fear of you; for to-morrow, he will return. In the meanwhile I am here, as another MICAIAH, and will lay down my life to prove all those things true, which he hath taught out of Holy Scripture; and to this combat I challenge thee before God and all equaljudges; even unto thee, CURWIN, I say, which art one of the four hundred false prophets, into whom the spirit of lying is entered, and seekest by adultery to establish a succession, betraying the King into endless perdition.'

82. STOEE, who relates this in his Chronicle, says that ELSTOW "waxed hot, so that they could not make him cease his speech, until the King himself bade him hold his peace. The two friars were brought the next day before the King's council, who rebuked them, and told them, that they deserved to be put into a sack. and thrown into the Thames. "Whereupon ELSTOW said, smiling: "Threaten these things to rich and dainty persons, who are clothed in purple, fare deliciously, and have their chiefest hope in this world; for we esteem them not, but are joyful, that, for the discharge of our duty, we are driven hence: and with thanks to God, we know the way to heaven to be as ready by water as by land."

83. It is impossible to speak with sufficient admiration of the conduct of these men. Ten thousand victories by land or sea would not bespeak so much heroism in the winners of those victors as was shown by these friars. If the bishops, or only a fourth part of them, had shown equal courage, the tyrant would have stopped in that career which was now on the eve of producing so many horrors. The stand made against him by these two poor friars was the only instance of bold and open resistance, until he had actually got into his murders and robberies; and, seeing that there never was yet found even a Protestant pen, except the vile pen of BURNET, to offer so much as an apology for the deeds of this tyrant, one would think that the heroic virtue of PEYTO and ELSTOW ought to be sufficient to make us hesitate before we talk of "monkish ignorance and superstition," Recollect, that there was no wild fanaticism in the conduct of those men; that they could not be actuated by any selfish motive; that they stood forward in the cause of morality, and in defence of a person, whom they had never personally known, and that, too, with the certainty of incurring the most severe punishments, if not death itself. Before their conduct, how the heroism of the Hampdens and the Russells sinks from our sight!

84. We now come to the consideration of that copious source of blood, the suppression of the POPE'sS SUPREMACY. To deny the King's supremacy was made *high treason*, and, to refuse to take an oath, acknowledging that supremacy, was deemed a denial of it. Sir THOMAS MORE, who was the Lord Chancellor, and JOHN FISHER, who was Bishop of Rochester, were put to death for refusing to take this oath. Of all the men in England, these were the two most famed for learning, for integrity, for piety, and for long and faithful services to the King and his father. It is no weak presumption in favour of the POPE's supremacy that these two men, who had exerted their talents to prevent its suppression, laid their heads on the block rather than sanction that suppression. But, knowing, as we do, that it is the refusal of our Catholic fellow subjects to take this same oath, rather than take which MORE and

FISHER died; knowing that this is the cause of all that cruel treatment which the Irish people have so long endured, and to put an end to which ill treatment they are now so arduously struggling; knowing that it is on this very point that the fate of England herself may rest in case of another war; knowing these things, it becomes us to inquire with care what is the nature, and what are the effects, of this papal supremacy, in order to ascertain, whether it be favourable, or otherwise, to true religion and to civil liberty.

85. The Scripture tells us, that Christ's Church was to be ONE. We, in repeating the Apostle's Creed, say, "I believe in the Holy Catholic Church." Catholic, as we have seen in paragraph **3**, means universal. And how can we believe in an universal church, without believing that that Church is ONE, and under the direction of one head? In the Gospel of Saint John, chap. 10, v. 16, Christ says, that he is the good shepherd, and that "there shall be one fold and one shepherd." He afterwards deputes PETER to be his shepherd in his stead. In the same gospel, chap. 17, v. 10 and 11, Christ says, "And all mine are thine, and thine are mine, and I am glorified in them. And now I am no more in the world, but they are in the world, and I come to thee. Holy Father, keep through thine own name, those whom thou hast given me, that they may be ONE, as we are." Saint Paul, in his second epistle to the Corinthians, says, "Finally, brethren, farewell: be perfect, be of good comfort, be of ONE MIND." The same Apostle, in his epistle to the Ephesians, chap. 4, v. 3, says, "Endeavouring to keep the *unity* of the spirit in the bond of peace. There is *one* body and *one* spirit, even as ye are called in *one* hope of your calling; *one* lord, ONE FAITH, ONE BAPTISM, one God and Father of all." Again, in his first epistle to the Corinthians, chap. 1, v. 10. "Now, I beseech you, brethren, by the name of our Lord Jesus Christ, that ye all speak the same thing, and that there be no divisions amongst you; but that ye be perfectly joined together in the same mind and the same judgment."

86. But besides these evidences of Scripture, besides our own creed, which we say we have from the Apostles, there is the reasonableness of the thing. It is perfectly monstrous to suppose that there can be TWO true faiths. It cannot be: one of the two must be false. And will any man say, that we ought to applaud a measure which, of necessity, must produce an indefinite number of faiths? If our eternal salvation depend upon our believing the truth, can it be good to place people in a state of necessity to have different beliefs? And does not that, which takes away the head of the Church, inevitably produce such a state of necessity? How is the faith of all nations to continue to be ONE, it there be, in every nation, a head of the Church, who is to be appealed to, in the last resort, as to all questions, as to all points of dispute, which may arise? How, if this be the case, is there to be "*one* fold and *one* shepherd"? How is there to be "*one* faith and *one* baptism"? how are the "*unity* of the spirit and the *bond* of peace" to be preserved? We shall presently see what unity and what peace there were in England, the moment that the King became the head of the Church.

87. To give this supremacy to a King is, in our case, to give it occasionally to a *woman*; and still more frequently to a *child*, even to a *baby*. We shall very soon see it devolve on a boy nine years of age, and we shall see the monstrous effects that it produced. But if his present Majesty and all his royal brothers were to die to-morrow (and they are all mortal), we should see it devolve on a little girl only about five years old. She would be the "one shepherd;" she, according to our own creed, which we repeat every Sunday, would be head of the "Holy Catholic Church"! She would have a council of regency. Oh! then there would be a whole troop of shepherds. There must be a pretty "*unity* of spirit" and a pretty "*bond* of peace."

88. As to the POPE's interference with the authority of the King or state, the sham plea set up was, and is, that he divided the government with the King, to whom belonged the sole supremacy with regard to every thing within his realm. This doctrine, pushed home, would shut out Jesus Christ himself, and make the King an object of adoration. Spiritual and temporal authority are perfectly distinct in their nature, and ought so to be kept in their exercise; and that, too, not only for the sake of religion, but also for the sake of civil liberty. It is curious enough that the Protestant sectarians, while they most cordially unite with the established Clergy in crying out against the POPE for "usurping" the King's authority, and against the Catholics for countenancing that "usurpation," take special care to deny, that this same King has any spiritual supremacy over themselves! The Presbyterians have their Synod, the Methodists their Conference, and all the other motley mongrels some *head* or other of their own. Even the "meek" and money-making followers of George Fox have their Elders and Yearly Meeting. All these *heads* exercise an absolute power over their members. They give or refuse their sanction to the appointment of the bawlers; they remove them, or break them, at pleasure. We have recently seen the Synod in Scotland ordering a preacher of the name of FLETCHER to cease preaching in London. He appears not to have obeyed; but the whole congregation has, it seems, been thrown into confusion in consequence of this disobedience. Strange enough, or, rather, impudent enough, is it, in these sects, to refuse to acknowledge any spritual supremacy in the King, while they declaim against the Catholics, because they will not take an oath acknowledging that supremacy: and is it not, then, monstrous, that persons belonging to these sects can sit in Parliament, can sit in the King's council, can be generals or admirals or judges, while from all these posts, and many others, the Catholics are excluded, and that, too, only because their consciences, their honourable adherence to the religion of their fathers, will not allow them to acknowledge this supremacy, but bids them belong to the "one fold and the one shepherd," and to know none other than "one Lord one faith, and one baptism"?

89. But the POPE was a foreigner exercising spiritual power in England; and this the hypocrites pretended was a degradation to the King and country. This was something to tickle JOHN BULL, who has, and, I dare say, always has had, an instinctive dislike to foreigners. But, in the first place, the POPE might be an Englishman, and we have, in paragraph **42**, seen one instance of this. Then how could it be a thing degrading to this nation, when the same thing existed with regard to all other nations? Was King ALFRED, and were all the long line of kings, for 900 years, degraded beings? Did those who really conquered France, not by subsidies and bribes, but by arms; did they not understand what was degrading, and what was not? Does not the present King of France, and do not the present French people, understand this matter? Are the sovereignty of the former, and the freedom of the latter, less perfect, because the papal supremacy is distinctly acknowledged. and has full effect in France? And if the Synod in Scotland can exercise its supremacy in England, and the Conference in England exercise its supremacy in Scotland, in Ireland, and in the Colonies; if this can be without any degradation of king or people, why are we to look upon the exercise of the papal supremacy as degrading to either?

90. Ay; but there was the money. The money ot England went to the POPE. Popes cannot live, and keep courts and ambassadors, and maintain great state, without money, any more than other people. A part of the money of England went to the POPE; but a part also of that of every other Christian nation took the same direction. This money was not, however, thrown away. It was so much given for the

preservation of unity of faith, peace, good will and charity, and morality. We shall, in the broils that ensued, and in the consequent subsidies and bribes to foreigners, soon see that the money which went to the POPE, was extremely well laid out. But how we Protestants strain at a gnat, while we swallow camels by whole caravans! Mr. PERCEVAL gave more to foreigners in one single year than the Popes ever received from our ancestors in four centuries. We have bowed, for years, to a DUTCHMAN, who was no heir to the crown any more than one of our workhouse paupers, and who had not one drop of English blood in his veins; and we now send annually to Hanoverians and other foreigners, under the name of half-pay, more money than was ever sent to the POPE in twenty years. From the time of the "Glorious Revolution," we have been paying two thousand pounds a year to the heirs of "Marshal SCHOMBERG," who came over to help the DUTCHMAN; and this is, mind, to be paid as long as there are such heirs of Marshal SCHOMBERG, which, to use the elegant and logical and philosophical phrase of our great "Reformation" poet, will, I dare say, be "for ever and a day." And have we forgotten the BENTINCKS and all the rest of the DUTCH tribe, who had estates of the Crown heaped upon them: and do we talk, then, of the degradation and the loss of money occasioned by the supremacy of the POPE! It is a notorious fact, that not a German soldier would have been wanted in this kingdom, during the last war, had it not been for the disturbed and dangerous state of Ireland, in which the German troops were very much employed. We have long been paying, and have now to pay, and shall long have to pay, upwards of a hundred thousand pounds a year to the half-pay officers of these troops, one single penny of which, we now should not have had to pay, if we had dispensed with the oath of supremacy from the Catholics. Every one to his taste; but, for my part, if I must pay foreigners for keeping me in order, I would rather pay "pence to PETER" than pounds to Hessian Grenadiers. Alien Priories, the establishment of which was for the purpose of inducing learned persons to come and live in England, have been a copious source of declamatory complaint. But, leaving their utility out of the question, I, for my particular part, prefer Alien Priories to Alien Armies, from which latter this country has never been, except for very short intervals, wholly free, from the day that the former were suppressed. I wish not to set myself up as a dictator in matters of taste; but, I must take leave to say, that I prefer the cloister to the barrack; the chaunting of matins to the reveille by the drum; the cowl to the brass-fronted hairy cap; the shaven crown to the mustachio, though the latter be stiffened with black-ball; the rosary, with the cross appendant, to the belt with its box of bullets; and, beyond all measure, I prefer the penance to the point of the bayonet. One or the other of these set of things, it would seem, we must have; for, before the "Reformation," England never knew, and never dreamed, of such a thing as a standing soldier; since that event she has never, in reality, known what it was to be without such soldiers: till, at last, a thundering standing army, even in time of profound peace, is openly avowed to be necessary to the "preservation of our happy constitution in CHURCH AND STATE."

91 . However, this money part of the affair is *now* over, with regard to the POPE . No one proposes to give him any money at all, in any shape whatever. The Catholics believe, that the unity of their church would be destroyed, that they would, in short, cease to be Catholics, if they were to abjure his supremacy; and, therefore, they will not abjure it: they insist that their teachers shall receive their authority from him: and what do they, with regard to the POPE, insist upon, more than is insisted upon and acted upon by the Presbyterians, with regard to their Synod?

92. Lastly, as to this supremacy of the POPE, what was its effect with regard to civil liberty; that is to say, with regard to the security, the rightful enjoyment, of men's property and lives? We shall, by-and-by, see that civil liberty fell by the same tyrannical hands that suppressed the POPE's supremacy. But *whence came* our civil liberty? Whence came those laws of England which LORD COKE calls "the *birth-right*" of Englishmen, and which each of the States of America, declare, in their constitutions, to be the "*birth-right* of the people thereof?" Whence came these laws? Are they of Protestant origin? The bare question ought to make the revilers of the Catholics hang their heads for shame. Did Protestants establish the three courts and the twelve judges, to which establishment, though, like all other human institutions, it has sometimes worked evil, England owes so large a portion of her fame and her greatness? Oh, no! This institution arose when the POPE's supremacy was in full vigour. It was not a gift from Scotckmen, nor Dutchmen, nor Hessians; from Lutherans, Calvinists, nor Huguenots; but was the work of our own brave and wise English Catholic ancestors; and CHIEF JUSTICE Annon is the heir, in an unbroken line of succession, to that BENCH, which was erected by ALFRED, who was, at the very same time, most zealously engaged in the founding of churches and of monasteries.

93. If, however, we still insist, that the POPE's supremacy and its accompanying circumstances, produced ignorance, superstition and slavery, let us act the part of sincere, consistent and honest men. Let us knock down, or blow up, the cathedrals and colleges and old churches; let us sweep away the three courts, the twelve judges, the circuits, and the jury-boxes; let us demolish all that we inherit from those whose religion we so unrelentingly persecute, and whose memory we affect so heartily to despise: let us demolish all this, and we shall have left, all our own, the capacious jails and penitentiaries; stock-exchange; the hot and ancle- and knee-swelling, and lung-destroying cotton-factories; the whiskered standing army and its splendid barracks; the parson-captains, parson-lieutenants, parson-ensigns and parson-justices; the poor-rates and the pauper houses; and, by no means forgetting, that blessing which is peculiarly and doubly and "gloriously" Protestant, the NATIONAL DEBT. Ah! people of England, how have you been deceived!

94. But, for argument's sake, counting the experience of antiquity for nothing, let us ask ourselves what a chance civil liberty can stand, if all power, spiritual and lay, be lodged in the hands of the same man? That man must be a despot, or his power must be undermined by an Oligarchy, or by something. If the President, or the Congress, of the United States, had a spiritual supremacy; if they appointed the Bishops and Ministers, though they have no benefices to give, and would have no tenths and first fruits to receive, their government would be a tyranny in a very short time. MONTESQUIEU observes, that the people of Spain and Portugal would have been absolute slaves, without the power of the Church, which is, in such a case, "the only check to arbitrary sway." Yet, how long have we had "papal usurpation and tyranny" dinned in our ears! This charge against the POPE surpasseth all understanding. How was the POPE to be an usurper, or tyrant, in England? He had no fleet, no army, no judge, no sheriff, no justice of the peace, not even a single constable or beadle at his command. We have been told of "the thunders of the Vatican" till we have almost believed, that the POPE's residence was in the skies; and, if we had believed it quite, the belief would not have surpassed in folly, our belief in numerous other stories hatched by the gentry of the "Reformation." The truth is, that the POPE had no power but that which he derived from the free will of the people. The people were frequently

on his side, in his contests with Kings; and, by this means, they, in numerous instances, preserved their rights against the attempts of tyrants. If the POPE had had no power, there must have sprung up an Oligarchy, or a something else, to check the power of the King: or, every king might have been a Nero, if he would. We shall soon see a worse than Nero in Henry VIII.; we shall soon see him laying all law prostrate at his feet; and plundering his people, down even to the patrimony of the poor. But, reason says that it must be so; and, though this spiritual power be now nominally lodged in the hands of the King, to how many tricks and contrivances have we resorted, and some of them most disgraceful and fatal ones, in order to prevent him from possessing the reality of this power! We are obliged to effect by influence and by faction that is to say, by means indirect, disguised, and frequently flagitiously immoral, not to say almost seditious into the bargain, that which was effected by means direct, avowed, frank, honest, and loyal. It is curious enough, that while all Protestant ministers are everlastingly talking about "papal usurpation and tyranny," all of them, except those who profit from the establishment, talk not less incessantly about what they have no scruple to call, "that two-headed monster, *Church and State*." What a monster would it have been, then, if the Catholics had submitted to the "VETO;" that is to say, to give the King a rejecting voice in the appointment of Catholic Bishops; and thus to make him, who is already "the *Defender* of the *Faith*," against which he protests, an associate with the Sovereign Pontiff in carrying on the affairs of that church, to which the law strictly forbids him to belong!

95. Thus, then, this so much abused papal supremacy was a most salutary thing: it was the only check, then existing, on despotic power, besides it being absolutely necessary to that unity of faith, without which there could be nothing worthy of the name of a Catholic Church. To abjure this supremacy was an act of apostasy, and also, an act of base abandonment of the rights of the people. To require it of any man was to violate Magna Charta and all the laws of the land; and to put men to death for refusing to comply with the request was to commit unqualified murder. Yet, without such murder, without shedding innocent blood, it was impossible to effect the object. Blood must flow. Amongst the victims to this act of outrageous tyranny, were, Sir THOMAS MORE and Bishop FISHER. The former had been the LORD HIGH CHANCELLOR for many years. The character given of him by his contemporaries, and by every one, to the present day, is that of as great perfection for learning, integrity and piety, as it is possible for a human being to possess. He was the greatest lawyer of his age, a long-tried and most faithful servant of the King and his father; and was, besides, so highly distinguished beyond men in general for his gentleness and humility of manners, as well as for his talents and abilities, that his murder gave a shock to all Europe. FISHER was equally eminent in point of learning, piety, and integrity. He was the only surviving privy-councillor of the late King, whose mother (the grandmother of Henry VIII.) having out lived her son and daughter, besought with her dying breath, the young King to listen particularly to the advice of this learned, pious, and venerable prelate; and, until that advice thwarted his brutal passions, he was in the habit of saying, that no other prince could boast of a subject to be compared with FISHER. He used, at the council-board, to take him by the hand and call him his father; marks of favour and affection which the Bishop repaid by zeal and devotion which knew no bounds other than those prescribed by his duty to God, his King and his country. But, that sacred duty bade him object to the divorce and to the King's supremacy; and then the tyrant, forgetting, at once, all his services, all his devotion, all his unparalleled attachment, sent him to the block, after fifteen months of imprison ment, during which he lay, worse than a common felon, buried in filth and

almost destitute of food; sent him, who had been his boast, and whom he had called his father, to perish under the axe; dragged him forth, with limbs tottering under him, his venerable face and hoary locks begrimed, and his nakedness scarcely covered with the rags left on his body; dragged him thus forth to the scaffold, and, even when the life was gone, left him to lie on that scaffold like a dead dog! Savage monster! Rage stems the torrent of our tears, hurries us back to the horrid scene, and bids us look about us for a dagger to plunge into the heart of the tyrant.

96. And yet, the calculating, cold-blooded and brazen BURNET has the audacity to say, that "such a man as Henry VIII. was necessary to bring about the Reformation!" He means, of course, that such measures as those of Henry were necessary; and, if they were necessary, what must be the nature and tendency of that "Reformation?"

97. The work of blood was now begun, and it proceeded with steady pace. All who refused to take the oath of supremacy; that is to say, all who refused to become apostates, were considered and treated as traitors, and made to suffer death accompanied with every possible cruelty and indignity. As a specimen of the works of BURNET's necessary reformer, and to spare the reader repetition on the subject, let us take the treatment of JOHN HOUGHTON, Prior of the Charter-house in London, which was then a convent of Carthusian monks. This Prior, for having refused to take the oath, which, observe, he could not take without committing perjury, was hanged at TYBURN. He was scarcely suspended when the rope was cut, and he alive on the ground. His clothes were then stripped off; his bowels were ripped up; his heart and entrails were torn from his body and flung into a fire; his head was cut from his body; the body was divided into quarters and parboiled; the quarters were then subdivided and hung up in different parts of the city; and one arm was nailed to the wall over the entrance into the monastery!

98. Such were the means, which BURNET says were necessary to introduce the Protestant religion into England. How different, alas! from the means by which the Catholic religion had been introduced by POPE GREGORY and Saint AUSTIN! These horrid butcheries were perpetrated, mind, under the primacy of Fox's great Martyr, CRANMER, and with the active agency of another ruffian, named THOMAS CROMWELL, whom we shall soon see sharing with CRANMER the work of plunder, and finally sharing, too, in his disgraceful end.

99. Before we enter on the grand subject of plunder, which was the mainspring of the "Reformation," we must follow the King and his primate through their murders of Protestants, as well as Catholics. But, first, we must see how the Protestant religion arose, and how it stood at this juncture. Whence the term, Protestant, came, we have seen in paragraph 3. It was a name given to those who declared, or protested, against the Catholic, or universal church. This work of protesting was begun in Germany, in the year 1517, by a friar, whose name was MARTIN LUTHER, and who belonged to a convent of Augustin friars, in the electorate of Saxony. At this time the POPE had authorised the preaching of certain indulgences, and this business having been entrusted to the Order of Dominicans, and not to the order to which LUTHER belonged, and to which it had been usual to commit such trust, here was one of the motives from which LUTHER's opposition to the POPE proceeded. He found a protector in his sovereign, the Elector of Saxony, who appears to have had as strong a relish for plunder, as that with which our English tyrant and his courtiers and parliament were seized a few years afterwards.

100. All accounts agree that LUTHER was a most profligate man. To change his religion he might have thought himself called by his conscience; but, conscience could not call upon him to be guilty of all the abominable deeds of which he stands convicted even by his own confessions, of which I shall speak more fully, when I come to the proper place for giving an account of the numerous sects into which the Protestants were soon divided, and of the fatal change which was, by this innovation in religion, produced, even according to the declaration of the Protestant leaders themselves, in the morals of the people and the state of society. But, just observing, that the Protestant sects had, at the time we are speaking of, spread themselves over a part of Germany, and had got into Switzerland and some other states of the Continent, we must now, before we state more particulars relating to LUTHER and the sects that he gave rise to, see how the King of England dealt with those of his subjects who had adopted the heresy.

101. The Protestants immediately began to disagree amongst themselves; but, they all maintained, that faith alone was sufficient to secure salvation; while the Catholics maintained, that good works were also necessary. The most profligate of men, the most brutal and bloody of tyrants may be a stanch believer; for the devils themselves believe; and, therefore, we naturally, at first thought, think it strange, that Henry VIII. did not instantly become a zealous Protestant, did not become one of the most devoted disciples of LUTHER, He would, certainly; but LUTHER began his "Reformation" a few years too soon for the King. In 151 7, when LUTHER began his works, the King had been married to his first wife only eight years; and he had not then conceived any project of divorce. If LUTHER had begun twelve years later, the King would have been a Protestant at once, especially after seeing that this new religion allowed LUTHER and seven other of his brother leaders in the "Reformation" to grant, under their hands, a licence to the LANGRAVE OF HESSE to have TWO WIVES at one and the same time! So complaisant a religion would have been, and, doubtless was, at the time of the divorce, precisely to the King's taste; but, as I have just observed, it came twelve years too soon for him; for, not only had he not adopted this religion, but had opposed it, as a Sovereign; and, which was a still more serious affair, had opposed it, as an AUTHOR! He had in 1521, written a BOOK against it. His vanity, his pride, were engaged in the contest; to which may be added, that Luther, in answering his book, had called him "a pig, an ass, a dunghill, the spawn of an adder, a basilisk, a lying buffoon dressed in a king's robes, a mad fool with a frothy mouth and a whorish face;" and had afterwards said to him, "you *lie*, you stupid and sacrilegious King."

102. Therefore, though the tyrant was bent on destroying the Catholic Church, he was not less bent on the extirpation of the followers of LUTHER and his tribe of new sects. Always under the influence of some selfish and base motive or other, he was, With regard to the Protestants, set to work by revenge, as, in the case of the Catholics, he had been set to work by lust, if not by lust to be gratified by incest. To follow him, step by step, and in minute detail, through all his butcheries and all his burnings, would be to familiarize one's mind to a human slaughter-house and a cookery of cannibals. I shall, therefore, confine myself to a general view of his works in this way.

103. His book against LUTHER had acquired him the title of "*Defender of the Faith*," of which we shall see more by-and-by. He could not, therefore, without recantation, be a Protestant; and, indeed, his pride would not suffer him to become the proselyte of a man, who had, in print, too, proclaimed him to be a pig, an ass, a fool, and a liar. Yet he could not pretend to be a Catholic. He was, therefore, compelled to

make a religion of his own. This was doing nothing, unless he enforced its adoption by what he called law. Laws were made by him and by his servile and plundering parliament, making it heresy in, and condemning to the flames, all who did not expressly conform, by acts as well as by declarations, to the faith and worship, which, as head of the Church, he invented and ordained. Amongst his tenets there were such as neither Catholics nor Protestants could, consistently with their creeds, adopt. He, therefore, sent both to the stake, and sometimes, in order to add mental pangs to those of the body, he dragged them to the fire on the same hurdle, tied together in pairs back to back, each pair containing a Catholic and a Protestant, Was this the way that Saint AUSTIN and Saint PATRICK propagated their religion? Yet, such is the malignity of BURNET, and of many, many others, called Protestant "divines," that they apologise for, if they do not absolutely applaud, this execrable tyrant, at the very moment that they are compelled to confess that he soaked the earth with Protestant blood, and filled the air with the fumes of their roasting flesh.

104. Throughout the whole of this bloody work, CRANMER, who was the primate of the King's religion, was consenting to, sanctioning, and aiding and abetting in, the murdering of Protestants well as of Catholics; though, and I pray you to mark it well, HUME, TILLOTSON, BURNET, and all his long list of eulogists, say, and make it matter of merit in him, that, all this while, he was himself a sincere Protestant in his heart! And, indeed, we shall, by-and-by, see him openly avowing those very tenets, for the holding of which he had been instrumental in sending, without regard to either age or sex, others to perish in the flames. The progress of this man in the paths of infamy, needed incontestible proof to reconcile the human mind to a belief in it. Before he became a priest he had married: after he became a priest, and had taken the oath of celibacy, he being then in Germany, and having become a Protestant, married another wife, while the first was still alive. Being the primate of Henry's Church, which still forbade the clergy to have wives, and which held them to their oath of celibacy, he had his wife brought to England in a chest, with holes bored in it to give her air. As the cargo was destined for Canterbury, it was landed at Gravesend, where the sailors, not apprised of the contents of the chest, set it up on one end, and the wrong end downwards, and had nearly broken the neck of the poor *frow!* Here was a pretty scene! A German *frow*, with a litter of half German half English young ones, kept in hugger-mugger, on that spot, which had been the cradle of English Christianity; that spot, where Saint AUSTIN had inhabited, and where THOMAS À BECKET had sealed with his blood his opposition to a tyrant, who aimed at the destruction of the Church and at the pillage of the people! Here is quite enough to fill us with disgust; but, when we reflect, that this same primate, while he had under his roof his *frow* and her litter, was engaged in assisting to send Protestants to the flames, because they dissented from a system that forbade the clergy to have wives, we swell with indignation, not against CRANMER, for, though there are so many of his atrocious deeds yet to come, he has exhausted our store; not against HUME, for he professed no regard for any religion at all; but, against those who are called "divines," and who are the eulogists of CRANMER; against BURNET, who says that CRANMER "did all with a good conscience;" and against Dr. STURGES, or rather, the Dean and Chapter of Winchester, who clubbed their "talents" in getting up the "Reflections on Popery," who talk of the "respectable CRANMER," and who have the audacity to put him, in point of integrity, upon a level with Sir THOMAS MORE! As Dr. MILNER, in his answer to STURGES, observes, they resembled each other in that the name of both was Thomas; but in all other things, the dissimilarity was as great, as

that which the most vivid imagination can ascribe to the dissimilarity between hell and heaven.

105. The infamy of CRANMER in assisting in sending people to the flames for entertaining opinions, which he afterwards confessed that he himself entertained at the time that he was so sending them, can be surpassed by nothing of which human depravity is capable; and it can be equalled by nothing but that of the King, who, while he was, as he hoped and thought, laying the axe to the root of the Catholic faith, still styled himself its *defender!* He was not, let it be borne in mind, defender of what he might, as others have, since his day, and in his day, called the Christian Faith. He received the title from the POPE, as a reward for his written defence of the Catholic faith against Luther. The POPE conferred on him this title, which was to descend to his posterity. The title was given by POPE Leo X. in a bull, or edict, beginning with these words: "Leo, servant of the servants of the Lord, to his most dear Son, Henry, King of England, Defender of the Faith, all health and happiness." The bull then goes on to say, that the King, having, in defence of the faith of the Catholic Church, written a book against Martin Luther, the POPE and his Council had determined to confer on him and his successors the title of *Defender of the Faith.* "We," says the bull, "sitting in this Holy See, having, with mature deliberation, considered the business with our brethren, do with their unanimous counsel and consent, grant unto your Majesty, your heirs and successors, the title of Defender of the Faith; which we do, by these presents, confirm unto you, commanding all the Faithful to give your Majesty this title."

106. What are we to think, then, of the man who could continue to wear this title, while he was causing to be acted before him a farce, in which the POPE and his Council were exposed to derision, and was burning, and ripping up the bowels, of people, by scores, only because they remained firm in that faith of which he had still the odious effrontery to call himself the defender? All justice, everything like law, every moral thought must have been banished before such monstrous enormity could have been suffered to exist. They were all banished from the seat of power. An iron despotism had, as we shall see in the next Number, come to supply the place of the papal supremacy. Civil liberty was wholly gone; no man had any thing that he could call property; and no one could look upon his life as safe for twenty-four hours.

107. But, there is a little more to be said about this title of *Defender of the Faith,* which, for some reason or other that one can hardly discover, seems to have been, down to our time, a singularly great favourite. EDWARD VI., though his two "Protectors," who succeeded each other in that office, and whose guilty heads we shall gladly see succeeding each other on the block, abolished the Catholic faith by law; though the Protestant faith was, with the help of Foreign troops, established in its stead, and though the greedy ruffians, of his time, robbed the very altars, under the pretext of extirpating that very faith, of which his title called him the Defender, continued to wear this title throughout his reign. ELIZABETH continued to wear this title, during her long reign of "mischief and of misery," as WITAKER justly calls it, though during the whole of that reign she was busily engaged in persecuting, in ruining, in ripping up the bowels of those who entertained that faith, of which she styled herself the Defender, in which she herself had been born, in which she had lived for many years, and to which she adhered, openly and privately, till her self-interest called upon her to abandon it. She continued to wear this title while she was tearing the bowels out of her subjects for hearing mass; while she was refusing the last comforts of the Catholic religion to her cousin, MARY, Queen of Scotland, whom she

put to death by a mockery of law and jus tice, after, as WITAKER has fully proved, having long endeavoured in vain to find amongst her subjects, a man base and bloody enough to take her victim off by assassination. This title was worn by that mean creature, JAMES I., who took as his chief councillor the right worthy son of that father who had been the chief contriver of the murder of his innocent mother, and whose reign was one unbroken series of base plots and cruel persecutions of all who professed the Catholic faith. But, not to anticipate further matter which will, hereafter, find a more suitable place, we may observe, that, amongst all our sovereigns, the only real Defenders of the Faith, since the reign of MARY, have been the late King and his son, our present sovereign: the former, by assent ing to a repeal of a part of the penal code, and by his appointing a special commission to try, condemn, and execute the leaders of the ferocious mob who set fire to, and who wished to sack, London, in 1780, with the cry of "NO POPERY" in their mouths, and from pretended zeal for the Protestant religion: and the latter, by his sending, in 1814, a body of English troops to assist, as a guard of honour, at the re-instalment of the POPE. Let us hope, that his defence of the faith is not to stop here; but that unto him is reserved the real glory of being the Defender of the Faith of all his subjects, and of healing for ever those deep and festering wounds, which, for more than two centuries, have been inflicted on so large and so loyal a part of his people.

108. From the sectarian host no man can say, what ought to be expected! but, from the "divines" of the established Church, even supposing them dead to the voice of justice, one would think, that, when they reflect on the origin of this title of their sovereign, common decency would restrain their revilings. It is beyond all dispute that the King holds this title from the POPE and from nobody else. His divine right to the crown is daily disputed; and he himself has disclaimed it. But, as to Defender of the Faith, he owes it entirely to the POPE. Will, then, the Protestant divines boldly tell us, that their and our sovereign wears a title, which, observe, finds its way, not only into every treaty, but into every municipal act, deed, or covenant; will they tell us, that he holds this title from the "Man of Sin, Antichrist, and the scarlet whore"? Will they thus defame that sovereign, whom they, at the same time, call on us to honour and obey? Yet this they must do; or they must confess, that their revilings, their foul abuse of the Catholic Church, have all been detestably false.

109. The King's predecessors had another title. They were called Kings of France; a title of much longer standing than that of Defender of the Faith. That title, a title of great glory, and one of which we were very proud, was not won by "Gospellers" or Presbyterians, or New Lights, with Saint Noel or Saint Butterworth at their head. It was, along with the Three Feathers, which the King so long wore, won by our brave Catholic ancestors. It was won while the POPE's supremacy; while confessions to priests, while absolutions, indulgences, masses, and monasteries existed in England. lit was won by Catholics in the "dark ages of monkish ignorance and superstition." It was surrendered in an age enlightened by a "heaven-born" Protestant and pledge-breaking Minister. It was won by valour and surrendered by fear; and fear, too, of those whom, for years, we had been taught to regard as the basest (as they certainly had been the bloodiest) of all mankind.

110. It would be time now, after giving a rapid sketch of the progress which the tyrant had made in prostrating the liberties of his people, and in despatching more of his wives, to enter on the grand scene of plunder, and to recount the miseries which immediately followed; but these must be the subject of the next Letter.

LETTER IV.

HORRID TYRANNY. BUTCHERY OF THE COUNTESS OF SALISBURY.
CELIBACY OF THE CLERGY.-- BISHOPS OF WINCHESTER.
HUME'S CHARGES AND BISHOP TANNER'S ANSWER.

Kensington, 28th February, 1825.

MY FRIENDS,

111. WE have seen, then, that the "Reformation" was engendered in beastly lust, brought forth in hypocrisy and perfidy, and we have had some specimens of the acts by which it caused innocent blood to be shed. We shall now, in this Letter and the next, see how it devastated and plundered the country, what poverty and misery it produced, and how it laid the sure foundation for that pauperism, that disgraceful immorality, that fearful prevalence of crimes of all sorts, which now so strongly mark the character of this nation, which was formerly the land of virtue and of plenty.

112. When, in paragraph **97**, we left the King and CRANMER at their bloody work, we had come to the year 1536, and to the 27th year of the King's reign. In the year 1528, an act had been passed to exempt the King from paying any sum of money that he might have borrowed; another act followed this for a similar purpose; and thus thousands of persons were ruined. His new Queen, JANE SEYMOUR brought him, in 1537, a son, who was afterwards King, under the title of EDWARD VI.; but the mother died in Child-birth, and according to Sir RICHARD BAKER, "had her body ripped up to preserve the child"! In this great "Reformation" man all was of a piece: all was consistent: he seemed never to have any compassion for the suffering of any human being; and this is a characteristic which WITAKER gives to his daughter ELIZABETH.

113. Having a son for a successor, he, with his Parliament, enacted, in 1537, that MARY and ELIZABETH, his two daughters, were bastards, and that, in case of a want of lawful issue, the King should be enabled, by letters patent, or by his last will, to give the crown to whomsoever he pleased! To cap the whole, to complete a series of acts of tyranny such as was never before heard of, it was enacted, in 1537, and in the 28th year of his reign, that, except in cases of mere private right; "the King's Proclamations should be of the same force as Acts of Parliament"! Thus, then, all law and justice were laid prostrate at the feet of a single man, and that man a man with whom law was a mockery, on whom the name of justice was a libel, and to whom mercy was wholly unknown.

114. It is easy to imagine that no man's property or life could have security with power like this in the hands of such a man. MAGNA CHARTA had been trampled under foot from the moment that the POPE's supremacy was assailed. The famous Act of EDWARD THE THIRD, for the security of the people against unfounded charges of high treason, was wholly set aside. Numerous things were made high treason, which were never before thought criminal at all. The trials were, for a long while, a mere mockery; and at last, they were altogether, in many cases, laid aside, and the accused were condemned to death, not only without being arraigned and heard in their defence; but, in numerous cases, without being apprised of the crimes, or pretended crimes, for which they were executed. We have read of Deys of Algiers and of Beys of Tunis; but, never have heard of their, even in the most exaggerated accounts, deeds to be, in point of injustice and cruelty, compared with those of this man, whom

BURNET calls, "the first-born son of the English 'Reformation.'" The objects of his bloody cruelty generally were, as they naturally would be, chosen from amongst the most virtuous of his subjects; because from them such a man had the most to dread. Of these his axe hewed down whole families and circles of friends. He spared neither sex nor age, if the parties possessed, or were suspected of possessing, that integrity which made them disapprove of his deeds. To look awry excited his suspicion, and his suspicion was death. England, before his bloody reign, so happy, so free, knowing so little of crime as to present to the judges of assize scarcely three criminals in a county in a year, now saw upwards of sixty thousand persons shut up in her gaols at one and the same time. The purlieus of the court of this "first-born son of the Reformation" were a great human slaughter-house, his people, deserted by their natural leaders, who had been bribed by plunder, or the hope of plunder, were the terrified and trembling flock, while he, the master-butcher, fat and jocose, sat in his palace issuing orders for the slaughter, while his High Priest, CRANMER, stood ready to sanction and sanctify all his deeds.

115. A detail of these butcheries could only disgust and weary the reader. One instance, however, must not be omitted; namely, the slaughtering of the relations, and particularly the mother, of Cardinal POLE. The Cardinal, who had, when very young, and before the King's first divorce had been agitated, been a great favourite with the King, and had pursued his studies and travels on the Continent at the King's expense, disapproved of the divorce, and of all the acts that followed it; and though called home by the King, he refused to obey. He was a man of great learning, talent, and virtue, and his opinions had great weight in England. His mother, the Countess of SALISBURY, was descended from the PLANTAGENETS, and was the last living descendant of that long race of English Kings. So that the Cardinal, who had been by the POPE raised to that dignity, on account of his great learning and eminent virtues, was, thus, a relation of the King, as his mother was of course, and she was, too, the nearest of all his relations. But the Cardinal was opposed to the King's proceedings; and that was enough to excite and put in motion the deadly vengeance of the latter. Many were the arts that he made use of, and great in amount was the treasure of his people that he expended, in order to bring the Cardinal's person within his grasp; and, these having failed, he resolved to wreak his ruthless vengeance on his kindred and his aged mother. She was charged by the base THOMAS CROMWELL (of whom we shall soon see enough) with having persuaded her tenants not to read the new translations, of the Bible, and also with having received bulls from Rome, which the accuser said, were found at COURDRAY HOUSE, her seat in Sussex. CROMWELL also showed a *banner*, which had, he said, been used by certain rebels in the North, and which he said he found in her house. All this was, however, so very barefaced, that it was impossible to think of a trial. The judges were then asked, whether the parliament could not *attaint* her; that is to say, *condemn* her, *without giving her a hearing?* The judges said, that it was a dangerous matter; that they could not, in their courts, act in this manner, and that they thought the parliament never would. But, being asked, whether, if the parliament were to do it, it would remain good in law, they answered in the affirmative. That was enough. A bill was brought in, and thus was the Countess, together with the Marchioness of EXETER and two gentlemen, relations of the Cardinal, condemned to death. The two latter were executed, the Marchioness was pardoned, and the Countess shut up in prison as a sort of hostage for the conduct of her son. In a few months; however, an insurrection having broken out on account of his tyrannical acts, the King chose to suspect, that the rebels had been instigated by Cardinal POLE, and, forth he dragged his mother to the scaffold. She,

who was upwards of seventy years of age, though worn down in body by her imprison ment, maintained to the last a true sense of her character and noble descent. When bidden to lay her head upon the block: "No," answered she, "my head shall never bow to tyranny: it never committed treason; and, if you will have it, you must get it as you can," The executioner struck at her neck with his axe, and, as she ran about the scaffold with her gray locks hanging down her shoulders and breast, he pursued, giving her repeated chops, till, at last, he brought her down!

116. Is it a scene in Turkey or in Tripoli that we are contemplating? No; but, in England, where MAGNA CHARTA had been so lately in force. where nothing could have been done contrary to law; but where all power, ecclesiastical as well as lay, being placed in the hands of one man, bloody butcheries like this, which would have roused even a Turkish populace to resistance, could be perpetrated without the smallest danger to the perpetrator. HUME, in his remarks upon the state of the people in this reign, pretends, that the people never hated the King, and "that he seems even, in some degree, to have possessed to the last, their love and affection." He adds, that it may be said with truth, that the "English, in that age, were so thoroughly subdued, that, like Eastern slaves, they were inclined to admire even those acts of violence and tyranny which were exercised over themselves, and at their own expense." This lying historian every where endeavours to gloss over the deeds of those who destroyed the Catholic Church, both in England and Scotland. Too cunning, however, to applaud the bloody Henry himself, he would have us believe, that, after all, there was something amiable in him, and this belief he would have us found on the fact of his having been to the last, seemingly, beloved by his people.

117. Nothing can be more false than this assertion, if repeated insurrections against him, accompanied with the most bitter complaints and reproaches, be not to be taken as marks of popular affection. And, as to the remark, that the English, "in that age were so thoroughly subdued," while it seems to refute the assertion as to their affection for the tyrant, it is a slander, which the envious Scotch writers all delight to put forth and repeat. One object, always uppermost with HUME, is to malign the Catholic religion; it, therefore, did not occur to him, that this sanguinary tyrant was not effectually resisted, as King John and other bad kings had been, because this tyrant had the means of bribing the natural leaders of the people to take part against them; or, at the least, to neutralize those leaders. It did not occur to him to tell us, that Henry VIII. found the English as gallant and just a people as his ancestors had found them; but that, having divided them, having by holding out to the great an enormous mass of plunder as a reward for abandoning the rights of the people, the people became, as every people without leaders must become, a mere flock, or herd, to be dealt with at pleasure. The malignity and envy of this Scotchman blinded him to this view of the matter, and induced him to ascribe to the people's admiration of tyranny that submission, which, after repeated struggles, they yielded merely from the want of those leaders, of whom they were now, for the first time, wholly deprived. What? have we never known any country, consisting of several millions of people, oppressed and insulted, even for ages, by a mere handful of men? And, are we to conclude, that such a country submits from admiration of the tyranny under which they groan? Did the English submit to CROMWELL from admiration; and, was it from admiration that the French submitted to ROBESPIERRE? The latter was punished, but CROMWELL was not: he, like HENRY, died in his bed; but, to what mind except to that of the most malignant and perverse, would it occur that CROMWELL'S impunity arose from the willing submission and the admiration of the people?

118. Of the means by which the natural leaders of the people were seduced from them; of the kind and the amount of the prize of plunder, we are now going to take a view. In paragraph **4**, I have said, that the "Reformation" was cherished and fed by plunder and devastation: In paragraph **37**, I have said, that it was not a Reformation, but a devastation of England; and that this devastation impoverished and degraded the main body of the people. These statements I am now about to prove to be true.

119. In paragraphs from **55** to **60** inclusive, we have seen how monasteries arose, and what sort of institutions they were. There were, in England, at the time we are speaking of, 645 of theee institutions; besides 90 Colleges, 110 Hospitals, and 2374 Chantries and Free-Chapels. The whole were seized on, first and last, taken into the hands of the King, and by him granted to those who aided and abetted him in the work of plunder.

120. I pray you, my friends, sensible and just English men, to observe here, that this was a great mass of landed property; that this property was not by any means used for the sole benefit of monks, friars, and nuns; that, for the far greater part, its rents flowed immediately back amongst the people at large; and, that, if it had never been an object of plunder, England never would, and never could, have heard the hideous sound of the words pauper and poor-rate. You have seen, in paragraph **52**, in what manner the tithes arose and how they were disposed of; and you are, by-and-by, to see how the rents of the monasteries were distributed.

121 . You have, without doubt, fresh in your recollection all the censures, sarcasms, and ridicule, which we have, from our very infancy, heard against the monastic life. What drones the monks and friars and nuns were; how uselessly they lived; how much they consumed to no good purpose whatever; and particularly how ridiculous, and even how wicked it was to compel men and women to live unmarried, to lead a life of celibacy, and, thus, either to deprive them of a great natural pleasure, or to expose them to the double sin of breach of chastity and breach of oath.

122. Now, this is a very important matter. It is a great moral question; and, therefore, we ought to endeavour to settle this question; to make up our minds completely upon it, before we proceed any further. The monastic state necessarily was accompanied with vows of celibacy; and, therefore, it is, before we give an acccunt of the putting down of these institutions in England, necessary to speak of the tendency, and, indeed, of the natural and inevitable consequences of those vows.

123. It has been represented as "unnatural" to compel men and women to live in the unmarried state, and as tending to produce propensities, to which it is hardly proper even to allude. Now, in the first place, have we heard, of late days, of any propensities of this sort? Have they made their odious appearance amongst clergymen and bishops? And, if they have, have those clergymen and bishops been Catholics, or have they been Protestants? The answer, which every one now living in England and Ireland can instantly give to these questions, disposes of this objection to vows of celibacy. In the next place, the Catholic Church compels nobody to make such vow. It only says, that it will admit no one to be a priest, monk, friar, or nun, who rejects such vow. Saint PAUL strongly recommends to all Christian teachers an unmarried life. The Church has founded a rule on this recommendation; and that, too, for the same reason that the recommendation was given; namely, that those who have flocks to watch over, or, in the language of our own Protestant Church, who have the care of souls, should have as few as possible of other cares, and should, by all means, be free from those incessant, and, sometimes, racking cares, which are inseparable from a

wife and family. What priest, who has a wife and family, will not think more about them than about his flock? Will he, when any part of that family is in distress, from illness or other cause, be wholly devoted, body and mind, to his flock? Will he be as ready to give alms, or aid of any sort, to the poor, as he would be if he had no family to provide for? Will he never be tempted to swerve from his duty, in order to provide patronage for sons, and for the husbands of daughters? Will he always as boldly stand up and reprove the Lord or the 'Squire for their oppressions and vices, as he would do if he had no son for whom to get a benefice, a commission, or a sinecure? Will his wife never have her partialities, her tattlings, her bickerings, amongst his flock, and never, on any account, induce him to act towards any part of that flock, contrary to the strict dictates of his sacred duty? And to omit hundreds, yes, hundreds of reasons that might, in addition, be suggested, will the married priest be as ready as the unmarried one to appear at the bed-side of sickness and contagion? Here it is that the calls on him are most imperative, and here it is that the married priest will, and with nature on his side, be deaf to those calls. From amongst many instances that I could cite, let me take one. During the war of 1776, the King's house at Winchester was used as a prison for French prisoners of war. A dreadfully contagious fever broke out amongst them. Many of them died. They were chiefly Catholics, and were attended in their last moments by two or three Catholic Priests residing in that city. But, amongst the sick prisoners, there were many Protestants; and these requested the attendance of Protestant Parsons. There were the parsons of all the parishes at Winchester. There were the Dean and all the Prebendaries, But, not a man of them went to console the dying Protestants, in consequence of which several of them desired the assistance of the priests, and, of course, died Catholics. Doctor MILNER, in his Letters to Doctor STURGES (page 56,) mentions this matter, and he says, "the answer" (of the Protestant Parsons) "I understand to have been this: We are not more afraid, as individuals, to face death than the priests are; but we must not carry poisonous contagion into the bosoms of our families." No, to be sure! But, then, not to call this the cassock's taking shelter behind the petticoat, in what a dilemma does this place the Dean and Chapter? Either they neglected their most sacred duty, and left Protestants to flee, in their last moments, into the arms of "popery;" or that clerical celibacy, against which they have declaimed all their lives and still declaim, and still hold up to us, their flocks, as something both contemptible and wicked, is, after all, necessary to that "care of souls," to which they profess themselves to have been called, and for which they receive such munificent reward.

124. But, conclusive, perfectly satisfactory, as these reasons are, we should not, if we were to stop here, do any thing like justice to our subject; for, as to the parochial clergy, do we not see, ay, and feel too, that they, if with families, or intending to have families, find little to spare to the poor of their flocks? In short, do we not know that a married priesthood and pauperism and poor-rates, all came upon this country at one and the same moment? And what was the effect of clerical celibacy with regard to the higher orders of the clergy? A bishop, for instance, having neither wife nor child, naturally expended his revenues amongst the people in his diocese. He expended a part of them on his Cathedral Church, or in some other way sent his revenues back to the people. If WILLIAM OF WYKHAM had been a married man, the parsons would not now have had a COLLEGE at Winchester; nor would there have been a College either at Eton, Westminster, Oxford, or Cambridge, if the bishops, in those days, had been married men. Besides, who is to expect of human nature, that a bishop with a wife and family will, in his distribution of the church preferment, consider nothing but the interest of religion? We are not to expect of man more than that, of which we,

from experience, know that man is capable. It is for the lawgiver to interpose, and to take care that the community suffer not from the frailty of the nature of individuals, whose private virtues even may, in some cases, and those not a few, not have a tendency to produce public good. I do not say that married bishops ever do wrong, because I am not acquainted with them well enough to ascertain the fact; but, in speaking of the diocese in wnich I was born, and with which I am best acquainted, I may say that it is certain, that, if the late Bishop of Winchester had lived in Catholic times, he could not have had a wife, and that he could not have had a wife's sister, to marry Mr. EDMUND POULTER, in which case, I may be allowed to think it possible, that Mr. POULTER would not have quitted the bar for the pulpit, and that he would not have had the two livings of Meon-Stoke and Soberton, and a Prebend besides; that his son BROWNLOW POULTER would not have had the two livings of Buriton and Petersfield; that his son CHARLES POULTER would not have had the three livings of Alton, Binstead and Kingsley; that his son-in-law OGLE would not have had the living of Bishop's Waltham; and that his son-in-law HAYGARTH would not have had the two livings of Upham and Durley. If the Bishop had lived in Catholic times, he could not have had a son, CHARLES AUGUSTUS NORTH, to have the two livings of Alverstoke and Havant and to be a Prebend; that he could not have had another son, FRANCIS NORTH, to have the four livings of Old Alresford, Medstead, New Alresford, and St. Mary's, Southampton, and to be, moreover, a Prebend and Master of St. Cross; that he could not have had a daughter to marry Mr. WiLLIAM GARNIER, to have the two livings of Droxford and Brightwell Baldwin, and to be a Prebend and a Chancellor besides; that he could not have had Mr. William Gamier's brother, THOMAS GARNIER, for a relation, and this latter might not, then, have had the two livings of Aldingbourn and Bishop's Stoke; that he could not have another daughter to marry Mr. THOMAS DE GREY, to have the four livings of Calbourne, Fawley, Merton, and Rounton, and to be a Prebend and also an Archdeacon besides! In short, if the late Bishop had lived in Catholic times, it is a little too much to believe, that these twenty-four Livings, five Prebends, one Chancellorship, one Archdeaconship, and one Mastership, worth perhaps, all together. more than twenty thousand pounds a-year, would have fallen to the ten persons above named. And, may we not reasonably suppose, that the Bishop, instead of leaving behind him (as the newspapers told us he did) savings to nearly the amount of three hundred thousand pounds in money, would, if he had had no children nor grand-children, have expended a part of his money on that ancient and magnificent Cathedral, the roof of which has recently been in danger of falling in, or, would have been the founder of something for the public good and national honour, or would have been a most munificent friend and protector of the poor, and would never, at any rate, have suffered SMALL BEER TO BE SOLD OUT OF HIS EPISCOPAL PALACE AT FARNHAM? With an excise licence, mind you! I do not say, or insinuate, that there was any smuggling carried on at the palace. Nor do I pretend to censure the act. A man who has a large family to provide for must be allowed to be the best judge of his means; and, if he happen to have an overstock of small beer, it is natural enough for him to sell it, in order to get money to buy meat, bread, groceries, or other necessaries. What I say is, that I do not think that WILLIAM of WYKHAM ever sold small beer, either by wholesale or retail; and I most distinctly assert, that this was done during the late Bishop's life-time, from his Episcopal Palace at Farnham! WILLIAM OF WYKHAM (who took his surname from a little village in Hampshire) was not Bishop of Winchester half so long as the late Bishop: but, out of his revenues, he built and endowed one of the Colleges at Oxford, the College of Winchester, and did numerous other most munificent things, in some of which, however, he was ot without examples in his predecessors, nor without imitators in his successors as long as the Catholic Church remained; but, when a married clergy came, then ended all that was munificent in the Bishops of this once famous city.

125. It is impossible to talk of the small beer and of the Master of Saint Cross, without thinking of the melancholy change which the "Reformation" has produced in this ancient establishment. Saint Cross, or Holy Cross, situated in a meadow about half a mile from Winchester, is an hospital, or place for hospitality, founded and endowed by a Bishop of Winchester, about seven hundred years ago. Succeeding Bishops added to its endowments, till, at last, it provided a residence and suitable maintenance for forty-eight decayed gentlemen, with priests, nurses, and other servants and attendants; and, besides this, it made provision for a dinner every day for a hundred of the most indigent men in the city. These met daily in a hall, called "the hundred men's hall." Each had a loaf of bread, three quarts of small beer and "two messes," for his dinner; and they were allowed to carry home that which they did not consume upon the spot. What is seen at the hospital of Holy Cross now? Alas! TEN poor creatures creeping about in this noble building, and THREE out-pensioners; and to those an attorney from Winchester carries, or sends, weekly, the few pence, whatever they may be, that are allowed them! But the place of the "Master" is, as I have heard, worth a round sum annually. I do not know exactly what it is; but, the post being a thing given to a son of the Bishop, the reader will easily imagine that it is not a trifle. There exists, however, here, that which, as Dr. MILNER observes, is probably, the last remaining vestige of "old English hospitality;" for here, any traveller who goes and knocks at the gate, and asks for relief, receives gratis a pint of good beer and a hunch of good bread. The late Lord Henry Stuart told me that he once went and that he received both.

126. But (and I had really nearly forgotten it) there is a Bishop of Winchester now! And, what is he doing? I have not heard that he has founded, or is about to found, any colleges or hospitals. All that I have heard of him in. the EDUCATION way, is, that, in his first charge to his Clergy (which he published) he urged them to circulate amongst their flocks the pamphlets of a society in London, at the head of which is Mr. JOSHUA WATSON, wine and spirit merchant, of Mincing-lane; and, all I have heard of him in the Charity way, is, that he is VICE-PATRON of a self-created body, called the "Hampshire Friendly Society," the object of which is, to raise subscriptions amongst the poor, for "their mutual relief and maintenance;" or, in other words, to induce the poor labourers to save out of their earnings the means of supporting themselves, in sickness or in old age, without coming for relief to the poor-rates! Good God! Why WILLIAM OF WYKHAM, Bishop Fox, Bishop WYNEFLEET; Cardinal BEAUFORT, HENRY DE BLOIS, and, if you take in all the Bishops of Winchester, even back to Saint SWITHIN himself; never would they have thought of a scheme like this for relieving the poor! Their way of promoting learning was, to found and endow colleges and schools; their way of teaching religion was, to build and endow churches and chapels; their way of relieving the poor and the ailing was, to found and endow hospitals: and all these at their own expense; out of their own revenues. Never did one of them, in order to obtain an interpretation of "Evangelical truth" for their flocks, dream of referring his Clergy to a Society, having a wine and brandy merchant at its head. Never did there come into the head of any one of them a thought so bright as that of causing the necessitous to relieve themselves! Ah! but they, alas lived. in the "dark ages of monkish ignorance and superstition." No wonder

that they could not see that the poor were the fittest persons in the world to relieve the poor! And, besides, they had no wives and children! No sweet babes to smile on, to soften their hearts. If they had, their conjugal and paternal feelings would have taught them, that true charity begins at home; and that it teaches men to sell small beer, and not give it away.

127. Enough now about the celibacy of the Clergy: but, it is impossible to quit the subject without one word to Parson MALTHUS. This man is not only a Protestant, but a parson of our Church. Now, he wants to compel the labouring classes to refrain, to a great extent, from marriage; and Mr. SCARLETT actually brought a bill into parliament, having, in one part of it, this object avowedly in view; the great end, proposed by both, being to cause a diminution of the poor-rates. Parson MALTHUS does not call this recommending celibacy; but "moral restraint." And, what is celibacy but moral restraint? So that, here are these people reviling the Catholic Church for insisting on vows of celibacy on the part of those who choose to be priests, or nuns; and, at the same time, proposing to compel the labouring classes to live in a state of celibacy, or to run the manifest risk of perishing (they and their children) from starvation! Is all this sheer impudence, or is it sheer folly? One or the other it is, greater than ever was before heard from the lips of mortal man. They affect to believe that the clerical vow of celibacy must be nugatory, because nature is constantly at work to overcome it. This is what Dr. STURGES asserts. Now, if this be the case with men of education; men on whom their religion imposes abstinence, fasting, almost constant prayer, and an endless number of austerities; if this be the case with regard to such men, bound by a most solemn vow, a known breach ot which exposes them to indelible infamy; if such be the case with such men, and if it be, therefore, contemptible and wicked, not to compel them, mind, to make such vows, but to permit them voluntarily to do it, what must it be to compel young men and women labourers to live in a state of celibacy, or be exposed to absolute starvation? Why, the answer is, that it is the grossest of inconsistency, or of premeditated wickedness; but that, like all the other wild schemes and cruel projects relative to the poor, we trace it at once back to the" Reformation," that great source of the poverty and misery and degradation of the main body of the people of this kingdom. The "Reformation" despoiled the working classes of their patrimony; it tore from them that which nature and reason had assigned them; it robbed them of that relief for the necessitous, which was theirs by right imprescriptable, and which had been confirmed to them by the law of God and the law of the land. It brought a compulsory, a grudging, an unnatural mode of relief, calculated to make the poor and rich hate each other, instead of binding them together, as the Catholic mode did, by the bonds of Christian charity. But of all its consequences that of introducing a married clergy has, perhaps, been the most prolific in mischief. This has absolutely created an order for the procreation of dependants on the state; for the procreation of thousands of persons annually, who have no fortunes of their own, and who must be, some how or other, maintained by burdens imposed upon the people. Places, commissions, sinecures, pensions; something or other must be found for them; some sort of living out of the fruit of the rents of the rich and the wages of labour. If no excuse can be found; no pretence of public service; no corner of the pension list open; then they must come as a direct burden upon the people; and, thus it is that we have, within the last twenty years, seen sixteen hundred thousand pounds voted by the parliament out of the taxes, for the "relief of the poor Clergy of the Church of England;" and at the very time that this prernium on the procreation of idlers was annually being granted, the parliament was pestered with projects for compelling the working part of the community to lead a life

of celibacy! What that is evil, what that is monstrous, has not grown out of this Protestant "Reformation"!

128. Thus, then, my friends, we have, I think, settled this great question; and, after all that we have, during our whole lives, heard against that rule of the Catholic Church. which imposed a vow of celibacy on those who chose the clerical, or the monastic life, we find, whether we look at this rule in a religious, in a moral, in a civil, or in a political, point of view, that it was founded in wisdom, that it was a great blessing to the people at large, and that its abolition is a thing to be deeply deplored.

129. So much, then, for this topic of everlasting railing against the Catholic Church. We must, before we come to an account of the deeds of the ruffian, THOMAS CROMWELL, who conducted the work of plunder, say something in answer to the *general charge* which Protestant writers, and particularly the malignant Scotch historians, have preferred against the Monasteries; for, if what they say were *true*, we might be disposed to think (as, indeed, we have been taught to think), that there was not so much harm in the plunderings that we are about to witness. We will take this *general charge* from the pen of HUME, who (Vol. iv. p. 160), speaking of the reports made by THOMAS CROMWELL and his myrmidons, says, "it is safest to credit the existence of vices *naturally* connected with the very *institution* of the monastic life. The cruel and inveterate factions and quarrels, therefore, which the commissioners mentioned, are VERY CREDIBLE among men, who, being confined together within the same walls, can never forget their mutual animosities, and who, being cut off from all the most endearing connections of nature, are commonly cursed with hearts more selfish, and tempers more unrelenting, than fall to the share of other men. The pious frauds, practised to increase the devotion and liberality of the people, may be regarded AS CERTAIN, in an order "founded on illusion, lies and superstition. The SUPINE IDLENESS, also, and its attendant, PROFOUND IGNORANCE, with which the convents were reproached, ADMIT OF NO QUESTION. No manly or elegant knowledge could be expected among men, whose life, condemned to a tedious uniformity, and deprived of all emulation, afforded nothing to raise the mind or cultivate the genius."

130. I question whether monk ever wrote sentences con taining worse grammar than these contain: but, as to the facts; these "very credible," these "certain," these "unquestionable," facts, are, almost upon the face of them, a tissue of malignant lies. What should there be "factions" and "quarrels" about, amongst men living so "idle" and "unambitious" a life? How much harder are the hearts of unmarried, than those of married ecclesiastics we have seen above, in the contrast between the charities of Catholic, and those of Protestant, bishops. It is quite "credible," that men, lost in "supine idleness," should practise frauds to get money, which their very state prevented them from either keeping or bequeathing, and who were totally destitute of all "emulation." The malignity of this liar exceeded his cunning, and made him not perceive, that he was, in one sentence, furnishing strong presumptive proof against the truth of another sentence. Yet, as his history has been, and is, much read, and, as it has deceived me, along with so many thousands of others, I shall, upon this subject, appeal to several authorities, all Protestants, mind, in contradiction to these, his false and base assertions, just remarking, by the way, that he himself never had a family, or a wife, and that he was a great, fat fellow, fed, in considerable part, out of public money, without having merited it by any real public services.

131. In his History of England, he refers, not less than two hundred times, to Bishop TANNER, who was Bishop of St. Asaph in the reign of George the Second. Let us hear, then, what Bishop TANNER; let us hear what this Protestant Bishop says, of the character and effects of the Monasteries, which the savages under Henry VIII. destroyed; Let us see how this high authority of HUME agrees with him on this, one of the most interesting and important points in our history. We are about to witness a greater act of plunder, a more daring contempt of law and justice and humanity, than ever was, in any other case, witnessed in the whole world. We are going to see thousands upon thousands of persons stripped, in an instant, of all their property; torn from their dwellings, and turned out into the wide world to beg or starve; and all this, too, in violation, not only of natural justice, but of every law. of the country, written and unwritten. Let us, then, see what was the character of the persons thus treated, and what were the effects of the institutions to which they belonged. And, let us see this, not in the description given by an avowed enemy not only of the Catholic, but of the Cluttian religion; but, in that descrIption which has been given us uy a Protestant Bishop, and in a book written expressly to give "An account of all the abbeys, priories, and friaries, formerly existing in England and Wales;" bearing in mind, as we go along, that HUME has, in his History of England, referred to this very work, upwards of two hundred times, taking care, however, not to refer to a word of it, relating to the important question now before us.

132. Bishop TANNER, before entering on his laborious account of the several monastic institutions, gives us, in pages 19, 20 and 21 of his preface, the following general description of the character and pursuits of the Monasteries, and of the effects of their establishments. I beg you, my friends, to keep, as you read, Bishop TANNER's description, the description of HUME constantly in your minds. Remember, and look, now-and-then, back at his charges of "supine idleness," "profound ignorance," want of all "emulation and all manly and Segant knowledge;" and, above all things, remember his charge of selfishness, his charge of "*frauds*" to get money from the people. The Bishop speaks thus upon the subject.

133. "In every great abbey, there was a large room called the Scriptorium, where several writers made it their whole business to transcribe books for the use of the library. They sometimes, indeed, wrote the ledger books of the house, and the missals, and other books, used in divine service, but they were generally upon other works, viz.: the Fathers, Classics, Histories, &c. &c. JOHN WHETHAMSTED, Abbot of St. Albans, caused above eighty books to be thus transcribed (there was then no printing) during his abbacy. Fifty-eight were transcribed by the care of one Abbot, at Glastonbury; and so zealous were the Monks in general for this work, that they often got lands given, and churches appropriated, for the carrying of it on. In all the greater abbeys, there were also persons appointed to take notice of the principal occurrences of the kingdom, and at the end of every year to digest them into annals. In these records they particularly preserved the memoirs of their founders, and benefactors, the years and days of their births and deaths; their marriages, children, and successors; so that recourse was sometimes bad to them for proving persons' ages, and genealogies though it is to be feared, that some of those pedigrees were drawn up from tradition only: and that, in most of their accounts, they were favourable to their friends, and severe upon their enemies. The constitutions of the clergy in their national and provincial synods, and (after the Conquest) even Acts of Parliament, were sent to the abbeys to be recorded: Which leads me to mention the use and advantage of these religious houses. For, FIRST, the choicest records and treasures in the kingdom were

preserved in them. An exemplification of the charter of liberties, granted by King Henry I. (MAGNA CHARTA) was sent to some abbey in every county to be preserved. Charters and Inquisitions relating to the county of Cornwall were deposited in the Priory of Bodmin; a great many rolls were lodged in the Abbey of Leicester, and Priory of Kenilworth, till taken from thence by King Henry III. King Edward I. sent to the religious houses to search for his title to the kingdom of Scotland, in their ledgers and chronicles, as the most authentic records for proof of his right to that crown. When his sovereignty was acknowledged in Scotland, he sent letters to have it inserted in the chronicles of the Abbey of Winchomb, and the Priory of Norwich, and probably of many other such like places. And when he decided the controversy relating to the crown of Scotland, between Robert Brus and John Baliol, he wrote to the Dean and Chapter of St. Paul's, London, requiring them to enter into their chronicles the exemplification therewith sent of that decision. The learned Mr. SELDEN hath his greatest evidences for the dominion of the narrow seas, belonging to the King of Great Britain, from Monastic records. The evidences and money of private families were oftentimes sent to these houses to be preserved. The seals of noblemen were deposited there upon their deaths. And even the King's money was sometimes lodged in them. -- SECONDLY, they were schools of learning and education, for every convent had one person or more appointed for this purpose; and all the neighbours, that desired it, might have their children taught grammar and church music without any expense to them. In the Nunneries also young women were taught to work) and to read English, and sometimes Latin also. So that not only the lower rank of people who could not pay for their learning, but most of the noblemen's and gentlemen's daughters were educated in those places. -- THIRDLY, all the Monasteries were, in effect, great hospitals. And were most of them obliged to relieve many poor people every day. There were likewise houses of entertainment for almost all travellers. Even the nobility and gentry, when they were upon the road, lodged at one religious house, and dined at another, and seldom, or never, went to inns. In short, their hospitality was such, that in the Priory of Norwich, one thousand five hundred quarters of malt, and above eight hundred quarters of wheat, and all other things in proportion, were generally spent every year. -- FOURTHLY, the nobility and gentry provided not only for their old servants, in these houses by corrodies, but for their younger children, and impoverished friends, by making them, first, monks and nuns, and in time, priors and prioresscs, and abbots and abbesses -- FIFTHLY, they were of considerable advantage to the Crown:
1. By the profits received from the death of one Abbot or Prior, to the election, or, rather, confirmation, of another.
2. By great fines paid for the confirmation of their liberties.
3. By many corrodies granted to old servants of the Crown, and pensions to the King's clerks and chaplains, till they get preferment. -- SIXTHLY, they were likewise of considerable advantage to the places where they had their sites and estates:--
1. By causing great resort to them, and getting grants of fairs and markets for them.
2 By freeing them from the forest laws.
3. By letting their lands at easy rates.
-- LASTLY, they were great ornaments to the country: many of them were really noble buildings; and though not actually so grand and neat, yet, perhaps, as much admired in their times, as Chelsea and Greenwich Hospitals are now. Many of the abbey churches were equal, if not superior, to our present Cathedrals; and they must have been as much an ornament to the country, and employed as many workmen in building, and keeping them in repair, as noblemen's and gentlemen's seats now do."

134. Now, then, malignant HUME, come up, and face this Protestant bishop, whose work you have quoted more than two hundred times, and who here gives the lie direct to all and every part of your description. Instead of your "supine idleness," we have industry the most patient and persevering; instead of your "profound ignorance," we have, in even convent, a school for teaching, gratis, all useful science; instead of your want of all "manly and elegant knowledge," we have the study, the teaching, the transcribing, the preserving, of the Classics; instead of your "selfishness" and your "pious frauds" to get the money from the people, we have hospitals for the sick, doctors and nurses to attend them, and the most disinterested, the most kind, the most noble hospitality; instead of that "slavery," which, in fifty parts of your history, you assert to have been taught by the monks, we have the freeing of people from the forest laws, and the preservation of the Great Charter of English liberty; and you know as well as I, that when this Charter was renewed by King JOHN, the renewal was, in fact, the work of Archbishop LANGTON, who roused the Barons to demand it, he having, as TANNER observes, found the Charter deposited in an abbey! Back, then; down, then, malignant liar, and tell the devil that the Protestant Bishop TANNER hast sent thee!

135. Want of room compels me to stop; but, here, in this one authority, we have ten thousand times more than enough to answer the malignant liar, HUME, and all the revilers of monastic life, which lies and revilings it was necessary to silence before proceeding, as I shall in the next Letter, to describe the base, the cruel, the bloody means by which these institutions were devastated and de stroyed.

LETTER V.

AUTHORITIES RELATING TO THE EFFECTS OF THE MONASTIC
INSTITUTIONS.
THEIR GREAT UTILITY AND THE POLITICAL WISDOM IN WHICH THEY
WERE FOUNDED.
THE APPOINTMENT OF THE RUFFIAN THOMAS CROMWELL.
HIS PROCEEDINGS IN THE WORK OF PLUNDER AND DEVASTATION.
THE FIRST ACT OF PARLIAMENT AUTHORISING THE PLUNDER.

Kensington, 31st March, 1825.

MY FRIENDS,

136. WHEN, at the close of the foregoing Letter, I appeared to content myself with
the authority of the Protestant Bishop TANNER, as a defender of Monastic
Institutions against the attacks, the malignant lies, of HUME, I had in reserve other
authorities in abundance, some of which I should then have cited, if I had had room.
Bishop TANNER goes, indeed, quite home to every point; but, the matter is of such
great importance, when we are about to view the destruction of these institutions, that,
out of fifty authorities that I might refer to, I will select four or five. I will take one
Foreign and four English; and observe, they are all Protestant authorities.

137. MALLET. *History of the Swiss, Vol. I. p. 105.* "The monks softened by their
instructions the ferocious manners of the people, and opposed their credit to the
tyranny of the nobility, who knew no other occupation than war, and grievously
oppressed their neighbours. On this account the government of Monks was preferred
to theirs. The people sought them for Judges. It was an usual saying, that it was better
to be governed by the Bishop's crosier than the Monarch's sceptre."

138. DRAKE. *Literary Hours, Vol. ii. p. 435.* "The monks of CASSINS, observes
WHARTON, were distinguished not only for their knowledge of sciences, but their
attention to polite learning, and an acquaintance with the Classics. Their learned
Abbot Desiderius, collected the best Greek and Roman authors. The fraternity not
only composed learned treatises on Music, Logic, Astronomy, and Vitruvium
Architecture, but likewise employed a portion of their time in transcribing Tacitus,
&c. This laudable example was, in the 11th and 12th centuries, followed with great
spirit and emulation by many English Monasteries."

139. TURNER, *History of England, Vol. 11. p. 332 and 361.* "No tyranny was ever
established that was more unequivocally the creature of popular will, nor longer
maintained by popular support; in no point did personal interest, and public welfare,
more cordially unite, than in the encouragement of Monasteries."

140. BATES. *Rural Philosophy, p. 322.* "It is to be lamented, that, while the Papists
are industriously planting Nunneries and other religious Societies in this Kingdom,
some good Protestants, are not so far excited to imitate their example, as to form
establishments for the education and protection of young women of serious
disposition, or who are otherwise unprovided, where they might enjoy at least a
temporary refuge, be instructed in the principles of religion, and in all such useful and
domestic arts, as might qualify them, who were inclined to return into the world, for a
pious and laudable discharge of the duties of common life. Thus might the comfort

and welfare of many individuals be promoted, to the great benefit of society at large, and the interests of Popery, by improving on its own principles, be considerably counteracted."

141. QUARTERLY REVIEW. *December 1811.* "The world has never been so indebted to any body of men as to the illustrious order of Benedictine Monks; but historians, in relating the evil of which they were the occasion, too frequently forget the good which they produced. Even the commonest readers are acquainted with the arch miracle-monger, St. Dunstan, whilst the most learned of our countrymen scarcely remember the names of those admirable men, who went forth from England, and became the Apostles of the North, Tinian and Juan Fernandez are not more beautiful spots on the ocean, than Malmesbury , Lindisfarne and Jarrow, were, in the ages of our heptarchy. A community of pious men, devoted to literature and to the useful arts as well as to religion, seems, in those days, like a green Oasis amid the desert. Like stars on a moonless night, they shine upon us with a tranquil ray. If ever there was a man, who could truly be called venerable, it was he, to whom the appellation is constantly fixed, BEDE, whose life was passed in instructing his own generation, and preparing records for postenty. In those days, the Church offered the only asylum from the evils to which every country was exposed -- amidst continual wars, the Church enjoyed peace -- it was regarded as a sacred realm by men, who, though they hated one another, believed and feared the same God. Abused as it was by the worldly-minded and ambitious, and disgraced by the artifices of the designing, and the follies of the fanatic, it afforded a shelter to those who were better than the world in their youth, or weary of it in their age. The wise as well as the timid and gentle fled to this Goshen of God, which enjoyed its own light and calm, amidst darkness and storms."

142. This is a very elegant passage; but, as TURNER's Protestantism impels him to apply the term "*tyranny*" to that which honest feeling bids him say was the "creature of the popular will," and was produced and upheld by" a cordial union of personal interest and public welfare," so the Protestantism of the REVIEWERS leads them to talk about "evil" occasioned by an Order to whom "the world is more indebted than to any other body of men"; and it also leads them to repeat the hackneyed charge against St. DUNSTAN, forgetting, I dare say, that he is one of the Saints in our Protestant Church Calendar! However, here is more than enough to serve as an answer to the whole herd of writers who have put forth their venom against the Monastic Orders.

143. Can we refer to these authorities, can we see all the indubitable proofs of the real Christian charity and benevolence which were essentially connected with the religion of our forefathers, without feeling indignation against those who, from our infancy to our manhood, have been labouring to persuade us, that the Catholic Church produced selfishness, hardness of heart, greediness in the clergy, and particularly a want of feeling for the poor? Undeniable as is the fact, that the "Reformation" robbed the poor of their patrimony; clear as we shall, by-and-by, see the proofs of its power in creating paupers, and in taking from the higher all compassion for the lower classes, how incessant have been the efforts, how crafty the schemes, to make us believe precisely the contrary! If the salvation of their souls had been the object they had in view, the deceivers could not have laboured with more pains and anxiety. They have particularly bent their attention to the implanting of their falsehoods in the minds of children. The press has teemed, for two centuries and more, with cheap books having this object principally in view. Of one instance of this sort I cannot refrain from making particular mention; namely, a FABLE, in a Spelling-book, by one FENNING,

which has been in use in England for more than half a century. The fable is called: "The priest and the jester." A man, as the fable says, went to a "Romish Priest," and asked charity of him. He began by asking for a guinea, but lowered the sum till it came to a farthing, and still the priest refused. Then the beggar asked for a "blessing," which the priest readily consented to give him: "No," said the beggar; "if it were worth but one single farthing you would not give it me." How indefatigable must have been these deceivers, when they could resort to means like these! What multitudes of children, how many millions of people, have, by this book alone, had falsehood, the most base and wicked, engraven upon their minds!

144. To proceed now with our inquiry relative to the effects of the Monastic Institutions, we may observe, that authorities, in this case, seemed necessary. The lies were of long standing: hypocritical selfishness, backed by every species of violence, tyranny and cruelty, had been at work for ages to delude the people of England. Those who had fattened upon the spoils of the church and the poor, and who wished still to enjoy the fatness in quiet, naturally laboured to persuade the people, that those who had been despoiled were unworthy people; that the institutions, which gave them much property were, at least, useless; that the possessors were lazy, ignorant, and base creatures, spreading darkness over the country instead of light; devouring that which ought to have sustained worthy persons. When the whole press and all the pulpits of a country are leagued for such a purpose, and supported in that purpose by the State; and when the reviled party is, by terrors hardly to be described, reduced to silence; in such a case, the assailants must prevail; the mass of the people must believe what they say. Reason, in such a state of things, is out of the question. But TRUTH is immortal; and though she may be silenced for a while, there always, at last, comes something to cause her to claim her due and to triumph over falsehood.

143. There is now come that which is calculated to give our reasoning faculties fair play. We see the land covered at last with pauperism, fanaticism and crime. We hear an increase of the people talked of as a calamity; we hear of projects to check the breeding of the people; we hear of Scotch *"feelosofers,"* prowling about the country, reading lectures to the manufacturers and artisans to instruct them in the science of preventing their wives from being mothers; and, in one instance, this has been pushed so far as to describe, in print, the mechanical process for effecting this object! In short, we are now arrived at a point which compels us to inquire into the cause of this monstrous state of things. The immediate cause we find to be the poverty and degradation of the main body of the people; and these, through many stages, we trace back to the "Reformation," one of the effects of which was to destroy those Monastic institutions which, as we shall now see, retained the produce of labour in the proper places, and distributed it in a way naturally tending to make the lives of the people easy and happy.

146. The authorities that I have cited ought to be of great weight in the question; but supposing there to be no authorities on the side of these institutions, of what more do they stand in need than the unfettered exercise of our reason? Reason, in such a ease, is still better than authorities; but who is to resist both? Let us ask, then, whether reason do not reject with disdain the slander that has been heaped on the Monastic Institutions. They flourished in England for nine hundred years; they were beloved by the people; they were destroyed by violence, by the plunderer's grasp, and the murderer's knife. Was there ever any thing, vicious in itself, or evil in its effects, held in veneration by a whole people for so long a time? Even in our own time, we see the people of Spain rising in defence of their Monasteries; and we hear the Scotch

"feelosofers" abuse them, because they do not like to see the property of those Monasteries transferred to English Jews.

147. If the Monasteries had been the cause of evil, would they have been protected with such care by so many wise and virtuous kings, legislators, and judges? Perhaps ALFRED was the greatest man that ever lived. What writer of eminence, whether poet, lawyer, or historian, has not selected him as the object of his highest praises? As king, as soldier, as patriot, as lawgiver, in all his characters he is, by all, regarded as having been the greatest, wisest, most virtuous of men. And is it reasonable, then, for us to suppose, that he, whose whole soul was wrapped up in the hope of making his people free, honest, virtuous, and happy; is it reasonable to suppose, that he would have been, as he was, one oc the most munificent founders of Monasteries, if those institutions had been vicious in themselves, or had tended to evil? We have not these institutions and their effects immediately before our eyes. We do not actually see the Monasteries. But we know of them two things; namely, that they were most anxiously cherished by ALFRED and his tutor, Saint SWITHIN; and that they were destroyed by the bloody tyrant HENRY THE EIGHTH, and the not less bloody ruffian, THOMAS CROMWELL. Upon these two facts alone we might pretty safely decide on the merits of these institutions.

148. And what answer do we ever obtain to this argument? Mr. MERVYN ARCHDALL, in the Preface to his History of the Irish Monasteries, says: "When we contemplate the universality of that religious zeal which drew thousands from the elegance and comforts of society to sequestered solitude and austere maceration: when we behold the greatest and wisest of mankind the dupes of a fatal delusion, and even the miser expending his store to partake in the felicity of mortified ascetics: again, when we find the tide of enthusiasm subsided, and sober reason recovered from her delirium, and endeavouring, as it were, to demolish every vestige of her former frenzy, have a concise sketch of the history of Monachism, and no common instance of that mental weakness and versatility which stamp the character of frailty on the human species. We investigate these phenomena in the moral world with a pride arising from assumed superiority in intellectual powers, or higher degrees of civilization: our vanity and pursuit are kept alive by a comparison so decidedly in favour of modern times"? Indeed, Mr. ARCHDALL! And where are we to look for the proofs, or signs, of this "assumed superiority"; this "comparison so decidedly in favour of modern times"? Are we to find them in the ruins of those noble edifices, of the plunder and demolition of which you cite us an account? Are we to find them in the total absence of even an attempt to ornament your country with any thing to equal them in grandeur or in taste? Are we to look for this "superiority" in the numerous tithe-battles, pistol in hand, like that of SKIBEEREEN? Are modern times proved to be "decidedly superior" to former times by the law that shuts Irishmen up in their houses from sunset to sunrise? Are the people' s living upon pig-diet, their nakedness, their hunger, their dying by hundreds from starvation while their ports weree crowded with ships carrying provisions from their shores, and while an army was fed in the country, the business of which army was to keep the starving people quiet: are these amongst the facts on which you found your "comparison so decidedly in favour of modern times"? What, then, do you look with "PRIDE" to the ball at the Opera-house, for the relief of the starving people of ireland, the BALL-room "DECORATED with a transparency exhibiting an Irishman, as large as life, EXPIRING FROM HUNGER"? And do you call the "greatest and wisest of mankind" dupes; do you call them "the dupes of a fatal delusion," when they founded institutions which rendered a thought of

Opera-house relief impossible? Look at the present wretched and horrible state of your country; then look again at your list of ruins; and then (for you are a church-parson, I see,) you will, I have no doubt, say, that, though the former have evidently come from the latter, it was "sober reason," and not thirst for plunder, that produced those ruins, and that it was "frenzy and mental weakness" in the "greatest and wisest of mankind" that produced the foundations of which those ruins are the melancholy memorials!

149. The hospitality and other good things proceeding from the Monasteries, as mentioned by the Protestant Bishop TANNER, are not to be forgotten; but we must take a close view of the subject, in order to do full justice to these calumniated institutions. It is our duty to show, that they were founded in great political wisdom as well as in real piety and charity. That they were not, as the false and malignant and selfish HUME has described them, mere dolers out of bread and meat and beer; but that they were great diffusers of general prosperity, happiness and content; and that one of their natural and necessary effects was, to prevent that state of things which sees but two classes of people in a community, masters and slaves, a very few enjoying the extreme of luxury, and millions doomed to the extreme of misery.

150. From the land all the good things come. Somebody must own the land. Those who own it must have the distribution of its revenues . If these revenues be chiefly distributed amongst the people, from whose labour they arise, and in such a way as to afford to them a good maintenance on easy terms, the community must be happy. If the revenues be alienated in very great part; if they be carried away to a great distance, and expended amongst those, from whose labour no part of them arise, the main body of the community must be miserable: poor houses, gaols, and barracks must arise. Now, one of the greatest advantages attending the Monasteries was, that they, of necessity, caused the revenues of a large part of the lands of the country to be spent on the spot whence those revenues arose. The hospitals and all the other establishments of the kind had the same tendency. There were, of the whole, great and small, not less, on an average, than fifty in each county; so that the revenues of the land diffused themselves, in great part, immediately amongst the people at large. We all well know how the state of a parish becomes instantly changed for the worse, when a noble or other great land-owner quits the mansion in it, and leaves that mansion shut up. Every one knows the effect which such a shutting up has upon the poor-rates of a parish. It is notorious, that the non-residence of the Clergy and of the noblemen and gentlemen is universally complained of as a source of evil to the country. One of the arguments, and a great one it is, in favour of severe game laws, is, that the game causes noblemen and gentlemen to reside. What, then, must have been the effect of twenty rich Monasteries in every county, expending constantly a large pan of their incomes on the spot? The great cause of the miseries of Ireland, at this moment, is "absenteeship"; that is to say, the absence of the land-owners , who draw away the revenues of the country, and expend them in other countries. If Ireland had still her seven or eight hundred Monastic Institutions, great and small, she would be, as she formerly was, prosperous and happy. There would be no periodical famines and typhus f evers; no need of sun-set and sun-rise laws; no Captain Rocks; no projects for preventing the people from increasing; no schemes for getting rid of a "surplus population"; none of that poverty and degradation that threaten to make a desert of the country, or to make it the means of destroying the greatness of England herself.

151. Somebody must own the lands; and the question is, whether it be best for them to be owned by those who constantly live, and constantly must live, in the country and

in the midst of their estates; or, by those who always may, and who frequently will and do, live at a great distance from their lands, and draw away the revenues of them to be spent elsewhere. The monastics are, by many, called drones. Bishop TANNER has shown us that this charge is very false. But, if it were true; is not a drone in a cowl as good as a drone in a hat and top-boots? By drones, are meant those who do not work; and, do land-owners usually work? The lay land-owner and his family spend more of their revenues in a way not useful to the people than the monastics possibly could. But, besides this, besides the hospitality and charity of the monastics, and besides, moreover, the lien, the legal lien, which the main body of the people had, in many cases, to a share, directly or indirectly, in the revenues of the Monasteries, we are to look at the monks and nuns in the very important capacity of landlords and landladies. All historians, however Protestant or malignant, agree, that they were "easy landlords"; that they let their lands at low rents, and on leases of long terms of years; so that, says even HUME, "the farmers regarded themselves as a species of proprietors, always taking care to renew their leases before they expired." And was there no good in a class of landlords of this sort? Did not they naturally and necessarily create, by slow degrees, men of property? Did they not thus cause a class of yeomen to exist, real yeomen, independent of the aristocracy? And was not this class destroyed by the "Reformation," which made the farmers rack-renters and absolute dependants, as we see them to this day? And, was this change favourable, then, to political liberty? Monastics could possess no private property, they could save no money, they could bequeath nothing. They had a life interest in their estate, and no more. They lived, received, and expended in common. Historians need not have told us, that they were "easy landlords." They must have been such, unless human nature had taken a retrograde march expressly for their accommodation. And, was it not happy for the nation, that there was such a class of landlords? What a jump for joy would the farmers of England now give, if such a class were to return to-morrow, to get them out of the hands of the squandering and needy lord and his grinding land-valuer!

152. Then, look at the monastics as causing, in some of the most important of human affairs, that fixedness which is so much the friend of rectitude in morals, and which so powerfully conduces to prosperity, private and public. The Monastery was a proprietor that never died; its tenantry had to do with a deathless landlord; its lands and houses never changed owners; its tenants were liable to none of many uncertainties that other tenants were; its oaks had never to tremble at the axe of the squandering heir; its manors had not to dread a change of lords; its villagers had all been born and bred up under its eye and care; their character was of necessity a thing of great value, and, as such, would naturally be an object of great attention. A Monastery was the centre of a circle in the country, naturally drawing to it all that were in need of relief, advice, and protection, and containing a body of men, or of women, having no cares of their own, and having wisdom to guide the inexperienced, and wealth to relieve the distressed. And was it a good thing, then, to plunder and devastate these establishments; was it a reformation to squander estates, thus employed, upon lay persons, who would not, who could not, and did not, do any part or particle of those benevolent acts, and acts of public utility, which naturally arose out of the monastic institutions?

153. Lastly, let us look at the Monasteries as a resource for the younger Sons and daughters of the aristocracy, and as the means of protecting the government against the injurious effects of their clamorous wants. There cannot exist an aristocracy, or

body of nobility, without the means, in the hands of the government, of preventing that body from falling into that contempt, which is, and always must be, inseparable from Noble-poverty. "Well," some will say, "why need that be any such body?" That is quite another question; for we have it; and have had it for more than a thousand rears; except during a very short interval, at the end of which our ancestors eagerly took it back again. I must, too. though it really has nothing to do with the question before us, repeat my opinion, many times expressed, that we should lose more than we should gain by getting rid of our aristocracy. The basest and most corrupt government that I ever knew any thing, or heard any thing of, is the republican government of PENNSYLVANIA, and, withal, the most truly tyrannical: base and corrupt from bottom to top; from the root to the topmost twig; from the trunk to the extreme point of every branch. And, if any PENNSYLVANIAN, who has a name, and who will put it as a challenge to me to prove my words, I will, before the face of all Europe, prove them in the most complete and ample manner. I am not, therefore, for republican government; and, then, it follows, that I am for an aristocracy; for, without it, there can be no limit to a kingly government.

134. However, this has nothing at all to do with the present question; we have the aristocracy, and we must, by a public provision of some sort, for the younger branches of it, prevent it from falling into the degradation inseparable from poverty. This provision was, in the times of which we are speaking, made by the Monasteries, which received a great number of its monks and nuns from the families of the nobles. This rendered those odious and burdensome things, pensions and sinecures, unnecessary. It, of course, spared the taxes. It was a provision that was not degrading to the receivers; and it created no grudging and discontent amongst the people, from whom the receivers took nothing. Another great advantage arising from this mode of providing for the younger branches of the nobility was, that it secured the government against the temptation to give offices and to lodge power in unfit hands. Look at our pension and sinecure list; look at the list of those who have commands, and who fill other offices of emolument; and you will, at once, see the great benefit which must have been derived from institutions, which left the government quite free to choose commanders, ambassadors, governors and other persons, to exercise power, and to be entrusted in the carrying on of the public affairs. These institutions tended, too, to check the increase of the race of nobles; to prevent the persons connected with that order from being multiplied to the extent to which they naturally would, otherwise, be multiplied. They tended also to make the nobles not so dependant on the Crown, a provision being made for their poor relations without the Crown's assistance; and, at the same time, they tended to make the people less dependant on the nobles than they otherwise would have been. The Monasteries set the example, as masters and landlords; an example that others were, in a great degree, compelled to follow. And thus, all ranks and degrees were benefited by these institutions, which, with malignant historians, have been a subject of endless abuse, and the destruction of which they have recorded with so much delight, as being one of the brightest features in the "Reformation"!

155. Nor must we, by any means, overlook the effects of these institutions on the mere face of the country. That soul must be low and mean indeed, which is insensible to all feeling of pride in the noble edifices of its country. Love of country, that variety of feelings which, altogether, constitute what we properly call patriotism, consist in part of the admiration of, and veneration for, ancient and magnificent proofs of skill and of opulence. The monastics built as well as wrote for posterity. The never-dying

nature of their institutions set aside, in all their undertakings, every calculation as to time and age. Whether they built or planted, they set the generous example of providing for the pleasure, the honour, the wealth and greatness of generations upon generations yet unborn. They executed every thing in the very best manner: their gardens, fish-ponds, farms; in all, in the whole of their economy, they set an example tending to make the country beautiful, and to make it an object of pride with the people, and to make the nation truly and permanently great. Go into any county, and survey, even at this day, the ruins of its, perhaps, twenty Abbeys and Priories: and, then, ask yourself, "What have we in exchange for these"? Go to the site of some once-opulent Convent. Look at the cloister, now become, in the hands of a rack-renter, the receptacle for dung, fodder and fagot-wood: see the hall, where, for ages, the widow, the orphan, the aged and the stranger, found a table ready spread; see a bit of its walls now helping to make a cattleshed, the rest having been hauled away to build a workhouse: recognise, in the side of a barn, a part of the once magnificent chapel: and, if, chained to the spot by your melancholy musings, you be admonished of the approach of night by the voice of the screech-owl, issuing from those arches, which once, at the same hour, resounded with the vespers of the monk, and which have, for seven hundred years, been assailed by storms and tempests in vain: if thus admonished of the necessity of seeking food, shelter, and a bed, lift your eyes and look at the white-washed and dry-rotten shell on the hill, called the "gentleman's house;" and, apprised of the "board-wages" and the spring-guns, suddenly turn your head; jog away from the scene of devastation; with "old English Hospitality" in your mind, reach the nearest inn, and there, in a room half-warmed and half-lighted, and with reception precisely proportioned to the presumed length of your purse, sit down and listen to an account of the hypocritical pretences, the base motives, the tyrannical and bloody means, under which, from which, and by which, that devastation was effected, and that hospitality banished from ever front the land.

156. We have already seen something of these pretences, motives and acts of tyranny and barbarity; we have seen that the beastly lust of the chief tyrant was the groundwork of what is called the "Reformation"; we have seen that he could not have proceeded in his course without the concurrence of the Parliament; we have seen that, to obtain that concurrence, he held out to those who composed it a participation in the spoils of the Monasteries; and, when we look at the magnitude of their possessions, when we consider the beauty and fertility of the spots on which they, in general, were situated, when we think of the envy which the love borne them by the people must have excited in the hearts of a great many of the noblemen and gentlemen; when we thus reflect, we are not surprised, that these were eager for a "Reformation" that promised to transfer the envied possessions to them.

157. When men have power to commit, and are resolved to commit, acts of injustice, they are never at a loss for pretences. We shall presently see what were the prefences under which this devastation of England was begun: but, to do the work, there required a workman; as, to slaughter an ox, there requires a butcher. To turn the possessors of so large a part of the estates out of those estates, to destroy establishments venerated by the people from their childhood, to set all law, divine as well as human, at defiance, to violate every principle on which property rested, to rob the poor and helpless of the means of sustenance, to deface the beauty of the country, and make it literally a heap of ruins; to do these things, there re quired a suitable agent; and that agent the tyrant found in THOMAS CROMWELL, whose name, along with that of CRANMER, ought "to stand for aye accursed in the calendar." This

CROMWELL was the son of a blacksmith of Putney, in Surrey. He had been an underling of some sort in the family of CARDINAL WOLSEY, and had recommended himself to the King by his sycophancy to him, and his treachery to his old master. The King, now become Head of the Church, and having the supremacy to exercise, had very judiciously provided himself with CRANMER as a primate; and, to match him, he provided himself with CROMWELL, who was equal to CRANMER in impiousness and baseness, rather surpassed him in dastardliness, and exceeded him decidedly in quality of ruffian. All nature could not, perhaps, have afforded another man so fit to be the "ROYAL VICEGERENT and VICAR-GENERAL" of the new head of the English Church.

158. Accordingly, with this character the brutal blacksmith was invested. He was to exercise "all the spiritual authority belonging to the King, for the due administration uf justice in all cases touching the ecclesiastical jurisdiction, and the godly reformation and redress of errors, heresies, and abuses in the said church." We shall very soon see proofs enough of the baseness of this nan, for whom ruffian is too gentle a term. What chance, then, did the Monasteries stand in his hands? He was created a peer. He sat before the primate in parliament, he sat above all the bishops in assemblies of the clergy, he took precedence of all the nobles, whether in office or out of office, and, as in character, so in place, he was second only to the chief tyrant himself.

159. In order to begin the "godly Reformation"; that is to say, the work of plunder, the "Vicegerent" blacksmith set on foot a visitation of the Monasteries! Dreadful visitation! He, active as he was in wickedness, could not do all the work himself. He, therefore, appointed deputies to assist in making this visitation. The kingdom was divided into districts for this purpose, and two deputies were appointed to visit each district. The object was to obtain grounds of accusation against the monks and nuns. \\then we consider what the object was, and what was the character of the man, to whom the work was committed, we may easily imagine what sort of men these deputies were. They were, in fact, fit to be the subalterns of such a chief. Some of the very worst men in all England; men of notoriously infamous characters; men who had been convieted of heinous crimes; some who had actually been branded; and, probably, not one man who had not repeatedly deserved the halter. Think of a respectable, peaceful, harmless and pious family, broken in upon, all of a sudden, by a brace of burglars with murder written on their scowling brows, demanding an instant production of their title-deeds, money and jewels; imagine such a scene as this, and you have then some idea of the visitations of these monsters, who came with the threat of the tyrant on their lips, who menaced the victims with charges of high treason, who wrote in their reports not what was, but what their merciless employers wanted them to write.

160. The monks and nuns, who had never dreamed of the possibility of such proceedings, who had never had an idea that Magna Charta and all the laws of the land could be set aside in a moment, and whose recluse and peaceful lives rendered them wholly unfit to cope with at once crafty and desperate villany, fell before these ruffians as chickens fall before the kite. The reports, made by these villains, met with no contradiction; the accused parties had no means of making a defence; there was no court for them to appear in; they dared. not, even if they had the means, to offer a defence or make a complaint; for they had seen the horrible consequences, the burnings, the rippings up, of all those of their brethren who had ventured to whisper their dissent from any dogma or decree of the tyrant. The project was to despoil

people of their property; and yet the parties, from whom the property was to be taken, were to have no court in which to plead their cause, no means of obtaining a hearing, could make even no complaint but at the peril of their lives. They, and those who depended on them, were to be, at once, stripped of this great mass of property, without any other ground than that of reports, made by men, sent, as the malignant HUME himself confesses, for the express purpose of finding a pretence for the dissolution of the Monasteries and for the King's taking to himself property that had never belonged to him or his predecessors.

161. HUME dares not, in the face of such a multitude of facts that are upon record to the contrary, pretend that these reports were true; but, he does his best to put a gloss upon them, as we have seen in paragraph **129**. He says, in order to effect by insinuation that which he does not venture to assert, that "it is, indeed, probable, that the blind submission of the people, during those ages, rendered the friars and nuns more unguarded and more dissolute than they are in any Roman Catholic country at present." Oh! say you so? And why more blind than now? It is just the same religion, there are the same rules, the peoples if blind then, are blind now; and, it would be singular indeed, that, when dissoluteness is become more common in the world, the "friars and nuns" should have become more guarded! However, we have here his acquittal of the Monasteries of the present day; and that is no small matter. It will be difficult, I believe, to make it appear "probable," that they were more unguarded, or more dissolute, in the sixteenth century; unless we believe, that the profound piety (which HUME calls superstition) of the people was not partaken of by the inhabitants of convents. Before we can listen to his insinuations in favour of these reports, we must believe that the persons belonging to the religious communities were a body of cunning creatures, believing in no part of that religion which they professed, and we must extend this our belief even to those numerous communities of women, who devoted their whole lives to the nursing of the sick poor!

162. However, upon reports thus obtained, an Act of Parliament was passed, in March, 1536, the same year that saw the end of ANNE BOLEYN, for the suppression, that is to say, confiscation, of three hundred and seventy-six monasteries, and for granting their estates, real and personal, to the King and his heirs! He took plate, jewels, gold and silver images and ornaments. This act of monstrous tyranny was, however, base as the Parliament was, and full as it was of greedy plunderers, not passed without some opposition. HUME says, "that it does not appear that any opposition was made to this important law." He frequently quotes SPELMAN as an historical authority; but, it did not suit him to quote SPELMAN's "History of Sacrilege," in which this Protestant historian says, that "the bill stuck long in the Lower House, and could get no passage, when the King commanded the Commons to attend him in the fore-noon in his gallery, where he let them wait till late in the afternoon, and then, coming out of his chamber, Walking a turn or two amongst them, and looking angrily on them, first on one side and then on the other, at last, 'I hear (saith he) that my bill will not pass; but, I will have it pass, or I will have some of your heads'; and, without other rhetoric, returned to his chamber. Enough was said; the bill passed, and all was given him as he desired."

163. Thus, then, it was an act of sheer tyranny; it was a pure Algerine proceeding at last. The pretences availed nothing: the reports of CROMWELL's myrmidons were not credited; every artifice had failed: resort was had to the halter and the axe to accomplish that "Reformation," of which the Scotch historian, BURNET, has called this monster the first-born son! So such man, he says, was necessary, to bring about

this "great and glorious event." What! was ever good yet produced by wickedness so atrocious? Did any man but this BURNET and his countryman, HUME, ever affect to believe, that such barefaced injustice and tyranny were justified on the ground of their tending to good consequences?

164. In the next Number, when I shall have given an account of the whole of that devastation and sacking, of which we have, as yet, only seen a mere beginning, I shall come to the consequences, not only to the monks and nuns, but to the people at large; and shall show how a foundation was, in this very Act of Parliament, laid for that pauperism, misery, degradation and crime, which are now proposed to checked by laws to render the women barren, or to export the people to foreign lands.

LETTER VI.

CONFISCATION OF THE MONASTERIES.
BASE AND CRUEL MEANS OF DOING THIS.
THE SACKING AND DEFACING OF THE COUNTRY.
BREAKING UP THE TOMB OF ALFRED.
MORE WIVES DIVORCED AND KILLED.
DEATH OF THE MISCREANT CROMWELL.
DEATH OF THE TYRANT HIMSELF.

Kensington, 30th April, 1825.

MY FRIENDS,

165. AT the close of the foregoing Letter, we saw the beginning only of the devastation of England. In the present letter, we shall see its horrible progress as far as there was time for that progress during the reign of the remorseless tyrant Henry VIII. We have seen in what manner was obtained the first Act for the suppression of Monasteries: that is to say, in reality, for robbing the proprietors of estates, and also the poor and the stranger. But I must give a more full and particular account of the Act of Parlia ment itself before I proceed to the deeds committed in consequence of it.

166. The Act was passed in the year 1 536, and in the 27th year of the King's reign. The preamble of the Act contains the reasons for its enactments; and as this Act really began the ruin and degradation of the main body of the people of England and Ireland; as it was the first step taken, in legal form, for robbing the people under pretence of reforming their religion; as it was the precedent on which the future plunderers proceeded, until they had com pletely impoverished the country; as it was the first of that series of deeds of rapine, by which this formerly well-fed and well-clothed people have, in the end, been reduced to rags and to a worse than gaol-allowance of food, I will insert its lying and villanous preamble at full length. Englishmen in general suppose, that there were always poor-laws and paupers in England. They ought to remember, that, for nine hundred years, under the Catholic religion, there were neither. Then ought, when they hear the fat parson cry "No-popery," to answer him by the cry of "No-pauperism." They ought, above all things,to endeavour to ascertain, how it came to pass, that this land of roast beef was changed, all of a sadden, into a land of dry bread, or of oatmeal por ridge. Let them attend, then, to the base and hypocritical pretences that they will find in the following preamble to this atrocious act of pillage.

167. "Forasmuch as manifest synne, vicious, carnal and abominable living is dayly used and committed commonly in such little and small Abbeys, Priories and other Religious Houses of Monks, Canons and Nuns, where the Congregation of such Religious Persons is under the Number of twelve Persons, whereby the Governors of such Religious Houses, and their Convent, spoyle, destroye, consume and utterly waste, as well their Churches, Monasteries, Priories, principal Farms, Granges, Lands, Tenements and Hereditaments, as the Ornaments of their Churches, and their Goods and Chattels, to the high Displeasure of Almighty God, Slander of good Religion, and to the great Infamy of the King's Highness and the Realm, if Redress should not be had thereof. And albeit that many continual Visitations hath been heretofore had, by the Space of two hundred years and more, for an honest and charitable Reformation of

such unthrifty, carnal and abominable Living, yet neverthelesse little or none Amendment is hitherto had, but their vicious Living shamelessly increaseth and augmenteth, and by a cursed Custom so rooted and infected, that a great Multitude of the Religious Persons in such small Houses do rather choose to rove abroad in Apostacy, than to conform themselves to the observation of good Religion; so that without such small Houses be utterly suppressed, and the Religious Persons therein committed to great and honourable Monasteries of Religion in this Realm, where they may be compelled to live religiously for Reformation of their Lives, the same else be no redress nor Reformation in that Behalf. In Consideration whereof, the King's most Royal Majesty, being supreme Head on Earth , under God, of the Church of England, dayly studying and devising the Increase, Advancement and Exaltation of true Doctrine and Virtue in the said Church, to the only Glory and Honour of God, and the total extirping and Destruction of Vice and Sin, having Knowledge that the Premises be true, as well as the Accompts of his late Visitations, as by sundry credible Informations, considering also that divers and great solemn Monasteries of this Realm wherein (Thanks be to God) Religion is right well kept and observed, be destitute of such full Number of Religious Persons as they ought and may keep, hath thought good that a plain Declaration should be made of the Premises, as well to the Lords Spiritual and Temporal, as to other his loving Subjects the Commons, in this present Parlia ment assembled: Whereupon the said Lords and Commons, by a great Deliberation, finally be resolved, that it is and shall he much more to the Pleasure of Almighty God, and for the Honour of this his Realm, that the Possessions of such small Religious houses, now being spent, spoiled and wasted for Increase and Maintenance of sin, should be used and committed to better uses, and the unthrifty Religious Persons, so spending the same, to be compelled to reform their lives."

168. This preamble was followed by enactments, giving the whole of the property to the King, his heir and assigns, to do and use therewith according to their own wills, to the pleasure of Almighty God, and to the honour and profit of this realm." Besides the lands and houses and stock, this tyrannical Act gave him the household goods and the gold, silver, jewels, and every other thing belonging to these Monasteries. Here was a breach of Magna Charta in the first place; a robbery of the monks and nuns in the next place; and, in the third place, a robbery of the indigents, the widow, the orphan and the stranger. The parties robbed, even the actual possessors of the property, were never heard in their defence; there was no charge against any particular convent; the charges were loose and general, and levelled against all convents, whose revenues did not exceed a certain sum. This alone was sufficient to show that the charges were false; for, who will believe that the alleged wickedness extended to all whose revenues did not exceed a certain sum, and that, when those revenues got above that point, the wickedness stopped? It is clear, that the reason for stopping at that point was, that there was yet something to be clone with the nobles and gentry, before a seizure of the great Monasteries could be safely attempted. The weak were first attacked, but means were very soon found for attacking and sacking the remainder.

169. The moment the tyrant got possession of this class of the Church estates, he began to grant them away to his "assigns" as the Act calls them. Great promises had been held out, that the King, when in possession of these estates, would never more want taxes from the people; and it is possible, that he thought. that he should be able to do without taxes; but, he soon found, that he was not destined to keep the plunder to himself; and that, in short, he must make a sudden stop, if not actually undo all that he had done, unless he divided the spoil with others, who instantly poured in upon

him for their share, and they so beset him, that he had not a moment's peace. They knew that he had good things; they had taken care to enable him to have "assigns;" and they, as they intended from the first, would give him no rest, until he, "to the pleasure of Almighty God and to the honour and profit of the realm," made them those "assigns."

170. Before four years had passed over his head, he found himself as poor as if had never confiscated a single convent, so sharp-set were the pious reformers, and so eager to "please Almighty God." When complaining to CROMWELL of the rapacity of the applicants for grants, he exclaimed, "By our Lady, the cormorants, when they have got the garbage, will devour the dish." CROMWELL reminded him, that there was much more yet to come, "Tut, man," said the King, "my whole realm would not stanch. their maws." However, he attempted this, very soon after; by a seizure of the larger Monasteries.

171. We have seen, in paragraph **167**, that the Parliament. when they enabled him to confiscate the smaller Monasteries, declared, that, in the "great and solemn Monasteries, (thanks be to God) religion is right well kept and observed.." It seemed, therefore to be a work of some difficulty to discover (in so short a time after this declaration was made) reasons for the confiscation of these larger Monasteries. But tyranny stands in need of no reasons and, in this Case, no reasons were alleged. CROMWELL and his myrmidons beset the heads of these great establishments; they threatened, they promised, they lied, and they bullied. By means the most base that Can be conceived, they obtained from some few what they called a "voluntary surrender." However, where these unjust and sanguinary men met with sturdy opposition, they resorted to false accusation, and procured the murder of the parties, under pretence of their having committed high treason. It was under this infamous pretence that the tyrant hanged and ripped up and quartered the Abbot of the famous Abbey of GLASTONBURY, whose body was mangled by the executioner, and whose head and limbs were hung up on what is called the torre, which overlooks the abbey. So that the surrender, wherever it did take place, was precisely of the nature of those " voluntary surrenders " which men make of their purses, when the robber's pistol is at their temple, or his blood-stained knife at their throat.

172. After all, however, even to obtain a pretence of voluntary surrender was a work too troublesome for CROMWELL and his ruffian visitors, and much too slow for the cormorants who waited for the plunder. Without more ceremony, therefore, an Act was passed (31 Hen. VIII. chap. 13,) giving all these "surrendered" Monasteries to the King, his heirs and assigns, and also ALL OTHER MONASTERIES; and all hospitals and colleges into the bargain! It is useless to Waste our time in uttering exclamations, or inventing curses on the memory of the monsters, who thus made a general sacking of this then fine, rich and beautiful country, which, until now, had been, for nine hundred years, the happiest country, and the greatest country too, that Europe had ever seen.

173. The carcass being thus laid prostrate, the rapacious vultures, who had assisted in the work, flew on it, and began to tear it in pieces. The people, here and there, rose in insurrection against the tyrant's satellites; but, deprived of their natural leaders, who had, for the most part, placed themselves on the side of tyranny and plunder, what were the mere common people to do? HUME affects to pity the ignorance of the people (as our stock-jobbing writers now affect to pity the ignorance of the country people in Spain) in showing their attachment to the monks. Gross ignorance, to be

sure, to prefer easy landlords, leases for life, hospitality and plenty!; "gross ignorance and superstition" to prefer these to grinding rack-rents, buying small beer at Bishops' palaces, and living on parish pay. We shall see, shortly, how soon horrid misery followed these tyrannical proceedings; but we must trace CROMWELL and his ruffians in their work of confiscating, plundering, pillaging and devastating.

1 74 . Tyrants have often committed robberies on their people; but, in all Cases but this, in England at least, there was always something of legal process observed. In this case there was no such thing. The base Parliament, who were to share, and who did most largely share, in the plunder, had given not only the lands and houses to the tyrant, or, rather, had taken them to themselves; but had disposed, in the same short way, of all the moveable goods, stock on farms, crops, and which was of more consequence, of the gold, silver, and jewels. Let the reader judge of the ransackings that now took place. The poorest of the convents had some images, vases, and other things, of gold or silver. Many of them possessed a great deal in this way. The altars of their churches were generally enriched with the precious metals, if not with costly jewels; and, which is not to be overlooked, the people, in those days, were honest enough to suffer all these things to remain in their places, without a standing army and without police officers.

175. Never, in all probability, since the world began, was there so rich a harvest of plunder. The ruffians of CROMWELL entered the convents; they tore down the altars to get away the gold and silver; ransacked the chests and drawers of the monks and nuns; tore off the covers of books that were ornamented with the precious metals. These books were all in manuscript. Single books had taken, in many cases, half a long life-time to compose and to copy out fair. Whole libraries, the getting of which together had taken ages upon ages and had cost immense sums of money, were scattered abroad by these hellish ruffians, when they had robbed the covers of their rich ornaments. The ready money, in the convents, down to the last shilling, was seized. in short, the most rapacious and unfeeling soldiery never. in town delivered up to be sacked, proceeded with greediness, shamelessness and brutality to be at all compared with those of these heroes of the Protestant Reformation; and this, observe, towards persons, women as well as men, who had committed no crime known to the laws, who had had no crime regularly laid to their charge, Who had had no hearing in their defence, a large part of whom had, within a year, been declared, by this same Parliament, to lead most godly and useful lives, the whole of whose possessions were guaranteed to them by the great Charter as much as the Kings crown was to him, and whose estates were enjoyed for the benefit of the poor as well as for that of these plundered possessors themselves,

176. The tyrant was, of course, the great pocketter of this species of plunder. CROMWELL carried or sent it to him in parcels, twenty ounces of gold at one time, fifty ounces at another; now a parcel of precious stones of one sort, then a parcel of another, HUME, whose main object is to blacken the Catholic religion, takes every possible occasion for saying something or other in praise of its destroyers. He could not, he was too cunning, to ascribe justice or humanity to a monster whose very name signifies injustice and cruelty. He, therefore, speaks of his high spirit, his magnificence and generosity. It was a high-spirited, magnificent and generous King, to be sure, who sat in his palace, in London, to receive with his own hands the gold, silver, jewels, and pieces of money, of which his unoffending subjects had been robbed by ruffians sent by himself to commit the robbery. One of these items runs in these words:-- "ITEM, Delivered unto the King's royal Majesty, the same day, of the

same stuffe, foure chalices of golde, with foure patens of golde to the same; and a spoon of golde, weighing altogether an hundred and six ounces."
"Received: HENRY REX."

177. There are high-spirit, magnificence, and generosity! Amongst the stock of this "generous prince's" pawnbroker's shop; or, rather, his store-house of stolen goods, were images of all sorts, candlesticks, sockets, cruets, cups, pixes, goblets, basons, spoons, diamonds, sapphires, pearls, finger-rings, ear-rings, pieces of money of all values, even down to shillings, bits of gold and silver torn from the covers of books, or cut and beaten out of the altars. In cases where the wood-work, either of altars, crosses, or images, was inlaid with precious metal, the wood was frequently burnt to get at the metal. Even the Jew-thieves of the present day are not more expert in their trade than the myrmidons of CROMWELL were. And, with these facts before us; these facts, undenied and undeniable; with these facts before us, must we not be the most profound hypocrites that the world ever saw; must we not be the precise country of that which Englishmen have always been thought to be, if we still affect to believe, that the destruction of the shrines of our forefathers arose from motives of conscience?

178. The parcel of plunder, mentioned in the last paragraph but one, brought into this royal PEACHUM, was equal in value to about eight thousand pounds of money of the present day; and that parcel was, perhaps, not a hundredth part of what he received in this way. Then, who is to suppose that the plunderers did not keep a large share to themselves? Did subaltern plunderers ever give in just accounts? It is manifest that, from, this specimen, the whole amount of the goods of which the Convents were plundered must have been enormous. The reforming gentry ransacked the Cathedral Churches, as well as the Convents and their Churches. Whatever pile contained the greatest quantity of the "the same stuffe," seemed to be the object of their most keen rapacity. Therefore, it is by no means surprising, that they directed, at a very early stage of their pious and honest progress, their hasty steps towards Canterbury, which, above all other places, had been dipped in the "manifest synne" of possessing rich altars, tombs, gold and silver images, together with "manifestely synneful" diamonds and other precious stones. The whole of this city, famed as the cradle of English Christianity, was prize; and the "Reformation" people hastened to it with that alacrity, and that noise of anticipated enjoyment which we observe in the crows and magpies, when flying to the spot where a horse or an ox has accidentally met with its death.

179. But there were, at Canterbury, two objects by which the "Reformation" birds of prey were particularly attracted; namely, the monastery of Saint AUSTIN and the tomb of THOMAS À BECKET. The former of these renowned men, to whose preaching and whose long life of incessant and most disinterested labour England owed the establishment of Christianity in the land, had, for eight or nine centuries, been regarded as the Apostle of England. His shrine was in the monastery dedicated to him; and as it was, in all respects, a work of great magnificence, it offered a plenteous booty to the plunderers, who, if they could have got at the tomb of Jesus Christ himself, and had found it equally rich, would, beyond all question, have torn it to pieces. But, rich as this prize was, there was a greater in the shrine of Thomas à Becket, in the Cathedral Church. BECKET, who was Archbishop of Canterbury, in the reign of Henry II., who resisted that king, when the latter was manifestly preparing to rob the Church, and to enslave and pillage the people, had been held in the highest veneration all over Christendom for more than three hundred years, when the Reformation plunderers assailed his tomb; but especially was his name venerated in

England, where the people looked upon him as a martyr to their liberties as well as their religion, he having been barbarously murdered by ruffians sent from the King, and for no other cause than that he persevered in resisting an attempt to violate the Great Charter. Pilgrimages were continually made to his tomb; offerings incessantly poured into it; churches and hospitals and other establishments of piety and charity were dedicated to him, as, for instance, the church of St. Thomas, in the City of London, the Monastery of Sende, in Surrey, the Hospital of St. Thomas, in the Borough of Southwark, and things of this sort, in great numbers, all over the country. The offerings at his shrine had made it exceedingly rich and magnificent. A king of France had given to it a diamond, supposed to be the most valuable then in Europe. HUME, never losing sight of the double object of maligning the Catholic religion and degrading the English nation, ascribes this sort of half-adoration of BECKET to the craft of the priests and to the folly and superstition of the people. He is vexed to death to have to relate, that more than a hundred thousand pilgrims to BECKET's shrine have been assembled at one time in Canterbury. Indeed! why, then, there must have been some people living in England, even in those old times; and those people must have had some wealth too; though, according to the whole tenor of the lying book, which the Scotch call our history, this was, at the time I am now speaking of, a poor, beggarly, scarcely-inhabited country. The City of Canterbury does not now contain men, women, and children, all counted and well-puffed out, more than twelve thousand seven hundred and twenty souls! Poor souls! How could they find lodging and entertainment for a hundred thousand grown persons! And this, too, observe, at one corner of the Island. None but persons of some substance could have performed such a journey. Here is a fact that just slips out sideways, which is of itself much more than enough to make us reflect and inquire before we swallow what the Scotch philosophers are now presenting to us on the subjects of national wealth and population. And, then, as to the craft and superstition which HUME says produced this concourse of pilgrims. Just as if either were necessary to produce unbounded veneration for the name of a man, of whom it was undeniably true, that he had sacrificed his life, and that, too, in the most signal manner, for the rights and liberties and religion of his country. Was it "folly and superstition," or was it wisdom and gratitude and real piety to show, by overt acts, veneration for such a man? The bloody tyrant, who had sent MORE and FISHER to the block, and who, of course, hated the name of BECKET, caused his ashes to be dug up and scattered in the air, and forbade the future insertion of his name in the CALENDAR. We do not, therefore, find it in the Calendar in the Common Prayer Book; but, and it is a most curious fact, we find it in Moore's ALMANACK; in that almanack it is for this very year, 1825; and thus, in spite of the ruthless tyrant, and in spite of all the liars of the "Reformation," the English nation has always continued to be just and grateful to the memory of this celebrated man.

180. But, to return to the Reformation robbers; here was a prize! This tomb of BECKET was of wood, most exquisitely wrought, inlaid abundantly with the precious metals, and thickly set with precious stones of all sorts. Here was an object for "Reformation" piety to fix its godly eyes upon! Were such a shrine to be found in one of our churches now, how the swaddlers would cry out for another "Reformation"! The gold, silver, and jewels, filled two chests, each of which required six or eight men of that day (when the labourers used to have plenty of meat) to move them to the door of the Cathedral! How the eyes of HUME's "high-minded, magnificent and generous prince" must have glistened when the chests were opened! They vied, I dare say, with the diamonds themselves. No robbers, of which we have ever had an account,

equalled these robbers in rapacity, in profligacy, and in insolence. But, where is the wonder? The tyrant's proclamations had now the force of laws; he had bribed the people's natural leaders to his side; his will was law; and that will constantly sought plunder and blood.

181. The Monasteries were now plundered, sacked, gutted; for, this last is the proper word whereby to describe the deed. As some comfort, and to encourage us to endure the horrid relation, we may here bear in mind, that we shall, by-and-by see the base ruffian, CROMWELL, after being the chief instrument in the plunder, laying his miscreant head on the block; but, to seize the estates and to pillage the churches and apartments of the monasteries was not all. The noble buildings, raised in the view of lasting for countless ages; the beautiful gardens; these ornaments of the country must not be suffered to stand, for, they continually reminded the people of the rapacity and cruelty of their tyrant and his fellow-plunderers and partakers in the plunder. How the property in the estates was disposed of we shall see further on; but, the buildings must come down. To go to work in the usual way would have been a labour without end; so that, in most instances, GUNPOWDER was resorted to; and thus, in a few hours, the most magnificent structures, which it had required ages upon ages to bring to perfection, were made heaps of ruins, pretty much such as many of them remain even unto this day. In many cases, those who got the estates were bound to destroy the buildings, or to knock them partly down, so that the people should, at once, be deprived of all hope of seeing a revival of what they had lost, and in order to give them encouragement to take leases under the new owners.

182. The whole country was, thus, disfigured; it had the appearance of a land recently invaded by the most brutal barbarians: and this appearance, if we look well into it, it has even to this day. Nothing has ever yet come to supply the place of what was then destroyed. This is the view for us to take of the matter, it is not a mere matter of religion; but a matter of rights, liberties, real wealth, happiness and national greatness. If all these have been strengthened, or augmented, by the "REFORMATION," even. then we must not approve of the horrible means; but, if they have all been weakened, or lessened, by that "Reformation," what an outrageous abuse of words is it to call the event by that name! And, if I do not prove, that this latter has been the case; if I do not prove, clear as the daylight, that, before the "Reformation," England was greater, more wealthy, more moral, and more happy, than she has ever been since; if I do not make this appear as clearly as any fact ever was made to appear, I will be content to pass, for the rest of my life, for a vain pretender.

183. If I look at the county of Surrey, in which I myself was born, and behold the devastation of that county, I am filled with indignation against the ruffian devastators. Surrey has very little of natural wealth in it. A very considerable part of it is mere heath-land. Its present comparative opulence is a creature of the fictitious system of funding. Yet this county was, from one end of it to the other, ornamented and benefited by the establishments which grew out of the Catholic Church. At BERMONDSEY there was an Abbey; at St. MARY OVERY there was a Priory, and this convent founded that very St. Thomas's Hospital which now exists in Southwark. This Hospital also was seized by the ruffians, but the building was afterwards given to the City of London. At NEWINGTON there was an Hospital, and, after its revenues were seized, the master obtained a licence to beg! At MERTON there was a Priory. Then, going across to the Sussex side, there was another Priory at REIGATE, Coming again near the Thames, and more to the West, there was a Priory at SHENE. Still more to the West, there was an Abbey at CHERTSEY. At TANDRIGE there was a

Priory. Near GUILDFORD, at SENDE, there was a Priory. And, at the lower end of the county, at WAVERLEY, in the parish of Farnham, was an Abbey. To these belonged cells and chapels at a distance from the convents themselves: so that it would have been a work of some difficulty for a man so to place himself, even in this poor heathy county, at six miles distance from a place where the door of hospitality was always open to the poor, to the aged, the orphan, the widow, and the stranger. Can any man, now, place himself, in that whole county, within any number of miles of any such door? No; nor in any other county. All is wholly changed, and all is changed for the worse. There is now no hospitality in England. Words have changed their meaning. We now give entertainment to those who entertain us in return. We entertain people because we like them personally; and, very seldom, because they stand in need of entertainment. An hospital, in those days, meant a place of free entertainment; and not a place merely for the lame, the sick and the blind; and the very sound of the words "Old English Hospitality," ought to raise a blush on every Protestant cheek. But, besides this hospitality exercised invariably in the Monasteries, the weight of their example was great with all the opulent classes of the community; and thus, to be generous and kind was the character of the nation at large: a niggardly, a base, a money-loving disposition could not be in fashion, when those institutions to which all men looked with reverence, set an example which condemned such a disposition.

184. And, if I am asked why the thirteen monks of WAVERLEY, for instance, should have had 196*l*. 13*s*. 1*d*. a year to spend, making about four thousand pounds a year of the money of the present day, I may answer by asking, why they should not have had it? And I may go on, and ask, why any body should have any property at all? Ay, but, they never worked; they did nothing to increase the nation's store! Let us see how this is. They possessed the lands of WAVERLEY, a few hundred acres of very poor land with a mill, and, perhaps, about twenty acres of very indifferent meadow-land, on one part of which, sheltered by a semicircle of sand-hills, their Abbey stood, the river Wey (about twenty feet wide) running close by the outer wall of the convent. Besides this, they possessed the impropriated tithes of the parish of Farnham, and a pond or two on the commons adjoining. This estate in land belongs to a Mr. THOMPSON, who lives on the spot, and the estate in tithes to a Mr. HALSEY, who lives at a distance from the parish. Now, without any disparagement to these gentlemen, did not the monks work as much as they do? Did not their revenue go to augment the nation's store as much as the rents of Mr. THOMPSON, or the tithes of Mr. HALSEY? Ay, and which is of vast importance, the poor of the parish of Farnham, having this Monastery to apply to, and having for their neighbour a Bishop of Winchester, who did not sell small beer out of his palace, stood in no need of poor-rates, and had never heard the horrid word pauper pronounced. Come, my townsmen of Farnham, you, who, as well as I, have, when we were boys, climbed the ivy-covered ruins of this venerable Abbey (the first of its order in England); you, who, as well as I have, when looking at those walls, which have outlived the memory of the devastators but not the malice of those who still taste time sweets of the devastation; you, who, as well as I, have many times wondered what an abbey was, and how and why this one came to be devastated; you shall be judge in this matter, You know what poor-rates are and you know what church-rates are. Very well, then, there were no poor-rates nor church-rates as long as Waverley Abbey existed and as long as Bishops had no wives. This is a fact wholly undeniable. There was no need of either. The Church shared its property with the poor and the stranger, and left the people at large to possess their own earnings. And, as to matters of faith and worship, look at that immense heap of earth round the church, where your

parents and my parents, amid where our progenitors, for twelve hundred years, lie buried; then bear in mind, that, for nine hundred years out of the twelve, they were all of the faith and worship of the monks of Waverley; and, with that thought in your mind, find, if you can, the heart to say, that the monks of Waverley, by whose hospitality your fathers and my fathers were, for so many ages, preserved from bearing the hateful name of pauper, taught an idolatrous and damnable religion.

185. That which took place in Surrey, took place in every other county, only to a greater extent in proportion to the greater wealth and resources of the spot. Defacing followed closely upon the heels of confiscation and plunder. If buildings could have been murdered, the tyrant and his plunderers would have made short work of it. As it was, they did all they could: they knocked down, they blowed up, they annihilated as far as they could. Nothing, indeed, short of diabolical malice was to be expected from such men; but, there were two Abbeys in England, which one might have hoped, that even these monsters would spare; that which contained the tomb of ST. AUSTIN and that which had been founded by, and contained the remains of, ALFRED We have seen how they rifled the tomb of ST. AUSTIN at Canterbury. They tore down the church and the Abbey, and with the materials built a menagerie for wild beasts, and a palace for the tyrant himself. The tomb of ALFRED was in an Abbey, at Winchester, founded by that king himself. The Abbey and its estates were given by the tyrant to WRIOTHESLEY, who was afterwards made Earl of Southampton, and who got a pretty good share of the confiscations in Hampshire. One almost sickens at the thought of a man capable of a deed like the destruction of this Abbey. Where is there one amongst us, who has read anything at all, who has not read of the fame of ALFRED? What book can we open, even for our boyish days, that does not sound his praise? Poets, moralists, divines, historians, philosophers, lawyers, legislators, not only of our own country, but of all Europe, have cited him, and still cite him, as a model of virtue, piety, wisdom, valour, and Patriotism; as possessing every excellence, without a single fault. He, in spite of difficulties such as no other human being on record ever encountered, cleared his harassed and half-barbarized country of horde after horde of cruel invaders, who, at one time, had wholly subdued it, and compelled him, in order to escape destruction, to resort to the habit and the life of a herdsman. From this state of depression he, during a not long life, raised himself and his people to the highest point of happiness and of fame. He fought, with his armies and fleets, more than fifty battles against the enemies of England. He taught his people by his example as well as by his precepts, to be sober, industrious, brave, and just. He promoted learning in all the sciences; he planted the University of Oxford; to him, and not to a late Scotch lawyer, belongs "Trial by Jury "; Blackstone calls him. the founder of Common Law; the counties, the hundreds, the tithings, the courts of justice, were the work of ALFRED; he, in fact, was the founder of all those rights, liberties and laws, which made England to he what England has been, which gave her a character above that of all other nations, which made her rich and great and happy beyond all her neighbours, and which still give her whatever she possesses of that pre-eminence. if there be a name under heaven, to which Englishmen ought to bow with reverence approaching towards adoration, it is the name of ALFRED. And we are not unjust and ungrateful in this respect, at any rate; for, whether Catholics or Protestants, where is there an Englishman to be found, who would not gladly make a pilgrimage of a thousand miles to take off his hat at the tomb of this maker of the English name? Alas! that tomb is nowhere to be found. The barbarians spared not even that. It was in the Abbey before-mentioned, called HYDE ABBEY, which had been founded by ALFRED himself, and intended as the place of his burial. Besides the remains of

ALFRED, this Abbey contained those of ST. GRIMBALD, the Benedictine monk, whom ALFRED brought into England to begin the teaching at Oxford. But, what cared the plunderers for remains of public benefactors? The Abbey was knocked down, or blowed up: the tombs were demolished; the very lead of the coffins was sold; and, which fills one with more indignation than all the rest, the estates were so disposed of as to make the loan-makers, the BARINGS, at this day, the successors of ALFRED the Great!

186. WRIOTHESLEY got the manors of MICHELDEVER and STRATTON, which, by marriage, came into the hands of the family of RUSSELL, and, from that family, about thirty years ago, they were bought by the BARINGS, and are now in possession of Sir THOMAS BARING. It is curious to observe how this Protestant "Reformation" has worked. if it had not been, there would have been no paupers at Micheldever and Stratton; but, then the Russells would not have had the estates, and they could not have sold them to the Barings; ay, but then there would have been, too, no national debt, as well as no paupers, and there would have been no loan-makers to buy the estates of the Russells. Besides this, there would have been no bridewell erected upon the precise spot where the abbey-church stood; no tread-mill, perhaps, Over the very place where the ashes of ALFRED lay; and, what is more, there would have been no need of bridewell or tread-mill. It is related of ALFRED, that he made his people so honest, that he could hang bracelets up by the way side, without danger of their being touched. Alas! that the descendants of that same people should need a tread-mill! Ay, but, in the days of ALFRED there were no paupers; no miserable creatures compelled to labour from month's end to month's end without seeing meat; no thousands upon thousands made thieves by that hunger, which acknowledges no law, human or divine.

187. Thus, then, was the country devastated, sacked and defaced; and I should now proceed to give an account of the commencement of that poverty and degradation, which were, as I have pledged myself to show, the consequences of this devastation; and which I shall show, not by bare assertion, nor from what are called "histories of England;" but, from Acts of Parliament, and from other sources, which every one can refer to, and the correctness of which is beyond all dispute. But, before we come to this important matter, we must see the end of the ruffian "Vicegerent," and also the end of the tyrant himself, who was, during the events that we have been speaking of, going on marrying and divorcing, or killing, his wives; but, whose career, was, after all, not very long.

188. After the death of JANE SEYMOUR, who was the mother of Edward VI., and who was the only one of all the tyrant's wives who had the good luck to die a queen, and to die in her bed; after her death, which took place in 1537, he was nearly two years hunting up another wife. None, certainly, but some very gross and unfeeling woman could be expected to have, voluntarily, anything to do with a man, whose hands were continually steeped in blood. In 1539 he found, however, a mate in ANNE, the sister of the Duke of Cleves. When she arrived in England he expressed his dislike of her person; but he found it prudent to marry her. In 1540, about six or seven months after the marriage, he was divorced from her, not daring, in this case, to set his myrmidons to work to bring her to the block. There was no lawful pretence for the divorce. The husband did not like his wife: that was all: and this was alleged, too, as the ground of the divorce. CRANMER, who had divorced him from two wives before, put his irons into the fire again for this occasion; and produced, in a little time, as neat a piece of work as ever had come from the shop of the famous "Reformation." Thus the King and Queen were single people again; but, the former had another young

and handsome wife in his eye. This lady's name was CATHERINE HOWARD, a niece of the Duke of NORFOLK. This Duke, as well as most of the old nobility, hated CROMWELL; and now was an opportunity of inflicting vengeance on him. CROMWELL had been the chief cause of the King's marriage with ANNE of Cleves; but, the fact is, his plundering talent was no longer wanted, and it was convenient to the tyrant to get rid of him.

189 . CROMWELL had obtained enormous wealth, from his several offices, as well as from the plunder of the church and the poor. He had got about thirty of the estates belonging to the monasteries; his house, or rather palace, was gorged with the fruits of the sacking; he had been made Earl of Essex; he had precedence of every one but the King; and he, in fact, represented the King in the Parliament, where he introduced and defended all his confiscating and murdering laws. He had been barbarous beyond all description towards the unfortunate and unoffending monks and nuns; without such an instrument the plunder never could have been effected: but, he was no longer wanted; the ruffian had already lived too long; the very walls of the devastated convents seemed to call for public vengeance on his head. On the morning of the 10th of June, 1540, he was all-powerful: in the evening of the same day he was in prison as a traitor. He lay in prison only a few days before he had to experience the benefit of his own way of administering justice. He had, as we have seen in the last Number, invented a way of bringing people to the block, or the gallows, without giving them any form of trial; without giving them even a hearing; but merely by passing a law to put them to death. This was what this abominable wretch had brought about in the case of the Countess of SALISBURY; and this was what was now to fall on his own head. He lived only about forty-eight days after his arrest; not half long enough to enable him to enumerate, barely to enumerate, the robberies and murders committed under his orders. His time seems, however, to have been spent, not in praying to God to forgive him for these robberies and murders, but in praying to the tyrant to spare his life. Perhaps, of all the mean and dastardly wretches that ever died, this was the most mean and dastardly. He, who had been the most insolent and cruel of ruffians, when he had power, was now the most disgustingly slavish and base. He had, in fact, committed no crime against the King; though charged with heresy and treason, he was no more a heretic than the King was; and, as to the charge of treason, there was not a shadow of foundation for it. But, he was just as guilty of treason as the abbots of Reading, Colchester, and Glastonbury, all of whom, and many more, he had been the chief instrument in putting to death. He put them to death in order to get possession of their property; and, I dare say, to get at his property, to get the plunder back from him, was one of the motives for bringing him to the block. This very ruffian had superintended the digging up of the ashes of THOMAS À BECKET, and scattering them in the air; and now, the people who had witnessed that, had to witness the letting of the blood out of his dirty body, to run upon the pavement, to be licked up by hogs or dogs. The cowardly creature seems to have had, from the moment of his arrest, no thought about any thing but saving his life. He wrote repeatedly to the King, in hope of getting pardoned: but, all to no purpose: he had done what was wanted of him; the work of plunder was nearly over; he had, too, got a large share of the plunder, which it was not convenient to leave in his hands; and, therefore, upon true "Reformation" principles, it was time to take away his life. He, in his letters to the King, most vehemently protested his innocence. Ay; no doubt of that: but, he was not more innocent than were the butchered abbots and monks; he was not more innocent than any one out of those thousands upon thousands, whom he had quartered, hanged, burned, or plundered; and, amongst all those thousands upon thousands, there never

was seen one, female or male, so complete a dastard as him self. In these letters to the tyrant, he fawned on him in the most disgusting manner; compared his smiles and frowns to those of God; besought him to suffer him "to kiss his balmy hand once more, that the fragrance thereof might make him fit for heaven"! The base creature deserved his death, if it had only been for writing these letters. Fox, the "Martyr" man, calls this CROMWELL the "valiant soldier of the Reformation." Yes, there have been few soldiers to understand sacking better: he was full of valour on foraging parties; and when he had to rifle monks and nuns and to rob altars: a brave fellow when he had to stretch monks and nuns on the rack, to make them confess treasonable words or thoughts; but when death began to stare him in the face, he was, assuredly, the most cowardly caitiff that ever died. it is hardly necessary to say, that this man is a great favourite of HUME, who deeply laments CROMWELL's fate, though he has not a word of compassion to bestow upon all the thousands that had been murdered or ruined by him. He, as well as other historians, quotes from the conclusion of one of CROMWELL's letters to the King, these abject expressions: "I, a most woful prisoner, am ready to submit to death, when it shall please God and your Majesty; and yet the frail flesh incites me to call on your grace for mercy and pardon of mine offences. -- Written at the Tower with the heavy heart and trembling hand of your Highness's most miserable prisoner and poor slave, THOMAS CROMWELL -- Most gracious prince, I cry for mercy, mercy, mercy!" This is the language of Fox's "valiant soldier." Fox meant valiant, not in the field, or on the scaffold, but in the convent, pulling the rings from women's fingers, and tearing the gold clasps from books: that was the Protestant valour of the "Reformation." HUME says, that "CROMWELL deserved a better fate." Never was fate more just or more appropriate. He had been the willing, the officious, the zealous, the eager agent in the execution of all the tyrannical, sacrilegious, and bloody deeds of his master; and had, amongst other things, been the very man who first suggested the condemning of people to death without trial. What could be more just than that he should die in the same way? Not a tear was shed at his death, which produced on the spectators an effect such as is produced when the foulest of murderers expiate their crimes on the gallows.

190. During the seven years that the tyrant himself survived this his cruel and dastardly Vicegerent, he was beset with disappointments, vexations and torments of all sorts. He discovered, at the end of a few months, that his new Queen had been, and still was, much such another as ANNE BOLEYN. He with very little ceremony, sent her to the block, together with a whole posse of her relations, lovers, and cronies. He raged and foamed like a wild beast, passed laws most bloody to protect himself against lewdness and infidelity in his future wives, and got, for his pains, the ridicule of the nation and of all Europe. He, for the last time, took another wife; but, this time, none would face his laws but a widow; and she very narrowly escaped the fate of the rest. He, for some years before he died, became, from his gluttony and debaucheries, an unwieldy and disgusting mass of flesh, moved about by means of mechanical inventions. But, still he retained all the ferocity and bloody-mindedness of his former days. The principal business of his life was the ordering of accusations, executions, and confiscations. When on his death-bed, every one was afraid to intimate his danger to him, lest death to the intimater should be the consequence; and he died before he was well aware of his condition, leaving more than one death-warrant unsigned for want of time!

191. Thus expired, in the year 1547, in the fifty-sixth year of his age and the thirty-eighth of his reign, the most unjust, hard-hearted, meanest and most sanguinary tyrant

that the world had ever beheld, whether Christian or Heathen. That England, which he found in peace, unity, plenty and happiness, he left torn by factions and schisms, her people wandering about in beggary and misery. He laid the foundations of immorality, dishonesty and pauperism, all which produced an abundant harvest in the reigns of his unhappy, barren, mischievous and miserable children, with whom, at the end of a few years, his house and his name were extinguished for ever. How he disposed of the plunder of the church and the poor; how his successors completed that work of confiscation which he had carried on so long; how the nation sunk in point of character and of wealth; how pauperism first arose in England; and how were sown the seeds of that system of which we now behold the effects in the impoverishment and degradation of the main body of the people of England and Ireland; all these will be shown in the next Letter and shown, I trust, in a manner which will leave, in the mind of every man of sense, no doubt, that, of all the scourges that ever afflicted this country, none is to be put in comparison with the Protestant "Reformation."

LETTER VII.

EDWARD VI. CROWNED.
PERJURY OF THE EXECUTORS OF HENRY VIII.
NEW CHURCH "BY LAW ESTABLISHED,"
ROBBERY OF THE CHURCHES,
INSURRECTIONS OF THE PEOPLE.
TREASONS OF CRANMER AND HIS ASSOCIATES,
DEATH OF THE KING.

Kensington, 31st May, 1825.

My FRIENDS,

192. HAVING, in the preceding Letters, shown, that the thing, impudently called the "REFORMATION," was engendered in beastly lust, brought forth in hypocrisy and perfidy, and cherished and fed by plunder, devastation, and by rivers of innocent English and Irish blood, I intended to show, in the present Letter, how the main body of the people were, by these doings, impoverished and degraded up to this time; that is to say, I intended to trace the impoverishment and degradation down to the end of the reign of the bloody tyrant, Henry VIII. But, upon reviewing the matter, I think it best *first* to go through the whole of my account of the plunderings, persecutions and murderings of the "Reformation" people; and, when we have seen all the robberies and barbarities that they committed under the hypocritical Pretence of religious zeal; or, rather, when we have seen such of those robberies and barbarities as we can find room for; then I shall conclude with showing how enormously the nation lost by the change; and, how that change made the main body of the people poor and wretched and degraded. By pursuing this plan, I shall, in one concluding Letter, give, or, at least, endeavour to give, a clear and satisfactory history of this impoverishment. I shall take the present Protestant labourer, with his cold potatoes and water, and show him how his Catholic forefathers lived; and if those cold potatoes and water, if this poorer than pig-diet, have not quite taken away all the natural qualities of English blood, I shall make him execrate the plunderers and hypocrites by whom was produced that change, which has finally led to his present misery. and to nine-tenths of that mass of corruption and crime, public and private, which now threaten to uproot society itself.

193. In pursuance of this plan and in conformity with my promise to conclude my little work in Ten Numbers, I shall distribute my matter thus: in Number VIII (the. present), the deeds and events of the reign of Edward VI. In Number VIII those of the reign of Queen Mary. In number IX, those of the reign of Queen Elizabeth; and, in Number X, the facts and arguments to establish my *main point*; namely, that the thing, impudently called the "Reformation," impoverished and degraded the main body of the people. In the course of the first three of these Numbers, I shall not touch, except incidentally, upon the impoverishing and degrading effects of the change; but, shall reserve these for the last number, when, having witnessed the horrid means, we will take an undivided view of the consequences. tracing those consequences down to the present day.

194. In paragraph **190** we had the satisfaction to see the savage tyrant expire at a premature old age, with body swelled and bursting from luxury, and with a mind torn by contending passions. One of his last acts was a will, by which he made his infant

son his immediate successor, with remainder, in case he died without issue, to his daughter Mary first, and then, in default of issue again, to his daughter ELIZABETH; though, observe, both the daughters still stood bastardized by Act of Parliament, and, though the latter was born of ANNE BOLEYN while the King's first wife the mother of MARY, was alive.

195. To carry this will into execution and to govern the kingdom, until Edward, who was then ten years of age. should be eighteen years of age, there were sixteen executors appointed, amongst whom was SEYMOUR, Earl of Hertford, and the "honest CRANMER." These sixteen worthies began by taking, in the most solemn manner, an *oath* to stand to and maintain the last will of their master. Their second act was to break that oath by making HERTFORD, who was a brother of JANE SEYMOUR, the King's mother, protector, though the will gave equal powers to all the executors. Their next step was to give new peerages to some of themselves. The fourth, to award to the new peers grants of the public money. The fifth was to lay aside, at the Coronation, the ancient English custom of asking the people if they were willing to have and obey the King. The sixth was "to attend at a solemn high mass." And the seventh was to begin a series of acts for the total subversion of all that remained of the Catholic religion in England, and for the effecting of all that Old Harry had left uneffected in the way of plunder.

196. The Monasteries were gone; the cream had been taken off; but there remained the skimmed milk of church-altars, chanteries, and guilds. Old Harry would, doubtless, if he had lived much longer, have plundered these; but, he had not done it, and he could not do it without openly becoming Protestant, which, for the reasons stated in paragraph **101**, he would not do. But HERTFORD and his fifteen brother worthies had in their way no such obstacle as the ruffian King had had. The church-altars, the chanteries, and the guilds contained something valuable; and they longed to be at it. The power of the POPE was gotten rid of; the country had been sacked; the poor had been despoiled; but, still there were some pickings left. The piety of ages had made every church, however small, contain some gold and silver appertaining to the altar. The altars, in the parish churches, and, generally, in the cathedrals, had been left, as yet, untouched; for, though the wife-killer had abjured the POPE, whose power he had taken to himself, he still professed to be of the Catholic faith, and he maintained the *mass* and the *sacraments* and *creeds* with fire and fagot. Therefore he had left the church-altars unplundered. But, they contained gold, silver, and other valuables, and the worthies saw these with longing eyes and itching fingers.

197. To seize them, however, there required a pretext, and what pretext could there be short of declaring, at once, that the Catholic religion was false and wicked, and, of course, that there ought to be no altars, and, of course, no gold and silver things appertaining to them! The sixteen worthies, with HERTFORD at their head, and with CRANMER amongst them, had had the King crowned as a Catholic: he, as well as they, had taken the oaths as Catholics; they had sworn to uphold that religion; they had taken him. to a high mass after his coronation; but, the altars had good things about them; there was plunder remaining; and to get at this remaining plunder, the Catholic religion must be wholly put down . There were, doubtless, *some* fanatics; *some* who imagined that the religion of nine hundred years standing ought not to be changed; *some* who had not plunder and plunder only in view; but, it is impossible for any man of common sense, of unperverted mind, to look at the history of this transaction, at this open avowal of Protestantism, at this change from the religion of

England to that of a part of Germany, without being convinced that the principal authors of it had plunder and plunder only in view.

198. The old tyrant died in 1547; and by the end of 1549, CRANMER, who had tied so many Protestants to the stake for not being Catholics, had pretty nearly completed a system of Protestant worship. He first prepared a. book of homilies and a catechism, in order to pave the way. Next came a law to allow the clergy to have wives; and then, when all things had been prepared, came the Book of Common Prayer and Administration of the Sacraments. GARDINER, who was Bishop of Winchester, reproached CRANMER with his duplicity; reminded him of the zeal with which he had upheld the Catholic worship under the late King, and would have made him hang himself, or cut his throat, if he had had the slightest remains of shame in him.

199. This new system did not, however, go far enough for the fanatics; and there instantly appeared arrayed against it whole tribes of new lights on the continent. So that CRANMER, cunning as he was, soon found that he had undertaken no easy matter. The proclamations put forth, upon this occasion, were disgustingly ridiculous, coming, as they did, in the name of a King only ten years of age, and expressed in words so solemnly pompous and so full of arrogance. However, the chief object was the plunder; and to get at this nothing was spared. There were other things to attract the grasp; but, it will be unnecessary to dwell very particularly on any thing but the *altars* and the *churches*. This was the real "Reformation reign "; for, it was a reign of robbery and hypocrisy without any thing to be compared with them; any thing in any country or in any age. *Religion, conscience*, was always the pretext; but in one way or another, robbery, plunder was always the end. The People, once so united and so happy, became divided into innumerable sects, no man knowing hardly what to believe; and, indeed, no one knowing what it was lawful for him to say; for it soon became impossible for the common people to know what was heresy and what was not heresy.

200. That prince of hypocrites, CRANMER, who, during the reign of Henry, had condemned people to the flames for not believing in transubstantiation, was now ready to condemn them for believing in it. We have seen, that LUTHER was the beginner of the work of "Reformation "; but, he was soon followed by further reformers on the continent. These had made many attempts to propagate their doctrines in England; but, old Henry had kept them down. Now, however, when the churches were to he robbed of what remained in them, and when, to have a pretext for that robbery, was necessary to make a complete change in the form of worship, these sectarians all flocked to England, which became one great scene of religious disputation. Some were for the Common Prayer Book; others proposed alterations in it; others were for abolishing it altogether and there now began that division, that multiplicity of hostile opinions, which has continued to the present day. CRANMER employed a part of the resources of the country to feed and fatten those of these religious, or, rather, impious, adventurers, who sided with him, and who chose the best market for their doctrines. England was over-run by these foreign traders in religion; and this nation, so jealous of foreign influence, was now compelled to bend its haughty neck, not only to foreigners, but to foreigners of the most base and infamous character and description. CRANMER could not find Englishmen sufficiently supple to be his tools in executing the work that he had in hand. The Protector Hertford, whom we must now call SOMERSET (the child king having made him Duke of SOMERSET), was the greatest of all "reformers" that had yet appeared in the world, and, as we shall soon see, the greatest and most audacious of all the

plunderers that this famous Reformation has produced, save and except old Harry himself. The total abolition of the Catholic worship was necessary to his projects of plunder; and, therefore, he was a great encourager of these greedy and villainous foreigners. Perhaps the world has never, in any age, seen a nest of such atrocious miscreants as LUTHER, ZUINGLIUS, CALVIN, BEZA, and the rest of the distinguished reformers of the Catholic religion. Every one of them was notorious for the most scandalous vices, even according to the full confession of his own followers. They agreed in nothing but in the doctrine, that good works were useless; and their lives proved the sincerity of their teaching; for there was not a man of them whose acts did not merit a halter.

201. The consequences to the *morals* of the people were such as were naturally to be expected. All historians agree, that vice of all sorts and crime of every kind was never so great and so numerous before. This was confessed by the teachers themselves; and yet the Protestants have extolled this reign as the reign of *conscience* and religion! it was so manifest that the change was a bad one, that men could hot have proceeded in it from *error*. Its mischiefs were all manifest before the death of the old tyrant; that death afforded an opportunity for returning into the right path but, there was plunder remaining, and the plunderers went on. The "reformation" was not the work of virtue, of fanaticism, of error, of ambition; but of a love of plunder. This was its great animating principle in this it began, and in this it proceeded till there was nothing left for it to work on.

202. The old tyrant had, in certain cases, enabled his minions to rob the bishoprics; but, now, there was a grant! sweep at them. The PROTECTOR took the lead, and his example was followed by others. They took so much from one, so much from another, and some they wholly suppressed, as that of Westminster, and took their estates to themselves. There were many chanteries (private property to all intents and purposes); free chapels, also private property; alms-houses; hospitals; guilds, or fraternities, the property of which was as much private property as the funds of any Friendly Society now are. All these became lawful plunder. And yet there are men, who pretend, that what is now possessed by the Established Church is of so sacred a nature as not to be touched by Act of Parliament This was the reign in which this our present Established Church was founded; for, though the fabric was overset by MARY, it was raised again by ELIZABETH, Now it was that it was made, it was made, and the new worship along with it, by Acts of Parliament, and it now seems to be high time, that, by similar Acts, it should be unmade, it had its very birth in division, disunion, discord; and its life has been worthy of its birth. The property it possesses was taken, nominally, from the Catholic Church; but, in reality, from that Church, and *also* from the widow, the orphan, the indigent and the stranger. The pretext for making it was, that it would cause an union of sentiment amongst the people; that it would compose all dissensions. The truth, the obvious truth, that there could be but *one* true religion, was acknowledged and loudly proclaimed; and, it was not to be denied, that there were already *twenty*, the teachers of every one of which declared that all the others were false; and, of course, that they were, at the very least, no better than no religion at all. Indeed, this is the language of common sense; though it is now so fashionable to disclaim the doctrine of exclusive salvation. I ask the Unitarian parson, or prater, for instance, why he takes upon him that office; why he does not go and follow some trade, or why he does not work in the fields? His answer is, that he is more usefully employed in teaching. If I ask, of what use his teaching is, he tells me, he must tell me, that his teaching is necessary to the salvation of souls. Well, say I, but, why not

leave that business to the Established Church, to which the people all pay tithes? Oh, no! says he; I cannot do that, because the Church does not teach the *true* religion. Well, say I; but true or false, if it serve for salvation, what signifies it? Here I have him penned up in. a corner. He is compelled to confess., that he is a fellow wanting to lead an easy life by pandering to the passions or whims of conceited persons; or, to insist, that his sort of belief and teaching are absolutely necessary to salvation: as he will not confess the former, he is obliged to insist on the latter; and here, after all his railing against the intolerance of the Catholics, he maintains the doctrine of exclusive salvation.

203. *Two* true religions, *two* true creeds, differing from each other, contradicting each other, present us with an impossibility. What, then, are we to think of twenty or forty creeds, each differing from all the rest? If deism, or atheism, he something not only wicked in itself, but so mischievous in its effects as to call, in case of the public profession of it, for imprisonment for years and years; if this be the case what are we to think of laws, the same laws, too, which inflict that cruel punishment, tolerating and encouraging a multiplicity of creeds, all but *one* of which must he false? A code of laws acknowledging and tolerating but one religion is consistent in punishing the deist and the atheist; but if it acknowledge or tolerate *more* than one, it acknowledges or tolerates one *false* one; and let divines say, whether a false religion is not as had as deism or atheism? Besides, is it just to punish the deist or the atheist for not believing in the Christian religion at all, when he sees the laws tolerate so many religions, all but one of which must be false? What is the natural effect of men seeing constantly before their eyes a score or two of different sects, all calling themselves Christians, all tolerated by the law, and each openly declaring that all the rest are false? The natural, the necessary effect is., that many men will believe that none of them have truth on their side; and, of course, that the thing is false altogether, and invented solely for the benefit of those who teach it, and who dispute about it.

204. The law should acknowledge and tolerate but one religion: or it should know nothing at all about the matter. The Catholic code was consistent. It said, that there was but *one* true religion; and it punished as offenders those who dared openly to profess any opinion contrary to that religion. Whether that were the true religion or not, we have not now to inquire; but, while its long continuance, and in so many nations too, was a strong presumptive proof of its good moral effects upon the people, the disagreement amongst the Protestants was, and is, a presumptive proof, not less strong, of its *truth.* If, as I observed upon a former occasion, there be forty persons, who, and whose fathers, for countless generations, have, up to this day, entertained a certain belief; and, if thirty-nine of these say, at last, that this belief is erroneous, we may naturally enough suppose, or, at least, we may think it possible, that the *truth,* so long hidden, is, though late, come to light. But, if the thirty-nine begin, aye, and instantly begin, to entertain, instead of the *one* old belief, thirty-nine new beliefs, each differing from all the other thirty-eight, must we not, in common justice, decide, that the old belief must have been the true one? What; shall we hear these thirty-nine protestors against the ancient faith each protesting against all the other thirty-eight, and still believe that their joint protest was just? Thirty-eight of them must now be in error; this *must* be: and are we still to believe in the correctness of their former decision; and that, too, relating to the same identical matter? If, in a trial, relating to the dimensions of a piece of land, which had been proved to have always been, time without mind, taken for *twenty* acres, there were one surveyor to swear it contained twenty acres, and each of thirty-nine other surveyors to swear to each of the other

number of acres, between *one* and *forty*, what judge and jury would hesitate a moment in crediting him who swore to the twenty, and in wholly rejecting the testimony of all the rest?

205. Thus the argument would stand, on the supposition that thirty-nine parts out of forty of all Christendom had protested; but, there were not, and there are not, even unto this day, two parts out of fifty. So that here we have thirty-nine persons breaking off from about two thousand, protesting against the faith which the whole, and their fathers, have held; we have each of these thirty-nine instantly protesting that all the other thirty-eight have protested upon false grounds; and yet we are to believe, that their joint protest against the faith of the two thousand, who are backed by all antiquity, was wise and just! Is this the way in which we decide in other cases? Did honest men, and men not blinded by passion, or by some base motive, ever decide thus before? Besides, if the Catholic faith were so false as it is by some pretended to he, how comes it not to have been extirpated before now? When, indeed, the POPE had very great power; when even kings were compelled to bend to him, it might he said, and pretty fairly said, that no one dared to use the weapons of reason against the Catholic faith. But, we have seen the POPE a prisoner in a foreign land; we have seen him almost with out food and raiment; and we have seen the press of more than half the world at liberty to treat him and his faith as it pleased to treat them. But have we not seen the Protestant sects at work for three hundred years to destroy the Catholic faith? Do we not see, at the end of those three hundred years, that that faith is still the reigning faith of Christendom? Nay, do we not see that it is gaining ground at this very moment, even in this kingdom itself, where a Protestant hierarchy receives eight millions sterling a year, and where Catholics arc still rigidly excluded from all honour and power, and, in some cases, from all political and civil rights, under a constitution founded by their Catholic ancestors? Can it be, then, that this faith is false? Can it he that this worship is idolatrous? Can it be that it was necessary to abolish them in England, as far as law could do it? Can it be that it was for our good, our honour, to sack our country, to violate all the rights of property, to deluge the country with blood, in order to change our religion?

206. But, in returning, now, to the works of the plunderers, we ought to remark, that, in discussions of this sort, it is a common, but a very great error, to keep our eyes so exclusively fixed on mere matters of religion. The Catholic Church included in it a great deal more than the business of teaching religion and of practising worship and administering sacraments. It had a great deal to do with the temporal concerns of the people. It provided, and amply provided, for all the wants of the poor and distressed, It received back, in many instances, what the miser and extortioner had taken unfairly, and applied it to works of beneficence. It contained a great body of land proprietors, whose revenues were distributed, in various ways, amongst the people at large, upon terms always singularly advantageous to the latter. It was a great and powerful estate, independent both of the aristocracy and the crown, and naturally siding with the people. But, above all things, it was a provider for the poor and a keeper of hospitality. By its charity, and by its benevolence towards its tenants and dependants, it mitigated the rigour of proprietorship, and held society together by the ties of religion rather than by the trammels and terrors of the law. It was the great cause of that description of tenants called life-holders, who formed a most important link in the chain of society, coming after the proprietors in fee, and before the tenant at will, participating, in some degree, of the proprietorship of the estate, and yet, not whom without dependence on the proprietor. This race of persons, formerly so numerous in

England, has, by degrees, become almost wholly extinct, their place having been supplied by a comparatively few rack-renters, and by swarms of miserable paupers. The Catholic Church held the lending of money for interest, or gain, to be directly in the face of the Gospel. It considered all such gain as *usurious*, and, of course, criminal. It taught the making of loans without interest; and thus it prevented the greedy-minded from amassing wealth in that way in which wealth is most easily amassed. Usury amongst Christians was wholly unknown, until the wife-killing tyrant had laid his hands on the property of the Church and the poor. The principles of the Catholic Church all partook of generosity; it was their great characteristic, as selfishness is the characteristic of that Church which was established in its stead.

207 . The plunder which remained after the seizure of the monasteries was comparatively small; but, still, the very leavings of the old tyranny, the mere gleanings of the harvest of plunder, were something; and these were not suffered to remain. The plunder of the churches, parochial as well as collegiate, was preceded by all sorts of antics played in those churches. CALVIN had got an influence opposed to that of CRANMER; so that there was almost open war amongst these Protestants, which party should have the teaching of the people. After due preparation in this way, the robbery was set about in due form. Every church altar had, as I have before observed, more or less of gold and silver. A part consisted of images, a part of censers, candlesticks, and other things used in the celebration of the *mass*. The mass was, therefore, abolished, and there was no longer to be an *altar*, but a *table* in its stead. The fanatical part of the reformers amused themselves with quarrelling about the part of the church where the table was to stand; about the shape of it, and whether the head of it was to be placed to the North, the East, the West, or the South; and whether the people were to stand, kneel, or sit at it! The plunderers, however, thought about other things; they thought about the value of the images, censers, and the like.

208. To reconcile the people to these innovations the plunderers had a Bible contrived for the purpose, which Bible was a perversion of the original text wherever it was found to be necessary. Of all the acts of this hypocritical and plundering reign, this was, perhaps, the basest. In it we see the true character of the heroes of the "Protestant Reformation"; and the poor and miserable labourers of England, who now live upon potatoes and water, feel the consequences of the deeds of the infamous times of which I am speaking. Every preparation being made, the robbery began, and a general plunder of churches took place by royal and parliamentary authority! The robbers took away every thing valuable, even down to the vestments of the priests. Such mean rapacity never was heard of before, and, for the honour of human nature, let us hope that it will never be heard of again. It seems that England was really become a den of thieves, and of thieves, too, of the lowest and most despicable character.

209. The Protector, SOMERSET, did not forget himself. Having plundered four or five of the bishoprics, he needed a palace in London. For the purpose of building this palace, which was erected in the Strand, London, and which was called "SOMERSET-HOUSE," as the place is called to this day, he took from three bishops their town-houses; he pulled these down, together with a parish church, in order to get a suitable spot for the erection. The materials of these demolished buildings being insufficient for his purpose, he pulled down a part of the buildings appertaining to the then cathedral of St. Paul; the church of St. John, near Smithfield; Barking Chapel, near the Tower; the college church of St. Martin-le-Grand; St. Ewen's church, Newgate; and the parish church of St. Nicholas. He, besides these, ordered the pulling

down of the parish church of Saint Margaret, Westminster; but, says Dr. HEYLIN, "the workmen had no sooner advanced their scaffolds, when the parishioners gathered together in great multitudes, with bows and arrows, and staves and clubs; which so terrified the workmen that they ran away in great amazement, and never could be brought again upon that employment." Thus arose SOMERSET-HOUSE, the present grand seat of the power of fiscal grasping. It was first erected literally with the ruins of churches, and it now serves, under its old name, as the place from which issue the mandates to us to give up the fruit of our earnings to pay the interest of a DEBT, which is one of the evident and great consequences of the " Protestant Reformation," without which that DEBT never could have existed.

210. I am, in the last Number, to give an account of the impoverishment and degradation that these and former Protestant proceedings produced amongst the people at large; but I must here notice, that the people heartily detested these Protestant tyrants and their acts; General discontent prevailed, and this, in some cases, broke out into open insurrection. It is curious enough to observe the excuses that HUME, in giving an account of these times, attempts to make for the plunderers and their "reformation." It was his constant aim to blacken the Catholic institutions, and particularly the character and conduct of the Catholic clergy. Yet he could not pass over these discontents and risings of the people; and as there must have been a cause for these, he is under the necessity of ascribing them to the badness of the change, or to find out some other cause. He, therefore, goes to work in a very elaborate manner to make his readers believe, that the people were in error as to the tendency of the change. He says, that "scarce any institution can be imagined less favourable, in the main, to the interests of mankind," than that of the Catholic; yet, says he, "as it was followed by many good effects, which had ceased with the suppression of the monasteries, that suppression was very much regretted by the people." He then proceeds to describe the many benefits of the monastic institutions; says that the monks always residing on their estates caused a diffusion of good constantly around them; that, "not having equal motives to avarice with other men, they were the best and most indulgent landlords;" that, when the church lands became private property, the rents were raised, the money spent at a distance from the estates, and the tenants exposed to the rapacity of stewards; that whole estates were laid waste; that the tenants were expelled; and that even the cottagers were deprived of the commons on which they formerly fed their cattle; that a great decay of the people, as well as a diminution of former plenty, was remarked in the kingdom; that, at the same time, the coin had been debased by Henry, and was now further debased; that the good coin was hoarded or exported: that the common people were thus robbed of part of their wages; that complaints were heard in every part of the kingdom."

211 . Well; was not this change a *bad one*, then? And what are the excuses which are offered for it by this calumniator of the Catholic institutions? Why, he says, that "their hospitality and charity gave encouragement to idleness, and prevented the increase of public wealth;" and that "as it was by an addition alone of toil, that the people were able to live, this increase of industry was, at last, the effect of the PRESENT SITUATION, an effect *very beneficial* to society." What does he mean by the "present situation"? The situation of the country, I suppose, at the time when he wrote; and, though the "reformation" had not then produced pauperism and misery and DEBT and taxes equal to the present, it was on the way to do it. But what does he mean by "public riches"? The Catholic institutions "provided against the pressure of want amongst the people"; but prevented the increase of "public riches"! What, again

I ask, is the meaning of the words, "public riches"? What is, or ought to be, the end of all government and of every institution? Why, the happiness of the people. But this man sees, like ADAM SMITH, and indeed, like almost every Scotch writer, to have a notion, that there may be great public good, though producing individual misery. They seem always to regard the people as so many cattle, working for an indescribable something that they call "the "public." The question with them, is, not whether the people, for whose good all government is instituted, be well off, or wretched; but, whether, the "public" gain, or lose, money or money's worth. I am able to show, and I shall show, that England was a *greater country* before the "reformation" than since; that it was greater positively and relatively; that its real wealth was greater. But, what we have, at present, to observe, is, that thus far, at any rate, the reformation had produced general misery amongst the common people; and that, accordingly, complaints were heard from one end of the kingdom to the other.

212. The Book of Common Prayer was to put an end to all dissensions; but, its promulgation and the consequent robbery of the churches, were followed by open insurrection, in many of the counties, by battles, and executions by martial law. The whole kingdom was in commotion; but, particularly to the great honour of those counties, in Devonshire and Norfolk. In the former county the insurgents were superior in force to the hired troops, and had besieged Exeter. Lord RUSSELL was sent against them, and, at last, reinforced by GERMAN TROOPS, he defeated them, executed many by martial law, and most gallantly hanged a priest on the top of the tower of his church! This, I suppose, Mr. BROUGHAM reckons amongst those services of the family of Russell, which, he tells us, England can never repay! In Norfolk the insurrection was still more formidable; but was finally suppressed by the aid of FOREIGN TROOPS, and was also followed by the most barbarous executions. The people of Devonshire complained of the alterations in religion; that, as Dr. HEYLIN (a Protestant divine) expresses it, "that the freeborn commonalty was oppressed by a small number of gentry, who glutted themselves with pleasures, while the poor commons, wasted by daily labour, like pack-horses, live in extreme slavery; and that holy rites, established by their fathers, were abolished, and a new form of religion obtruded"; and they demanded, that the *mass* and a part of the monasteries should be restored, and that priests should not be allowed to marry. Similar were the complaints and the demands every where else. But, CRANMER's Prayer Book and the Church "by law established," backed by *foreign bayonets*, finally triumphed, at least for the present, and during the remainder of this hypocritical, base, corrupt, and tyrannical reign.

213. Thus *arose* the Protestant Church, as by *law* established. Here we see its *origin*. Thus it was that it commenced its career. How different, alas! from the commencement of that Church of England, which arose under St. AUSTIN at Canterbury, which had been cherished so carefully by ALFRED the Great, and, under the wings of which the people of England had, for nine hundred years, seen their country the greatest in the world, and had them selves lived in ease and *plenty* and real freedom, superior to those of all other nations!

214. SOMERSET, who had brought his own brother to the block in 1549, chiefly because he had opposed himself to his usurpations (though both were plunderers), was, not long after the commission of the above cruelties on the people, destined to come to that block himself. DUDLEY, Earl of Warwick, who was his rival in baseness and injustice, and his superior in talent, had out-intrigued him in the Council; and, at last, he brought him to that end which he so well merited. On what grounds

this was done is wholly uninteresting. It was a set of most wicked men circumventing, and, if necessary, destroying each other; but, it is worthy of remark, that, amongst the crimes alleged against this great culprit, was, his having brought foreign troops into the kingdom! This was, to be sure, rather ungrateful in the pious reformers; for, it was those troops that established for them their new religion. But, it was good to see them putting their leader to death, actually cutting off his head, for having caused their projects to succeed. It was, in plain words, a dispute about the *plunder*. Somerset had got more than his brother-plunderers deemed his share. He was building a palace for himself; and if each plunderer could have had a palace, it would have been peace amongst them; but, as this could not be, the rest called him a "traitor," and as the king, the Protestant St. Edward, had signed the death-warrant of one uncle at the instigation of another uncle, he now signed the death-warrant of that other, the "Saint" himself being, even now, only fifteen years of age!

215. WARWICK, who was now become Protector, was made Duke of Northumberland, and got granted to him the immense estates of that ancient house, which had fallen into the hands of the crown. This was, if possible, a more zealous Protestant than the last Protector; that is to say, still more profligate, rapacious, and cruel. The work of plundering the church went on, until there remained scarcely anything worthy of the name of clergy. Many parishes were, in all parts of the kingdom, united in one, and having but one priest amongst them. But, indeed, there were hardly any persons left worthy of the name of clergy. All the good and all the learned had either been killed, starved to death, banished, or had gone out of the country; and those who remained were, during this reign of mean plunders so stripped of their incomes, so pared down, that the parochial clergy worked as carpenters, smiths, masons, and were not unfrequently menial servants in gentlemen's houses. So that this Church of England "as by law (and German troops) established," became the scorn, not only of the people of England, but of all the nations of Europe.

216. The king, who was a poor sickly lad; seems to have had no distinctive characteristic except that of hatred to the Catholics and their religion, in which hatred CRANMER and others had brought him up. His life was not likely to be long, and NORTHUMBERLAND, who was now his keeper, conceived the project of getting the crown into his own family, a project quite worthy of a hero of the "Reformation." In order to carry this project into effect, he married one of his sons, Lord GUILFORD DUDLEY, to Lady JANE GREY, who next after MARY and ELIZABETH and MARY Queen of Scotland, was heiress to the throne. Having done this, he got Edward to make a *will*, settling the crown on this Lady Jane to the exclusion of his two sisters. The advocates of the "Reformation," who, of course, praise this boy-king, in whose reign the new church was invented , tell us long stories about the way in which NORTHUMBERLAND persuaded "Saint Edward" to do this act of injustice; but, in all probability, there is not a word of truth in the story. However, what they say is this: that Lady JANE was a *sincere* Protestant; that the young king knew this; and that his *anxiety* for the security of the Protestant religion induced him to consent to NORTHUMBERLAND's proposition.

217. The settlement met with great difficulty when it came to be laid before the lawyers, who, some how or other, always contrived to keep *their* heads out of the halter. Even Old Harry's Judges used, when hard pressed, to refer him to the Parliament for the committing of violations of law. The Judges, the Lord Chancellor, the Secretaries of State, the Privy Council; all were afraid to put their names to this transfer of the crown. The thing was, however, at last accomplished, and with the

signature of CRANMER to it, though he, as one of the late king's executor's, and the first upon that list, had sworn in the most solemn manner, to maintain his will, according to which will, the two sisters, in case of no issue by the brother, were to succeed that brother on the throne. Thus, in addition to his fourth act of notorious perjury, this maker of the Common Book of Prayer became clearly guilty of high treason. He now, at last, in spite of all his craft, had woven his own halter, and that, too, beyond all doubt, for the purpose of preserving his bishopric. The Princess MARY was next heir to the throne. He had divorced her mother; he had been the principal agent in that unjust and most wicked transaction; and, besides, he knew that MARY was immoveably a Catholic, and that, of course, her accession must be the death of his office and his church . Therefore he now committed the greatest crime known to the laws, and that, too, from the basest of motives.

218. The king having made this settlement, and being kept wholly in the hands of Northumberland, who had placed his creatures about him, would naturally, as was said at the time, not live long! In short he died on the 6th of July, 1553, in the sixteenth year of his age, and the seventh of his reign, expiring on the same day of the year that his savage father had brought Sir THOMAS MORE to the block. These were seven of the most miserable and most inglorious years that England had ever known. Fanaticism and roguery, hypocrisy and plunder, divided the country between them. The people were wretched beyond all description; from the plenty of Catholic times, they had been reduced to general beggary; and, then, in order to repress this beggary, laws the most ferocious were passed to prevent even starving creatures from asking alms. Abroad, as well as at home, the nation sunk in the eyes of the world. The town of Boulogne, in France, which had been won by Catholic Englishmen, the base Protestant rulers now, from sheer cowardice, surrendered; and from one end of Europe to the other, were heard jeering and scoffing at this formerly great and lofty nation. HUME, who finds goodness in every one who was hostile to the Catholic institutions, says, "*All* English historians dwell with *pleasure* on the excellences of this young king, whom the flattering promises of hope, joined to many real virtues, had made an object of the most tender affections of the public. He possessed mildness of disposition, a capacity to learn and to judge, and attachment to equity and justice." Of his mildness we have, I suppose, a proof in his assenting to the burning of several Protestants, who did not protest in his way; in his signing of the death-warrants of his two uncles; and in his wish to bring his sister MARY to trial for not conforming to what she deemed blasphemy, and from doing which he was deterred only by the menaces of the Emperor her cousin. So much for his mildness. As for his justice, who can doubt of that, who thinks of his will to disinherit his two sisters, even after the judges had unanimously declared to him, that it was contrary to law? The "tender affection" that the people had for him was, doubtless, evinced, by their rising in insurrection against his ordinances from one end of the kingdom to the other, and by their demanding the restoration of that religion, which all his acts tended wholly to extirpate. But, besides these internal proofs of the falsehood of HUME's description, Dr. HEYLIN, who is, at least, one of "*all* the English historians," and one, too, whom HUME himself refers to no less than twenty-four times in the part of his history relating to this very reign, does not "dwell with *pleasure* on the excellences of this young prince," of whom he, in the 4th Paragraph of his preface, speaks thus: "King EDWARD, whose death I cannot reckon for an infelicity to the Church of England; for, being ill principled in himself, and easily inclined to embrace such counsels as were offered him, it is not to be thought but that the rest of the bishoprics (before sufficiently impoverished) would have followed that of Durham, and the poor church

be left as destitute as when she came into the world in her natural nakedness." Aye, but this was his great merit in the eyes of HUME. He should have said so then, and should have left his good character of the tyrant in the egg to rest on his own opinion; and not have said, that "all English historians dwelt with pleasure on his excellences,"

219. The settlement of the crown had been kept a secret from the people, and so was the death of the King for three whole days. In the meanwhile NORTHUMBERLAND seeing the death of the young "Saint" approaching, had, in conjunction, observe, with CRANMER and the rest of his council, ordered the two princesses to come near to London, under pretence that they might be at hand to comfort their brother; but with the real design of putting them into prison the moment the breath should be out of his body. Traitors, foul conspirators, villains of all descriptions, have this in common, that they, when necessary to their own interest, are always ready to betray each other. Thus it happened here; for the Earl of ARUNDEL, who was one of the council, and who went with Dudley and others, on the tenth of July, to kneel before Lady Jane as Queen, had, in the night of the sixth, sent a secret messenger to MARY, who was no farther off than Hoddesden, informing her of the death of her brother, and of the whole of the plot against her. Thus warned, she set off on horseback, accompanied only by a few servants, to Kinninghall in Norfolk, whence she proceeded to Framlingham, in Suffolk, and thence issued her commands to the council to proclaim her as. their sovereign, hinting at, but not positively accusing them with, their treasonable designs. They had, on the day before, proclaimed Lady JANE to be Queen! They had taken all sorts of precautions to ensure their success: army, fleet, treasure, all the powers of government were in their hands. They, therefore, returned her a most insolent answer, and commanded her to submit, as a dutiful subject, to the lawful Queen, at the bottom of which command CRANMER's name stood first.

220. Honesty and sincerity exult to contemplate the misgivings, which, in a few hours afterwards, seized this band of almost unparalleled villains. The nobility and gentry had instantly flocked to the standard of Mary; and the people, even in London, who were most infected with the pestiferous principles of the foreign miscreants that had been brought from the continent to teach them the new religion, had native honesty enough left to make them disapprove of this last and most daring of robberies. RIDLEY, the Protestant Bishop of London, preached at St. Paul's, to the Lord Mayor and a numerous assemblage, for the purpose of persuading them to take part against Mary; but, it was seen, that he preached in vain. Northumberland himself marched from London on the 13th of July, to attack the Queen. But, in a few days, she was surrounded by twenty or thirty thousand. men, all volunteers in her cause, and refusing pay. Before Northumberland reached Bury St. Edmunds, he began to despair; he marched to Cambridge, and wrote to his brother conspirators for reinforcements. Amongst these, dismay first, and then perfidy, began to appear. In a few days, these men, who had been so audacious, and who had sworn solemnly to uphold the cause of Queen Jane, sent Northumberland an order to disband his army, while they themselves proclaimed Queen Mary, amidst the unbounded applause of the people.

221. The master-plotter had disbanded his army, or, rather, it had deserted him, before the order of the council reached him. This was the age of "reformation" and of baseness. Seeing himself abandoned, he, by the advice of Dr. SANDS, the Vice-Chancellor of the University, who, only four days before, had preached against Mary, went to the market place of Cambridge, and proclaimed her Queen, tossing, says STOWE, "his cap into the air, in token of his joy and satisfaction." In a few hours afterwards he was arrested by the Queen's order, and that, too, by his brother

conspirator, the Earl of Arundel, who had been one of the very first to kneel before Lady Jane! No reign, no age, no country, ever witnessed rapacity, hypocrisy, meanness, baseness, perfidy such as England witnessed in those, who were the destroyers of the Catholic, and the founders of the Protestant, Church. This DUDLEY, who had for years been a plunderer of the Church; who had been a promoter of every ruffian-like measure against those who adhered to the religion of his fathers; who had caused a transfer of the crown because, as he alleged, the accession of Mary would endanger the Protestant religion; this very man, when he came to receive justice on the block, confessed his belief in the Catholic faith; and, which is more, exhorted the nation to return to it He, according to Dr. HEYLIN (a Protestant mind), exhorted them "To stand to the religion of their ancestors, rejecting that of later date, which had occasioned all the misery of the foregoing thirty years; and that, if they desired to present their souls unspotted, before God, and were truly affected to their country, they should expel the preachers of the reformed religion. For himself," he said, "being blinded by ambition, he made a rack of his conscience, by temporizing, and so acknowledged the justice of his sentence." Fox, author of the lying "Book of Martyrs," of whose lies we shall see more by-and-by, asserts that DUDLEY made this confession in consequence of a promise of pardon. But, when he came on the scaffold, he knew that he was not to be pardoned; and besides, he himself expressly declared the contrary at his execution; and told the people, that he had not been moved by any one to make it, and had not done it from any hope of saving his life. However, we have yet to see CRANMER himself recant, and to see the whole band of Protestant plunderers on their knees before the POPE's legates confessing their sins of heresy and sacrilege, and receiving absolution for their offences!

222. Thus ended this reign of "reformation," plunder, wretchedness, and disgrace. Three times the form of the new worship was changed, and yet those who adhered to the old worship, or who went beyond the new worship, were punished with the utmost severity. The nation became every day more and more despised abroad, and more and more distracted and miserable at home. The Church, "as by law established," arose, and was enforced under two protectors, or chief ministers, both of whom deservedly suffered death as traitors. Its principal author was a man who had sent both Protestants and Catholics to the stake; who had burnt people for adhering to the POPE, others for not believing in transubstantiation, others for believing in it, and who now burnt others for disbelieving in it for reasons different from his own; a man, who now openly professed to disbelieve in that, for not believing in which he had burnt many of his fellow-creatures, and who, after this, most solemnly declared, that his own belief was that of these very persons! As this Church, by "law established," advanced, all the remains of Christian charity vanished before it. The indigent, whom the Catholic Church had so tenderly gathered under her wings, were now, merely for asking alms, branded with red-hot irons and made slaves, though no provision was made to prevent them from perishing from hunger and cold; and England, so long famed as the land of hospitality, generosity, ease, plenty, and security to person and property, became, under a Protestant Church, a scene of repulsive selfishness, of pack-horse toil, of pinching want, and of rapacity and plunder and tyranny that made the very names of law and justice a mockery.

LETTER VIII.

MARY'S ACCESSION TO THE THRONE.
HER MILD AND BENEVOLENT LAWS.
THE NATION RECONCILED TO THE CHURCH.
THE QUEEN'S GREAT GENEROSITY AND PIETY.
HER MARRIAGE WITH PHILIP.
FOX'S "MARTYRS,"

Kensington, 30th June, 1825.

MY FRIENDS,

223 . We are now entering upon that reign, the punishments inflicted during which have furnished such a handle to the calumniators of the Catholic Church, who have left no art untried to exaggerate those punishments in the first place, and, in the second place, to ascribe them to the Catholic religion, keeping out of sight, all the while, the thousand times greater mass of cruelty occasioned by Protestants in this kingdom. Of all cruelties I disapprove. I disapprove also of all corporal and pecuniary punishments on the score of religion. Far be it from me, therefore, to defend all the punishments inflicted, on this score, in the reign of Queen MARY; but, it will be my duty to show, *first*, that the mass of punishment then inflicted on this account, has been monstrously exaggerated; *second*, that the circumstances under which they were inflicted found more apology for the severity than the circumstances under which the Protestant punishments were inflicted; *thirdly*, that they were in amount as a single grain of wheat is to a whole bushel, compared with the mass of punishments under the Protestant Church, "as by law established;" *lastly*, that, be they what they might, it is a base perversion of reason to ascribe them to the principles of the Catholic religion; and that, as to the Queen herself, she was one of the most virtuous of human. beings, and was rendered miserable, not by her own disposition or misdeeds, but by the misfortune and misery entailed on her by her two immediate predecessors, who had uprooted the institutions of the country, who had plunged the kingdom into confusion, and who had left no choice but that of making severe examples, or, of being an encourager of, and a participator in, heresy, plunder, and sacrilege. Her reign our deceivers have taught us to call the reign of "BLOODY QUEEN MARY"; while they have taught us to call that of her sister, the "GOLDEN DAYS OF GOOD QUEEN BESS." They have taken good care never to tell us, that, for every drop of blood that Mary shed, Elizabeth shed a pint; that the former gave up every fragment of the plunder of which the deeds of her predecessors had put her in possession, and that the latter resumed this plunder again, and took from the poor every pittance which had, by oversight, been left them; that the former never changed her religion, and that the latter changed from Catholic to Protestant, then to Catholic again, and then back again to Protestant; that the former punished people for departing from that religion in which she and they and their fathers had been born, and to which she had always adhered; and that the latter punished people for not departing from the religion of her and their fathers, and which religion, too, she herself professed and openly lived in even at the time of her coronation. Yet, we have been taught to call the former "bloody" and the latter "good"! How have we been deceived! And is it not time, then, that this deception, so injurious to our Catholic fellow-subjects and so debasing to

ourselves, should cease? It is, perhaps, too much to hope, that I shall be able to make it cease; but, towards accomplishing this great and most desirable object, I shall do something, at any rate, by a plain and true account of the principal transactions of the reign of Mary.

224. The Queen, who, as we have seen in paragraph **219**, was in Framlingham, in Suffolk, immediately set off for London, where, having been greeted on the road with the strongest demonstrations of joy at her accession, she arrived on the 31st of July, 1553. As she approached London the throngs thickened; Elizabeth, who had kept cautiously silent while the issue was uncertain, went out to meet he, and the two sisters, riding on horseback, entered the city, the houses being decorated, the streets strewed with flowers, and the people dressed in their gayest clothes. She was crowned soon afterwards, in the most splendid manner, and after the Catholic ritual, by GARDINER, who had, as we have seen, opposed CRANMER's new Church, and whom she found a prisoner in the Tower, he having been deprived of his Bishopric of Winchester; but whom we are to see one of the great actors in restoring the Catholic religion. The joy of the people was boundless. It was a coronation of greater splendour and more universal joy than ever had before been witnessed. This is agreed on all hands. And this fact gives the lie to HUME, who would have us believe that the people did not like the Queen's principles. This fact has reason on its side as well as historical authority; for, was it not natural that the people, who, only three years before, had actually risen in insurrection in all parts of the kingdom against the new church, and its authors, should be half mad with joy at the accession of a Queen, who they were sure would put down that church, and put down those who had quelled them by the aid of German troops?

225. Mary began her reign by acts the most just and beneficent. Generously disregarding herself, her ease and her means of splendour, she abolished the debased currency, which her father had introduced and her brother had made still baser; she paid the debts due by the crown; and she largely remitted taxes at the same time. But that which she had most at heart, was, the restoration of that religion, under the influence of which the kingdom had been so happy and so great for so many ages, and since the abolition of which it had known nothing but discord, disgrace, and misery. There were in her way great obstacles; for, though the pernicious principles of the German and Dutch and Swiss reformers had not, even yet, made much progress amongst the people, except in London, which was the grand scene of the operations of those hungry and fanatical adventurers, there were the plunderers to deal with, and these plunderers had power. It is easy to imagine, which, in deed, was the undoubted fact, that the English people, who had risen in insurrection, in all parts of the kingdom, against CRANMER's new church; who had demanded the restoration of the mass and of part, at least, of the monasteries, and who had been silenced only by German bayonets, and halters and gibbets following martial law; it is easy to imagine, that this same people would, in only three years afterwards, hail with joy indescribable, the prospect of seeing the new church put down, and the ancient one restored, and that, too, under a Queen, on whose constancy and piety and integrity they could so firmly rely. But, the plunder had been so immense, the plunderers were so numerous, they were so powerful, and there were so few men of family of any account who had not participated, in one way or another, in deeds hostile to the Catholic Church, that the enterprise of the Queen was full of difficulty. As to CRANMER's Church, "by law established," that was easily disposed of. The gold and silver and cups and candlesticks and other things, of which the altar-robbers of young

"Saint Edward's" reign had despoiled the churches, could not, indeed, be restored; but, the altars themselves could, and speedily were; and the tables which had been put in their stead, and the married priests along with them, were soon seen no longer to offend the eyes of the people. It is curious to observe, how tender-hearted HUME is upon this subject. He says, "Could any notion of law, justice, or reason, be attended to, where superstition predominates, the priests would never have been expelled for their past marriages, which, at that time, were permitted by the laws of the kingdom." I wonder why it never occurred to him to observe, that monks and nuns ought not, then, to have been expelled! Were not their institutions "permitted by the laws of the kingdom"? Aye, and had been permitted by those laws for nine hundred years, and guaranteed too by Magna Charta. He applauds the expelling of them; but this "new thing," though only of three years and a half standing, and though "established" under a boy-king, who was under two protectors, each of whom was justly beheaded for high treason, and under a council who were all conspirators against the lawful sovereign; these married priests, the most of whom had, like LUTHER, CRANMER, KNOX, HOOPER, and other great "Reformers," broken their vows of celibacy, and were, of course, perjurers; no law was to be repealed, however contrary to public good such law might be, if the repeal injured the interests of such men as these! The Queen had, however, too much justice to think thus, and these apostates were expelled, to the great joy of the people, many of whom had been sabred by German troops, because they demanded, amongst other things, that priests might not be permitted to marry. The Catholic bishops, who had been turned out by CRANMER, were restored, and his new bishops were, of course, turned out. CRANMER himself was, in a short time, deprived of his ill-gotten see, and was in prison, and most justly, as a traitor. The mass was, in all parts of the country, once more celebrated, the people were no longer burnt with red-hot irons, and made slaves merely for asking alms, and they began to hope, that England would be England again, and that hospitality and charity would return.

226. But there were the plunderers to deal with! And, now, we are about to witness a scene, which, were not its existence so well attested, must pass for the wildest of romance. What? That Parliament, who had declared CRANMER's divorce of Catherine to be lawful, and who had enacted that Mary was a bastard, acknowledge that same Mary to be the lawful heir to the throne! That Parliament which had abolished the Catholic worship and created the Protestant worship, on the ground that the former was idolatrous and damnable, and the latter agreeable to the will of God, abolish the latter and restore the former! What? Do these things? And that, too, without any force; without being compelled to do them? No: not exactly so: for it had the people to fear, a vast majority of whom were cordially with the Queen as far as related to these matters, respecting which it is surprising what dispatch was made. The late King died only in July, and before the end of the next November, all the work of CRANMER, as to the divorce as well as to the worship, was completely overset, and that, too, by Acts of the very Parliament who had confirmed the one and "established" the other. The first of these Acts declared, that Henry and Catherine had been lawfully married, and it laid all the blame upon CRANMER by name! The second Act called the Protestant Church, "as by law established," a "new thing imagined by a few singular opinions," though the Parliament when it established it, asserted it to have come from the "Holy Ghost." What was now said of it was true enough: but it might have been added, established by German bayonets. The great inventor, CRANMER, who was, at last, in a fair way of receiving the just reward of his numerous misdeeds, could only hear of the overthrow of his work; for, having, though clearly as guilty of high treason as DUDLEY himself, been, as yet, only confined to his palace at

Lambeth, and hearing that mass had been celebrated in his Cathedral Church at Canterbury, he put forth a most inflammatory and abusive declaration, (which, mind, he afterwards recanted) for which declaration, as well as for his treason, he was committed to the Tower, where he lay at the time when these Acts were passed. But, the new church required no law to abolish it. It was, in fact, abolished by the general feeling of the nation; and, as we shall see in the next Number, it required rivers of blood to re-establish it in the reign of Elizabeth. HUME, following Fox, the "Martyr"-man, complains bitterly of "the court" for its "contempt of the laws, in celebrating, "before the two Houses, at the opening of the Parliament a mass of Latin, with all the ancient rites and ceremonies, though abolished by Act of Parliament!" Abolished! Why, so had CROMWELL and his canting crew abolished the kingly government by Act of Parliament, and by the bayonet; and yet this did not induce Charles to wait for a repeal before he called himself king. Nor did the bringers over of the "deliverer," WILLIAM, wait for an Act of Parliament to authorize them to introduce the said "deliverer." The "new thing" fell of itself. It had been forced upon the people and they hated it.

227. But, when the question came, whether the Parliament should restore the PAPAL SUPREMACY, the plunder was at stake; for, to take the Church property was sacrilege, and, if the POPE regained his power in the kingdom, he might insist on restitution. The greater part of this property had been seized on eighteen years before. In many cases it bad been divided and sub-divided; in many, the original grantees were dead. The common people, too, had, in many cases, become dependent on the new proprietors: and, besides, they could not so easily trace the connexion between their faith and that supremacy, as they could between their faith and the mass and the sacraments. The Queen, therefore, though she most anxiously wished to avoid giving, in any way whatever, her sanction to the plunder, was reduced to the necessity of risking a civil war for the POPE's supremacy; to leave her kingdom unreconciled to the Church; and to keep to herself the title of Head of the Church, to her so hateful; or to make a compromise with the plunderers. She was induced to prefer the latter; though it is by no means certain that civil war would not have been better for the country, even if it had ended in the triumph of the plunderers, which, in all human probability, it would not. But, observe in how forlorn a state, as to this question, she was placed. There was scarcely a nobleman, or gentleman of any note, in her kingdom, who had not, in one way or another, soiled his hands with the plunder. The Catholic bishops, all but FISHER, had assented to the abolition of the POPE's supremacy. Bishop GARDINER, who was now her High Chancellor, was one of these, though he had been deprived of his bishopric and imprisoned in the Tower, because he opposed CRANMER's further projects. These Catholic bishops, and GARDINER especially, must naturally wish to get over this matter as quietly as possible; for, how was he to advise the Queen to risk a civil war for the restoration of that, the abolition of which he had so fully assented to, and so strenuously supported? And how was she to do any thing without councillors of some sort?

228. Nevertheless the Queen, whose zeal was equal to her sincerity, was bent on the restoration; and, therefore, a compromise with the plunderers was adopted. Now, then, it was fully proved to all the world, and now this plundered nation, who had been reduced to the greatest misery by what had been impudently called the "Reformation," saw as clearly as they saw the light of day, that all those who had abetted the "Reformation;" that all the railings against the POPE; that all the accusations against the monks and nuns; that all the pretences of abuses in the Catholic Church; that all

the confiscations, sackings, and bloodshed; that all these, from first to last, had proceeded from the love of plunder; for, now, the two Houses of Parliament, who had, only about three or four years before, established CRANMER's Church, and declared it to be "the work of the Holy Ghost;" now these pious "Reformation" men, having first made a firm bargain to keep the plunder, confessed (to use the words even of HUME) "that they had been guilty of a most horrible defection from the true Church; professed their sincere repentance for their past transgressions; and declared their resolution to repeal all laws enacted in prejudice of the POPE's authority"! Are the people of England aware of this? No: not one man out of fifty thousand. These, let it be remembered, were the men who made the Protestant religion in England!

229. But this is a matter of too much importance to be dismissed without the mention of some particulars. The Queen had not about her one single man of any eminence, who had not, in some degree, departed from the straight path, during one or the other, or both, of the two last reigns. But there was Cardinal POLE, of whom, and of the butchery of whose aged and brave mother, we have seen an account in paragraph **115**. He still remained on the Continent; but now he could with safety return to his native country, on which the fame of his talents and virtues reflected so much honour. The Cardinal was appointed by the POPE to be his Legate, or representative, in England. The Queen had been married on the 25th of July, 1554, to PHILIP, Prince of Spain, son and heir of the Emperor CHARLES V., of which marriage I shall speak more fully by-and-by.

230. In November, the same year, a Parliament was called, and was opened with a most splendid procession of the two Houses, closed by the King and Queen, the first on horseback, the last in a litter, dressed in robes of purple. Their first act was a repeal of the attainder of POLE, passed in the reign of the cruel Henry VIII. While, this was going on, many noblemen, and gentlemen had gone to Brussels, to conduct POLE to England; and it is worth observing, that amongst these was that Sir WILLIAM CECIL who was afterwards so bitter and cruel an enemy of the Catholics and their religion, in the reign of ELIZABETH. POLE was received at Dover with every demonstration of public joy and exultation; and, before he reached Gravesend, where he took water for Westminster, the gentlemen of the country had flocked to his train, to the number of nearly two thousand horsemen. Here is a fact, which, amongst thousands of others, shows what the populousness and opulence of England then were.

231. On the 29th of November the two Houses petitioned the King and Queen. In this petition they expressed their deep regret at having been guilty of defection from the Church; and prayed their Majesties, who had not participated in the sin, to intercede with the Holy Father, the POPE, for their forgiveness, and for their re-admission into the fold of Christ. The next day, the Queen being seated on the throne, having the King on her left, and POLE, the POPE's Legate, on her right, the Lord High Chancellor, Bishop GARDINER, read the petition; the King and Queen then spoke to POLE, and he, at the close of a long speech, gave, in the name of the POPE, to the two Houses and to the whole nation, absolution in the name of the Father, Son and Holy Ghost, at which words the members of the two Houses, being on their knees, made the hall resound with AMEN!

232. Thus was England once more a Catholic country. She was restored to the "fold of Christ"; but the fold had been plundered of its hospitality and charity; and the plunderers, before they pronounced the "Amen," had taken care that the plunder should not be restored. The POPE had hesitated to consent to this; Cardinal POLE,

who was a man full of justice, had hesitated still longer; but, as we have seen before, GARDINER, who was now the Queen's prime minister, and, indeed, all her council, were for the compromise; and therefore, these "Amen" people, while they confessed that they had sinned by that defection, in virtue of which defection, and of that alone, they got the property of the Church and the poor; while they prayed for absolution for that sin; while they rose from their knees to join the Queen in singing TE DEUM in thanksgiving for that absolution; while they were doing these things, they enacted, that all the holders of Church property should keep it, and that any person who should attempt to molest or disturb them therein should be deemed guilty of *præmunire*, and be punished accordingly!

233. It, doubtless, went to the heart of the Queen to assent to this act, which was the very worst deed of her whole reign, the monstrously exaggerated fires of Smithfield not excepted. We have seen how she was situated as to her councillors, and particularly as to GARDINER, who, besides being a most zealous and active minister, was a man of the greatest talents. We have seen, that there was scarcely a man of any note, who had not, first or last, partook of the plunder; but still, great as her difficulty certainly was, she would have done better to follow the dictates of her own mind, insisting upon doing what was right, and leaving the consequences to God, as she had so nobly done, when CRANMER. and the rest of the base council of Edward VI., commanded her to desist from hearing mass and most cruelly took her chaplains from her.

234. However, she was resolved to keep none of the plunder herself. Old HARRY, as "Head of the Church," had taken to himself the tenths and first fruits; that is to say, the tenth part of the annual worth of each church benefice and the first whole year's income of each, These had, of course, been kept by King Edward. Then there were some of the Church estates, some of the hospitals, and other things, and these amounting to a large sum altogether, that still belonged to the crown; and of which the Queen was, of course, the possessor. In November, 1555, she gave up to the Church the tenths, and first fruits; which, together with the tithes, which her two immediate predecessors had seized on and kept, were worth about 63,000*l.* a year in money of that day, and were equal to about a million a year of the present money! Have we ever heard of any other sovereign doing the like? "Good Queen Bess" we shall find taking them back again to herself; and, though we shall find Queen ANNE giving them up to the Church, we are to bear in mind, that, in Mary's days, the Crown and its officers, ambassadors, judges, pensioners, and all employed by it, were supported out of the landed estate of the Crown itself, the remains of which estate we now see in the pitiful rest of "Crown-lands." Taxes were never, in those days, called for, but for wars, and other really national purposes; and Mary was Queen two years and a half, before she imposed upon her people a single farthing of tax in any shape whatever! So that this act of surrendering the tenths and first fruits was the effect of her generosity and piety; and of hers alone too; for it was done against the remonstrances of her council, and it was not without great opposition that the bill passed in parliaments where it was naturally feared that this just act of the Queen would awaken the people's hatred of the plunderers. But the Queen persevered, saying, that she would be "Defender of the Faith" in reality, and not merely in name. This was the woman, whom we have been taught to call "the Bloody Queen Mary"!

235. The Queen did not stop here, but proceeded to restore all the Church and Abbey lands, which were in her possession, being, whatever might be the consequence to her, firmly resolved not to be a possessor of the plunder. Having called some members of

her council together, she declared her resolution to them, and bade them prepare an account of those lands and possessions, that she might know what measures to adopt for the putting of her intention in execution. Her intention was to apply the revenues, as nearly as possible, to their ancient purposes. She began with Westminster Abbey, which had, in the year 610, been the site of a church immediately after the introduction of Christianity by St. AUSTIN, which church had been destroyed by the Danes, and, in 958, restored by King Edgar and St. Dunstan, who placed twelve Benedictine monks in it: and which became, under Edward the Confessor, in 1049, a noble and richly endowed abbey, which when plundered and suppressed by Henry, had revenues to the amount of 3,977*l.* a year of good old rent, in money of that day, and, therefore, equal to about eighty thousand pounds a year of money of this day! Little of this, however, remained, in all probability, to the Queen, the estates having, in great part, been parcelled out amongst the plunderers of the two last reigns. But, whatever there remained to her she restored; and Westminster Abbey once more saw a convent of Benedictine monks within its walls. She next restored the Friary at Greenwich, to which had belonged friars PEYTO and ELSTOW, whom we have seen, in paragraphs **81** and **82**, so nobly pleading, before the tyrant's face, the cause of her injured mother, for which they had felt the fury of that ferocious tyrant. She re-established the Black-Friars in London. She restored the Nunnery at Sion near Brentford, on the spot where Sion-House now stands. At Sheen she restored the Priory. She restored and liberally endowed the Hospital of St. John, Smithfield. She re-established the Hospital in the Savoy, for the benefit of the poor, and allotted to it a suitable yearly revenue out of her own purse; and, as her example would naturally have great effect, it is, as Dr. HEYLIN (a Protestant, and a great enemy of her memory,) observes, "hard to say how far the nobility and gentry might have done the like, if the Queen had lived some few years longer."

236. These acts were so laudable, so unequivocally good, so clearly the effect of justice, generosity and charity, in the Queen, that, coming before us, as they do, in company with great zeal for the Catholic religion, we are naturally curious to hear what remarks they bring from the unfeeling and malignant HUME. Of her own free will, and even against the wish of very powerful men, she gave up, in this way, a yearly revenue of probably not less than a million and a half of pounds of our present money. And for what? Because she held it unjustly; because it was plunder; because it had been taken to the Crown in violation of Magna Charta and all the laws and usages of the realm; because she hoped to be able to make a beginning in the restoring of that hospitality and charity which her predecessors had banished from the land; and because her conscience, as she herself declared, forbade her to retain these ill-gotten possessions, valuing, as she did (she told her council) , "her conscience more than ten kingdoms." Was there ever a more praiseworthy act? And were there ever motives more excellent? Yet HUME, who exults in the act in which the plunderers insisted on, to secure their plunder, calls this noble act of the Queen an "impudent" one, and ascribes it solely to the influence of the new POPE, who, he tells us, told her ambassadors, that the English would never have the doors of Paradise opened to them unless the whole of the church property was restored. How false this is, in spite of HUME's authorities, is clear from this undeniable fact; namely, that she gave the Tenths and First Fruits to the Bishops and Priests of the Church in England, and not to the POPE, to whom they were formerly paid. This, therefore, is a malignant misrepresentation. Then again, he says, that the POPE's remonstrances on this score, had "little influence "with the nation." With the plunderers, he means; for, he has been obliged to confess, that, in all parts of the country, the people, in Edward's reign,

demanded a restoration of a part of the monasteries; and, is it not clear, then, that they must have greatly rejoiced to see their sovereign make a beginning in that restoration? But, it was his business to lessen, as much as possible, the merit of these generous and pious acts of this basely calumniated Queen.

237. Events soon proved to this just and good, but singularly unfortunate, Queen, that she would have done better to risk a civil war against the plunderers than assent to the Act of Parliament by which was secured to them the quiet possession of their plunder. Her generous example had no effect upon them; but on the contrary, made them dislike her, because it exposed them to odium, presenting a contrast with their own conduct, so much to their disadvantage. From this cause, more than from any other, arose those troubles, which harassed her during the remainder of her short reign.

238. She had not been many months!on the throne before a rebellion was raised against her, instigated by the "Reformation" preachers, who had bawled in favour of Lady JANE GREY, but who now discovered, amongst other things, that it was contrary to God's word to be governed by a woman. The fighting rebels were defeated, and the leaders executed, and, at the same time, the Lady Jane herself, who had been convicted of high treason, who had been kept in prison, but whose life had hitherto been spared, and would evidently still have been spared, if it had not manifestly tended to keep alive the hopes of the traitors and disaffected. And, as this Queen has been called "the bloody," is another instance to be found of so much lenity shown towards one, who had been guilty of treason to the extent of actually proclaiming herself the sovereign? There was another rebellion afterwards, which was quelled in like manner, and was followed by the execution of the principal traitors, who had been abetted by a Protestant faction in France, if not by the Government of that country, which was bitterly hostile towards the Queen on account of her marriage with Philip, the Prince of Spain, which marriage became a great subject of invective and false accusation with the Protestants and disaffected of all sorts.

239. The Parliament, almost immediately after her accession, advised her to marry; but not to marry a foreigner. How strangely our taste is changed! The English had always a deep-rooted prejudice against foreigners, till, for pure love of the Protestant religion, they looked out for, and soon felt the sweets of one who began the work of funding, and of making national debts! The Queen, how ever, after great deliberation, determined to marry Philip, who was son and heir to the Emperor Charles V., and who, though a widower, and having children by his first wife, was still much younger than the Queen, who was now (in July, 1554) in the 39th year of her age, while Philip was only 27. Philip arrived at Southampton in July, 1554, escorted by the combined fleets of England, Spain, and the Netherlands; and on the 25th of that month the marriage took place in the Cathedral of Winchester, the ceremony being performed by GARDINER, who was the bishop of the see, and being attended by great numbers of nobles from all parts of Christendom. To show how little reliance is to be placed on HUME, I will here notice, that he says the marriage took place at Westminster, and to this adds many facts equally false. His account of the whole of this transaction is a mere romance, made up from Protestant writers, even whose accounts he has shamefully distorted to the prejudice of the views and character of the Queen.

240. As things then stood, sound and evident good to England dictated this match. Leaving out ELIZABETH, the next heir to the throne was Mary Queen of Scots, and she was betrothed to the Dauphin of France; so that England might fall to the lot of the French King; and, as to Elizabeth, even supposing her to survive the Queen, she

now stood bastardized by two Acts of Parliament; for the Act which had just been passed, declaring Catherine to be the lawful wife of her father, made her mother (what, indeed, CRANMER had declared her) an adulteress in law, as she was in fact. Besides, if France and Scotland were evidently likely to become the patrimony of one and the same Prince, it was necessary that England should take steps for strengthening herself also in the way of preparation. Such was the policy that dictated this celebrated match, which the historical calumniators of Mary have attributed to the worst and most low and disgusting of motives; in which, however, they have only followed the example of the malignant traitors of the times we are referring to, it being only to be lamented that they were not then alive to share in their fate.

241. Nothing ever was, nothing could he more to the honour of England than every part of this transaction; yet did it form the pretences of the traitors of that day, who, for the obvious reasons mentioned in the last paragraph, were constantly encouraged and abetted by France, and as constantly urged on by the disciples of CRANMER and his crew of German and Dutch teachers. When the rebels had, at one time, previous to Mary's marriage, advanced even to London, she went to the Guildhall, where she told the citizens, that, if she thought the marriage were injurious to her people, or to the honour of the state, she would not assent to it; and that, if it should not appear to the Parliament to be for the benefit of the whole kingdom, she would never marry at all. "Wherefore," said she, "stand fast against these rebels, your enemies and mine; fear them not; for I assure ye, that I fear them nothing at all." Thus she left them, leaving the Hall resounding with their acclamations.

242. When the marriage articles appeared, it was shown that, on this occasion, as on all others, the Queen had kept her word most religiously: for even HUME is obliged to confess, that these articles were "as favourable as possible for the interest and security and even the grandeur of England." What more was wanted, then? And if, as HUME says was the case, "these articles gave no satisfaction to the nation," all that we can say, is, that the nation was very unreasonable and ungrateful. This is, however, a great falsehood; for, what HUME here ascribes to the whole nation, he ought to have confined to the plunderers and the fanatics, whom, throughout his romance of this reign, he always calls the nation. The articles quoted from RYMER by HUME himself, were, that, though Philip should have the title of King, the administration should be wholly in the Queen; that no foreigner should hold any office in the kingdom; that no change should be made in the English laws, customs, and privileges; that sixty thousand pounds a year (a million of our present money) should be settled on the Queen as her jointure to be paid by Spain if she outlived him; that the male issue of this marriage should inherit together with England, both Burgundy and the low Countries; and that, if Don Carlos, Philip's son by his former marriage, should die leaving no issue, the Queen's issue, whether male or female, should inherit Spain, Sicily, Milan, and all the other dominions of Philip. Just before the marriage ceremony was performed, an envoy from the Emperor, Philip's father, delivered to the English Chancellor, a deed resigning to his son the kingdom of Naples and the Duchy of Milan, the Emperor thinking it beneath the dignity of the Queen of England to marry one that was not a king.

243. What transaction was ever more honourable to a nation than this transaction was to England? What queen, what sovereign, ever took more care of the glory of a people? Yet the fact appears to be, that there was some jealousy in the nation at large, as to this foreign connection; and, I am not one of those who are disposed to censure this jealousy. But, can I have the conscience to commend, or, even to abstain from

censuring, this jealousy in our Catholic forefathers, without feeling as a Protestant, my cheeks burn with shame at what has taken place in Protestant times, and even in my own time! When another Mary, a Protestant Mary, was brought to the throne, did the Parliament take care to keep the administration wholly in her, and to give her husband the mere title of king? Did they take care then that no foreigners should hold offices in England? Oh, no! That foreign, that Dutch husband, had the administration vested in him; and he brought over whole crowds of foreigners, put them into the highest offices, gave them the highest titles, and heaped upon them large parcels of what was left of the Crown estate, descending to that Crown, in part at least, from the days of ALFRED himself! And this transaction is called "glorious"; and that, too, by the very men, who talk of the "inglorious" reign of Mary! What, then, are sense and truth never to reign in England? Are we to be duped unto all generations?

244. And, if we come down to our own dear Protestant days, do we find the Prince of SAXE COBURG the heir to mighty dominions? Did he bring into the country, as Philip did, twenty-nine chests of bullion, leading to the Tower twenty-two carts and ninety-nine pack horses? Do we find him settling on his wife's issue great states and kingdoms? Do we find his father making him a king, on the eve of the marriage, because a person of lower title would be beneath a Queen of England? Do we find him giving his bride, as a bridal present, jewels to the amount of half a million of our money? Do we find him settling on the Princess Charlotte a jointure of a million sterling a year, if she should outlive him? No; but (and come and boast of it, you shameless revilers of this Catholic Queen!) we find our Protestant parliament settling ON HIM fifty thousand pounds a year, to come out of taxes raised on us, if he should outlive her; which sum we now duly and truly pay in full tale, and shall possibly have to pay it for forty years yet to come! How we feel ourselves shrink, when we thus compare our conduct with that of our Catholic forefathers!

245. In my relation, I have not adhered to the exact chronological order, which would have too much broken my matter into detached parcels , but, I should here observe, that the marriage was previous to the reconciliation with the POPE, and also previous to the Queen's generous restoration of the property, which she held of the Church and the poor. It was also previous to those dreadful punishments which she inflicted upon heretics, of which punishments I am now about to speak, and which, though monstrously exaggerated by the lying Fox and others, though a mere nothing compared with those inflicted afterwards on Catholics by Elizabeth, and though hardly to be called cruel, when set in comparison with the rivers of Catholic blood that have flowed in Ireland, were, nevertheless, such as to be deeply deplored by every one, and by nobody more than the Catholics, whose religion, though these punishments were by no means caused by its principles, has been reproached as the cause, and the sole cause, of the whole of them.

246. We have seen, in paragraph **200** and **201**, what a Babel of opinions and of religions had been introduced by CRANMER and his crew; and we have also seen, that immoralitv, that vice of all sorts, that enmity and strife incessant, had been the consequence. Besides this, it was so natural that the Queen should desire to put down all these sects, and that she should be so anxious on the subject, that we are not at all surprised that, if she saw all other means ineffectual for the purpose, she should resort to means of the utmost severity that the laws of the land allowed of, for the accomplishment of that purpose. The traitors and the leading rebels of her reign were all, or affected to be, of the new sects. Though small in number, they made up for that disadvantage by their indefatigable malignity; by their incessant efforts to trouble the

state, and indeed, to destroy the Queen herself. But I am for rejecting all apologies for her, founded on provocations given to her: and also for rejecting all apologies founded on the disposition and influence of her councillors; for, if she had been opposed to the burning of heretics, that burning would, certainly, never have taken place. That burning is fairly to be ascribed to her; but, as even the malignant HUME gives her credit for sincerity, is it not just to conclude, that her motive was to put an end to the propagation, amongst her people, of errors which she deemed destructive of their souls, and the permission of the propagation of which she deemed destructive of her own? And, there is this much to be said in defence of her motive, at any rate, that these new lights, into however many sects they might be divided, all agreed in teaching the abominable doctrine of salvation by faith alone, without regard to works.

24 7 . As a preliminary to the punishment of heretics there was an Act of Parliament passed in December, 1554 (a year and a half after the Queen came to the throne) , to restore the ancient statutes, relative to heresy. These statutes were first passed against the LOLLARDS in the reigns of RICHARD II. and HENRY IV. And they provided, that heretics, who were obstinate, should be burnt. These statutes were altered in the reign of HENRY VIII., in order that he might get the property of heretics; and, in that of EDWARD, they were repealed. Not out of mercy, however; but because heresy was, according to those statutes, to promulgate opinions contrary to the Catholic Faith; and this did, of course, not suit the state of things under the new church, "as by law established." Therefore, it was then held, that heresy was punishable by common law, and, that, in case of obstinacy, heretics might be burnt; and, accordingly, many were punished and some burnt, in that reign, by process at common law; and these were, too, Protestants dissenting from CRANMER's Church, who himself condemned them to the flames. Now, however, the Catholic religion being again the religion of the country, it was thought necessary to return to ancient statutes; which, accordingly, were re-enacted. That which had been the law, during seven reigns, comprising nearly two centuries, and some of which reigns had been amongst the most glorious and most happy that England had ever known, one of the Kings having won the title of King of France and another of them having actually been crowned at Paris; that which had been the law for so long a period was now the law again: so that here was nothing new, at any rate. And, observe, though these statutes were again repealed, when ELIZABETH's policy induced her to be a Protestant, she enacted others to supply their place, and that both she and her successor, JAMES I., burnt heretics; though they had, as we shall see, a much more expeditious and less noisy way of putting out of the world those who still had the constancy to adhere to the religion of their fathers.

248. The laws, being passed, were not likely to remain a dead letter. They were put in execution chiefly in consequence of condemnations, in the spiritual court, by BONNER, Bishop of London. The punishment was inflicted in the usual manner; dragging to the place of execution, and then burning to death, the sufferer being tied to a stake, in the midst of a pile of fagots, which, when set on fire, consumed him. Bishop GARDINER, the Chancellor, has been, by Protestant writers, charged with being the adviser of this measure. I can find no ground for this charge, while all agree that POLE, who was now become Archbishop of Canterbury, in the place of CRANMER, disapproved of it. It is also undeniable, that a Spanish friar, the confessor of Philip, preaching before the Queen, expressed his disapprobation of it. Now, as the Queen was much more likely to be influenced, if at all, by POLE, and especially by PHILIP, than by GARDINER, the fair presumption is, that it was her own measure. And, as to BONNER, on whom so much blame has been thrown on this account, he

had, indeed, been most cruelly used by CRANMER and his Protestants; but, there was the Council continually accusing all the Bishops (and he more than any of the rest) of being too slow in the performance of this part of their duty. Indeed, it is manifest, that, in this respect, the Council spoke the then almost universal sentiment; for though the French ceased not to hatch rebellions against the Queen, none of the grounds of the rebels ever were, that she punished heretics. Their complaints related almost solely to the connexion with Spain; and never to the "flames of Smithfield," though we of latter times have been made to believe, that nothing else was thought of; but, the fact is, the persons put to death were chiefly of very infamous character, many of them foreigners, almost the whole of them residing in London, and called, in derision by the people at large, the "London Gospellers." Doubtless, out of two hundred and seventy-seven persons (the number stated by HUME on authority of Fox) who were thus punished, some may have been real martyrs to their opinions, and have been sincere and virtuous persons; but, in this number of 277, many were convicted felons, some clearly traitors, as RIDLEY and CRANMER. These must be taken from the number, and we may; surely, take such as were alive when Fox first published his book, and who expressly begged to decline the honour of being enrolled amongst his "Martyrs." As a proof of Fox's total disregard of truth, there was, in the next reign, a Protestant parson, as Anthony Wood (a Protestant) tells us, who, in a sermon, related, on authority of Fox, that a Catholic of the name of GRIMWOOD had been, as Fox said, a great enemy of the Gospellers, had been "punished by a judgment of God," and that his "bowels fell out of his body." GRIMWOOD was not only alive at the time when the sermon was preached, but happened to be present in the church to hear it; and he brought an action of defamation against the preacher! Another instance of Fox's falseness relates to the death of Bishop GARDINER. Fox and BURNET, and other vile calumniators of the acts and actors in Queen Mary's reign, say, that GARDINER, on the day of the execution of LATIMER and RIDLEY, kept dinner waiting till the news of their suffering should arrive, and that the Duke of Norfolk, who was to dine with him, expressed great chagrin at the delay; that, when the news came, "transported with joy," they sat down to table, where GARDINER was suddenly seized with the disury, and died, in horrible torments, in a fortnight after wards. Now, LATIMER. and RIDLEY were put to death on the 16th of October; and COLLIER, in his Ecclesiastical History, p. 386, states, that GARDINER opened the Parliament on the 21st of October; that he attended in Parliament twice afterwards; that he died on the 12th of November, of the gout, and not of disury; and that, as to the Duke of Norfolk, he had been dead a year when this event took place! What a hypocrite, then, must that man he, who pretends to believe in this Fox! Yet, this infamous book has, by the arts of the plunderers and their descendants, been circulated to a boundless extent amongst the people of England, who have been taught to look upon all the thieves, felons, and traitors, whom Fox calls "Martyrs," as sufferers resembling St. Stephen, St. Peter, and St. Paul!

249. The real truth about these "Martyrs," is, that they were, generally, a set of most wicked wretches, who sought to destroy the Queen and her Government, and under the pretence of conscience and superior piety, to obtain the means of again preying upon the people. No mild means could reclaim them: those means had been tried: the Queen had to employ vigorous means, or, to suffer her people to continue to be torn by the religious factions, created, not by her, but by her two immediate predecessors, who had been aided and abetted by many of those who now were punished, and who were worthy of ten thousand deaths each, if ten thousand deaths could have been endured. They were, without a single exception, apostates, perjurers, or plunderers;

and, the greater part of them had also been guilty of flagrant high treason against Mary herself, who had spared their lives; but whose lenity they had requited by every effort within their power to overset her authority and the Government. To make particular mention of all the ruffians that perished upon this occasion, would be a task as irksome as it would be useless; but, there were amongst them, three of CRANMER's Bishops and himself! For, now, justice, at last, overtook this most mischievous of all villains, who had justly to go to the same stake that he had unjustly caused so many others to be tied to; the three others were HOOPER, LATIMER, and RIDLEY, each of whom was, indeed, inferior in villany to CRANMER, but to few other men that have ever existed.

250. HOOPER was a MONK; he broke his vow of celibacy and married a Flandrican; be, being the ready tool of the Protector Somerset, whom he greatly aided in his plunder of the churches, got two Bishoprics, though he himself had written against pluralities; he was a co-operator in all the monstrous cruelties inflicted on the people, during the reign of Edward, and was particularly active in recommending the use of German troops to bend the necks of the English to the Protestant yoke. LATIMER began his career, not only as a Catholic priest, but as a most furious assailant of the Reformation religion. By this he obtained from Henry VIII. the Bishopric of Worcester. He next changed his opinions; but he did not give up his Catholic Bishopric! Being suspected, he made abjuration of Protestantism; he thus kept his Bishopric for twenty years, while he inwardly reprobated the principles of the Church, and which Bishopric he held in virtue of an oath to oppose, to the utmost of his power, all dissenters from the Catholic Church; in the reigns of Henry and Edward he sent to the stake Catholics and Protestants for holding opinions, which he himself had before held openly, or that he held secretly at the time of his so sending them. Lastly, he was a chief both in the hands of the tyrannical Protector SOMERSET in that black and unnatural act of bringing his brother Lord THOMAS SOMERSET, to the block, RIDLEY had been a Catholic bishop in the reign of Henry VIII., when he sent to the stake Catholics who denied the King's supremacy, and Protestants, who denied transubstantiation. In Edward's reign he was a Protestant bishop, and denied transubstantiation himself; and then he sent to the stake Protestants who differed from the creed of CRANMER. He, in Edward's reign, got the Bishopric of London by a most roguish agreement to transfer the greater part of its possessions to the rapacious ministers and courtiers of that day. Lastly, he was guilty of high treason against the Queen, in openly (as we have seen in paragraph **220**), and from the pulpit, exhorting the people to stand by the usurper Lady JANE; and thus endeavouring to produce civil war and the death of his sovereign, in order that he might, by treason, be enabled to keep that bishopric which he had obtained by simony, including perjury.

251. A pretty trio of Protestant "Saints," quite worthy, however, of "SAINT" MARTIN LUTHER, who says, in his own work, that it was by the arguments of the Devil (who, he says, frequently ate, drank, and slept with him) that he was induced to turn Protestant: three worthy followers of that LUTHER, who is, by his disciple MELANCTHON, called "a brutal man, void of piety and humanity, one more a Jew than a Christian:" three followers altogether worthy of this great founder of that Protestantism, which has split the world into contending sects: but, black as these are, they bleach the moment CRANMER appears in his true colours. But, alas! where is the pen, or tongue, to give us those colours! Of the 65 years that he lived, and of the 35 years of his manhood, 29 years were spent in the commission of a series of acts, which, for wickedness in their nature and for mischief in their consequences, are

absolutely without any thing approaching to a parallel in the annals of human infamy. Being a fellow of a college at Cambridge, and having, of course, made an engagement (as the fellows do to this day), not to marry while he was a fellow, he married secretly, and still enjoyed his fellowship. While a married man he became at priest, and took the oath of celibacy; and, going to Germany, he married another wife, the daughter of a Protestant "saint;" so that he had now two wives at one time, though his oath bound him to have no wife at all. He, as Archbishop, enforced the law of celibacy, while he himself secretly kept his German frow in the palace at Canterbury, having, as we have seen in paragraph **104**, imported her in a chest. He, as ecclesiastical judge, divorced Henry VIII. from three wives, the grounds of his decision in two of the cases being directly the contrary of those which he himself had laid down when he declared the marriages to be valid; and, in the case of ANNE BOLEYN, he, as ecclesiastical judge, pronounced, that Anne had never been the King's wife; while, as a member of the House of Peers, he voted for her death, as having been an adulteress, and, thereby, guilty of treason to. her husband. As Archbishop under Henry (which office he entered upon with a premeditated false oath on his lips) he sent men and women to the stake because they were not Catholics, and he sent Catholics to the stake, because they would not acknowledge the King's supremacy, and thereby perjure themselves as he had so often done. Become openly a Protestant, in Edward's reign, and openly professing those very principles, for the professing of which he had burnt others, he now burnt his fellow-Protestants, because their grounds for protesting were different from his. As executor for the will of his old master, Henry, which gave the crown (after Edward) to his daughters, Mary and Elizabeth, he conspired with others to rob those two daughters of their right, and to give the Crown to Lady JANE, that Queen of nine days, whom he, with others, ordered to be proclaimed. Confined, notwithstanding his many monstrous crimes, merely to the palace of Lambeth, he, in requital of the Queen's lenity, plotted with traitors in the pay of France to overset her government. Brought, at last, to trial and to condemnation as a heretic, he professed himself ready to recant. He was respited for six weeks, during which time he signed six different forms of recantation, each more ample than the former. He declared that the Protestant religion was false; that the Catholic religion was the only true one; that he now believed in all the doctrines of the Catholic Church; that he had been a horrid blasphemer against the sacrament; that he was unworthy of forgiveness; that he prayed the People, the Queen and the POPE, to have pity on, and to pray for his wretched soul; and that he had made and signed this declaration without fear, and without hope of favour, and for the discharge of his con science, and as a warning to others. It was a question in the Queen's council, whether he should be pardoned, as other recanters had been; but it was resolved, that his crimes were so enormous that it would be unjust to let him escape; to which might have been added, that it could have done the Catholic Church no honour to see reconciled to it a wretch covered with robberies, perjuries, treasons and bloodshed. Brought, therefore, to the public reading of his recantation, on his way to the stake; seeing the pile ready, now finding that he must die, and carrying in his breast all his malignity undiminished, he recanted his recantation, thrust into the fire the hand that had signed it, and thus expired, protesting against that very religion in which, only nine hours before, he had called God to witness that he firmly believed!

252. And Mary is to be called the "Bloody", because she put to death monsters of iniquity like this! It is, surely, time to do justice to the memory of this calumniated Queen; and not to do it by halves, I must, contrary to my intention, employ part of the next Number in giving the remainder of her history.

LETTER IX.

MARY AT WAR WITH FRANCE.
THE CAPTURE OF CALAIS BY THE FRENCH.
THE DEATH OF QUEEN MARY.
ACCESSION OF QUEEN ELIZABETH.
HER CRUEL AND BLOODY LAWS RELATIVE TO RELIGION.
HER PERFIDY WITH REGARD TO FRANCE.
THE DISGRACE SHE BROUGHT UPON HER GOVERNMENT AND THE
COUNTRY BY THIS PERFIDY.
HER BASE AND PERPETUAL SURRENDER OF CALAIS.

Kensington, 31st July, 1825..

MY FRIENDS,

253. I NOW, before I proceed to the "Reformation" works in the reign of
ELIZABETH, must conclude the reign of MARY. "Few and full of sorrow" were the
days of her power. She had innumerable difficulties to struggle with, a most inveterate
and wicked faction continually plotting against her, and the state of her health, owing
partly to her weak frame, and partly to the anxieties of her whole life, rendered her
life so uncertain, that the unprincipled plunderers, though they had again become
Catholics, were continually casting an eye towards her successor, who, though she
was now a Catholic, was pretty sure to become Protestant whenever she came to the
throne, because it was impossible that the POPE should ever acknowledge her
legitimacy.

254. In the year 1557, the Queen was at war with France, on account of the
endeavours of that Court to excite rebellion against her in England. Her husband,
PHILIP, whose father, the Emperor, had now retired to a convent, leaving his son to
supply his place, and possess all his dominions, was also at war with France, the scene
of which war was the Netherlands and the North of France. An English army had
joined PHILIP, who penetrated into France, and gained a great and important victory
over the French. But a French army, under the Duke of GUISE, took advantage of the
naked state of Calais, to possess itself of that important town, which had been in
possession of the English for more than two hundred years. It was not Calais alone
that England held; but the whole country round for many miles, including Guisnesse,
Fanim, Ardres, and other places, together with the whole territory called the county of
Oye. EDWARD III. had taken Calais after a siege of nearly a year. It had always been
regarded as very valuable for the purposes of trade; it was deemed a great monument
of glory to England, and it was a thorn continually rankling in the side of France. Dr.
HEYLIN tells us, that Monsieur de CORDES, a nobleman who lived in the reign of
Louis XI., used to say "that he would be content to lie seven years in hell upon
"condition that this town were regained from the English."

255. The Queen felt this blow most severely, it hastened that death which overtook
her a few months after wards: and, when her end approached, she told her attendants,
that, "if they opened her body, they would find Calais at the bottom of her heart." This
great misfortune was owing to the neglect, if not perfidy, of her councillors, joined to
the dread of Philip to see Calais and its dependencies in the hands of MARY's
successor. Doctor HEYLIN (a Protestant, mind) tells us, that Philip, seeing that

danger might arise to Calais, advised the Queen of it, and "freely offered his assistance for the defence of it; but, that the English council, over-wisely jealous of Philip, neglected both his advice and proffer." They left the place with only five hundred men in it; and that they did this intentionally it is hardly possible to doubt. Still, however, if the Queen had lived but a little longer, Calais would have been restored. The war was not yet over. In 1558, Philip and the King of France began negotiations for peace; and one of the conditions of Philip (who was the most powerful, and who had beaten the French) was, that Calais should be restored to England; and this condition would unquestionably have been adhered to by Philip; but, in the midst of these. negotiations, Mary died!

256, Thus, then, it is to the "Reformation," which had caused the loss of Boulogne, in the plundering and cowardly reign of Edward VI., that we, even to this day, owe, that we have to lament, the loss of Calais, which was, at last, irretrievably lost by the selfishness and perfidy of Elizabeth. While all historians agree, that the loss of Calais preyed most severely upon the Queen, and hastened her death; while they all do this great honour to her memory, none of them attempt to say, that the loss of Boulogue had even the smallest effect on the spirits of her "Reformation" brother! He was too busy in pulling down altars and in confiscating the property of Guilds and Fraternities to think much about national honour; or, perhaps, though he, while he was pulling down altars, still called himself "Defender of the Faith," he might think, that territory and glory, won by Catholics, ought not to be retained by Protestants. Be this as it may, we have seen a loss to England much greater than that of Calais; we have seen the half of a continent cut off from the crown of England, and seen it become a most formidable rival on the seas; and we have never heard, that it preyed much upon the spirits of the sovereign, in whose reign the loss took place.

257. With the loss of Calais at the bottom of her heart, and with a well-grounded fear that her successor would undo, as to religion, all that she had done, the unfortunate Mary expired on the 17th of November, 1558, in the forty-second year of her age, and in the sixth year of her reign, leaving to her sister and successor the example of fidelity, sincerity, patience, resignation, generosity, gratitude, and purity in thought, word and deed; an example, however, which, in every particular, that sister and successor took special care not to follow. As to those punishments, which have served as the ground for all the abuse heaped on the memory of this Queen, what were they other than punishments inflicted on offenders against the religion of the country? The "fires of Smithfield" have a horrid sound; but, to say nothing about the burnings of Edward VI., Elizabeth, and James I., is it more pleasant to have one's bowels ripped out, while the body is alive (as was Elizabeth's favourite way), than to be burnt? Protestants have even exceeded Catholics in the work of punishing offenders of this sort. And, they have punished, too, with less reason on their side. The Catholics have one faith; the Protestants have fifty faiths: and yet, each sect, whenever it gets uppermost, punishes, in some way or other, the rest as offenders. Even at this very time, there are, according to a return, recently laid before the House of Commons, no less than fifty-seven persons, who have, within a few years, suffered imprisonment and other punishments added to it, as offenders against religion; and this, too, at a time, when men are permitted openly to deny the divinity of Christ, and others openly to preach in their synagogues, that there never was any Christ at all. A man sees the laws tolerate twenty sorts of Christians (as they all call themselves), each condemning all the rest to eternal flames; and, if, in consequence of this, he be led to express his belief, that they are all wrong, and that the thing they are disputing about is altogether

something unreal, he may be punished with six years (or his whole life) of imprisonment in a loathsome gaol! Let us think of these things, when we are talking of the "bloody Queen Mary." The punishments now-a-days proceed from the maxim that "Christianity is part and parcel of the law of the land." When did it begin? Before, or since, the "Reformation"? And, who, amongst all these sects, which, it would seem, this law tolerates; which of them is to tell us; from which of them are we to learn, what Christianity is?

258. As to the mass of suffering, supposing the whole of the 277 persons, who suffered in the reign of Mary, to have suffered solely for the sake of religion instead of having been, like CRANMER and RIDLEY, traitors and felons as well as offenders on the score of religion; let us suppose the whole 277 to have suffered for offences against religion, did the mass of suffering surpass the mass of suffering; on this same account, during the reign of the late King? And, unless Smithfield and burning have any peculiar agony, any thing worse than death, to impart, did Smithfield ever witness so great a mass of suffering as the Old Bailey has witnessed, on account of offences against that purely Protestant invention, bank notes? Perhaps this invention, expressly intended to keep out Popery, has cost ten times, if not ten times ten times, the blood that was shed in the reign of her, whom we still have the injustice, or the folly, to call the "bloody Queen Mary," all whose excellent qualities, all whose exalted virtues, all her piety, charity, generosity, sacred adherence to her faith and her word, all her gratitude, and even those feelings of anxiety for the greatness and honour of England, which feelings hastened her to the grave: all these, in which she was never equalled by any sovereign that sat on the English throne, ALFRED alone excepted, whose religion she sought to re-establish for ever; all these are to pass for nothing, and we are to call her the "bloody Mary," because it suits the views of those who fatten on the spoils of that Church which never suffered Englishmen to bear the odious and debasing name of pauper.

ELIZABETH.

259. To the pauper and ripping-up reign we now come. This is the reign of "good Queen Bess." We shall, in a short time, see how good she was. The Act of Parliament, which is still in force, relative to the poor and poor-rates, was passed in the 43rd year of this reign; but, that was not the only act of the kind: there were eleven acts passed before that, in consequence of the poverty and misery, into which the "Reformation" had plunged the people. However, it is the last Number of my work which is to contain the history of the rise and progress of English pauperism, from the beginning of the "Reformation" down to the present time. At present I have to relate what took place with regard to the affairs of religion.

260. ELIZABETH, during the reign of her brother, had been a Protestant, and during the reign of her sister, a Catholic. At the time of her sister's death, she not only went to mass publicly; but, she had a Catholic chapel in her house, and also a confessor. These appearances had not, however, deceived her sister, who, to the very last, doubted her sincerity. On her death bed, honest and sincere Mary required from her a frank avowal of her opinions as to religion. Elizabeth, in answer, prayed God that the earth might open and swallow her, if she were not a true Roman Catholic She made the same declaration to the Duke of Feria, the Spanish envoy, whom she so completely deceived, that he wrote to Philip, that the accession of Elizabeth would make no alteration in matters of religion, in England. In spite of all this, it was not

long before she began ripping up the bowels of her unhappy subjects, because they were Roman Catholics.

261. She was a bastard by law. The marriage of her mother had been, by law, which yet remained unrepealed, declared to be null and void from the beginning. Her accession having been, in the usual way, notified to foreign powers, that is, that "she had succeeded to the throne by hereditary right and the consent of the nation," the POPE answered, that he did not understand the hereditary right of a person not born in lawful wedlock So that he, of course, could not acknowledge her hereditary right. This was, of itself, a pretty strong inducement for a lady of so flexible a conscience as she had, to resolve to be a Protestant. But, there was another and even a stronger motive. Mary, Queen of Scotland, who had married the Dauphin of France, claimed the crown of England, as the nearest legitimate descendant of Henry VII. So that Elizabeth ran a manifest risk of losing the crown unless she became a Protestant, and crammed CRANMER's creed down the throats of her people. If she remained a Catholic, she must yield submission to the decrees from Rome: the POPE could have made it a duty with her people to abandon her; or, at the very least, he could have greatly embarrassed her. In short, she saw clearly, that, if her people remained Catholics, she could never reign in perfect safety. She knew that she had no hereditary right; she knew that the law ascribed her birth to adultery. She never could think of reigning quietly over a people the head of whose Church refused to acknowledge her right to the crown. And resolving to wear that crown, she resolved, cost what ruin or blood it might, to compel her people to abandon that very religion, her belief in which she had, a few months before, declared, by praying to "God that the earth might open and swallow her alive, if she were not a true Roman Catholic."

262. The POPE's answer was honest; but it was impolitic, and most unfortunate it was for the English and Irish people, who had now to prepare for sufferings such as they had never known before. The situation of things was extremely favourable to the Protestants. Mary, the Queen of Scots, the real lawful heir to the throne, was, as we have seen, married to the Dauphin of France. If Elizabeth were set aside, or, if she died without issue before Mary, England must become an appendage of France. The loss of Calais and of Boulogne had mortified the nation enough; but, for England herself to he to transferred France, was what no Englishman could think of with patience. So that she became strong from the dread that the people had of the consequences of her being put down. It was the betrothing of Mary, Queen of Scots, to the Dauphin, which induced Mary, Queen of England, to marry PHILIP, and thereby to secure an ally for England in case of Scotland becoming a dependance of France. How much more pressing was the danger now, when the Queen of Scots was actually married to the Dauphin (the heir apparent to the French throne), and when if she were permitted to possess the crown of England, England, in case of her having a son, must become a province of France!

263. This state of things was, therefore, most unfortunate for the Catholics. It made many, very many, of themselves cool in opposition to the change which the new Queen soon showed her determination to effect; for, how ever faithful as to their religion, they were Englishmen, and abhorred the thought of being the underlings of Frenchmen. They might hate the Queen for her apostacy and tyranny; but still they could not but desire that England should remain an independent state; and to keep her such, the upholding of Elizabeth seemed absolutely necessary. Those who eulogize Henry IV. of France, who became a Catholic expressly and avowedly for the purpose of possessing and keeping the throne of that country, cannot very consistently blame

Elizabeth for becoming a Protestant for an exactly similar reason. I do not attempt to justify either of them; but I must confess, that, if any thing would have induced me to uphold Elizabeth, it would have been, that she, as far as human foresight could go, was an instrument necessary to preserve England from subjection to France; and, beyond all doubt, this was the main reason for which, at the outset at least, she was upheld by many of the eminent and powerful men of that day.

264. But if we admit that she was justified in thus consulting her preservation as a Queen, and the nation's independence, at the expense of religious considerations; if we admit that she had a right to give a preference to Protestants, and to use all gentle means for the totally changing of the religion of her people; if we admit this, and that is admitting a great deal more than justice demands of as, who can refrain from being filled with horror at the barbarity which she so unsparingly exercised for the accomplishment of her purpose?

265. The intention to change the religion of the country became, in a short time, so manifest, that all the Bishops but one refused to crown her. She at last found one to do it; but even he would not consent to do the thing without her conformity to the Catholic ritual. Very soon, however, a series of acts were passed, which, by degrees, put down the Catholic worship, and re-introduced the Protestant; and she found the plunderers and possessors of plunder just as ready to conform to her ecclesiastical sway, as they had been to receive absolution from Cardinal Pole, in the last reign. CRANMER's book of Common Prayer, which had been ascribed by the Parliament to the suggestions of the "Holy Ghost," had been altered and amended even in Edward's reign. It was now revived, and altered and amended again; and still it was ascribed to the "dictates of the Holy Ghost"!

266. If these Acts of Parliament had stopped here, they would certainly have been bad and disgraceful enough. But such a change was not to be effected without blood. This Queen was resolved to reign: the blood of her people she deemed necessary to her own safety; and she never scrupled to make it flow. She looked upon the Catholic religion as her mortal enemy; and, cost what it might, she was resolved to destroy it, if she could, the means being, by her, those which best answered her end.

267. With this view, statutes the most bloody were passed. All persons were compelled to take the oath of supremacy, on pain of death. To take the oath of supremacy; that is to say, to acknowledge the Queen's supremacy in spiritual matters, was to renounce the POPE and the Catholic religion; or, in other words, to become an apostate. Thus was a very large part of her people at once condemned to death for adhering to the religion of their fathers; and moreover, for adhering to that very religion, in which she had openly lived till she became Queen, and to her firm belief in which she had sworn at her coronation!

268. Besides this act of monstrous barbarity, it was made high treason in a priest to say mass; it was made high treason in a priest to come into the kingdom from abroad; it was made high treason to harbour or to relieve a priest. And, on these grounds, and others of a like nature, hundreds upon hundreds were butchered in the most inhuman manner, being first hung up, then cut down alive, their bowels then ripped up, and their bodies chopped into quarters: and this, I again beg you, sensible and just Englishmen, to observe, only because the unfortunate persons were too virtuous and sincere to apostatize from that faith which this Queen herself had, at her coronation, in her coronation oath, solemnly sworn to adhere to and defend!

269. Having pulled down the altars, set up the tables; having ousted the Catholic priests and worship, and put in their stead a set of hungry, beggarly creatures, the very scum of the earth, with Cranmer's prayer-book amended in their hands; having done this, she compelled her Catholic subjects to attend in the churches under enormous penalties, which rose, at last, to death itself, in case of perseverance in refusal! Thus were all the good, all the sincere, all the conscientious people in the kingdom incessantly harassed, ruined by enormous fines, brought to the gallows, or compelled to flee from their native country. Thus was this Protestant religion watered with the tears and the blood of the people of England. Talk of Catholic persecution and cruelty! Where are you to find persecution and cruelty like this, inflicted by Catholic princes? Elizabeth put, in one way or another, more Catholics to death in one year, for not becoming apostates to the religion which she had sworn to be hers, and to be the only true one, than Mary put to death in her whole reign for having apostatized from the religion of her and their fathers, and to which religion she herself had always adhered. Yet, the former is called, or has been called, "good Queen Bess," and the latter "bloody Queen Mary." Even the horrid MASSACRE of ST. BARTHOLOMEW was nothing, when fairly compared with the butcheries and other cruelties of the reign of this Protestant Queen of England; yes, a mere nothing; and yet she put on mourning upon that occasion, and had the consummate hypocrisy to affect horror at the cruelties that the King of France had committed.

270. This massacre took place at Paris, in the year 1572, and in the 14th year of Elizabeth's reign; and, as it belongs to the history of that day, as it was, in fact, in part, produced by her own incessant and most mischievous intrigues, and as it has been made a great handle of in the work of calumniating the Catholics, even to this day, it is necessary that I give a true account of it, and that I go back to those civil wars in France which she occasioned, and in which she took so large a part, and which finally lost Calais and its territory to England. The "Reformation," which LUTHER said he was taught by the Devil, had found its way into France so early as in the year 1530, or thereabouts. The "reformers" there were called HUGUENOTS. For a long while they were of little consequence; but they, at last, in the reign of Charles IX., became formidable to the government by being taken hold of by those ambitious and rebellious leaders CONDÉ and COLIGNI. The faction, of which these two were the chiefs, wanted to have the governing of France during the minority of Charles, who came to the throne in the year 1561, at ten years of age. His mother, the Queen Dowager, gave the preference to the Duke of Guise and his party. The disappointed nobles, Condé and Coligni, needed no better motive for becoming most zealous Protestants, the Guises being zealous in the Catholic cause! Hence arose an open rebellion on the part of the former, fomented by the Queen of England, who seemed to think, that she never could be safe as long as there were Catholic prince, priest, or people left upon the face of the earth; and who never stuck at means, if they were but calculated to effect her end. She was herself an apostate; she wanted to annihilate that from which she had apostatized; and, by her endeavours to effect her purpose, she made her people bleed at every pore, and made no scruple upon any occasion, to sacrifice the national honour.

271. At her coming to the throne, she found the country at war with France, and Calais in its hands, that fortress and territory having, as we have seen in paragraph **254**, been taken by a French army under the Duke of Guise. She almost immediately made peace with France, and that, too, without getting CALAIS back, as she might have done, if she had not preferred her own private interest to the interest and honour

of England. The negotiations for peace (England, Spain, and France being the parties) were carried on at Cateau Cambresis, in France. All was soon settled with regard to Spain and France; but PHILIP (Mary's husband, remember), faithful to his engagements, refused to sign the treaty, until the new Queen of England should be satisfied with regard to Calais; and he even offered to Continue the war for six years, unless Calais were restored, provided Elizabeth would bind herself not to make a separate peace during that period. She declined this generous offer; she had begun to rip up her subjects, and was afraid of war; and she, therefore, clandestinely entered into negotiations with France, and it was agreed that the latter should keep Calais for eight years, or pay to England 500,000 crowns! Never was there a baser act than this treaty, on the part of England. But this was not all; for the treaty further stipulated, that if France committed any act of aggression against England during the eight years, or if England committed any act of aggression against France, during that time, the treaty should be void, and that the former should lose the right of retaining, and the latter the claim to the restoration, of this valuable town and territory.

272. This treaty was concluded in 1559, and it was a treaty not only of friendship, but of alliance between the parties. But, before three years out of the eight had passed away, "good Queen Bess," out of pure hatred and fear of the Catholics; from a pure desire to make her tyrannical sway secure; from the sole desire of being still able to fine, imprison, and rip up her unfortunate subjects, forfeited all claim to the restoration of Calais, and that too, by a breach of treaty more flagrant and more base than, perhaps, had ever before been witnessed in the world..

273. CONDÉ and COLIGNI, with their Huguenots, had stirred up a formidable civil war in France. "Good Queen Bess's" ambassador at that Court stimulated and assisted the rebels to the utmost of his power. At last, VIDAME, an agent of Condé and Coligni, came, secretly, over to England to negotiate for military, naval and pecuniary assistance. They succeeded with "good Bess," who, wholly disregarding the solemn treaties by which she was bound to Charles IX., King of France, entered into a formal treaty with the French rebels to send them an army and money, for the purpose of carrying on war against their sovereign, of whom she was an ally, having bound herself, in that character, by a solemn oath on the Evangelists! By this treaty she engaged to furnish men, ships, and money; and the traitors, on their part, engaged to put HAVRE DE GRACE at once into her hands, as a pledge, not only for the repayment of the money to be advanced, but for the restoration of Calais! This infamous compact richly deserved the consequences that attended it.

274. The French ambassador in London, when he found that an intercourse was going on between the Queen and the agents of the rebels, went to CECIL, the Secretary of State, carrying the treaty of Cateau Cambresis in his hand, and demanded, agreeably to the stipulations of that treaty, that the agents of the rebels should be delivered up as traitors to their sovereign; and he warned the English government, that any act of aggression on its part, would annihilate its claim to the recovery of Calais at the end of the eight years. But "good Bess" had caused the civil wars in France; she had, by her bribes, and other underhand means, stirred them up, and she believed that the success of the French rebels was necessary to her own security on her throne of doubtful right; and, as she hoped to get Calais in this perfidious way, she saw nothing but gain in the perfidy.

275. The rebels were in possession of DIEPPE, ROUEN, HAVRE DE GRACE, and had extended their power over a considerable part of Normandy. They at once put

HAVRE and DIEPPE into the hands of the English. So infamous and treacherous a proceeding roused the Catholics of France, who now became ashamed of that inactivity, which had suffered a sect, less than a hundredth part of the population, to sell their country under the blasphemous plea of a love of the Gospel. "Good Bess," with her usual mixture of hypocrisy and effrontery, sent her proclamations into Normandy, declaring, that she meant no hostility against her "good brother" the King of France; but merely to protect his Protestant subjects against the tyranny of the House of Guise; and that her "good brother" ought to be grateful to her for the assistance she was lending! This cool and hypocritical insolence added fury to the flame. All France could but recollect, that it was the skilful, the gallant, the patriotic Duke of Guise, who had, only five years before, ejected the English from Calais, their last hold in France; and they now saw these "sons of the Gospel," as they had the audacity to call themselves, bring those same English back again, and put two French seaports into their hands at once! Are we to wonder at the inextinguishable hatred of the people of France against this traitorous sect? Are we to wonder, that they felt a desire to extirpate the whole of so infamous a race, who had already sold their country to the utmost of their power?

276. The French nobility, from every province and corner of France, flew to the aid of their sovereign, whose army was commanded by the Constable, Montmorency, with the Duke of Guise under him. Condé was at the head of the rebel army, having Coligni as a sort of partner in the concern, and having been joined by the English troops under the Earl of Warwick, nephew of "good Bess's" paramour, DUDLEY, of whom the Protestant clergymen, Heylin and Witaker, will tell us more than enough by-and-by. The first movement of the French against this combined mass of hypocrisy, audacity, perfidy and treason, was the besieging of ROUEN, into which Sir Edward Poinings, who had preceded Warwick, had thrown an English reinforcement to assist the faithful "sons of the Gospel." In order to encourage the French, the Queen-Mother (Catherine de Medici), her son the young King, Charles (now twelve years of age), and the King of Navarre, were present at the siege. The latter was mortally wounded in the attack; but the Catholics finally took the town by assault, and put the whole of the garrison to the sword, including the English reinforcement sent by "good Queen Bess."

277. In the meanwhile the brother of Coligni had, by the money of "good Bess," collected together a body of German mercenary Gospellers, and had got them to ORLEANS, which was then the main hold of the Huguenots; while "good Bess," in order to act her part faithfully, ordered public prayers, during three whole days to implore God's blessing "upon her cause and the cause of the Gospel." Thus reinforced by another body of foreigners brought into their country, the base traitors, Condé and Coligni, first made a feint on the side of Paris; but, finding themselves too weak on that side, they took their way towards Normandy, in the hope of their having the aid of the English forces. But, the Catholics, still under Montmorency, followed the traitors, overtook them at DREUX, compelled them to fight, took Condé himself prisoner, and, though Montmorency was taken prisoner by the rebels, the Duke of Guise took the chief command, and drove the rebel Coligni and his army before him; and this, too, observe, in spite of "good Bess's" three whole days of prayers.

278. Nevertheless, Coligni kept the field, and pillaged Normandy pretty severely. "Good Bess" sent him some money, and offered to be bound for more, if he could get any merchants (that is, Jews) to lend it him; but, she sent him no troops; those, under the Earl of Warwick, being kept safe and sound in the strong fortress of Havre de

Grace, which place honest and "good Bess" intended to keep, let things go which way they might, which honest intention we shall, however, find defeated in the end. Coligni and his ruffians and German mercenary Gospellers cruelly plundered the Normans as far as they could extend their arms. The Catholics, now under the Duke of Guise, laid siege to Orleans. While this siege was going on, one POLTROT, a Huguenot, in the pay of Coligni, went, under the guise of being a deserter from that inveterate rebel chief, and entered into the service of the army under the Duke of Guise. In a short time this miscreant found the means to assassinate that gallant nobleman and distinguished patriot, instigated, and, indeed, employed for the express purpose by Coligni, and urged on by BEZA, the "famous preacher," as HUME calls him, but really one of the most infamous of all the "reforming" preachers, and, perhaps, second to none but LUTHER himself. This atrocious deed met, afterwards, with retaliation in the massacre of St. Bartholomew, when on Coligni's mangled body there might have been placarded the name of POLTROT. This wretch had been paid by Coligni, and the money had come from honest and sincere "good Queen Bess," whom we shall hereafter find plainly accused by Witaker (a clergyman of the Church of England) of plotting the assassination of her own cousin, and finding no man in her kingdom base enough to perform the deed.

279. This foul deed seems to have made Condé ashamed of his infamous associate and followers. Ambition had made him a rebel; but he had sense of honour enough left to make him shudder at the thought of being the leader of assassins: and he, with one drop of true blood in him, could not think without horror of such a man as the Duke of Guise, who had rendered such inestimable services to France, being swept from existence by so base a miscreant -- as that whom his late colleague had hired and paid for that purpose. If the son of the Duke of Guise could have destroyed Coligni and his whole crew, he would have been justified in so doing. And yet, the world has been stunned with the Protestant cries of horror at the death of this same Coligni and a small part of his followers!

280. Condé now sought to get rid of his miscreant associates by proposing, in February 1563, a pacification, and tendering his submission to his sovereign on condition of an act of oblivion. Coligni was included in the amnesty. The King granted to the Huguenots permission to practice their worship in one town in every bailiwick; and thus were all matters settled between the King and his rebellious subjects. Sad tidings for "good Queen Bess," who, as Witaker well observes, continually sought her safety in the divisions and misery of others. Condé, in his treaty with her, had stipulated not to conclude any peace without her consent; but, had she a right to complain of a want of good faith? She, who had broken her treaty and her oath with Charles IX., and who, in defiance of both, had entered into a treaty with rebels, in open arms against their King?

281. The French King, wishing to get her troops quietly out of Havre de Grace, and finding that she now pretended to hold it as a pledge for the surrender of Calais, at the end of the eight years, offered to renew the treaty of Cateau Cambresis, by which Calais was to be restored to England in 1567. But, she rejected this fair and reasonable proposal. She had got Havre; no matter how; and she said, that "a bird in hand was worth two in the bush," snapping her fingers at the same time, and, as was the common practice with her upon such occasions, confirming her resolution with a thundering oath, so becoming in a "Virgin Queen." Finding, however, that all parties in France were now united for the expulsion of the English, she reluctantly gave way. She authorised her ambassadors to present a new project of treaty; but, by this time,

the French army, under Montmorency, Condé, "good Bess's" late friend and ally being serving in the army, was on its way to regain Havre by force of arms, the King of France being well convinced, that treaties with "good Betsy" were things perfectly vain.

282. Still, it was not a trifling thing to take Havre out of the hands of the English. A great deal of taxes had been imposed upon this nation (to say nothing of the "prayers" in order to ensure the possession of this place. The Earl of Warwick, instead of sending troops to assist Bess's allies, had kept his army at Havre; had, with six thousand soldiers and seven hundred pioneers, rendered the place "impregnable;" had, as soon as he heard that the rebellion was at an end, expelled all the French people from Havre, to their utter ruin, and in direct breach of Bess's treaty with Condé and Coligni. But, in spite of all this, Montmorency was, at the end of a short time, ready to enter the place by assault, having made his breaches in preparation. The Queen-Mother and the King were present in the camp where they had the indescribable pleasure to see "good Queen Bess's" general humbly propose to surrender the place to its rightful sovereign, without any mention of Calais and its territory, and on no condition whatever, but that of being permitted to return to England with the miserable remnant of his army; and England, after all the treasure and blood expended to gratify the malignity of "good Bess," and after all the just imputations of perfidy that she had brought upon it, had to receive that remnant, that ratification of disgrace, greater than it had to support from the day when glorious Alfred finally expelled the Danes. And, yet, this woman is called, or has been called, "good Queen Bess," and her perfidious and butchering reign has been called glorious!

283. Great as the mortifications of "good Bess" now were, and great as were the misfortunes of the country, brought upon it by these her proceedings of hitherto unheard-of hypocrisy and breach of faith, we have, as yet, seen the full measure of neither the one nor the other. For, "glorious and good Bess" had now to sue for peace, and with that King, with whose rebel subjects she had so recently co-operated. Her ambassadors, going with due passports, were arrested and imprisoned. She stamped and swore, but she swallowed the affront, and took the regular steps to cause them to be received at the French court, who, on their part, treated her pressing applications with a contemptuous sneer, and suffered many months to pass away, before they would listen to any terms of peace. SMITH was one of her envoys, and the other was that same THROCKMORTON, who had been her ambassador at Paris, and who had been her agent in stirring up Condé and Coligni to their rebellion. The former was imprisoned at Melun, and the latter at Saint Germain's. Smith was released upon her application; but Throckmorton was detained, and was made use of for the following curious, and, to "good Bess," most humiliating purpose. The treaty of Cateau Cambresis, which stipulated for the restoration of Calais in eight years, or the forfeiture of 500,000 crowns by the French, contained a stipulation, that four French noblemen should be held by "good Bess" as hostages for the fulfilment of the treaty on the part of France. "Good Bess," by her aiding of the French rebels, had broken this treaty, had lost all just claim to Calais, and ought to have released the hostages; but, as "good Bess" very seldom did what she ought to; as she might, almost every day of her mischievous life, have, with perfect truth, repeated that part of the Prayer-Book "amended," which says, "we have done I those things which we ought not to do, and have left undone those things which we ought to do;" so, this "good" woman had kept the hostages, though she had forfeited all just claim to that for the fulfilment of which they had been put into her hands. Now, however, the French had got a "bird in

hand" too. They had got Throckrnorton, their old enemy, and he had got a large quantity of "good "Bess's" horrible secrets locked up in his breast! So that, after long discussions, during which Throckmorton gave very significant signs of his determination not to end his days in prison without taking revenge, of some sort, on his merciless employer, the "good" woman agreed to exchange the four French noblemen for him; and, as a quarter of a loaf was better than no bread, to take 125,000 crowns for the relinquishment of Calais to France in perpetuity!

284. Thus, then, it was "good Queen Bess," after all, glorious and Protestant Bess, that plucked this jewel from the English crown! Nor was this the only signal consequence of her unhallowed and unprincipled treaty and intrigues with the French rebels. The plague, which had got into the garrison of Havre de Grace, and which had left Warwick with only about two thousand out of his seven thousand men; this dreadful disease was brought by that miserable remnant of infected beings, to England, where HUME himself allows, that it "swept off great multitudes, especially in London, where above twenty thousand persons died of it in one year"! Thus was the nation heavily taxed, afflicted with war, afflicted with pestilence; thus were thousands upon thousands of English people destroyed, or ruined, or rendered miserable, merely to gratify this proud and malignant woman, who thought that she could never be safe until all the world joined in her flagrant apostacy. Thus, and merely for this same reason, was Calais surrendered for ever; Calais, the proudest possession of England; Calais, one of the two keys to the Northern Seas; Calais, that had been won by our Catholic forefathers two hundred years before; Calais, which they would have no more thought of yielding to France, than they would have thought of yielding Dover; Calais, the bare idea of a possibility of losing which had broken the heart of the honest, the virtuous, the patriotic and most calumniated Mary!

285. It is surprising what baseness HUME discovers in treating of the whole of this important series of transactions; how he glosses over all the breaches of faith and of oath, on the part of the "good Bess"; how he lets pass without censure the flagrant and malignant treason of the rebels; and even how he insinuates apologies for them; how he skips by the rare fidelity of Philip to his engagements; how he praises the black-hearted Coligni, while he almost censures Condé for seeking peace after the assassination of the Duke of Guise; how he wholly suppresses the deep humiliations of England in the case of Smith and Throckmorton; how he makes the last bill of sale 200,000 instead of the fourth part of 500,000; how he passes over the loss of Calais for ever, as nothing in "good Bess," though he had made the temporary loss of it everything in Mary; but, above all the rest, how he constantly aims his malignity at that skilful, brave, faithful, and patriotic noble man, the Duke of Guise, while he extols Condé as long as he was a rebel and a traitor, engaged in selling his country; and how he lauds the inveterate and treacherous Coligni to the last hour of that traitor's life.

286. Is there any man, who does not see the vast importance of Calais and its territory? Is there any man who does not see how desirable it would be to us to have it now? Is there an Englishman who does not lament the loss of it? And is it not clear as the sun at noon-day, that it was lost for ever by "good Bess's" perfidy in joining the rebels of France? If, when those rebels were formidable to their sovereign, she had pressed him to restore Calais at once, and to take an equivalent for such anticipated restoration, is it not obvious, that he would have consented, rather than risk her displeasure at such a moment? And what is the apology that HUME makes for her conduct in joining the rebels? "Elizabeth, besides the general and essential interest of

supporting the Protestants, and opposing the rapid progress of her enemy, the Duke of Guise" (how was he her enemy?) "had other motives which engaged her to accept this proposal. When she concluded the peace at Cateau Cambresis, she had good reason to foresee, that France would never voluntarily fulfil the article with regard to the restitution of Calais; and many subsequent incidents tended to confirm this suspicion. Considerable sums of money had been laid out on the fortifications; long leases had been granted of the lands; and many inhabitants had been encouraged to build and settle there, by assurances that Calais would never be restored to the English. The Queen, therefore, very wisely concluded, that, could she get possession of Havre, a place which commanded the mouth of the Seine, and was of much greater importance than Calais, she should easily constrain the French to execute the treaty, and should have the glory of restoring to the crown that ancient possession, which was so much the favourite of the nation."

287. Away, then, goes, at once,. all her professions of desire to defend the "cause of the Gospel;" she is a hypocrite the most profound at once; she breaks faith with the King of France and with the rebels too. But, if she really foresaw that the French would not voluntarily fulfil the treaty of Cateau Cambresis, why did she conclude it, when Philip was ready to aid her in compelling France to restore Calais at once? And, as to the "subsequent incidents," which had confirmed her suspicions, why should not the French government repair the fortifications, and why should they not give "assurances that the territory would never be restored to the English," seeing that she had bargained for the perpetual surrender of 500,000 crowns? The French meant, doubtless, to pay the money at the end of the eight years. They never, after she had rejected the offer of Philip, intended to give up Calais: that every body knew, and no body better than "good Bess:" she had hostages for the payment of the money; and she held those hostages after she had received Havre from the rebels as a security for the payment of that money! She had, she thought, two birds in the hand; but, though she "concluded very wisely," both birds escaped; she outwitted and overreached herself; and the nation has, to this day, to lament the consequences of her selfishness, bad faith, and atrocious perfidy.

288. I should now proceed to follow "good Bess" and her worthy friend Coligni down to the date of the massacre of St. Bartholomew, which was a sort of wholesale of the same work that "good Bess" carried on in detail: but, I have filled my paper; and I now see, that it will be impossible for me to do any thing like justice to my subject with out stretching my little work further than I intended.

LETTER X.

MASSACRE OF SAINT BARTHOLOMEW.
TAIL-PIECE TO IT.
A MAN'S HAND CUT OFF FOR THWARTING BESS IN HER LOVE-SICK FIT.
HER FAVOURITES AND MINISTERS.
HISTORY AND MURDER OF MARY, QUEEN OF SCOTLAND.

Kensington, August 31st, 1825.

MY FRIENDS,

289. THOUGH the massacre of St. BARTHOLOMEW took place in France, yet, it
has formed so fertile a source of calumny against the religion of our fathers; it has
served as a pretence with Protestant historians to justify, or palliate, so many atrocities
on the part of their divers sects; and the Queen of England and her Ministers had so
great a hand in first producing it, and then in punishing Catholics under pretence of
avenging it, that it is necessary for me to give an account of it.

29O. We have seen, in the paragraphs from **273** to **281**, the treacherous works of
Coligni, and in paragraph **278**, we have seen that this pretended Saint basely caused
that gallant and patriotic nobleman, the Duke of Guise; to be assassinated. But, in
assassinating this nobleman, the wretch did not take off the whole of his family. There
was a SON left to avenge that father, and the just vengeance of this son the
treacherous Coligni had yet to feel. We have seen, that peace had taken place between
the French King and his rebellious subjects; but, Coligni had all along discovered that
his treacherous designs only slept. The King was making a progress through the
kingdom about four years after the pacification; a plot was formed by Coligni and his
associates to kill or seize him; but by riding fourteen hours, without getting off his
horse, and without food or drink, he escaped, and got safe to Paris. Another civil war
soon broke out, followed by another pacification; but, such had been the barbarities
committed on both sides, that there could be, and was, no real forgiveness. The
Protestants had been full as sanguinary as the Catholics; and, which has been
remarked even by their own historians, their conduct was frequently, not to say
uniformly, characterised by plundering and by hypocrisy and perfidy, unknown to
their enemies.

291 . During this pacification, Coligni had, by the deepest dissimulation, endeavoured
to worm himself into favour with the young King, and upon the occasion of a
marriage between the King's sister and the young King of Navarre (afterwards the
famous Henry IV.), Coligni, who, Condé being now dead, was become the chief of his
sect, came to Paris, with a company of his Protestant adherents, to partake in the
celebration, and that, too, at the King's invitation. After he had been there a day or
two, some one shot at him, in the street, with a blunderbuss, and wounded him in two
or three places, but not dangerously. His partisans ascribed this to the young Duke of
Guise, though no proof has ever been produced in support of the assertion. They,
however, got about their leaders and threatened revenge, as was very natural. Taking
this for the ground of their justification, the Court resolved to anticipate the blow; and,
on Sunday, the 24th of August, 1572, it being St. BARTHOLOMEW's day, they put
their design in execution. There was great difficulty in prevailing upon the young
King to give his consent; but, at last, by the representations and entreaties of his

mother, those of the Duke of Anjou, his brother, and those of the Duke of Guise, he was prevailed upon. The dreadful orders were given; at the appointed moment the signal was made; the Duke of Guise with a band of followers rushed to and broke open the house of Coligni, whose dead body was soon thrown out of the window into the street. The people of Paris, who mortally hated the Protestants, and who could not have forgotten Coligni's having put the English in possession of Dieppe and Havre; who could not have forgotten, that, while the old enemy of France was thus again brought into the country by Coligni and his Protestants, this same traitor and his sect had basely assassinated that brave nobleman, the late Duke of Guise, who had driven the English from their last hold, Calais, and who had been assassinated at the very moment when he was endeavouring to drive this old enemy from Havre, into which this Coligni and his sect had brought that enemy: the people of Paris could not but remember these things, and remembering them they could not but hold Coligni and his sect in detestation indescribable. Besides this, there were few of them some one or more of whose relations had not perished, or suffered in some way or other, from the plunderings, or butcheries, of these marauding and murdering Calvinists, whose creed taught them, that good works were unavailing, and that no deeds, however base or bloody, could bar their way to salvation. These "Protestants," as they were called, bore no more resemblance to Protestants of the present day, than the wasp bears a resemblance to the bee. That name then was, and it was justly, synonymous with banditti; that is, robber and murderer; and the persons bearing it had been, by becoming the willing tool of every ambitious rebel, a greater scourge to France than foreign war, pestilence and famine united.

292. Considering these things, and, taking into view, that the people, always ready to suspect even beyond the limits of reason, heard the cry of "*Treason*" on all sides, is it any wonder that they fell upon the followers of Coligni, and that they spared none of the sect that they were able to destroy? When we consider these things, and especially when, we see the son of the assassinated Duke of Guise lead the way, is it not a most monstrous violation of truth to ascribe this massacre to the principles of the Catholic religion? With equal justice might we ascribe the act of BELLINGHAM (who sent for his Church Prayer-book the moment he was lodged in Newgate) to the principles of the Church of England. No one has ever been base and impudent enough to do this; why, then, are there men so base and impudent as to ascribe this French massacre to Catholic principles?

293. The massacre at Paris very far exceeded the wishes of the court; and, orders were instantly despatched to the great towns in the provinces to prevent similar scenes. Such scenes took place, however, in several places; but, though, by some Protestant writers, the whole number of persons killed, has been made to amount to 100,000, an account, published in 1582, and made up from accounts collected from the ministers in the different towns, made the number, for all France, amount to only 786 persons!

Dr. LINGARD (Note T. Vol. V.), with his usual fairness, says, "if we double this number, we shall not be far from the real amount." The Protestant writers began at 100,000; then fell to 70,000; then to 30,000; then to 20,000; then to 15,000; and, at last, to 10,000! All in round numbers! One of them, in an hour of great indiscretion, ventured upon obtaining returns of names from the ministers themselves; and, then, out came the 786 persons in the whole!

294. A number truly horrible to think of; but a number not half so great as that of those English Catholics whom "good Queen Bess" had, even at this time (the 14th year of her reign), caused to be ripped up, racked till the bones came out of their sockets, or caused to be dispatched, or to die, in prison, or in exile; and this, too, observe, not for rebellions, treasons, robberies and assassinations, like those of Coligni and his followers; but, simply and solely for adhering to the religion of their and her fathers, which religion she had openly practised for years, and to which religion she had most solemnly sworn that she sincerely belonged! The annals of hypocrisy conjoined with impudence afford nothing to equal her behaviour upon the occasion of the St. BARTHOLOMEW. She was daily racking people nearly to death to get secrets from them; she was daily ripping the bowels out of women as well as men for saying, or hearing, that mass, for the celebration of which the churches of England had been erected; she was daily mutilating, racking, and butchering her own innocent and conscientious subjects; and yet, she and her profligate courtwomen, when the French ambassador came with the King of France's explanation of the cause of the massacre, received him in deep mourning, and with all the marks of disapprobation. But, when she remonstrated with her "good "brother," the King of France, and added her hope that he would be indulgent to his Protestant subjects, her hypocrisy carried her a little too far; for the Queen-Mother, in her answer to "good Bess," observed, that, as to this matter, her son could not take a safer guide than his "good sister of England"; and that, while, like her, he forced no man's conscience; like her he was resolved to suffer no man to practise any religion but that which he himself practised. The French Queen-Mother was still short of "good Betsy's" mark; for she not only punished the practice of all religion but her own, she, moreover, punished people for not practising her religion; though she herself was a notorious apostate, and that, too, from motives as notoriously selfish. '

295 . But, there is a tail-piece, which most admirably elucidates "good Betsy's" sincerity upon this memorable occasion, and also that same quality in her which induced her to profess that she wished to live and die a virgin Queen. The Parliament and her Ministers, anxious for an undisputed succession, and anxious also to keep out the Scotch branch of the royal family. urged her, several times, to marry. She always rejected their advice. Her "virgin" propensity led her to prefer that sort of intercourse with men, which I need not more particularly allude to. Her amours with LEICESTER, of whom we shall see enough by-and-by, were open and notorious, and have been most amply detailed by many Protestant historians, some of whom have been clergymen of the Church of England; it is, moreover, well known, that these amours became the subject of a play, acted in the reign of Charles II. She was now, at the time of St. Bartholomew, in the, 39th year of her age; and she was, as she long had been, leading with Leicester the life that I have alluded to. Ten years afterwards, whether from the advanced age of Leicester, or from some other cause, the "virgin" propensity seemed, all of a sudden, to quit "good Betsy"; she became bent on wedlock; and, being now forty-nine years of age, there was, to be sure, no time to be lost in providing an hereditary successor to her throne. She had in the 13th year of her reign, assented to an Act that was passed, which secured the crown to her "natural issue," by which any bastard that she might have by any body, became heir to the throne; and it was, by the, same Act, made high treason to deny that such issue was heir to it. This Act, which is still in the Statute-Book, 13 Eliz. chap. 1. s. 2., is a proof of the most hardened profligacy that ever was witnessed in woman, and it is surprising, that such a mark of apparent national abjectness and infamy should have been suffered to remain in black and white to this day. However, at forty-nine "good

Betsy" resolved to lead a married life; and, as her savage father, whom she so much resembled, always looked out for a young wife, so "good virgin Betsy" looked out for a young husband; and, in order to convince the world of the sincerity of her horror at the massacre of St. Bartholomew, who should she fix on as a companion for life, who should she want to take to her arms, but the Duke of ANJOU, brother of Charles IX., and one of the perpetrators of those bloody deeds, on account of which she and the court ladies, all of her own stamp, had gone into mourning! The Duke was not handsome; but, he had what the French call la beauté da diable: he was young: only 28 years of age; and her old paramour LEICESTER, was now fifty! Betsy, though well stricken in years herself, had still a "colt's tooth." Her Ministers and the nation, who saw all the dangers of such a match to the independence of their country, protested against it most vehemently, and finally deterred her from it; but, a gentleman of Lincoln's inn, who had written and published a pamphlet against the marriage, was prosecuted, and had his right hand chopped off for this public-spirited effort in assisting to save England from the ruin about to be brought upon it for the mere gratification of the appetite of a gross, libidinous, nasty, shameless old woman. It was said of her monster of a father, who began the "Reformation," that "he spared no man in his anger, and no woman in his lust:" the very same, in substance, with a little change of the terms, might be said of this his monster of a daughter, who completed that "Reformation;" and, something approaching to the same degree of wickedness might be justly ascribed to almost every one who acted a conspicuous part in bringing about that, to England, impoverishing and degrading event.

296. Before we come to the three other great transactions of the long reign of this wicked woman, her foul murder of MARY STUART, Queen of Scotland; her war with Spain; and her scourging of Ireland, which unhappy country still bears the marks of her scorpion lash; before we come to these, it will be necessary to make ourselves acquainted with the names and characters of some of her principal advisers and co-operators; because, unless we do this, we shall hardly be able to comprehend many things, which we ought, nevertheless, to carry along clearly in our minds.

297. LEICESTER was her favourite, both in council and in the field. Doctor HEYLIN (History of the Reformation. Elizabeth, p. 168) describes him in these words: "Sir ROBERT DUDLEY, the second son of the Duke of Northumberland" (the odious traitor executed in the last reign), "she made, soon after she came to the throne, Lord Denbeigh and Earl of LEICESTER, having before made him her Master of Horse, Chancellor of the University of Oxford, and a Knight of the Garter; and she now gave him the fair manor of Denbeigh, with more gentlemen owing suit and service to it than any other in England in the hands of a subject, adding even to this the goodly castle and manor of Kenilworth. Advanced to this height, he engrossed unto himself the disposing of all offices in court and state, and of all preferments in the church, proving in fine so unappeasable in his malice, and so insatiable in his lusts, so sacrilegious in his rapines, so false in promises, and so treacherous in point of trust, and finally so destructive of the lives and properties of particular persons, that his little finger lay far heavier on the English subjects, than the loins of all the favourites of the two last Kings." And, mind, those "two Kings" were the plundering and confiscating Henry VIII. and Edward VI.! "And, that his monstrous vices might either be connived at, or not complained of, he cloaks them with a seeming zeal for true religion, and made himself the head of the Puritan faction, who spared no pains in setting forth his praises; nor was he wanting to caress them after such manner as he found most agreeable to these holy hypocrites, using no other language in his speech

and letters than the Scripture phrase, in which he was as dexterous as if he had received the same inspirations as the sacred penmen." We must bear in mind, that this character is drawn by a Doctor of the Church of England (Betsy's own Church), in a work, dedicated by permission to King Charles II. She, beyond all doubt, meaned to marry Leicester, who had, as all the world believed, murdered his own wife to make way for the match. She was prevented from marrying him by the reports from her ambassadors of what was said about this odious proceeding in foreign courts, and also by the remonstrances of her other ministers. HIGGONS, an historian of distinguished talent and veracity, states distinctly, that Leicester murdered his first wife for the purpose of marrying the Queen. He afterwards married, secretly, a second wife, and when she, upon his wanting to marry a third, refused to be divorced, he poisoned her; at least so said a publication, called Leicester's Republic, put forth in 1568. Yet, after all these things, this man, or, rather, this monster, continued to possess all his power and his emoluments, and all his favour with "the virgin Queen," to the last day of his life, which ended in 1588, after thirty years of plundering and oppressing the people of England. This was a " reformer" of religion, truly worthy of being enrolled with Henry VIII., Cranmer, Thomas Cromwell, and "good Queen Bess."

298. Sir WILLIAM CECIL was her next man. He was her Secretary of State; but, she afterwards made him a lord, under the title of Burleigh, and also made him Lord Treasurer. He had been a Protestant in the reign of Edward the Sixth, when he was Secretary, first under the Protector SOMERSET, who, when Dudley overpowered him, was abandoned by CECIL, who took to the latter, and was the very man that drew up the treasonable instrument, by which Edward, on his death-bed, disinherited his sisters Mary and Elizabeth. Pardoned for his treason by MARY, he became a most zealous Catholic, and was, amongst others, a volunteer to go over to Brussels to conduct Cardinal POLE to England. But, the wind having changed, he became Protestant again, and Secretary of State to "good Betsy," who never cared anything about the character or principles of those she employed, so that they did but answer her selfish ends. This CECIL, who was a man of extraordinary abilities, and of still greater prudence and cunning, was the chief prop of her throne for nearly forty of the forty-three years of her reign. He died in 1598, in the 77th year of his age; and, if success in unprincipled artifice; if fertility in cunning devices; if the obtaining of one's end without any regard to the means; if, in this pursuit, sincerity be to be set at nought, and truth, law, justice, and mercy, be to be trampled under foot; if, so that you succeed in your end, apostacy, forgery, perjury, and the shedding of innocent blood be to be thought nothing of, this CECIL was certainly the greatest statesman that ever lived. Above all others he was confided in by the Queen, who, when he grew old, and feeble in his limbs, used to make him sit in her presence, saying, in her accustomed masculine and emphatical style: "I have you, not for your weak legs, but for your strong head."

299. FRANCIS WALSINGHAM became Secretary of State after Cecil; but, he had been employed by the Queen almost from the beginning of her reign. He had been her ambassador at several courts, had negotiated many treaties, was an exceedingly prudent and cunning man, and wholly destitute of all care about means, so that he carried his end. He was said to have fifty-three agents and eighteen real spies in foreign courts. He was a most bitter and inflexible persecutor of the Catholics; but, before his death, which took place in 1590, he had to feel himself a little of that tyranny and ingratitude, and that want of mercy, which he had so long mainly assisted to make so many innocent persons feel.

300. PAULET ST. JOHN, Marquis of Winchester. This was not a statesman. He, like many more, was a backer-on. He presided at trials; and did other such-like work, These are unworthy of particular notice here, and PAULET is named merely as a specimen of the character and conduct of the makers and supporters of the famous "Reformation" This PAULET (the first noble of the family) was, at his outset, Steward to the Bishop of Winchester, in the time of Bishop Fox, in the reign of Henry VII. He was, by old brutal Harry VIII., made Treasurer of the King's household, and, zealously entering into all the views of that famous "Defender of the Faith," he was made Lord St. John. He was one of those famous executors, who were to carry into effect the will of Henry VIII. Though Harry had enjoined on these men to maintain his sort of half Catholic religion, PAULET now, in the reign of Edward, became a zealous Protestant, and continued to enjoy all his offices and emoluments, besides getting some new grants from the further spoils of the church and poor. Seeing that Dudley was about to supplant Somerset, which he finally did, Paulet joined Dudley, and actually presided at the trial and passed sentence of death on Somerset, "whose very name," says DR. MILNER, "had, a little more than two years before, "caused him to tremble." Dudley made him, first Earl of Wiltshire and then Marquis of Winchester, and gave him the palace of the Bishop of Winchester at Bishop's Waltham, together with other spoils of that Bishopric, When MARY came, which was almost directly afterwards, he became once more a Catholic, and continued to hold and enjoy all his offices and emoluments. Not only a Catholic, but a most furious Catholic, and the most active and vigorous of all the persecutors of those very Protestants, with whom he had made it his boast to join in communion only about two years before! We have heard a great deal about the cruelties of the "bloody Bishop BONNER"; but, nobody ever tells us, that this Marquis of Winchester, as President of the Council, repeatedly reprimanded Bonner, in very severe terms, for want of zeal and diligence in sending Protestants to the stake! Fox says, that "of the Council, the most active in these prosecutions was the Marquis of Winchester," But, now, Mary being dead, and Elizabeth being resolved to extirpate the Catholics, PAULET instantly became a Protestant again, a most cruel persecutor of the Catholics, president on several commissions for condemning them to death, and he was in such high favour with "good Bess," that she said, were he not so very old as he was, she would prefer him, as a husband, to any man in her dominions. He died in the 13th year of her reign, at the age of 97, having kept in place luring the reigns of five sovereigns, and having made four changes in his religion to correspond with the changes made by four out of the five. A French historian says, that Paulet being asked, how he had been able to get through so many storms not only unhurt, but rising all the while, answered, "En étant un saule, et non pas un chêne": "by being a willow, and not an oak." Our present Prime Minister, who, in 1822, while collections were making for the starving Irish, ascribed the distresses of the country to a surplus of food, seems also to be of this willow kind; for, with the exception of about fifteen months, he has been in place ever since he was a man. He was under Pitt the first time; Pitt went out, but he stuck in with Addington; Addington went out, but he stuck in again with Pitt a second time; he was pushed quite out by the "Whigs"; but in he came again with the Duke of Portland; he stuck in with Percival; and, at last, he got to the top, where he will remain for his natural life, unless the paper-money storm should tear even "willows" up by the roots. What this Bible-Saint would have done, if there had been a change of religion at every change of ministry, I shall not pretend to say.

301. Such were the tools with which "good Bess" had to work; and we have now to see in what manner they all worked with regard to MARY STUART, the celebrated

and unfortunate Queen of the Scotch. Without going into her history, it is impossible to make it clearly appear how Betsy was able to establish the Protestant religion in England in spite of the people of England; for it was, in fact, in spite of almost the whole of the people of all ranks and degrees. She actually butchered, that is to say, ripped up the bellies of some hundreds of them; she put many and many hundreds of them to the rack; she killed, in various ways, many thousands; and she reduced to absolute beggary as many as made the population of one of the smaller counties of England; to say nothing, at present, of that great slaughter-house, Ireland. It is impossible for us to see how she came to be able to do this; how she came to be able to get the Parliament to do the many monstrous things that they did; how they, without any force, indeed, came to do such barefaced things, as to provide that any bastard that she might have should inherit the throne, and to make it high treason to deny that such bastard was rightful heir to the throne. It is impossible to account for her being able to exist in England after that act of indelible infamy, the murder of Mary Stuart. It is impossible for us to see these things in their causes, unless we make ourselves acquainted with the history of Mary, and thereby show how the English were influenced at this most interesting period, the transactions of which were so decisive as to the fate of the Catholic religion in England.

302. MARY STUART, born in 1542 (nine years after the birth of Elizabeth), was daughter of James V. King of Scotland, and of Mary of Lorraine, sister of that brave and patriotic nobleman, the Duke of Guise, who, as we have seen, was so basely murdered by the vile traitor Coligni. Mary Stuart's father died when she was only eight days old; so that she became the reigning Queen of Scotland while in the cradle. Her father (James V.) was the son of James IV. and Margaret, the eldest sister of the old savage Henry VIII. This "Defender of the Faith" wished Mary Stuart to be betrothed to his son Edward, and by that means to add Scotland to the dominions of England. The family of Guise were too deep for the old "Defender." Mary Stuart (a Regency having been settled in Scotland) was taken to France, where she had her education, and. where her heart seemed to remain all her life. The French, in order to secure Scotland to themselves, as a constant ally against England, got Mary to be betrothed to Francis, Dauphin of France, son and successor of Henry II. King of France. She, at the age of seventeen years, was married to him, who was two years younger than herself, in 1 558, the very year that Elizabeth mounted the throne of England.

303. That very thing now took place which old Harry had been so much afraid of, and which, indeed, had been the dread of his councillors and his people. Edward was dead, Queen Mary was dead, and as Elizabeth was a bastard, both in law and in fact, Mary Stuart was the heiress to the throne of England; and she was now the wife of the immediate heir to the King of France. Nothing could be so fortunate for Elizabeth. The nation had no choice but one: to take her and uphold her; or, to become a great province of France. If Elizabeth had died at this time, or had died before her sister Mary, England must have become degraded thus; or, it must have created a new dynasty, or become a republic. Therefore it was, that all men, whether Catholics or Protestants, were for the placing and supporting of Elizabeth on the throne; and for setting aside Mary Stuart, though unquestionably she was the lawful heiress to the crown of England..

304. As if purposely to add to the weight of this motive, of itself weighty enough, Henry II, King of France, died in eight months after Elizabeth's accession; so that Mary Stuart was now, 1559, Queen Consort of France, Queen of Scotland, and called

WILLIAM COBBETT

herself Queen of England; she and her husband bore the arms of England along with those of France and Scotland; and the POPE had refused to acknowledge the right of Elizabeth to the English throne. Thus, as old Harry had foreseen, when he made his will setting aside the Scotch branch of his family, was England actually transferred to the dominion of France, unless the nation set at nought the decision of the POPE, and supported Elizabeth.

305. This was the real cause of Elizabeth's success in her work of extirpating the Catholic religion. According to the decision of the head of the Catholic Church, Elizabeth was an usurper; if she were an usurper, she ought to be set aside; if she were set aside, Mary Stuart and the King of France became Queen and King of England; if they became Queen and King of England, England became a mere province, ruled by Scotchmen and Frenchmen, the bare idea of which was quite sufficient to put every drop of English blood in motion. All men, therefore, of all ranks in life, whether Protestants or Catholics, were for Elizabeth. To preserve her life became an object dear to all her people; and, though her cruelties did, in one or two instances, arm Catholics against her life, as a body, they were as loyal to her as her Protestant subjects; and, even when her knife was approaching their bowels, they, without a single exception, declared her to be their lawful Queen. Therefore, though the decision of the POPE was perfectly honest and just in itself, that decision was, in its obvious and inevitable consequences, rendered, by a combination of circumstances, so hostile to the greatness, the laws, the liberties, and the laudable pride of Englishmen, that they were reduced to the absolute necessity of setting his decision at nought, or, of surrendering their very name as a nation, But, observe, by-the-bye, this dilemma and all the dangers and sufferings that it produced, arose entirely out of the "Reformation." Had the savage old Harry listened to Sir Thomas More and Bishop Fisher, there would have been no obstacle to the marrying of his son with Mary Stuart; and, besides, he would have had no children, whose legitimacy could have been disputed, and, in all human probability, several children to be, in lawful succession, heirs to the throne of England.

306. Here we have the great, and, indeed, the only cause, of Elizabeth's success in rooting out the Catholic religion. Her people were, ninety-nine hundredths of them, Catholics. They had shown this clearly at the accession of her sister Mary. Elizabeth was as great a tyrant as ever lived; she was the most cruel of women; her disgusting amours were notorious; yet, she was the most popular sovereign that had ever reigned since the days of Alfred; and we have thousands of proofs, that her people, of all ranks and degrees, felt a most anxious interest in everything affecting her life or her health. Effects like this do not come from ordinary causes. Her treatment of great masses of her people, her almost unparalleled cruelties, her flagrant falsehoods, her haughtiness, her insolence and her lewd life, were naturally calculated to make her detested, and to make her people pray for any thing that might rid them of her. But, they saw nothing but her between them and subjection to foreigners, a thing which they had always most laudably held in the greatest abhorrence. Hence it was, that the Parliament, when they could not prevail upon her to marry, passed an Act to make any bastard (" natural issue") of hers lawful heir to the throne. -- WITAKER (a clergyman of the Church of England) calls this a most infamous act. It was, in itself, an infamous act; but, that abjectness in the nation, which it now, at first sight, appears to denote, disappears, when we consider well what I have stated above. To be preserved from Mary Stuart, from the mastership of the Scotch and the French, was, at that time, the great object of anxiety with the English nation. HUME, whose head always runs upon

something hostile to the Catholic religion, ascribes Elizabeth's popularity to the dislike that her people had to what he calls the "Romish superstition." WITAKER ascribes the extirpation of the Catholic religion to the choice of her people, and not to her. The Catholic writers ascribe it to her cruelties; and they are right so far; but, they do not, as I have endeavoured to do, show how it came to pass that those numerous and unparalleled cruelties came to be perpetrated with impunity, to her and her Ministers. The question with the nation was, in short, the Protestant religion, Elizabeth, and independence; or, the Catholic religion, Mary Stuart, and subjection to foreigners. They decided for the former, and hence all the calamities, and the final tragical end of the latter lady.

307. MARY STUART was, in the year 1559, as we have seen in paragraph **303**, on the highest pinnacle of earthly glory, Queen Consort of France, Queen regnant of Scotland, Queen, in lawful right, of England, and was, besides, deemed one of the most beautiful women in the whole world. Never was fall like that of this Queen. Her husband, Francis II., died seventeen months after his accession, and was succeeded by Charles IX., then not more than three years old. Her husband's mother, CATHERINE DE MEDICI, soon convinced her, that to be any thing, she must return to Scotland. To Scotland she returned with a heavy heart, anticipating very little quiet in a country which was plunged in all the horrors of the "Reformation" even more deeply than England had been. Her long minority, together with her absence from her dominions, had given rise to contending factions of nobles who alternately triumphed over each other, and who kept the country in a state of almost incessant civil war, accompanied with deeds of perfidy and ferocity, of which there is scarcely any parallel to be found in history, ancient or modern. Added to this was the work of the new Saints, who had carried the work of "Reformation" much further than in England. The famous JOHN KNOX, an apostate monk, whom Dr. Johnson calls the "Ruffian of the Reformation," was leader of the "holy hypocrites" (as Dr. Heylin calls them) in Scotland. Mary, who had been bred a Catholic, and who had almost been deified in the court of France, was not likely to lead a happy life amongst people like these.

308. All this, however, Elizabeth and her Ministers and (for let us have no disguise) the English people, saw with great and ungenerous satisfaction. There was, for the present, at least, an end to the danger from the union of Scotland with France. But, Mary Stuart might marry again. There were the powerful family of Guise, her near relations; and she was still a formidable person, especially to Elizabeth. If Mary had been a man, Betsy would certainly have married her; but here was a difficulty too great even for Cecil to overcome. The English Queen soon began to stir up factions and rebellions against her cousin; and, indeed, by her intrigues with the religious factions and with the aspiring nobles, became, in a short time, with the aid of her money (a drug of infallible effect with the Scotch reformers), more the real ruler of Scotland than poor Mary was. She had, for the greater part of her whole reign, always a band of one faction or the other at, or about, her court. Her object was to keep Mary from possessing any real power, and to destroy her, if by any means short of detectable murder, she could effect that purpose.

309. In 1565, about three years after the return of Mary to Scotland, she was married to Henry Stuart, Earl of DARNLEY, her cousin, in which she over-reached the Queen of England, who, fearing that a visible heir to her own throne (as it actually happened) might come from this marriage, took desperate measures to prevent it; but, those measures came too late. Darnley, though young and handsome, proved to be a very foolish and disagreeable husband, and he was a Protestant into the bargain. She soon

treated him with great contempt, suffered him to have no real authority, and, in fact, as good as banished him from her court and disowned him. Darnley sought revenge. He ascribed his ill-treatment to Mary's being under the advice and control of her Catholic favourites, and particularly to the advice of Rizzio, a foreigner, her private secretary. Several malcontent "reformed" nobles joined with Darnley in agreeing to assist him in the assassinating of Rizzio, taking a bond from him to protect them against evil consequences. Mary was sitting at supper with some ladies of her court, Rizzio and other servants being in waiting, when the conspirators rushed in. Darnley went to the back of the Queen's chair; Rizzio, seeing their object, ran to the Queen for protection; she, who was in the sixth month of her pregnancy, endeavoured by entreaties and screams, to save his life. The ruffians stabbed him at her feet, and then dragged him out and covered his body with wounds.

310. This black and bloody transaction, for which not one of the assistants of Darnley was ever punished, was, in all probability, the cause, the chief cause, of the just, though illegal killing of Darnley himself. The next year after the murder of Rizzio, 1567, Mary having, in the meanwhile, brought forth a son (afterwards our James I., of half POPE and half Puritanical memory), Darnley was taken ill at Glasgow. The Queen went to visit him, treated him with great kindness, and, when he became better in health, brought him back to Edinburgh; but, for the sake of better air, lodged him in a house, at some distance from other houses, out of the town, where she visited him daily, and where, in a room immediately under his, she slept every night. But, on the night of the 10th of February (1567), she having notified it to him, slept at her palace, having promised to be present at the marriage of two of the attendants of her court, which marriage took place, and at which she was present: on this very night, the King's lodging-house was blown up by powder, and his dead body cast into an adjoining piece of ground! If the powder had given this base and bloody man time for thought, he would, perhaps, have reflected on the stabs he had given Rizzio in spite of the screams of a swooning and pregnant wife.

311. Now it was that the great and life-long calamities of this unfortunate Queen began. She had been repeatedly insulted and even imprisoned by the different factions, who, aided and abetted by the English Queen, alternately oppressed both her and her people; but, she was now to lead the life and die the death of a malefactor. It has been proved beyond all doubt, that the Earl of BOTHWEL, with other associates, bound in a "bloody bond," murdered Darnley. This was openly alleged, and, in placards about the streets, it was averred that Mary was in the plot. No positive proof has ever been produced to make good this charge; but, the subsequent conduct of the Queen was of a nature very suspicious . I shall simply state such facts as are admitted on all hands; namely, that Bothwel had, before the murder, been in great favour with the Queen, and possessed power that his talents and character did not entitle him to; that, after the murder, he was acquitted of it by a mock trial, which she might have prevented; that, on the 24th of April (53 days after the murder) she was, on her return from a visit to her infant son, seized by Bothwel at the head of 3,000 horsemen, and carried to his castle of Dunbar; that before she left the castle, on the 3d of May, she agreed to marry him; that he had a wife then alive; that a divorce, both Protestant and Catholic, in. one court for adultery and in the other for consanguinity, took place between Bothwel and his wife, in the space of six days; that, on the 12th of May, Bothwel led the Queen to the Sessions House, where, in the presence of the judges, she pardoned him for the violence committed on her person; that on the 15th of May, she openly married him; that the French Ambassador refused to appear at the

ceremony; and that Mary refused, in this case, to listen to the entreaties of the family of Guise.

312. Scores of volumes have been written, some in sup port of the assertion that Mary was consenting to the murder of her husband; and others in support of the negative of that proposition. Her enemies brought forward letters and sonnets, which they alleged to have been written by Mary to Bothwel, previous to her husband's murder. Her friends deny the authenticity of these; and I think they make their denial good. WITAKER, an Englishman, a Rector in the Church of England, mind; a man, too, who has written much against the Catholic religion, defends Mary against the charge of having consented, or having known of the intention, to murder her husband. But, nobody can deny, that she was carried off by Bothwel; that she, being at perfect liberty, pardoned him for that; and that she immediately married him, though it excited horror in the family of Guise, whom she had always heretofore listened to with the docility of a dutiful daughter.

313. This gross conduct, almost equal, in power of exciting odium, to the murder of such a wretch as Darnley, was speedily followed by tremendous punishment. A part of her subjects, armed against her, defeated Bothwel, who was compelled to flee the country, and who, in a few years afterwards, died in prison in Denmark. She herself be came a prisoner in the hands of her own subjects; and she escaped from their prison walls only to come and end her life within those of Elizabeth, her wily and deadly enemy.

314. The rebels were headed by the Earl of MURRAY, a natural son of Mary's father, and to her a most unnatural and cruel brother. He had imprisoned and deposed the Queen, had had her son crowned at thirteen months old, and had had himself elected Regent of the Kingdom. Murray had begun his life of manhood, not only as a Catholic, but as an ecclesiastic. He was prior of St. Andrew's; but, finding that he could gain by apostacy, he, like Knox, apostatized, and of course, broke his oath; and WITAKER says of him, that though "he was guilty of the most monstrous crimes, yet he was denominated a good man by the reformers of those days." His great object was to extirpate the Catholic religion, as the best means of retaining his power, and, being also a "bold liar" and a man that stuck at no forgery, no perjury, no bloody deed, that answered his purpose, he was a man after "good Queen Bess's" own heart.

315. She, however, at first affected to disapprove of his conduct, threatened to march an army to compel him to restore the Queen, gave the Queen positive assurances of her support, and invited her to take, in case of need, shelter, and receive protection, in England. In evil hour Mary, confiding in these promises and invitations, took, contrary to the prayers of her faithful friends, on their knees, the fatal resolution to throw herself into the jaws of her who had so long thirsted for her blood. At the end of three days she found that she had escaped to a prison. Her prison was, indeed, changed two or three times; but a prisoner she remained for nineteen long years; and was, at last, most savagely murdered for an imputed crime, which she neither did nor could commit.

316. During these nineteen years, Elizabeth was intriguing with Mary's rebellious subjects, tearing Scotland to pieces by means of her corruption spread amongst the different bands of traitors, and inflicting on a people, who had never offended her, every species of evil that a nation can possibly endure.

317. To enumerate, barely to enumerate, all, or one half, of the acts of hypocrisy, perfidy, meanness, and barbarity that "good Bess" practised against this unfortunate Queen, who was little more than twenty-five years of age when she was inveigled within the reach of her harpy claws; barely to enumerate these would require a space exceeding that of this whole Letter. While she affected to disapprove of Murray, she instigated him to accuse his queen and sister; while she pretended to assert the inviolability of sovereigns, she appointed a commission to try Mary for her conduct in Scotland; while she was vowing vengeance against the Scotch traitors for their rebellious acts against her cousin, she received, as presents from them, a large part of the jewels which Mary had received from her first husband, the King of France; and when, at last, she was compelled to declare Mary innocent of having consented to the murder, she not only refused to restore her, agreeably to her solemn promise repeatedly made, but refused also to give her her liberty, and, moreover, made her imprisoment more close, rigorous and painful than ever. Murray, her associate in perfidy, was killed in 1570 by a man whose estate he had unjustly confiscated; but, traitor after traitor succeeded him, every traitor in her pay, and Scotland bleeding all the while at every pore, because her cruel policy taught her that it was necessary to her own security. WITAKER produces a crowd of authorities to prove, that she endeavoured to get Mary's infant son into her hands, and that having failed in that, she endeavoured to cause him to be taken off by poison!

318. At last, in 1587, the tigress brought her long suffering victim to the block! Those means of dividing and destroying, which she had, all her life long, been employing against others, began now to be employed against herself, and she saw her life in constant danger. She thought and, perhaps, rightly, that these machinations against her arose from a desire in the Catholics (and a very natural desire it was) to rid the world of her and her horrid barbarities, and to make way for her Catholic, lawful successor, Mary; so that, now, nothing short of the death of this Queen seemed to her a competent guarantee for her own life. In order to open the way for the foul deed that had been resolved on, an Act of Parliament was passed, making it death for any one who was within the realm to conspire with others for the purpose of invading it, or, for the purpose of procuring the death of the Queen. A seizure was made of Mary's papers. What was wanting in reality was, as WITAKER. has proved, supplied by forgery, "a crime," says he, "which with shame to us, it must be confessed, belonged peculiarly to the Protestants." But, what right had Bess to complain of any hostile intention on the part of Mary? She was a queen as well as herself. She was held in prison by force; not having been made prisoner in war; but having been perfidiously entrapped and forcibly detained. Every thing had been done against her short of spilling her blood: and, had she not a clear and indisputable right to make war upon, and to destroy, her remorseless enemy, by all the means within her power? And, as to a trial, where was the law, or usage, that authorised one queen to invite another into her dominions, then imprison her, and then bring her to trial for alleged offences against her?

319. When the mode of getting rid of Mary was debated in "good Bess's" council: LEICESTER was for poison; others were for hardening her imprisonment, and killing her in that way; but WALSINGHAM was for death by means of a trial, a legal proceeding being the only one that would silence the tongues of the world. A commission was accordingly appointed, and Mary was tried and condemned; and that, too, on the evidence of papers, a part, at least, of which, were barefaced forgeries, all of which were copies, and the originals of none of which were attempted to be

produced! The sentence of death was pronounced in October. For four months the savage "good Queen Bess," was employed in devising plans for causing her victim to be assassinated, in order to avoid the odium of being herself the murderer! This is proved by WITAKER beyond all possibility of doubt: but, though she had entrusted the keeping of Mary to two men, mortal enemies of the Catholics, they, though repeatedly applied to for the purpose, perseveringly refused. Having ordered her Secretary, Davison, to write to them on the subject, Sir AMIAS PAULET, one of the keepers, returned for answer, that he "was grieved at the motion made to him, that he offered his life and his property to the disposal of her Majesty; but absolutely refused to be concerned in the assassination of Mary." The other keeper, Sir DRUE DRURY, did the same. When she read this answer, she broke out into reproaches against them, complained of the " daintiness of their consciences," talked scornfully of the niceness of such precise fellows," and swore that she would "have it done without their assistance." At the end, however, of four months of unavailing efforts to find men base and bloody enough to do the deed, she resorted to her last shift, the legal murder, which was committed on her hapless victim on the 8th of February, 1587, a day of everlasting infamy to the memory of the English Queen, "who, says WITAKER, had no sensibilities of tenderness, and no sentiments of generosity; who looked not forward to the awful verdict of history, and who shuddered not at the infinitely more awful doom of God. I blush as an Englishman to think that this was done by an English Queen, and one whose name I was taught to lisp in my infancy, as the honour of her sex, and the glory of our isle."

320. Ah! and thus was I taught; and thus have we all been taught. It is surely then our duty to teach our children to know the truth. Talk of "answers" to me, indeed! Let them deny, if they can, that this she "Head of the Church," this maker of it, was a murderer, and wished to be an assassin, in cold blood.

LETTER XI.

BESS'S HYPOCRISY AS TO THE DEATH OF MARY STUART.
SPANISH ARMADA.
POOR-LAWS .
BARBAROUS TREATMENT OF IRELAND.
BESS'S INQUISITION.
HORRID PERSECUTION OF THE CATHOLICS.
THE RACKS AND TORTURES SHE EMPLOYED.
HER DEATH.

Kensington, 30th Sept., 1825.

MY FRIENDS,

321 . DETESTABLY base as was the conduct of "good Queen Bess" in the act of murdering her unfortunate cousin, her subsequent hypocrisy was still more detestable. She affected the deepest sorrow for the act that had been committed, pretended that it had been done against her wish, and had the superlative injustice and baseness to imprison her Secretary, DAVISON, for having dispatched the warrant for the execution, though she, observe, had signed that warrant; and though, as WITAKER has fully proved, she had reviled DAVISON for not having despatched it, after she had, in vain, used all the means in her power to induce him to employ assassins to do the deed. She had, by a series of perfidies and cruelties wholly without a parallel. brought her hapless victim to the block, in that very country to which she had invited her to seek safety; she had, in the last sad and awful moments of that victim, had the barbarity to refuse her the consolations of a divine of her own communion; she had pursued her with hatred and malice that remained unglutted even when she saw her prostrate under the common hangman, and when she saw the blood gushing from her severed neck; unsated with the destruction of her body, she, Satan-like, had sought the everlasting destruction of her soul: and yet, the deed being done, she had the more than Satan-like hypocrisy to affect to weep for the untimely end of her "dear cousin"; and, which was still more diabolical, to make use of her despotic power to crush her humane secretary, under pretence that he had been the cause of the sad catastrophe! All expressions of detestation and honour fall short of our feelings, and our only consolation is, that we are to see her own end ten thousand times more to be dreaded than that of her victim.

322. Yet, such were the peculiar circumstances of the times, that this wicked woman escaped, not only for the present, but throughout her long reign, that general hatred from her subjects, which her character and deeds so well merited; nay, it perversely happened, that, immediately alter this foul deed, there took place an event which rallied all her people round her, and made her life, more than ever, an. object of their solicitude.

323. Philip II., King of Spain, who was also sovereign of the Low Countries, resolved on an invasion of England, with a fleet from Spain and with an army from Flanders. She had given him quite provocation enough; she had fomented rebellions against him, as she long had in France against the King of that country. Philip was the most powerful monarch in Europe; he had fleets and armies vastly superior to hers; the danger to England was really great; but, though these dangers had been brought upon

it solely by her malignity, bad faith, and perfidy, England was still England to her people, and they unanimously rallied round her. On this occasion, and, indeed, on all others, where love of country was brought to the test, the Catholics proved, that no degree of oppression could make them forget their duty as citizens, or as subjects. Even from HUME it is extorted, that the Catholic gentlemen, though her laws excluded them from all trust and authority, "entered as volunteers in her fleet or army. Some equipped ships at their own charge, and gave the command of them to Protestants: others were active in animating their tenants and vassals and neighbours, to the defence of their country: and, every rank of men, burying, for the present, all patty distinctions, seemed to prepare themselves with order as well as vigour, to resist these invaders." Charles I., James II., George I. and George II., and even George III., all saw the time, when they might have lamented the want of similar loyalty in Protestants. The first lost his head; the second his throne; the third and fourth were exposed to great danger of a similar loss; and the fifth lost America; and all by the doings of Protestants.

324. The intended invasion was prevented by a tremendous storm, which scattered and half destroyed the Spanish fleet, called the ARMADA, and, in all human probability, the invaders would not have succeeded, even if no storm had arisen. But, at any rate, there was great danger; no one could be certain of the result; the Catholics, had they listened to their just resentment, might have greatly added to the danger; and, therefore, their generous conduct merited some relaxation of the cruel treatment which they had hitherto endured under her iron sceptre. No such relaxation, however, took place: they were still treated with every species of barbarous cruelty; subjected to an inquisition infinitely more severe than that of Spain ever had or ever has been; and, even on the bare suspicion of disaffection, imprisoned, racked, and not unfrequently put to death.

325. As to Ireland, where the estates of the convents, and where the church property had been confiscated in the same way as in England, and where the greater distance of the people from the focus of power and apostacy and fanaticism, had rendered it more difficult to effect their "conversion" at the point of the bayonet, or by the halter, or the rack; as to this portion of her dominions, her reign was almost one unbroken series of robberies and butcheries. One greedy and merciless minion after another were sent to goad that devoted people into acts of desperation; and that, too, not only for the obvious purpose, but for the avowed purpose, of obtaining a pretence for new confiscations. The "Reformation" had, from its very outset, had plunder written on its front; but, as to Ireland, it was all plunder from the crown of its head to the sole of its foot. This horrible lynx-like she-tyrant could not watch each movement of the Catholics there, as she did in England; she could not so harass them in detail; she could find there no means of executing her dreadful police; and therefore she murdered them in masses. She sent over those parsons whose successors are there to the present day. The ever blood stained sword secured them the tithes and the church lands; but even that blood-stained sword could not then, and never did, though at one time wielded by the unsparing and double-distilled Protestant, CROMWELL, obtain them congregations. However, she planted, she watered with rivers of blood, and her long reign saw take fast root in the land, that tree, the fruit of which the unfortunate Irish taste to this hour; and which will, unless prevented by more wise and more just measures than appear to have been yet suggested, finally prove the overthrow of England herself.

326. I am to speak, further on, of the monstrous immoralities produced in England by the "Reformation," and also of the poverty and misery that it produced; and then I shall have to trace (through Acts of Parliament) this poverty and misery up to the "Reformation;" yes, for therein we shall see, clearly as we see the rivulet bubbling out of the bed of the spring, the bread and water of England and the potatoes of Ireland; but, even in this place, it is necessary to state the cause of the greater poverty and degradation of the Irish people. For ages that ill-treated people have, in point of clothing and food, formed a contrast with the English. Dr. FRANKLIN, in speaking of Ireland, says, that "one would think that the cast-off clothes of the working-people of England were sent over to be worn by the working-people here"

327. Whence comes it that this contrast has so long existed? The soil and the climate of Ireland are as good as those of England. The islands are but a few miles asunder. Both are surrounded by the same sea. The people of the. former are as able and as willing to labour as those of the latter; and of this they have given proof in all parts of the world, to which they have migrated, not to carry packs to cheat fools out of their money, not to carry the lash to make others work, but to share themselves, and cheerfully to share, in the hardest labours of those amongst whom they have sought shelter from the rod of unrelenting oppression. Whence comes it, then, that this contrast, so unfavourable to Ireland, has so long existed? The answer to this interesting question we shall find by attending to the different measures, dealt out to the two people, during the long and cruel reign of which we are now speaking; and we, at the same time, trace all the miseries of Ireland back, at once, to that "Reformation," the blessings of which have, with such persevering falsehood and hypocrisy, been dinned in our ears for ages.

328. We have seen in Letter III. of this little work, paragraphs **50, 51,** and **52,** that the Catholic Church was not, and is not, an affair of mere abstract faith; that it was not so very spiritual a concern as to scorn all cares relative to the bodies of the people; that one part, and that a capital part, of its business was, to cause works of charity to be performed; that this charity was not of so very spiritual a nature as not to be at all tangible, or obvious to the vulgar sense; that it showed itself in good works done to the needy and suffering; that the tithes and offerings and income from real property, of the Catholic Church, went in great part, to feed the hungry, to clothe the naked, to lodge and feed the stranger, to sustain the widow and the orphan, and to heal the wounded and the sick; that, in short, a great part, and indeed one of the chief parts, of the business of this Church was, to take care that no person, however low in life, should suffer from want either of sustenance or care; and that the priests of this Church should have as few selfish cares as possible to withdraw them from this important part of their duty, they were forbidden to marry. Thus, as long as this Church was the national Church, there were hospitality and charity in the land, and the horrid word "pauper" had never been so much as thought of.

329. But, when the Protestant religion came, and along with it a married priesthood, the poorer classes were plundered of their birthright, and thrown out to prowl about for what they could beg or steal. LUTHER and his followers wholly rejected the doctrine, that good works were necessary to salvation. They held, that faith, and faith alone, was necessary. They expunged from their Bible the Epistle of St. JAMES, because it recommends, and insists on the necessity of, good works; which Epistle Luther called, "An Epistle of straw." The "reformers" differed from each other, as widely as the colours of the rainbow, in most other things; but, they all agreed in this, that, good works were unnecessary to salvation, and that the" saints," as they had the

modesty to call themselves, could not forfeit their right to heaven by any sins, however numerous and enormous. By those, amongst whom plunder, sacrilege, adultery, polygamy, incest, perjury, and murder were almost as habitual as sleeping and waking; by those, who taught that the way to everlasting bliss could not be obstructed by any of these, nor by all of them put together; by such persons, charity, besides that it was a so well-known Catholic commodity, would be, as a matter of course, set wholly at nought.

330. Accordingly we see that it is necessarily excluded by the very nature of all Protestant establishments; that is to say, in reality; for the name of charity is retained by some of these establishments; but, the substance nowhere exists. The Catholic establishment interweaves deeds of constant and substantial charity with the faith itself. It makes the two inseparable. The DOUAY CATECHISM, which the Protestant parsons so much abuse, says that "the first fruit of the Holy Ghost is charity." And, then, it tells us what charity is; namely, "to feed the hungry, to give drink to the thirsty, to clothe the naked, to visit and ransom captives, to harbour the harbourless, to visit the sick, to bury the dead." Can you guess, my friends, why fat Protestant parsons rail so loudly against this "wicked Douay Catechism?" It is in the nature of man to love all this. This is what "the gates of hell will never prevail against ." This is what our fathers believed, and what they acted upon; and this it was that produced in them that benevolent disposition which, thank God , has not yet been wholly extirpated from the breasts of their descendants.

331. Returning now to paragraphs **50**, **51**, and **52**, just mentioned; it is there seen that the Catholic Church rendered all municipal laws about the poor wholly unnecessary; but, when that Church had been plundered and destroyed; when the greedy leading "reformers" had sacked the convents and the churches; when those great estates which of right belonged to the poorer classes, had been taken from them; when the parsonages had been first well pillaged, and the remnant of their revenues given to married men; then the poor (for poor there will and must be in every community) were left destitute of the means of existence, other than the fruits of begging, theft, and robbery. Accordingly, when "good Queen Bess" had put the finishing hand to the plundering of the Church and poor, once happy and free and hospitable England became a den of famishing robbers and slaves. STRIPE, a Protestant, and an authority to whom HUME appeals and refers many hundreds of times, tells us of a letter from a Justice of the Peace in Somersetshire to the Lord Chief Justice, saying: "I may justly say, that the able men that are abroad, seeking the spoil and confusion of the land, are able, if they were reduced to good subjection, to give the greatest enemy her Majesty hath a strong battle, and, as they are now, are so much strength to the enemy. Besides, the generation that daily springeth from them, is like to be most wicked. These spare neither rich nor poor; but, whether it be great gain or small, all is fish that cometh to net with them; and yet I say, both they and the rest are trussed up a-pace." The same Justice says: "In default of justice, many wicked thieves escape. For most commonly the most simple countrymen and women, looking no farther than to the loss of their own goods, are of opinion that they would not procure any man's death, for all the goods in the world." And while the "good Bess" complained bitterly of the non-execution of her laws, the same Protestant historian tells us, that "she executed more than five hundred criminals in a year, and was so little satisfied with that number, that she threatened to send private persons to see her penal laws executed for 'profit and gain's sake.' It appears that she did not threaten in vain; for soon after this a complaint was made in Parliament, that the stipendiary magistrate of that day was 'a kind of

living creature, who for half a dozen of chickens would dispense with a dozen of penal statutes.'" She did not, however, stop, with this "liberal" use of the gallows. Such was the degree of beggary, of vagabondage and of thievishness and robbery, that she resorted, particularly in London and its neighbourhood, to martial law. This fact is so complete a proof of the horrible effects of the "Reformation" upon the moral state of the people, and it is so fully characteristic of the Government, which the people of England had, in consequence of that "Reformation," become so debased as to submit to, that I. must take the statement as it stands in HUME, who gives the very words of "good and glorious Bess's" commission to her head murderer upon this occasion. "The streets of London were very much infested with idle vagabonds and riotous persons: the Lord Mayor had endeavoured to repress this disorder: the Star-chamber had exerted its authority, and inflicted punishment on these rioters. But the Queen, finding these remedies ineffectual, revived" [Revived? What does he mean by REVIVED?] "martial law, and gave Sir THOMAS WILFORD a commission as Provost-martial: 'Granting him authority, and commanding him, upon signification given by the justices of the peace in London or the neighbouring counties, of such offenders, worthy to be speedily executed by martial law, to take them, and according to the justice of martial law, to execute them upon the gallows or gibbet.' " And yet, this is she, whom we have been taught to call "good Queen Bess;" this is she, of the "glories" of whose reign there are men of learning base enough to talk, even to this day!

332. But, such were the natural consequences of the destruction of the Catholic Church, and of the plundering of the poor which accompanied that destruction, and particularly of lodging all power, ecclesiastical and civil, in the same hands. However, though this terrible she-tyrant spared neither racks nor halters, though she was continually reproving the executors of her bloody laws for their remissness while they were strewing the country with the carcasses of malefactors or alleged malefactors, all would not do; that hunger, which breaks through stone-walls, set even her terrors and torments at defiance; at last it was found to be absolutely necessary to make some general and permanent and solid provision for the poor; and in the 43rd year of her reign, was passed that Act, which is in force to this day, and which provides a maintenance for indigent persons, which maintenance is to come from the land, assessed and collected by overseers, and the payment enforced by process the most effectual and most summary. And here we have the great, the prominent, the staring, the horrible and ever-durable consequence of the "Reformation;" that is to say, pauperism established by law.

333. Yet this was necessary. The choice that the plunderers had in England was this: legal pauperism, or, extermination; and this last they could not effect, and if they could, it would not have suited them. They did not possess power sufficient to make the people live in a state of three-fourths starvation, therefore they made a legal provision for the poor: not, however, till they had tried in vain all other methods of obtaining a something to supply the place of Catholic charity. They attempted, at first, to cause the object to be effected by voluntary collections at the churches; but, alas! those who now entered those churches, looked upon LUTHER as the great teacher; and he considered St. JAMES's Epistle as an "Epistle of straw." Every attempt of this sort having failed, as it necessarily must, when the parsons who were to exhort others to charity, had enough to do to rake together all they could for their own wives and children; every Act (and there were many passed) short of a compulsory tax, enforced by distraint of goods and imprisonment of person, having failed, to this "glorious Bess" and her "Reformation" Parliament at last came; and here we have it to this day,

filling the country with endless quarrels and litigation, setting parish against parish, man against master, rich against poor, and producing, from a desire of the rich to shuffle out of its provisions, a mass of hypocrisy, idleness, fraud, oppression, and cruelty, such as was, except in the deeds of the original "reformers," never before witnessed in the world.

334. Nevertheless, it was, as far as it went, an act of justice. It was taking from the land and giving to the poor, a part, at least, of what they had been robbed of by the "Reformation." It was doing, in a hard and odious way, a part of that which had been done, in the most gentle and amiable way by the Church of our fathers. It was, indeed, feeding the poor like dogs, instead of like one's children; but it was feeding them. Even this, however, the "good Bess" and her plundering minions thought too much to do for the savagely-treated Irish people; and here we come to the real cause of that contrast, of which I have spoken in paragraph **235**; here we come to that which made Dr. FRANKLIN suppose, or, to say that any one might naturally suppose, that "the old clothes of the working classes in England had been sent over to be worn by the same class in Ireland."

335. We have seen how absolute necessity compelled "good Bess" and her plunderers to make a legal provision for the relief of the indigent in England; we have seen, that it was only restoring to them a part of that of which they had been plundered; and upon what principle was it, that they did not do the same with regard to the people of Ireland? These had been plundered in precisely the same manner that the former had; they had been plunged into misery by precisely the same means used under precisely the same hypocritical pretences; why were not they to be relieved from that misery in the same manner; and why was not the poor-law to be extended to Ireland?

336. Base and cruel plunderers! They grudged the relief in England; but, they had no compulsory means to be obtained out of England; and they found it impossible to make Englishmen to compel one another to live in a state of three-fourths starvation. But, they had England to raise armies in to send to effect this purpose in Ireland, especially when those English armies were urged on by promised plunder, and were (consisting as they did of Protestants) stimulated by motives as powerful, or nearly so, as the love of plunder itself. Thus it was, that Ireland was pillaged without the smallest chance of even the restoration which the English obtained; and thus have they, down unto this our day, been a sort of outcasts in their own country, being stripped of all the worldly goods that God and nature allotted them, and having received not the smallest pittance is return. We talk of "the outrages in Ireland;" we seem shocked at the violences committed there; and that sapient, profound, candid and modest gentleman, Mr. ADOLPHUS, the other day, in pleading at one of the police-offices in London (a sphere to which his talents are exceedingly well adapted,) took occasion, sought occasion, went out of his way to find occasion, to "thank God" that we, on this side of St. George's Channel, knew nothing of those outrages, which, when they were mentioned to the Irish, they ascribed to the misrule of ages. Now, it might be a little too much to expect an answer of any sort from a lawyer so dignified as this police-pleader; but, let me ask any English gentleman, or, any Englishman of any rank, except Mr. ADOLPHUS, what he thinks would be the consequences here, if the poor-laws were abolished to-morrow? Mr. ADOLPHUS can hardly help knowing, that Parson MALTHUS and his tribe have been preaching up the wisdom of such abolition; he may remember, too (for the example was terrific), that Mr. SCARLETT was "twisted down" in consequence of his having had the folly to mould this proposition of Malthus into the form of a BILL; but, Mr. ADOLPHUS may not know,

that petitions were preparing against that Bill, and that, too, from the payers of the poor-rates, stating, that, if such Bill were passed, there would be no safety for their property or their lives. Let us, then, have a little justice, at any rate; and, above all things, let us not, adding blasphemy to ignorance, insolence, and low, mob-courting sycophancy, "thank God" for the absence of outrages amongst us, as the wolf, in the fable, "thanked God" that he was not ferocious.

337. Why, there have been "ages of misrule" in Ireland, many, many ages too; or the landholders of England have, during those ages, been most unjustly assessed. But, they are sensible, or, at least, the far greater part of them, that a provision for the indigent, a settled, certain, legal provision, coming out of the land, is a right which the indigent possess, to use the words of BLACKSTONE, "in the very nature of civil society." Every man of reflection must know, that the labours, which the affairs of society absolutely demand, could never be performed but by persons who work for their bread; he must see, that a very large part of these persons will do no more work than is necessary to enable them to supply their immediate wants; and, therefore, he must see, that there always must be, in every community, a great number of persons who, from sickness, old age, from being orphans, widows, insane, and from other causes, will need relief from some source or other, This is the lot of civil society, exist wherever and however it may, and it will require a solider head than that which is on the shoulders of Mr. SCARLETT, to show, that this need of relief, to which all are liable, is not a necessary ingredient in the cement of civil society. The United States of America is a very happy country. The world has never yet seen a people better off. But, though the Americans cast off their allegiance to our king; though they abolished the monarchical rights; though they cast off the aristocracy of England; though they cast off the Church of England; they did not cast off the English poor-laws; and this very act of turbulent Bess, extorted from her by their English forefathers, is, at this moment, as completely in force in New York as it is in Old York, in New London as in Old London, in New Hampshire as in Old Hampshire, and in that whole country, from one end to the other, as it is in Old England herself.

338. Has it not, then, been a "misrule of ages" in Ireland? Have not that people been most barbarously treated by England? An Irishman, who has a thousand times been ready to expire from starvation in his native land, who has been driven to steal sea-weed to save himself from death, goes to America, feels hunger without having the means of relieving it; and there, in that foreign land, he finds, at once, be he where he may, an overseer of the poor, ready to give him relief! And, is such monstrous, such crying injustice as this still to be allowed to exist? The folly here surpasses, if possible, the injustice and the cruelty. The English landholders make the laws: we all know that. They subject, justly subject, their own estates to assessments for the relief of the poor in England; and, while they do this, they exonerate the estates of the Irish landowners from a like assessment, and choose rather to tax themselves and to tax us and tax the Irish besides, for the purpose of paying an army to keep that starving people from obtaining relief by force! Lord LIVERPOOL, when the Scotch Lords and others applied to him, in 1819, for a grant out of the taxes, to relieve the starving manufacturers in Scotland, very wisely and justly said, "No: have poor-laws, such as ours, and then your poor will be sure of relief." Why not say the same thing to the Irish landholders? Why not compel them to give to the people that which is their due? Why is Ireland to be the only civilised country upon the face of the earth, where no sort of settled, legal provision is made for the indigent, and where the Pastors are, at the same time, total strangers to the flocks, except in the season of shearing? Let us, at

least, as long as this state of things should be suffered to exist, have the decency not to cry out quite so loudly against the "outrages of the Irish."

339. I must now return from this digression (into which the mention of "good Bess's" barbarous treatment of Ireland has led me), in order to proceed with my account of her "reforming" projects. Betsy was a great Doctor of Divinity. She was extremely jealous of her prerogatives and powers, but particularly in what regarded her headship of the Church. She would make all her subjects be of her religion, though she had solemnly sworn, at her coronation, that she was a Catholic, and though, in turning Protestant. she had made a change in Cranmer's prayer-book and in his articles of faith. In order to bend the people's con sciences to her tyrannical will, which was the more unjust, because she herself had changed her religion, and had even changed the Protestant articles, she established an inquisition the most horrible that ever was heard of in the world. She gave what she called a Commission to certain Bishops and others, whose power extended over the whole kingdom, and over all ranks and degrees of the people. They were empowered to have an absolute control over the opinions of all men, and to punish all men according to their discretion, short of death. They might proceed legally, if they chose, in the obtaining of evidence against parties; but, if they chose, they were to employ imprisonment, the rack, or torture of any sort, for this purpose. If their suspicions alighted upon any man, no matter respecting what, and they had no evidence, nor even any hearsay, against him, they might administer an oath, called *ex-officio*, to him, by which he was bound, if called upon, to reveal his thoughts, and to accuse himself, his friend, his brother, or his father, upon pain of death. These subaltern monsters inflicted what fines they pleased; they imprisoned men for any length of time that they pleased. They put forth whatever new articles of faith they pleased; and, in short, this was a Commission exercising, in the name and for the purposes of "good Queen Bess," an absolute control over the bodies and the minds of that people, whom the base and hypocritical and plundering "reformers" pretended to have delivered from a "slavish subjection to the POPE," but whom they had, without any pretending, actually delivered from freedom, charity and hospitality.

340. When one looks at the deeds of this foul tyrant, when one sees what abject slavery she had reduced the nation to, and especially when one views this Commission, it is impossible for us not to reflect with shame on what we have so long been saying against the Spanish Inquisition, which, from its first establishment to the present hour, has not committed so much cruelty as this ferocious Protestant apostate committed in any one single year of the forty-three years of her reign. And, observe again, and never forget, that Catholics, where they inflicted punishments inflicted them on the ground, that the offenders had departed from the faith in which they had been bred and which they had professed; whereas the Protestant punishments have been inflicted on men because they refused to depart from the faith in which they had been bred, and which they had professed all their lives. And, in the particular case of the brutal hypocrite, they were punished, and that, too, in the most barbarous manner, for adhering to that very religion, which she had openly professed for many years of her life, and to which she, even at her coronation , had sworn that she belonged!

341 . It is hardly necessary to attempt to describe the sufferings that the Catholics had to endure during this murderous reign. No tongue, no pen is adequate to the task. To hear mass, to harbour a priest, to admit the supremacy of the POPE, to deny this horrid virago's spiritual supremacy. and many other things, which an honourable Catholic could scarcely avoid, consigned him to the scaffold and to the bowel-ripping knife. But, the most cruel of her acts, even more cruel than her butcheries, because of

far more extensive effect, and far more productive of suffering in the end, were the penal laws inflicting fines for recusancy, that is to say, for not going to her new-fangled Protestant church. And, was there ever tyranny equal to this? Not only were men to be punished for not confessing that the new religion was the true one; not only for continuing to practise the religion in which they and their fathers and children bad been born and bred; but also punished for not actually going to the new assemblages, and there performing what they must, if they were sincere, necessarily deem an act of open apostacy and blasphemy! Never, in the whole world, was there heard of before tyranny equal to this.

342. The fines were so heavy, and were exacted with such unrelenting rigour, and, for the offence of recusancy alone the sums were so enormous, that the whole of the conscientious Catholics were menaced with utter ruin. The priests who had never been out of England, and who were priests before the reign of this horrible woman, were, by, the 20th year of her reign, few in number, for the laws forbade the making of any new ones on pain of death, and, indeed none could be made in England, where there was no clerical authority to ordain them, the surviving Catholic bishops being forbidden to do it on pain of death. Then she harassed the remainder of the old priests in such a way, that they were, by the 20th year of her reign, nearly exterminated; and as it was death for a priest to come from abroad, death to harbour him, death for him to perform his functions in England, death to confess to him, there appeared to be an impossibility of preventing her from extirpating, totally extirpating from the land, that religion, under which England had been so great and so happy for ages so numerous; that religion of charity and hospitality; that religion which made the name of pauper unknown; that religion which had built the churches and cathedrals, which had planted and reared the Universities, whose professors had made Magna Charta and the Common Law, and who had performed all those glorious deeds in legislation and in arms, which had made England really "the "envy of surrounding nations and the admiration of the world": there now appeared to be an impossibility, and especially if the termagant tyrant should live for another twenty years (which she did), to prevent her from effecting this total extirpation. From accomplishing this object she was prevented by the zeal and talents of WILLIAM ALLEN, an English gentleman, now a priest, and who had before been of the University of Oxford. In order to defeat the she-tyrant's schemes for rooting out the Catholic religion, he formed a Seminary at DOUAY, in Flanders, for the education of English priests. He was joined by many other learned men; and, from this depot, though at the manifest hazard of their lives, priests came into England; and thereby the malignity of this inexorable apostate was defeated. There was the sea between her and ALLEN, but, while he safely defied her death-dealing power, she could not defy his, for she could not erect a wall round the island, and into it priests would come and did come; and, in spite of her hundreds of spies and her thousands of "pursuivants," as were called the myrmidons who executed her tormenting and bloody behests, the race of English priests was kept in existence, and the religion of their fathers along with it. In order to break up the seminary of ALLEN, who was afterwards made a Cardinal, and whose name can never be pronounced but with feelings of admiration, she resorted to all sorts of schemes; and, at last, by perfidiously excluding from her ports the fleet of the Dutch and Flemish insurgents, to whom she stood pledged to give protection, she obtained from the Spanish Governor, a dissolution of ALLEN's college; but, he found protection in France, from the House of Guise, by whom he and his college were, in spite of most bitter remonstrances from "good Bess" to the King of France, re-established at RHEIMS.

343. Thus defeated in all her projects for destroying the missionary trunk, she fell with more fury than ever on the branches and on the fruit. To say mass, to hear mass, to make confession, to hear confession, to teach the Catholic religion, to be taught it, to keep from her church service: these were all great crimes, and all punished with a greater or less degree of severity; so that the gallowses and gibbets and racks were in constant use, and the gaols and dungeons choking with the victims. The punishment for keeping away from her church was 20*l.* a lunar month, which, of money of the present day, was about 250*l.* Thousands upon thousands refused to go to her church; and thus she sacked their thousands upon thousands of estates; for, observe, here was, in money of this day, a fine of 3,250*l.* a year. And now, sensible and just reader, look at the barbarity of this "Protestant Reformation." See a gentleman of, perhaps, sixty years of age or more; see him, born and bred a Catholic, compelled to make himself and his children beggars, actual beggars, or to commit, what he deemed, an act of apostacy and blasphemy. Imagine, if you can, barbarity equal to this; and yet even this is not seen in its most horrible light, unless we take into view, that the tyrant who committed it, had, for many years of her life, openly professed the Catholic religion, and had, at her coronation, sworn that she firmly believed in that religion.

344. In the enforcing of these horrible edicts, every insult, that base minds could devise, was resorted to and in constant use. No Catholic, or reputed Catholic, had a moment's security or peace. At all hours, but generally in the night-times, the ruffians entered his house by breaking it open; rushed, in different divisions, into the rooms; broke open closets, chests, and drawers; rummaged beds and pockets; in short, searched every place and thing for priests, books, crosses, vestments, or any person or thing appertaining to the Catholic worship. In order to pay the fines, gentlemen were compelled to sell their estates piece by piece; when they were in arrear, the tyrant was, by law, authorised to seize all their personal property, and two thirds of their real estate every six months; and they were in some cases suffered, as a great indulgence, to pay an annual composition for the liberty of abstaining from what they deemed apostacy and blasphemy. Yet, whenever she took it into her suspicious head that her life was in danger, from whatever cause, and causes, and just causes enough there always were, she had no consideration for them on account of the fines or the composition. She imprisoned them, either in gaol, or in the houses of Protestants, kept them banished from their own homes for years. The Catholic gentleman's own house afforded him no security; the indiscretion of children or friends, the malice of enemies, the dishonesty or revenge of tenants or servants, the hasty conclusions of false suspicion, the deadly wickedness of those ready to commit perjury for gain's sake, the rapacity and corruption of constables, sheriffs, and magistrates, the virulent prejudice of fanaticism; to every passion hostile to justice, happiness, and peace; to every evil against which it is the object of just laws to protect a man, the conscientious Catholic gentleman lived continually exposed; and that, too, in that land which had become renowned throughout the world by those deeds of valour and those laws of freedom which had been performed and framed by his Catholic ancestors.

345. As to the poor conscientious "recusants," that is to say, keepers away from the tyrant's church, they, who had no money to pay fines with, were crammed into prison, until the gaols could (which was very soon) hold no more, and until the counties petitioned to be relieved from the charge of keeping them. They were then discharged, being first publicly whipped, or having their ears bored with a hot iron. This not answering the purpose, an act was passed to compel all "recusants," not worth twenty marks a year, to quit the country in three months after conviction, and to punish them

with death, in case of their return. The old "good Bess," defeated herself here; for, it was found impossible to cause the law to be executed, in spite of all her menaces against the justices and sheriffs, who could not be brought up to her standard of ferociousness; and they, therefore, in order to punish the poor Catholics, levied sums on them at their pleasure, as a composition for the crime of abstaining from apostacy and profanation.

346. The Catholics, at one time, entertained a hope, that, by a declaration of their loyalty, they should obtain from the Queen some mitigation, at least, of their sufferings. With this view they drew up a very able and most dutiful petition, containing an expression of their principles, their sufferings, and their prayers. Alas! they appealed to her to whom truth and justice and mercy were all alike wholly unknown. The petition being prepared, all trembled at the thought of the danger of presenting it to her. At last, RICHARD SHELLEY, of Michael Grove, Sussex, assumed the perilous charge. She had the (as it would have been in any other human being) incomparable baseness to refer him, for an answer, to the gloomy echoes of a pestiferous prison, where he expired, a victim to his own virtue and to her implacable cruelty.

347. Talk of Catholic tyrants! Talk of the Catholics having propagated their faith by acts of force and cruelty! I wonder that an English Protestant, even one whose very bread comes from the spoliation of the Catholics, can be found with so little shame as to talk thus. Our lying Protestant historians tell us, that the ships of the Spanish Armada were "loaded with RACKS," to be used upon the bodies of the English, who were preserved from these by the wisdom and valour of "good and glorious Queen Bess." In the first place, it was the storm, and not "glorious Bess," that prevented an invasion of the country; and, in the next place, the Spaniards might have saved themselves the trouble of importing RACKS, seeing that gentle Betsy had always plenty of them, which she kept in excellent order, and in almost daily use. It is to inflict most painful feelings on Protestants, to be sure; but, justice demands, that I describe one or two of her instruments of torture; because in them we see some of the most powerful of those means which she made use of for ESTABLISHING HER PROTESTANT CHURCH; and here I thank Dr. LINGARD for having, in note U of volume V. of his History, enabled me to give this description. One kind of torture, which was called "The Scavenger's Daughter, was a broad hoop of iron, consisting of two parts, fastened by a hinge. The prisoner was made to kneel on the pavement and to contract him self into as small a compass as he could. Then the executioner, kneeling on his shoulders, and having introduced the hoop under his legs, compressed the victim close together, till he was able to fasten the feet and hands together over the small of the back. The time allotted to this kind of torture was an hour and a half, during which time the blood gushed from the nostrils, and, sometimes, from the hands and feet." There were several other kinds of arguments of conversion that gentle Betsy made use of to eradicate the "damnable errors" of popery; but, her great argument was, the RACK. "This was a large open frame of oak, raised three feet from the ground. The prisoner was laid under it, on his back, on the floor. His wrists and ankles were attached by cords to two rollers at the ends of the frame: these were moved by levers in opposite directions till the body rose to a level with the frame. Questions were then put; and, if the answers did not prove satisfactory, the sufferer was stretched more and more till the bones started from their sockets."

348. There, Protestants; there, revilers of the Catholic religion; there are some of the means which" good Queen Bess" made use of to make her Church, "established by

law." Compare, oh! compare, if you have one particle of justice left in you; compare these means with the means made use of by those who introduced and established the Catholic Church!

349. The other deeds and events of the reign of this ferocious woman are now of little interest, and, indeed, do not belong to my subject; but, seeing that the pensioned poet, JAMMY THOMPSON, in that sickly stuff of his, which no man of sense ever can endure after he gets to the age of twenty, has told us about "the glories of the maiden reign," it may not be amiss, before I take my leave of this "good" creature, to observe, that "her glories" consisted in having broken innumerable solemn treaties and compacts; in having been continually bribing rebel subjects to annoy their sovereigns; in having had a navy of freebooters; in having had an army of plunderers; in having bartered for a little money the important town of Calais; and in never having added even one single leaf of laurel to that ample branch which had, for ages, been seated on the brows of England; and that, as to her maiden virtues, WITAKER (a Protestant clergyman, mind) says, that "her life was stained with gross licentiousness, and she had many gallants, while she called herself a maiden Queen." Her life, as he truly says, was a life of "mischief and of misery"; and, in her death (which took place in the year 1603, the 70th of her age and the 45th of her reign) she did all the mischief that it remained in her power to do, by sulkily refusing to name her successor, and thus leaving to a people, whom she had been pillaging and scourging for forty-five years, a probable civil war, as "a legacy of mischief after her death." Historians have been divided in opinion, as to which was the worst man that England ever produced, her father, or Cranmer; but, all mankind must agree, that this was the worst woman that ever existed in England, or in the whole world, Jezebel herself not excepted.

LETTER XII

ACCESSION OF JAMES I.
HORRID PERSECUTION OF THE CATHOLICS.
GUNPOWDER PLOT.
CHARLES I. QUALIFIED FOR THE RANK OF MARTYR.
"REFORMATION" THE SECOND, OR "THOROUGH GODLY REFORMATION."
CHARLES II. THE PLOTS AND INGRATITUDE OF HIS REIGN.
JAMES II.. HIS ENDEAVOURS TO INTRODUCE GENERAL TOLERATION.
DAWN OF "GLORIOUS" REVOLUTION.

Kensington, 31st October, 1825.

My FRIENDS,

350. IN the foregoing Letters, it has been proved, beyond all contradiction, that the "Reformation," as it is called; was, "engendered in beastly lust, brought forth in hypocrisy and perfidy, and cherished and fed by rivers of "innocent English and Irish blood." There are persons who publish what they call answers to me: but these answers (Which I shall notice again before I have done) all blink the main subject: they dwell upon what their authors assert to be errors in the Catholic Religion; this they do, indeed, without attempting to show how that Protestant Religion, which has about forty different sects, each at open war with all the rest, can be free from error; but, do they deny, that this new religion began in beastly lust, hypocrisy and perfidy; and do they deny, that it was established by plunder, by tyranny, by axes, by gallowses, by gibbets and by racks? Do they face with a direct negative either of these important propositions? No: there are the facts before them; there is the history; and (which they cannot face with a negative) there are the Acts of Parliament, written in letters of blood, and some of these remaining in force, to trouble and torment the people and to endanger the State, even to the present day. What do these answerers do, then? Do they boldly assert, that beastly lust, hypocrisy, perfidy, that the practice of plunder, that the use of axes, gallowses, gibbets and racks, are good things, and outward signs of inward evangelical purity and grace? No: they give no answer at all upon these matters; but rail against the personal character of priests and cardinals and popes, and against rites and ceremonies and articles of faith and rules of discipline, matters with which I have never meddled, and which have very little to do with my subject, my object, as the title of my work expresses, being to "show, that the 'Reformation' has impoverished and degraded the main body of the people of England and Ireland." I have shown that this change of religion was brought about by some of the worst, if not the very worst, people, that ever breathed: I have shown that the means were such as human nature revolts at; so far I can receive no answer from men not prepared to deny the authenticity of the statute-book; it now remains for me to show, from the same sources, the impoverishing and degrading consequences of this change of religion, and that, too, with regard to the nation as a whole, as well as with regard to the main body of the people.

351. But, though we have now seen the Protestant religion established, completely established, by the gibbets, the racks and the ripping knives, I must, before I come to the impoverishing and degrading consequences, of which I have just spoken, and of which I shall produce the most incontestable proofs; I must give an account of the

proceedings of the Reformation-people after they had established the system. The present Letter will show us the Reformation producing a second, and that, too (as every generation is wiser than the preceding), with "vast improvements;" the first being only "a godly Reformation," while the second we shall find to be "a thorough godly" one. The next (or thirteenth) Letter will introduce us to a third Reformation, commonly called the "glorious" Reformation, or revolution. The 14th Letter will give us an account of events still greater; namely, the American Reformation, or revolution, and that of the French. All these we shall trace back to the first Reformation as clearly as any man can trace the branches of a tree back to its root. And, then we shall in the remaining Letter, or Letters, see the fruit in the immorality, crimes, poverty and degradation of the main body of the people. It will be curious to behold the American and French Reformations, or revolutions, playing back the principles of the English Reformation-people upon themselves; and, which is not less curious, and much more interesting, to see them force the Reformation-people to begin to cease to torment the Catholics, whom they had been tormenting without mercy for more than two hundred years.

352. The "good and glorious and maiden" and racking and ripping-up Betsy, who, amongst her other "godly" deeds, granted to her minions, to whom there was no longer church-plunder to give, monopolies of almost all the necessaries of life, so that salt, for instance, which used to be about 2d. a bushel, was raised to 15s. or about seven pounds of our present money; the "maiden" Betsy, who had, as Witaker says, expired in sulky silence as to her successor, and had thus left a probable civil war as a legacy of mischief, was, however, peaceably succeeded by JAMES I., that very child of whom poor Mary Stuart was pregnant, when his father Henry Stuart, Earl of Darnley, and associates, murdered RIZZIO in her presence, as we have seen in paragraph **308**, and which child, when he came to man's estate, was a Presbyterian, was generally a pensioner of Bess, abandoned his mother to Bess's wrath, and, amongst his first acts in England, took by the hand, confided in and promoted, that CECIL, who was the son of the Old Cecil, who did, indeed, inherit the great talents of his father, but who had also been, as all the world knew, the deadly enemy of this new King's unfortunate mother.

353. like all the Stuarts, except the last, was at once prodigal and mean, conceited and foolish, tyrannical and weak; but the staring feature of his character was insincerity. It would be useless to dwell in the detail on the measures of this contemptible reign, the prodigalities and debaucheries and silliness of which did, however, prepare the way for that rebellion and that revolution, which took place in the next, when the double-distilled "Reformers" did, at last, provide a "martyr" for the hitherto naked pages of the Protestant Calendar. Indeed, this reign would, as far as my purposes extend, be a complete blank, were it not for; that "gunpowder plot," which alone has caused this Stuart to he remembered, and of which, seeing that it has been, and is yet, made a source of great and general delusion, I shall take much more notice than it would otherwise be entitled to.

354. That there was a plot in the year 1605 (the second year after James came to the throne), the object of which was to blow up the King and both Houses of Parliament, on the first day of the session; that Catholics, and none but Catholics, were parties to this plot; that the conspirators were ready to execute the deed; and that they all avowed this to the last; are facts which no man has ever attempted to deny, any more than any man has attempted to deny that the parties to the Cato-street plot did really intend to cut off the heads of Sidmouth and Castlereagh, which intention was openly

avowed by these parties from first to last, to the officers who took them, to the judge who condemned them, and to the people who saw their heads severed from their bodies.

355. But, as the Parliamentary Reformers in general were most falsely and basely accused of instigating to the commission of the last mentioned intended act, so were the Catholics in general, and so are they to this day, not less falsely and less basely accused of instigating to the intended act of 1605. But, as to the conspirators themselves; as to the extent of their crime, are we wholly to leave out of our consideration the provocation they had received? To strike a man is an assault; to kill a man is murder; but, are striking and killing always assault and murder? Oh, no; for we may justifiably assault and kill a robber or a house breaker. The Protestant writers have asserted two things; first, that the Catholics in general instigated to, or approved of, the gunpowder plot; and, second, that this is a proof of the sanguinary principles of their religion. As to the first, the contrary was fully and judicially proved to be the fact; and, as to the second, supposing the conspirators to have had no provocation, those of Cato-street were not Catholics at any rate, nor were those Catholics who qualified Charles I., for a post in the Calendar, and that, too, observe, after he had acknowledged his errors, and had made compensation to the utmost of his power.

356. However, these conspirators had provocation: and now let us see what that provocation was. The King, before he came to the throne, had promised to mitigate the penal laws, which, as we have seen, made their lives a burden. Instead of this, those laws were rendered even more severe than they had been in the former reign. Every species of insult as well as injury which the Catholics had had to endure under the persecutions of the Established Church was now heightened by that leaven of Presbyterian malignity and ferocity, which England had now imported from the North, which had then poured forth upon this devoted country endless hordes of the most greedy and rapacious and insolent wretches that God had ever permitted to infest and scourge the earth. We have seen, in paragraphs **340, 341, 342, 343, 344**, how the houses of conscientious Catholic gentlemen were rifled, how they were rummaged, in what constant dread these unhappy men lived, how they were robbed of their estates as a punishment for recusancy and other things called crimes; we have seen, that, by the fines, imposed on these accounts, the ancient gentry of England, whose families had, for ages, inhabited the same mansions and had been venerated and beloved for their hospitality and charity; we have seen how all these were gradually sinking into absolute beggary in consequence of these exorbitant extortions; but, what was their lot now! The fines, as had been the practice, had been suffered to fall in arrear, in order to make the fined party more completely at the mercy of the Crown; and JAMES, whose prodigality left him not the means of gratifying the greediness of his Scotch minions out of his own exchequer, delivered over the English Catholic gentry to these rapacious minions, who, thus clad with royal authority, fell, with all their well-known hardness of heart, upon the devoted victims, as the kite falls upon the defenceless dove. They entered their mansions, ransacked their closets, drawers and beds, seized their rent-rolls, in numerous instances drove their wives and children from their doors, and, with all their native upstart insolence, made a mockery of the ruin and misery of the uoffending persons whom they had despoiled.

357. Human nature gave the lie to all preachings of longer passive obedience, and, at last, one of these oppressed and insulted English gentlemen, ROBERT CATESBY, of Northamptonshire, resolved on making an attempt to deliver himself and his suffering brethren from this almost infernal scourge. But, how was he to obtain the means?

From abroad, such was the state of things; no aid could possibly be hoped for. Internal insurrection was, as long as the makers and executors of the barbarous laws remained, equally hopeless. Hence he came to the conclusion, that to destroy the whole of them afforded the only hope of deliverance; and to effect this there appeared to him no other way than that of blowing up the parliament-house when, on the first day of the session, all should be assembled together. He soon obtained associates; but, in the whole, they amounted to only about thirteen; and all, except three or four, in rather obscure situations in life, amongst whom was GUY FAWKES, a Yorkshireman who had served as an officer in the Flemish wars. He it was, who undertook to set fire to the magazine, consisting of two hogsheads and thirty-two barrels of gunpowder; he it was, who, if not otherwise to be accomplished, had resolved to blow himself up along with the persecutors of his brethren; he it was, who, on the 5th of November, 1605, a few hours only before the Parliament was to meet, was seized in the vault, with two matches in his pocket and a dark lantern by his side, ready to effect his tremendous purpose; he it was, who, when brought before the King and Council, replied to all their questions with defiance; he it was, who, when asked by a Scotch Lord of the Council, why he had collected so many barrels of gunpowder, answered, "To blow you Scotch beggars back to your native mountains," and, in this answer, proclaimed to the world the true immediate cause of this memorable conspiracy; an answer, which, in common justice, ought to be put into the mouth of those effigies of him, which crafty knaves induce foolish boys still to burn on the 5th of November. JAMES (whose silly conceit made him an author) was just, in one respect, at any rate. In his works, he called FAWKES, "the English SCÆVOLA"; and history tells us that that famous Roman, having missed his mark in endeavouring to kill a tyrant, who had doomed his country to slavery, thrust his offending hand into a hot fire, and let it burn, while he looked defiance at the tyrant.

358. Catesby and the other conspirators were pursued; he and three of his associates died with arms in their hands fighting against their pursuers. The rest of them (except Gresham, (who was poisoned in prison) were executed, and also the famous Jesuit, GARNET, who was wholly innocent of any crime connected with the conspiracy, and who, having come to a knowledge of it, through the channel of confession, had, on the contrary, done everything in his power to prevent the perpetrating of its object. He was sacrificed to that unrelenting fanaticism, which, encouraged by this and other similar successes, at last, as we are soon to see, cut off the head of the son and successor of this very King. The King and Parliament escaped from feelings of humanity in the conspirators . Amongst the disabilities imposed on the Catholics, they had not yet, and were not until the reign of Charles II., shut out of Parliament. So that, if the House were blown up, Catholics, Peers and Members, would have shared the fate of the Protestants. The conspirators could not give warning to the Catholics without exciting suspicions. They did give such warning where they could; and this led to the timely detection; otherwise the whole of the two Houses, and the King along with them, would have been blown to atoms; for, though CECIL evidently knew of the plot long before the time of intended execution; though he took care to nurse it till the moment of advantageous discovery arrived; though he was, in all probability, the author of a warning letter, which, being sent anonymously to a Catholic nobleman, and communicated by him to the Government, became the ostensible cause of the timely discovery; notwithstanding these well-attested facts, it by no means appears, that the plot originated with him, or, indeed, with any body but CATESBY, of whose conduct men will judge differently according to the difference in their notions about passive obedience and non-resistance.

359. This would be enough. of the famous gunpowder plot; but, since it has been ascribed to bloody-mindedness, as the natural fruit of the Catholic religion; since, in our COMMON PRAYER-BOOK, we are taught, in addressing God, to call all Catholics indiscriminately, "our cruel and blood-thirsty enemies," let us see a little what Protestants have attempted, and done, in this blowing-up way. This King James, as he himself averred, was nearly being assassinated by his Scotch Protestant subjects, Earl GOWRY and his associates; and, after that, narrowly escaped being blown up, with all his attendants, by the furious Protestant burghers of Perth. See COLLIER's Church History, vol. ii. p. 663, and 664. Then again the Protestants, in the Netherlands, formed a plot to blow up their governor, the Prince of Parma, with all the nobility and magistrates of those countries, when assembled in the city of Antwerp. But the Protestants did not always fail in their plots, nor were those who engaged in them obscure individuals. Fur, as we have seen in paragraph **310**, this very King James's father, the King of Scotland, was, in 1567, blown up by gunpowder and thereby killed. This was doing the thing effectually. Here was no warning given to anybody; and all the attendants and servants, of whatever religion and of both sexes, except such as escaped by mere accident, were remorselessly murdered along with their master. And who was this done by? By "blood-thirsty Catholics?" No; but by the lovers of the "Avangel," as the wretches called themselves; the followers of that KNOX, to whom a monument has just been erected, or is now erecting at Glasgow. The conspirators, on this occasion, were not thirteen obscure men, and those, too, who had received provocation enough to make men mad; but a body of noblemen and gentlemen, who really had received no provocation at all from MARY STUART, to destroy whom was more the object than it was to destroy her husband. Let us take the account of these conspirators in the words of WITAKER; and, let the reader recollect, that WITAKER, who published his book in 1790, was a parson of the Church of England, Rector of Ruhan-Lanyhorne in Cornwall, and that he was amongst those clergymen who were most strenuously opposed to the rites and ceremonies and tenets of the Catholic Church: but he was a truly honest man, a most zealous lover of truth and hater of injustice. Hear this staunch Church-Parson, then, upon the subject of this Protestant Gunpowder-Plot, concerning which he had made the fullest inquiry and collected together the clearest evidence. He (Vindication, of Mary, Queen of Scots, vol. iii. p. 235,) says, in speaking of the Plot, "The guilt of this wretched woman, ELIZABETH, and the guilt of that wretched man, CECIL, appear too evident, at last, upon the far of the whole. Indeed, as far as we can judge of the matter, the whole disposition of the murderous drama was this. The whole was originally planned and devised betwixt Elizabeth, Cecil, Morton and Murray; and the execution committed to Lethington, Bothwell, and Balfour; and Elizabeth, we may be certain, was to defend the original and more iniquitous part of the conspirators, Morton and Murray, in charging their own murder upon the innocent Mary." Did hell itself, did the devil, who was, as LUTHER himself says, so long the companion and so often the bed-fellow of this first "Reformer," ever devise wickedness equal to this Protestant plot? Let us hear no more, then, about the blood-thirstiness of the Catholic religion; and, if we must still have our 5th of November, let the "moral" disciples of KNOX, the inhabitants of "Modern Athens," have their tenth of February. Let them, too, (for it was Protestants that did the deed) have their 30th of January, the anniversary of the killing of the son of this same King James. Nobody knew better than James himself the history of his father's and his mother's end. He knew that they had both been murdered by Protestants, and that, too, with circumstances of atrocity quite unequalled in the annals of human infamy; and there fore he himself was not for

vigorous measures against the Catholics in general, on account of the plot; but love of plunder in his minions prevailed over him; and now began to blaze, with fresh fury, that Protestant Reformation spirit, which, at last, gave him a murdered son and successor, as it had already given him a murdered father and mother.

360. CHARLES I., who came to the throne on the death of his father, in 1625, with no more sense and with a stronger tincture of haughtiness and tyranny than his father, seemed to wish. to go back, in church matters, towards the Catholic rites and ceremonies, while his parliaments and people were every day becoming more and more puritanical. Divers were the grounds of quarrel between them, but the great ground was that of religion. The Catholics were suffering all the while, and especially those in Ireland, who were plundered and murdered by whole districts, and especially under WENTWORTH, who committed more injustice than ever had before been committed even in that unhappy country. But all this was not enough to satisfy the Puritans; and LAUD, the Primate of the Established Church, having done a great many things to exalt that church in point of power and dignity, the purer Protestants called for "another Reformation," and what they called "a thorough godly Reformation."

361 . Now, then, this Protestant Church and Protestant King had to learn that "Reformations," like comets, have tails. There was no longer the iron police of Old Bess, to watch and crush all gainsayers. The puritans artfully connected political grievances, which were real and numerous, with religious principles and ceremonies; and, having the main body of the people with them as to the former, while these were, in consequence of the endless change of creeds, become indifferent as to the latter, they soon became, under the name of "The Parliament," the sole rulers of the country; they abolished the Church and the House of Lords, and, finally brought, in 1649, during the progress of their "thorough godly Reformation," the unfortunate King himself to trial and to the block!

362. All very bad, to be sure; but all very natural, seeing what had gone before. If "some such man as Henry VIII.," were, as BURNET says he was, necessary to begin a "Reformation," why not "some such man" as CROMWELL to complete it? If it were right to put to death More, Fisher, and thousands of others, not forgetting the grand mother of Charles, on a charge of treason, why was Charles's head to be so very sacred? If it were right to confiscate the estates of the monasteries, and to turn adrift, or put to death, the abbots, priors, monks, friars, and nuns, after having plundered the latter of even the ear-rings and silver thimbles, could it be so very wrong to take away merely the titles of those who possessed the plundered property? And, as to the Protestant Church, if it were right to establish it on the ruins of the ancient Church, by German bayonets, by fines, gallowses and racks, could it be so very wrong to establish another newer one on its ruins by means a great deal milder? If, at the time we are now speaking of, one of "good Bess's" parsons, who had ousted a priest of Queen Mary, had been alive, and had been made to fly out of his parsonage-house, not with one of Bess's bayonets at his back, but on the easy toe of one of Cromwell's godly Bible-reading soldiers, could that parson have reasonably complained?

363. CROMWELL (whose reign we may consider as having lasted from 1649 to 1659), therefore, though he soon made the Parliament a mere instrument in his hands; though he was tyrannical and bloody; though he ruled with a rod of iron; though he was a real tyrant, was nothing more than the "natural issue," as "maiden" Betsy would have called him, of the "body" of the "Reformation." He was cruel towards the Irish;

he killed them without mercy; but, except in the act of selling 20,000 of them to the West Indies as slaves, in what did he treat them worse than Charles, to whom and to whose descendants they were loyal from first to last? And, certainly, even that sale did not equal, in point of atrociousness, many of the acts committed against them during the three last Protestant reigns; and, in point of odiousness and hatefulness, it fell far short of the ingratitude of the Established Church in the reign of Charles II.

364. But, common justice forbids us to dismiss the Cromwellian reign in this summary way; for, we are now to behold "Reformation" the second, which its authors and executors call "a thorough godly Reformation;" insisting that "Reformation" the first was but a half-finished affair, and that the "Church of England as by law established" was only a daughter of the "Old Whore of Babylon." This "Reformation" proceeded just like the former: its main object was plunder. The remaining property of the Church was now, as far as time and other circumstances would allow, confiscated and shared out amongst the "Reformers," who, if they had had time, would have resumed all the former plunder (as they did part of it) and have shared it out again! It was really good to see these "godly" persons ousting from the abbey-lands the descendants of those who had got them in "Reformation" the first, and, it was particularly good to hear the Church-bishops and parsons crying "sacrilege," when turned out of their palaces and parsonage-houses; ay, they who and whose Protestant predecessors had, all their lives long, been justifying the ousting of the Catholic bishops and priests who held them by prescription, and expressly by Magna Charta.

365. As if to make "Reformation" the second as much as possible like "Reformation" the first, there was now a change of religion made by laymen only; the Church clergy were calumniated just as the Catholic clergy had been; the bishops were shut out of Parliament as the abbots and Catholic bishops had been; the cathedrals and churches were again ransacked; Cranmer's tables (put in place of the altars) were now knocked to pieces; there was a general crusade against crosses, portraits of Christ, religious pictures, paintings on church windows, images on the outside of cathedrals, tombs in these and the churches. As the mass-books had been destroyed in "Reformation" the first, the church-books were destroyed in "Reformation" the second, and a new book, called the "DIRECTORY," ordered to be used in its place, a step which was no more than an imitation of Henry VIIIth's "CHRISTIAN MAN," and Cranmer's "PRAYER-BOOK." And, why not this "DIRECTORY"? If the mass-book, of nine hundred years' standing, and approved of by all the people, could be destroyed; surely, the Prayer-Book, of only one hundred years' standing, and never approved of by one half of the people, might also be destroyed. If it were quite right to put the former down, and that, too, as we have seen in paragraph 212, with the aid of the sword, wielded by German troops, it might naturally enough be thought, that it could not be very wrong to put the latter down with the aid of the sword, wielded by English troops, unless, indeed, there were, which we have not been told, something peculiarly agreeable to English men, in the cut of German steel.

366. It was a pair of "Reformations," as much alike as any mother and daughter ever were. The mother had a CROMWELL (see paragraph 157) as one of the chief agents in her work, and the daughter had a CROMWELL, the only difference in the two being, that one was a Thomas and the other an Oliver; the former Cromwell was commissioned to make "a godly reformation of errors, heresies and abuses in the church," and the latter was commissioned to make" a thorough godly reformation in the church;" the former Cromwell confiscated, pillaged and sacked the church, and just the same did the latter Cromwell, except that the latter did not, at the same time,

rob the poor, as the former had done; and, which seems a just distinction, the latter died in his bed, and the former, when the tyrant wanted his services no longer, died on a scaffold.

367. The heroes of "Reformation" the second were great Bible-readers, and almost every man became, at times, a preacher. The soldiers were uncommonly gifted in this way, and they claimed a right to preach as one of the conditions upon which they bore arms against the King. Every one interpreted the Bible in his own way: they were all for the Bible without note or comment. ROGER NORTH (a Protestant) in his "EXAMEN" gives an account of all sorts of blasphemies and of horrors committed by these people, who had poisoned the minds of nearly the whole of the community. Hence all sorts of monstrous crimes. At Dover a woman cut off the head of her child, alleging that, like Abraham , she had a particular command from God . A woman was executed at York, for crucifying her mother. She had, at the same time, sacrificed a calf and cock. These are only amongst the horrors of that "thorough godly Reformation;" only a specimen. And why not these horrors? We read of killings in the Bible; and, if every man be to be his own interpreter of that book, who is to say that he acts contrary to his own interpretation? Why not all these new and monstrous sects? If there could be one new religion, one new creed made, why not a thousand? What right had Luther to make a new religion, and then Calvin another new one, and Cranmer one differing from both these, and then "good Bess" to make an improvement upon Cranmer's? Were all these to make new religions, and were the enlightened soldiers of Cromwell's army to be deprived of this right? The former all alleged, as their authority, the "inspiration of the Holy Ghost." What, then, were Cromwell and his soldiers to be deprived of the benefit of this allegation? Poor "godly" fellows, why were they to be the only people in the world not qualified for choosing a religion for themselves and for those whom they had at the point of their bayonets? One of Cromwell's "godly" soldiers went, as NORTH relates, into the church of Walton-upon-Thames with a lantern and five candles, telling the people, that he had a message to them from God, and that they would be damned if they did not listen to him. He put out one light, as a mark of the abolition of the Sabbath; the second, as a mark of the abolition of all tithes and church dues; the third, as a mark of the abolition of all ministers and magistrates; and then the fifth light he applied to setting fire to a Bible, declaring that that also was abolished! These were pretty pranks to play; but, they were the natural, the inevitable, consequence of "Reformation" the first.

368. In one respect, however, these new reformers differed from the old ones. They did, indeed, make a new religion, and command people to follow it; and they inflicted punishments on the refractory; but, those punishments were beds of down compared with oak-planks, when viewed by the side of those inflicted by "good Bess" and her Church. They forbade the use of the Common Prayer-book in all churches, and also in private families; but, they punished the disobedient with a penalty of five pounds for the first offence, ten pounds for the second, and. with three years' imprisonment for the third; and did not hang them and rip out their bowels, as the Church of England sovereigns had done by those who said or heard mass. Bad as these fanatics were, wicked and outrageous as were their deeds, they never persecuted, nor attempted to persecute, with a hundredth part of the cruelty that the Church of England had done; ay, and that it did again, the moment it regained its power, after the restoration of Charles II., when it became more cruel to the Catholics even than it had been in the reign of "good Queen Bess "; and that, too, notwithstanding that the Catholics, of all

ranks and degrees, had signalized themselves, during the civil war, in every way in which it was possible for them to aid the royal cause.

369. This, at first sight, seems out of nature; but, if we consider, that this Church of England felt conscious, that its possessions did once belong to the Catholics, that the cathedrals and churches and the colleges, were all the work of Catholic piety, learning and disinterestedness; when we consider this, can we be surprised at these new possessors, who had got possession by such means, too, as we have seen in the course of this work; when we consider this, are we to be surprised, that they should do every thing in their power to prevent the people from seeing, hearing, and contracting a respect for those whom these new possessors had ousted? here we have the true cause of all the hostility of the Church of England clergy towards the Catholics. Take away the possessions, and the hostility would cease to-morrow; though there is, besides that, a wide, and, on their side, a very disadvantageous difference, between a married clergy, and one not married. The former will never have an influence with the people, any thing like approaching that of the latter. There is, too, the well-known superiority of learning on the side of the catholic clergy; to which may be added the notorious fact, that, in fair controversy, the Catholics have always triumphed. Hence the deep-rooted, the inflexible, the persevering and absolutely implacable hostility of this Established Church to the Catholics; not as men, but as Catholics. To what else are we to ascribe, that, to this day, the Catholics are forbidden to have steeples or bells to their chapels? They, whose religion gave us our steeples and our bells! To what else are we to ascribe, that their priests are, even now, forbidden to appear in the streets, or in private houses, in their clerical habiliments, and even when performing their functions at funerals? Why all this anxious pains to keep the Catholic religion out of sight? Men may pretend what they will, but these pains argue anything but consciousness of being right, on the part of those who take those pains. Why, when the English nuns came over to England, during the French revolution, and settled at Winchester, get a bill brought into Parliament (as the Church clergy did) to prevent them from taking Protestant scholars, and give up the bill only upon a promise that they would not take such scholars? Did this argue a conviction in the minds of the Winchester parsons, that Bishop North's was the true religion and that William of Wykham's was the false one? The Church parsons are tolerant enough towards the sects of all descriptions: quite love the Quaker, who rejects baptism and the sacrament; shake hands with the Unitarian, and allow him openly to impugn that, which they tell us in the Prayer-book, a man cannot be saved if he do not firmly believe in; suffer these, ay, and even JEWS, to present to church-livings, and refuse that right to Catholics, from whose religion all the church-livings came!

170. Who, then, can doubt of the motive of this implacable hostility, this everlasting watchfulness, this rancorous jealousy that never sleeps? The common enemy being put down by the restoration of Charles, the Church fell upon the Catholics with more fury than ever. This King, who came out of exile to mount the throne in 1660, with still more prodigality than either his father or grandfather, had a great deal more sense than both put together, and, in spite of all his well-known profligacy, he was, on account of his popular manners, a favourite with his people; but, he was strongly suspected to be a Catholic in his heart, and his more honest brother, JAMES, his presumptive heir, was an openly declared Catholic. Hence the reign of Charles II. was one continued series of plots, sham or real; and one unbroken scene of acts of injustice, fraud, and false-swearing. These were plots ascribed to the Catholics, but really plots against them. Even the great fire in London, which took place during this

reign, was ascribed to them, and there is the charge, to this day, going round the base of "the Monument," which POPE justly compares to a big, lying bully.

"Where London's column, pointing to the skies,
Like a tall bully, lifts its head, and lies."

The words are these: "This monument is erected in memory of the burning of this Protestant city, by the Popish faction, in Sept. AD. 1666, for the destruction of the Protestant religion and of old English liberty, and for the introduction of Popery and slavery. But the fury of the Papists is not yet satisfied." It is curious enough, that this inscription was made by order of Sir PATIENCE WARD, who, as ECHARD shows, was afterwards convicted of perjury. BURNET (whom we shall find in full tide by-and-by) says, that one HUBERT, a French Papist, "'confessed that he began the fire;" but HIGGONS (a Protestant, mind,) proves that HUBERT was a Protestant, and RAPIN agrees with Higgons! Nobody knew better than the King the monstrousness of this lie; but Charles II. was a lazy, luxurious debauchee. Such men have always been unfeeling and ungrateful; and this King, who had twice owed his life to Catholic priests, and who had, in fifty-two instances, held his life at the mercy of Catholics (some of them very poor) while he was a wandering fugitive, with immense rewards held out for taking him, and dreadful punishments for concealing him; this profligate King, whose ingratitude to his faithful Irish subjects is without a parallel in the annals of that black sin, had the meanness and injustice to suffer this lying inscription to stand. It was effaced by his brother and successor; but, when the Dutchman and the "glorious revolution" came, it was restored; and there it now stands, all the world, except the mere mob, knowing it to contain a most malignant lie.

371. By conduct like this, by thus encouraging the fanatical part of his subjects in their wicked designs, Charles II. prepared the way for those events by which his family were excluded from the throne for ever. To set aside his brother, who was an avowed Catholic, was their great object. This was, indeed, a monstrous attempt; but, legally considered, what was it more than to prefer the illegitimate Elizabeth to the legitimate Mary Stuart? What was it more, than to enact, that any "natural issue" of the former should be heir to the throne? And, how could the Protestant Church complain of it, when its great maker, Cranmer, had done his best to set aside both the daughters of Henry VIII., and to put Lady Jane Grey on the throne? In short, there was no precedent for annulling the rights of inheritance, for setting aside prescription, for disregarding the safety of property and of person, for violating the fundamental laws of the kingdom, that the records of the, "Reformation" did not amply furnish: and this daring attempt to set aside JAMES on account of his religion, might be truly said, as it was said, to be a Protestant principle; and it was, too, a principle most decidedly acted upon in a few years afterwards.

372. JAMES II. was sober, frugal in his expenses, economical! as to public matters, sparing of the people's purses, pious, and sincere; but weak and obstinate, and he was a Catholic, and his piety and sincerity made him not a match for his artful, numerous, and deeply-interested foes. If the existence of a few missionary priests in the country, though hidden behind wainscots, had called forth thousands of pursuivants, in order to protect the Protestant Church; if to hear mass in a private house bad been regarded as incompatible with the safety of that Church; what was to be the fate of that Church, if a Catholic King continued to sit on the throne! It was easy to see that the ministry, the army, the navy, and all the offices under the government, would soon contain few besides Catholics; and it was also easy to see that, by degrees, Catholics would be in the parsonages and in the episcopal palaces, especially as the King was as zealous as

he was sincere. The "Reformation" had made consciences to be of so pliant a nature, men had changed, under it, backward and forward so many times, that this last (the filling of the Church with Catholic priests and bishops) would, perhaps, amongst the people in general, and particularly amongst the higher classes, have produced but little alarm. But, not so with the clergy themselves, who soon saw their danger, and who, "passive" as they were, lost no time in preparing to avert it.

373. James acted, as far as the law would let him, and as far as prerogative would enable him to go beyond the law, on principles of general toleration. By this he obtained the support of the sectaries. But the Church had got the good things, and it resolved, if possible to keep them . Besides this, though the abbey lands and the rest of the real property of the Church and the poor, had been a long while in the peaceable possession of the then owners and their predecessors, the time was not so very distant but that able lawyers, having their opinions backed by a well organised army, might still find a flaw in, here and there, a grant of Henry VIII., Edward VI., and Old Betsy. Be their thoughts what they might, certain it is, that the most zealous and most conspicuous and most efficient of the leaders of the "Glorious Revolution" which took place soon afterwards, and which drove James from the throne, together with his heirs and his house, were amongst those whose ancestors bad not been out of the way at the time when the sharing of the abbey lands took place.

374. With motives so powerful against him, the King ought to have been uncommonly prudent and wary. He was just the contrary. He was severe towards all who opposed his views, however powerful they might be . Some bishops who presented a very insolent, but artful, petition to him, he sent to the Tower, had them prosecuted for a libel, and had the mortification to see them acquitted. As to the behaviour of the Catholics, prudence and moderation was not to be expected from them. Look at the fines, the burning-irons, the racks, the gibbets, and the ripping-knives of the. late reigns, and say if it were not both natural and just, that their joy and exultation should now be without bounds. These were, alas! of short duration, for a plan (we must not call it a plot) having been formed for compelling the King to give up his tolerating projects, and "to settle the kingdom," as it was called, the planners, without any act of Parliament, and without consulting the people in any way whatever, invited WILLIAM, the Prince of Orange, who was the Stadtholder of the Dutch, to come over with a Dutch army to assist them in "settling" the kingdom. All things having been duly prepared, the Dutch guards (who had been suffered to get from Torbay to London by perfidy in the English army) having come to the King's palace and thrusted out the English guards, the King, having seen one "settling" of a sovereign, in the reign of his father, and, apparently, having no relish for another settling of the same sort, fled from his palace and his kingdoms and took shelter in France, instead of fleeing to some distant English city and there rallying his people round him, which, if he had done, the event would, as the subsequent conduct of the people proved, have been very different from what it was.

375. Now came, then, the "glorious Revolution," or Reformation the third; and, when we have taken a view of its progress and completions we shall see how it, in its natural consequences, extorted, for the long-oppressed Catholics, that relief, which, by appeals to the justice and humanity of their persecutors, they had sought in vain for more than two hundred years.

LETTER XIII.

"GLORIOUS" REVOLUTION, OR REFORMATION THE THIRD.
THE DUTCH KING AND HIS DELIVERING ARMY.
THE "CRIMES" OF JAMES II., WITH ELUCIDATIONS.
PARLIAMENTARY PURITY.
THE PROTESTANT BISHOP, JOCELYN.
SIDNEY, AND OTHERS OF THE PROTESTANT PATRIOTS.
HABEAS CORPUS ACT.
SETTLEMENT OF AMERICAN COLONIES.

Kensington, 31st Oct., 1825.

MY FRIENDS,

376. AT the close of the last Letter, we saw a Dutchman invited over with an army to "settle" the kingdom; we saw the Dutch guards come to London and thrust out the English guards; we saw the King of England flee for his life, and take refuge in France, after his own army had been seduced to abandon him. The stage being now clear for the actors in this affair, we have now to see how they went to work, the manner of which we shall find as summary and as unceremonious as heart, however Protestant, could have possibly wished.

377. The King being gone, the Lord Mayor and Aldermen of London with a parcel of Common Councilmen, and such Lords and members of the late King Charles's Parliaments as chose to join them, went, in February 1688, without any authority from King, Parliament or people, and forming themselves into "a Convention," at Westminster, gave the Crown to William (who was a Dutchman) and his wife (who was a daughter of James, but who had a brother alive), and their posterity FOR EVER; made new oaths of allegiance for the people to take; enabled the new King to imprison, at pleasure, all whom he might suspect; banished, to ten miles from London, all Papists, or reputed Papists, and disarmed them all over the kingdom; gave the advowsons of Papists to the Universities; granted to their new Majesties excise duties, land-taxes and poll-taxes for the "necessary defence of the realm"; declared themselves to be the "Two Houses of Parliament as legally as if they had been summoned according to the usual form:" and this they called a "glorious Revolution," as we Protestants call it to this present day. After "Reformation" the second, and upon the restoration of CHARLES, the palaces and livings and other indestructible plunder, was restored to those from whom the "thorough godly" had taken it, except, however, to the Catholic Irish, who had fought for this King's father, who had suffered most cruelly for this King himself, and who were left still to be plundered by the "thorough godly," which is an instance of ingratitude such as, in no other case, has been witnessed in the world. However, there were, after the restoration, men enough to contend, that the episcopal palaces and other property, confiscated and granted away by the "'thorough godly," ought not to he touched; for that, if those grants were resumed, why not resume those of Henry VIII? Ay, why not indeed! Here was a question to put to the Church Clergy, and to the abbey-land owners! If nine hundred years of quiet possession, and Magna Charta at the back of it; if it were right to set these at nought for the sake of making only "a godly Reformation," why should not one hundred years of unquiet possession be set at nought for the sake of making "a

thorough godly Reformation"? How did the Church Clergy answer this question? Why, Dr. HEYLIN, who was Rector of Alresford in Hampshire, and afterwards Dean of Westminster, who was a great enemy of the "thorough godly," though not much less an enemy of the Catholics, meets the question in this way, in the Address, at the head of his History of Reformation the First, where he says, "that there certainly must needs be a vast disproportion between such contracts, as were founded upon acts of Parliament, legally passed by the King's authority, with the consent and approbation of the three estates, and those which have no other ground but the bare votes, and orders, of both Houses only. By the same logic it might be contended, that the two Houses alone have authority to depose a king."

378. This Church Doctor died a little too soon; or, he would have seen, not two Houses of Parliament, but a Lord Mayor of London, a parcel of Common Councilmen, and such other persons as chose to join them, actually setting aside one King and putting another upon the throne, and without any authority from King, Parliament, or people; he would have heard this called "a glorious" thing; and, if he had lived to our day, he would have seen other equally "glorious" things grow directly out of it; and, that notwithstanding BLACKSTONE had told the Americans, that a "glorious" revolution was a thing never to be repeated, Doctor Heylin would have heard them repeating, as applied to George III., almost word for word, the charges which the "glorious" people preferred against James II., though. they, naughty Yankees, knew perfectly well, that, after the "glorious" affair, a King of England (being a Protestant) could "do no wrong!" The Doctor's book, written to justify the "Reformation," did, as PIERRE ORLEANS tells us, convert James II. and his first wife to the Catholic religion; but his preface, above quoted, did not succeed so well with Protestants.

879. We shall, in due time, see something of the COST of this "glorious" revolution to the people; but, first, seeing that this revolution and the exclusion acts which followed it were founded upon the principle, that the Catholic religion was incompatible with public freedom and justice, let us see what things this Catholic King had really done, and in what degree they were worse than things that had been and that have been done under Protestant sovereigns. As William and his Dutch army have been called our deliverers, let us see what it really was, after all, that they delivered the people from; and, here, happily, we have the statute-book to refer to, in which there still stands the list of charges, drawn up against this Catholic King. However, before we examine these charges, we ought, in common justice, to notice certain things that James did not do. He did not, as PROTESTANT EDWARD VI. had done, bring German troops into the country to enforce a change of religion; nor did he, like that young Saint, burn his starving subjects with a hot iron on the breast or on the forehead and make them wear chains as slaves, as a punishment for endeavouring to relieve their hunger by begging. He did not, as PROTESTANT BETSY had done, make use of whips, boring-irons, racks, gibbets, and ripping-knives to convert people to his faith; nor did he impose even any fines for this purpose but, on the contrary, put, as far as he was able, an end to all persecution on account of religion: oh! but, I am forgetting: for this we shall find amongst his Catholic crimes: yes, amongst the proofs of his being a determined and intolerant Popish tyrant! He did not as PROTESTANT BETSY had done, give monopolies to his court-minions, so as to make salt, for instance, which, in his day, was about fourpence a bushel, fourteen pounds a bushel, and thus go on, till, at last, the Parliament feared, as they did in the time of "good Bess," that there would be a monopoly even of bread. These were

amongst the things which, being purely of Protestant birth, James, no doubt from "Catholic bigotry," did not do. And, now, let us come to the things which he really did, or, at least, which he was charged with having done.

380. Indictments do not generally come after judgment and execution; but, for some cause or other, the charges against James were postponed until the next year, when the crown had been actually given to the Dutchman and his wife. No matter: they came out at last; and there they stand, 12 in number, in Act 2, Sess. Wm. and M. chap. 2. We will take them one by one, bearing in mind, that they contained all that could even be said against this Popish King.

CHARGE I. "That he assumed and exercised a power of dispensing with and suspending laws, and the execution of laws, without consent of Parliament."-- That is to say, he did not enforce those cruel laws against conscientious Catholics, which had been enacted in former reigns. But, did not Betsy and her successor James I. dispense with, or suspend, laws, when they took a composition from recusants? Again, have we ourselves never seen any suspension of or dispensing with laws without consent of Parliament! Was there, and is there, no dispensing with the law, in employing foreign officers in the English army, and in granting pensions from the Crown to foreigners? And was there no suspension of the law, when the Bank stopped payment in 1797? And, did the Parliament give its assent to the causing of that stoppage? And, has it ever given its assent to the putting of foreigners in offices of trust, civil, or military, or to the granting of pensions from the Crown to foreigners? But, did James ever suspend the Habeas Corpus Act? Did his Secretaries of State ever imprison whom they pleased, in any gaol or dungeon that they pleased; let the captives out when they pleased? Ah! but what he and his Ministers did in this way (if they did any thing) was all done "without consent of Parliament;" and who is so destitute of discrimination as not to perceive the astonishing difference between a dungeon with consent of Parliament, and a dungeon without consent of Parliament!

CHARGE II. "That he committed and prosecuted divers worthy prelates, for humbly petitioning to be excused from concurring to the said assumed powers." He prosecuted them as libellers, and they were acquitted. But he committed them before trial and conviction; and, why? because they refused to give bail. And they contended that it was tyranny in him to demand such bail! Oh, heavens! How many scores of persons have been imprisoned for a similar refusal, or for want of ability to give bail on a charge of libel, during the last eight years! Would not Mr. CLEMENT have been imprisoned, the other day only, if he had refused to give bail, not on a charge of libel on a King upon his throne, but on a Protestant professor of humanity? And, do not six ACTS, passed by a Parliament, from which tyrannical Catholics are so effectually excluded, declare to us free Protestants, that this has always been the law of the land! And, is that all? Oh, no! For we may now be banished for life not only for libelling a King on his throne, but for uttering anything that has a TENDENCY to bring either House of Parliament into contempt!

CHARGE III. "That he issued a commission for erecting a Court, called the Court of Commissioners for Ecclesiastical Causes." Bless us! What! was this worse than "good Betsy's" real inquisition, under the same name? And, good God! have we no court of this sort now? And was not (no longer than about nine months ago) SARAH WALLIS (a labourer's wife of Hargrave in Norfolk), for having "brawled" in the churchyard, sentenced by this Court to pay 24l. 0s. 5d. costs; and was she not sent to gaol, for non-payment; and must she not have rotted in gaol, having not a shilling in the world, if humane persons had not stepped forward to enable her to get out by the Insolvent Act? And, cannot this Court now, agreeably to those of young Protestant Saint Edward's Acts, in virtue of which the above sentence was passed, condemn any one who attempts to fight in a church-yard, to have one ear cut off, and, if the offender "have no ears" (which speaks volumes as to the state of the people under PROTESTANT EDWARD) , then to be burnt with a hot iron in the cheek, and to be excommunicated besides? And, did not the revolution Protestants, who drew up the charges against James, leave this law in full force for our benefit?

CHARGE IV. "That he levied money for and to the use of the Crown by pretence of prerogative, for other time, and in other manner, than was granted by Parliament.." It is not pretended that he levied more money than was granted; but he was not exact as to the time and manner. Did the Parliament grant Betsy the right to raise money by the sale of monopolies, by compositions with offenders, and by various other of her means? But did we not lately hear of the hop-duty payment being shifted from one year to an other? Doubtless, with wisdom and mercy; but I very much doubt of James's ever having, in this respect, deviated from strict law to a greater amount, seeing that his whole revenue did not exceed (taking the difference in the value of money into account) much above sixteen times the amount of a good year's hop duty.

CHARGE V. "That he kept a standing army, in time of peace, without consent of Parliament." Ah! without consent of Parliament, indeed! That was very wicked. There were only seven or eight thousand men, to be sure, and such a thing as a barrack had never been heard of. But, without consent of Parliament! Think of the vast difference between the prick of a bayonet coming without consent of Parliament, and that of one coming with such consent! This King's father had been dethroned and his head had been cut off by an army kept up with consent of Parliament, mind that, however. Whether there were, in the time of James, any such affairs as that at Manchester, on the memorable 16th of August, 1819, history is quite silent; nor are we told, whether any of James's priests enjoyed military half-pay; nor are we informed, whether he gave half-pay, or took it away, at his pleasure, and without any "consent of Parliament": so that, as to these matters, we have no means of making a comparison. We are in the same situation with regard to foreign armies; for we do not find any account whatever of James's having brought any into England, and especially of his having caused foreign generals to command even the English troops, militia and all, in whole districts of England.

CHARGE VI. "That he caused several good subjects," being Protestants, to be disarmed, at the same time that papists were both armed and employed contrary to law." SIX ACTS disarmed enough of the King's subjects: ay, but, then, these were not "good" ones; they wanted a reform of the House of Commons. And besides, there was "law" for this. And, if people will not see what a surprising difference there is between being disarmed by law and disarmed by proclamation, it really is useless to spend valuable Protestant breath upon them.

CHARGE VII, "That he violated the freedom of election of Members to serve in Parliament." Oh, monstrous! Ay, and "notorious as the sun at noonday!" Come up, shades of sainted Perceval and Castlereagh; come, voters of Sarum and Gatton; assemble, ye sons of purity of election, living and dead, and condemn this wicked King for having "violated the freedom of elections"! But, come, we must not suffer this matter to pass off in the way of joke. Protestant reader, do you think that this violating of "the freedom of elections for Members to serve in Parliament" was a crime in King James? He is not accused of having done all these things with his own tongue, pen, or hands; but with having done them with the aid of "divers wicked ministers and councillors." Well; but do you, my Protestant readers, think that this violation of the freedom of elections was a bad thing, and a proof of the wicked principles of Popery? If you do, take the following facts, which ought to have a place in a work like this, which truth and honour and justice demand to be recorded, and which I state as briefly as I possibly can. Know, then, and be it for ever remembered, THAT Catholics have been excluded from the throne for more than a hundred years: THAT they have been excluded from the English Parliament ever since the reign of Charles II., and from the Irish Parliament ever since the 22d year of George III.: THAT therefore, the throne and the Parliament were filled exclusively with Protestants in the year 1809: THAT in 1779, long and long after Catholics had been shut out of the English Parliament, the House of Commons resolved, "That it is HIGHLY CRIMINAL for any Minister or Ministers, or any other servant of the Crown in Great Britain, directly or indirectly, to make use of the power of his office, in order to influence the election of Members of Parliament, and that an attempt to exercise that influence is an attack upon the dignity, the honour, and the independence of Parliament, an infringement of the rights and the liberties of the people, and an attempt to sap the basis of our free and happy constitution."-- THAT, in 1809, Lord Castlereagh, a Minister and a Privy Councillor, having been charged before the House with having had something to do about bartering a seat in the House, the House on the 25th of April of that year, resolved, "That while it was the bounden duty of that House to maintain at all times a jealous guard upon its purity, and not to suffer any attempt upon its privileges to pass unnoticed, the attempt, in the present instance (that of Lord Castlereagh and Mr. Reding), not having been carried into effect, that House did not think it then necessary to proceed to any criminating resolutions respecting the same." -- THAT on the 11th of May, 1809 (only sixteen days after this last resolution was passed), WILLIAM MADOCKS, Member for Boston, made a charge in the following words, to wit: "I affirm, then, that Mr. DICK purchased a seat in the House of Commons, for the Borough of Cashel, through the agency of the Honourable Henry Wellesley, who acted for, and on behalf of, the Treasury; that, upon a recent question of the last importance, when Mr. DICK had determined to vote according to his conscience, the noble Lord, CASTLEREAGH, did intimate to that gentleman the necessity of either his voting with the Government, or resigning his seat in that House; and that Mr. DICK, sooner than vote against his principles, did make choice of the latter alternative, and vacate his seat accordingly; and that to this transaction, I charge the right honourable gentleman, Mr. PERCEVAL, as being privy, and having connived at it. This I engage to prove by witnesses at your bar, if the House will give me leave to call them ." -- THAT, having made his charge, Mr. MADOCKS made a motion for INQUIRY into the matter;-- THAT, after a debate, the question was put to the vote: -- THAT there were three hundred and ninety-five Members in the House, all Protestants, mind:-- THAT (come up and hear it, you accusers of James and the Catholic religion!) there were EIGHTY-FIVE for an inquiry, and THREE HUNDRED AND TEN against it! -- THAT, this same PROTESTANT Parliament, did, in 1819, on the MOTION OF THAT VERY SAME LORD CASTLEREAGH, pass a law by which any of us may now be BANISHED FOR LIFE for publishing anything having a TENDENCY to bring THAT VERY HOUSE into CONTEMPT! -- THAT this LORD CASTLEREAGH was Secretary of State for Foreign Affairs.-- THAT he continued to be the leading Minister in the House of Commons (exclusively Protestant) until the close of the session of 1822, which took place on the 6th of

August of that year.-- THAT, on the 12th of that same month of August, he cut his own throat, and killed himself, at North Cray, in Kent; that a coroner's jury declared him to have been insane, and that the evidence showed, that he had been insane for several weeks, though he had been the leader of the House up to the 6th of August, and though he was, at the moment when he killed himself, Secretary of State for Foreign Affairs, and also temporary Secretary for the Home Department and that of the Colonies! -- THAT his body was buried in Westminster Abbey-church, mourned over by his colleagues, and that, as it was taken out of the hearse, a great assemblage of the people gave loud and long-continued cheers of exultation.

CHARGE VIII. "That he promoted prosecutions in the Court of King's Bench for matters and things cognizable only in Parliament; and that he did divers other arbitrary and unlawful things." That is to say, that he brought before a jury matters which the Parliament wished to keep to itself! Oh, naughty and arbitrary King! to have jury-trial for the deeds of Parliament-men instead of letting them try, themselves! As to the divers other such arbitrary things, they not being specified, we cannot say what they were.

CHARGE IX. "That he caused juries to be composed of partial, corrupt, and unqualified persons, who were not freeholders." Very bad, if true, of which, however, no proof, and no instance, is attempted to be given. One thing, at any rate, there were no special juries in those days. They, which are "appointed" by the Master of the Crown-office, came after Catholic Kings were abolished. But, not to mention that Protestant Betsy dispensed with juries altogether, when she pleased, and tried and punished even vagabonds and rioters by martial law, do we not now, in our own free and enlightened and liberal Protestant days, see many men transported for seven years WITHOUT ANY JURY AT ALL? Ay, and that, too, in numerous cases, only for being more than 15 minutes at a time out of their houses (which the law calls their castles) between sunset and sunrise? Ah! but this is with consent of Parliament! Oh! I had for gotten that. That's an answer.

CHARGE X. "That excessive bail hath" (by the Judges of course) "been required of persons committed in criminal cases, to elude the benefit of the laws made for the liberty of the subject."

CHARGE XI. "That excessive fines have been imposed, and illegal and cruel punishments inflicted."

CHARGE XII. "That he had made promises and grants of fines before conviction and judgment on the party."

381. I take these three charges together. As to fines and bail, look at Protestant Betsy's and Protestant James I.'s reigns. But, coming to our own times; I, for having expressed my indignation at the flogging of English local-militia men, in the heart of England, under a guard of German troops, was two years imprisoned in a felon's gaol, and, at the expiration of the time, had to pay a fine of a thousand pounds, and to give bail for SEVEN YEARS, myself in three thousand pounds, with two sureties in two thousand pounds each. The" Convention," who gave us the "Protestant Deliverer" does not cite any instances; but, while we cannot but allow, that the amiable lenity of our Protestant bail-works appeared most conspicuously, in 1822, in the 500*l.* bail taken of the Protestant Right Reverend Father in God, Percy Jocelyn, Bishop of Clogher, brother of the late and uncle of the present Earl of RODEN, which Protestant Bishop stood, on the oaths of seven witnesses, accused of (in conjunction with JOHN MOVELLY, a

soldier of the Foot Guards in London) an unnatural offence, and which Protestant Bishop finally fled from trial; though our Protestant bail-works appeared so gentle and so amiable here, and exacted only a bail of five hundred pounds, with two sureties in two hundred pounds each, from a PROTESTANT BISHOP (charged, on the oaths of seven witnesses, with such an enormous offence), whose income had, for many years, been about twelve or fifteen thousand a year; though our Protestant bail-works appeared so amiable, so dove-like in this case, and also in the case of the Soldier (partner of the Bishop), from whom bail of 200*l.* with two sureties in 100*l.* each was taken, and the Soldier, who was at once let out of prison, did, in imitation of the Bishop, flee from trial, though he was an enlisted soldier, and though his regiment was stationed in London: -- That, while we cannot but allow, that our Protestant bail-works were characterised by gentleness and mildness in these memorable cases; yet they have not always been in the same dove-like mood; for, THAT, in the year 1811 , JAMES BYRNE, a Catholic, who had been. a coachman in the Jocelyn family, having asserted that this same Protestant Bishop attempted to commit an unnatural offence on him, the said James Byrne was imprisoned at once, before indictment, and was, from his prison, brought to trial as a criminal: -- THAT, at this trial, the Protestant Bishop aforesaid, declared on his OATH, that Byrne had charged him FALSELY: -- THAT Byrne was sentenced, for this alleged libel, proved on the oath of this Protestant Bishop, to be imprisoned in a felon's gaol for two years, to be three times publicly whipped, and, at the end of the two years, to give bail for life, in 500*l.* himself, with two sureties in 200*l.* each: -- THAT James Byrne was carried into the gaol, having been first flogged half to death: -- THAT, at the end of two years, Byrne lay several months more in gaol for want of sureties: -- THAT this Protestant Bishop was, at this time, Bishop of FERNS, and that he was, after this, promoted to be Bishop of CLOGHER, and made a Commissioner of the Board of Education. So that our Protestant bail-works have not always been so very gentle. Nay, if we were to look into our gaols, even at this moment, we might find a man who has hardly a penny in the world, whose crime was libel, who has a fine of 600*l.* to pay, who has more than 500*l.* bail to find, with two sureties FOR LIFE, whose period of imprisonment has expired years ago, and who may, not only possibly but probably, end his life in that gaol from inability to pay his fine and to find the requisite bail. Until, therefore, some zealous admirer of the "glorious Revolution" will be pleased to furnish us with something specific as to the bail and fines in James's reign, we ought, in prudence, to abstain from even any mention of this charge against the unfortunate King; for, to talk of them in too censorious a strain, may possibly receive a no very charitable interpretation. -- But there had been illegal and cruel punishments in his reign. What punishments? There had been no people burnt, there had been no racks, as there had been in the reigns of Protestants Betsy and James 1. Why, Sir John Cox Hippesley, in a petition to Parliament, a year or two ago, asserted that the tread-mill was "cruel and illegal." Yet it stands, and that, too, for very trifling offences. Sir John might be wrong; but this shows that there might also be two opinions about punishments in the time of James; and we have to lament that those who brought in "the deliverer" were so careless as to specify none of those instances, which might have enabled us to make, as to this matter, a comparison between a Catholic King and a Protestant one. -- But, he granted away fines before the conviction of the party. Indeed! What, then, we have, in our happy day, under a Protestant King, no fines granted before-hand to informers of any sort? Ah! but this is with consent of Parliament! I had forgotten that again. I am silenced!

382. These were the offences of King James; these were the grounds, as recorded in the statute-book of the "glorious Revolution," made, as" the same Act expresses, to "deliver this kingdom from Popery and arbitrary power, and to prevent the Protestant religion from being subverted;" and, seeing that this was immediately followed by a perpetual exclusion of Catholics, and those who should marry with Catholics, from the throne, it is clear that this was a revolution entirely Protestant, and that it was an event directly proceeding from the "Reformation." This being the case, I should now proceed to take a view of the consequences, and particularly of the costs of this grand change, which was "Reformation" the third. But there are still to notice some things, which lying history and vulgar prejudice urge against this unfortunate Catholic King, who has been asserted to have been the adviser of his late brother, in all those deeds which have been deemed wicked, and especially in the putting of Lord RUSSELL and ALGERNON SIDNEY to death for high treason.

383. Alas! how have we been deluded upon this subject! I used to look upon these as two murdered men. A compulsion to look into realities, and discard romance, has taught me the contrary. The Protestants were, in the reign of Charles II., continually hatching Popish plots, and, by contrivances the most diabolical, bringing innocent Catholics to the scaffold and the gibbet; and, in the course of these their proceedings, they were constantly denying the prerogative of the King to pardon, or to mitigate the punishment of, their victims. But, at last, the King got real proof of a Protestant plot! The King was ill, and a conspiracy was formed for setting aside his brother by force of arms, if the King should die. The King recovered, but the Protestant plot went on, The scheme was, to rise in arms against the Government, to pay and bring in an army of Protestants from Scotland, and, in short, to make now that sort of "Reformation" the third, which did not take place till, as we have seen, some years afterwards. In this Protestant plot, RUSSELL and SIDNEY were two great leaders. Russell did not attempt to deny that he had had a part in the conspiracy; his only complaint was, that the indictment was not agreeable to law; but, he was told, which was true, that it was perfectly agreeable to numerous precedents in cases of trials of Popish plotters! When brought to the place of execution, Russell did not deny his guilt, but did not explicitly confess it. That part of his sentence, which ordered his bowels to be ripped out, while he was yet alive, and his body to he quartered, was, at the intercession of his family, remitted by the King, who, in yielding to their prayer, cuttingly said, "My Lord Russell shall find, that I am possessed "of that prerogative, which, in the case of Lord Stafford, "he thought fit to deny me."

384. As to SIDNEY, he had been one of the leading men in the "thorough godly" work of the last reign, and had even been one of the Commissioners for trying Charles I. and bringing him to the block, though, it is said by his friends, he did not actually sit at the trial. At the restoration of Charles II., he had taken refuge abroad. But, having confessed the errors of his younger years, and promised to be loyal in future, this King, under the guidance of a Popish brother, pardoned him, great as his offences had been. Yet, after this, he conspired to destroy the Government of that King, or, at the very least, to set aside that brother, and this, too, observe, by force of arms, by open rebellion against the King who had pardoned him, and by plunging into all the horrors of another civil war of that country, which he had before assisted to desolate. If any man ever deserved an ignominious death, this SIDNEY deserved his . He did not deny, he could not deny, that the conspiracy had existed, and that he was one of its chiefs. He had no complaint but one, and that related to the evidence against him. There was only one parole witness, to his acts, and, in cases of high treason, the law

of England required two. And, here it was that a blush might (if it were possible) have been raised upon the cheeks of these revilers of Popery; for, this very law, this law, which has saved the lives of so many innocent persons; this law which ought to engrave gratitude to its author on the heart of every Englishman; this law came from that very Popish QUEEN MARY, whom artful knaves have taught generations of thoughtless people to call "the bloody," while, too, she was the wife of, and had for coadjutor, that PHILIP II. whom to hold up as a sanguinary Popish tyrant has been a great object with all our base deluders.

385. Seeing, however, that SIDNEY had such a strong attachment to this Popish law, and that there really was but one witness against him; seeing that he could not bear the thought of dying without two witnesses against him, the Crown lawyers (all Protestants, mind, who had abjured the "damnable errors of Popery") contrived to accommodate him with a couple, by searching his drawers and making up a second witness out of his own papers! It was in vain, that he rested upon this flaw in the proceedings; all men knew that hundreds of Catholics had suffered death upon evidence slight, indeed, compared with that against him: men were not to be amused with this miserable special plea; and all men of sense and justice concurred in the opinion, that he received substantial justice, and no more.

386. So much for the "good old cause, for which Hampden died in the field and Sidney on the scaffold." What credulous creatures we have been; and who more so than myself! Ay, but these Protestant patriots on]y contemplated insurrection and the introduction of foreign armies. And with what more was O'QUIGLY charged, only about twenty seven years ago? With what more were the SHEARSES and Lord EDWARD FITZGERALD and WATT and DOWNIE and DESPARD, and scores of others charged? And were THISTLEWOOD, INGS, BRUNT and TIDD charged with more? Oh, no: but with a great deal less; and they suffered, not for compassing the death of the King, but of his Ministers, a crime made high treason, for the first time, in our own Protestant days, and by a Parliament from which tyrannical Popish people are wholly excluded. There was one KEILING, who, from a Protestant plotter, became an informer, and he, in order to fortify his own evidence, introduced his brother-in-law to the conspirators, in order to betray them, and bring them to justice. Well, but have we not had our CASTLESES, our OLIVERS and our EDWARDSES, and has not Mr. BROUGHAM said in the House of Commons, that while "there are such men as INGS in the world, there must be such men as EDWARDS "? However, no historian, Protestant as he may have been, enemy as he may have been of Charles's and James's memory, ever had the impudence to impute to either of them the having employed people to instigate others to commit acts of high treason, and then bringing those others to the block, while they rewarded the instigators.

387. It is said, and I think truly, that Charles II. was, at one time, in pecuniary treaty with the King of France, for the purpose of re-establishing the Catholic Church in England. Well, had he not as much right to do this, as Edward VI. had to bring over German troops to root out that ancient Church which had been established for 900 years, and which was guaranteed to the people by Magna Charta? And, if doing this by means of French troops were, intended by Charles, can that be complained of by those who approve of the bringing in of Dutch troops to "settle" the kingdom? After all, however, if it were such a deadly sin for a popishly-advised King of England to be in a pecuniary treaty with the King of France, which treaty neither King nor Catholics ever acted upon, what was it in the Protestant and Catholic-hating Sidney, and the younger Hampden and Armstrong and others to be real and bonâ fide and money-

touching pensioners of that same King of France, which fact has become unquestionable from Dalrymple's Memoirs, page 315 of Appendix?

388. But, now, if James be to be loaded with all those which have been called the *bad* deeds of his brother's reign, we cannot, with common justice, refuse him the merit of the good deeds of that reign. This reign gave us, then, the Act of Habeas Corpus, which Blackstone calls "the second great charter of English liberty." There are many other acts of this reign, tending to secure the liberties and all the rights of the people; but, if there had been only this one Act, ought it not alone to have satisfied the people, that they had nothing to apprehend from a popishly-inclined King on the throne? Here these "Popish tyrants," Charles and James, gave up, at one stroke of the pen, at a single writing of Charles's name, all prerogatives enabling them, as their predecessors had been enabled, to put people into prison, and to keep them there in virtue of a mere warrant, or order, from a Minister. And, was this a proof of that arbitrary disposition, of which we hear them incessantly accused? We are always boasting about this famous act of Habeas Corpus: but, never have we the gratitude to observe, that it came from those against whom Russell and Sidney conspired, and the last of whom was finally driven from his palace by the Dutch guards, in 1688.

389. Then, again, was this act ever suspended during the reigns of these Popish kings? Never; not even for a single day. But, the moment the "glorious Revolution," or Reformation the third came, the Dutch "deliverer" was, by the Protestant "Convention," whose grand business it was to get rid of "arbitrary power"; the moment that this "glorious" affair had taken place, that moment was the Dutch "deliverer" authorised to put in prison, and to keep there, any Englishman that he or his Ministers might suspect! But, why talk of this? We ourselves have seen this "second great charter of English liberty" suspended for seven years at a time; and, besides this, we have seen the King and his Ministers authorised to imprison any one whom they chose to imprison, in any gaol that they chose, in any dungeon that they chose; to keep the imprisoned person from all communication with friends, wives, husbands, fathers, mothers and children; to prevent them from the use of pen, ink, paper and books; to deny them the right of being confronted with their accusers; to refuse them a specification of their offence and the names of their accusers; to put them out of prison (if alive) when they pleased, without any trial; and, at last, to hold them to bail for good behaviour, and that too, mind, still without stating to them the names of the witnesses against them, or even the nature of their offence! All this we have seen done in our own dear Protestant times, while our Parliament House and our pulpits ring with praises of the "glorious Revolution" that "delivered us from Popery and slavery."

390. There was another great thing, too, done in the reigns of these Popish kings; namely, the settling of the Provinces (now States) of America. Virginia had been attempted to be settled under "good Bess," by that unprincipled minion, Sir WALTER RALEIGH, who, in the next reign, lost, on the scaffold, that life which he ought to have lost thirty years before; but the attempt wholly failed. A little, and very little, was done, in the two succeeding reigns. It was not until that of Charles II. that charters and patents were granted, that property became real, and that consequent population and prosperity came. This was a great event; great in itself, and greater in its consequences, some of which consequences we have already felt, others we are now feeling, but others, and by far of greater moment, we have yet to feel.

391. All these fine colonies were made by this popishly-inclined King, and by his really Popish brother. Two of them, the Carolinas, take their name from the King himself; another, and now the greatest of all, New York, from the King's brother, who was duke of the city of that name in Old England. These were the men who planted these the finest and happiest colonies that the sun ever lighted and warmed. They were planted by these Popish people; from them, from their "mere motion," as the law calls it, came those charters and patents, without which those countries might, to this hour, have been little better than a wilderness. From these Popish kings the colonies came. By whom were they lost? Not by abused and calumniated Papists, at any rate. Our Popish ancestors had, at different times, made England mistress of different parts of France. Protestant Edward VI. lost Boulogne, and Protestant Betsy bartered away Calais and the county of Oye for 100,000 crowns, and thus put her Protestant seal to England's ever lasting expulsion from the Continent of Europe! After one more Protestant reign, inglorious beyond all example, came these two Popish kings, who planted countries which were more than a compensation for the European loss. Then came that " lorious" affair, and it furnished all those principles, by which, at the end of only about seventy years, this compensation was wrested from us; and not only this, but by which was created a power, a great maritime power, at the very name of which, affect what they may, Englishmen, once so high and daring, now grow pale.

392. We shall, before the close of the next Letter, and after we have taken a view of the torments inflicted on the Catholics (Irish and English) in the reigns of William, Anne, and the Georges, trace this "Reformation" the fourth, directly back to "Reformation" the third; we shall show, that, in spite of the fine reasoning of BLACKSTONE, the deeds of the "Convention" were things to be imitated; we shall find that the List of Charges against James, drawn up by the "Lord Mayor of London, Aldermen, Common-Councilmen, and others," was as handy in 1776 as it had. been in 1688; we shall find this Reformation the third producing, in its progress, that monster in legislation, that new and heretofore unheard-of species of tyranny, called Bills of Pains and Penalties, which are of pure Protestant origin; and we shall finally see, that this famous and "glorious" affair, all Protestant as it was, did, at last, bring, though it crossed the Atlantic to fetch it, that dawn of liberty, which the Catholics began to behold at the end of a night of cruel slavery, which had lasted for more than two hundred years. But, I must not even here, lest it should not occur to my mind again, omit to notice, and to request the reader to notice, that, of the above mentioned colonies, the only ones that wholly abstained from religious persecution, the only ones that, from the first settling, proclaimed complete religious liberty, were those granted by patent to the Duke of YORK (afterwards the Catholic James II.) to Lord BALTIMORE, a Catholic nobleman, and to WILLIAM PENN, who suffered long imprisonment for his adherence to this Popish King. We shall, by-and-by, find all the colonies cordially united in declaring the character of a Protestant King to be "marked by every act that may define a tyrant;" but, this much we know, at any rate, that the colonies granted to and settled by Catholics, and by PENN, an adherent of James, were the only ones that had, from first to last, proclaimed and strictly adhered to, complete freedom as to matters of religion; and that, too, after the Protestants, at home, had, for more than a hundred years, been most cruelly and unremittingly persecuting the Catholics.

LETTER XIV.

WILLIAM'S TRIUMPH OVER JAMES AND THE CATHOLICS.
A "NO-POPERY" WAR REQUIRES MONEY TO CARRY IT ON.
BURNET'S SCHEME OF BORROWING AND FUNDING.
ORIGIN OF BANKS AND BANK NOTES.
HEAVY TAXES, EXCISE, SEPTENNIAL BILL.
ATTEMPT TO TAX THE AMERICANS.
AMERICANS REVOLT IN THE FACE OF THE DOCTRINES OF BLACKSTONE.
THEIR CHARGES AGAINST GEORGE III.

Kensington, 31st Dec., 1825.

MY FRIENDS,

393. WE have seen, in the foregoing Letter, that Reformation the Third, commonly called the "Glorious Revolution," grew directly out of Reformation the Second; and we are now to see Reformation the Fourth, commonly called "the American Revolution," grow directly out of Reformation the Third; and we are, before we get to the end of this present Letter, to see how severely the English people have been scourged, and how much more severely they are likely still to be scourged, in consequence of these several "Reformations," which have all proceeded from Reformation the First, as naturally as the stem and the branches of the tree proceed from the root.

394. We have seen, that King James and his family were set aside, because they were Catholics; and we are to bear that in mind, not forgetting at the same time, that ALFRED the Great was a Catholic, and that those Kings of England, who really conquered France, and won that title of King of France, which George III. gave up, were also Catholics. But we are now particularly to bear in mind, that James, an Englishman , was set aside, that William, a Dutchman, was made King in his stead, and that James's heirs were set aside, too, because he and they were Catholics. Bearing these things constantly in mind, we shall now see what took place, and how the " PROTESTANT REFORMATION" worked, till it produced the DEBT, the BANKS, the STOCK-JOBBERS, and the American Revolution.

395. James found faithful adherents in his IRISH subjects, who fought and bled in his cause with all that bravery and disregard of life of which so many Irishmen have given proof. But, with the aid of Dutch and German armies, paid by England, the "deliverer" finally triumphed over James and the Irish, and the whole kingdom submitted to the sway of the former. It is hardly necessary to say, that the Catholics were now doomed to suffer punishments heretofore unknown; and that, if their faith still existed in the kingdom, it could scarcely be owing to any thing short of the immediate superintendence of Providence. The oppressions which they had had to endure under former sovereigns were terrible enough; but now began a series of acts against them, such as the world never heard of before. I shall, further on, have to give a sketch, at least, of these acts, which we shall find going on increasing in number and in severity, and, at last, presenting a mass of punishments which, but to think of makes one's blood run cold, when, all of a sudden, in the 18th year of GEORGE III.,

came the American Revolution, which grew out of the English Revolution, and (mark the justice of God!) which produced the first relaxation in this most dreadfully penal code.

396. But now did the American Revolution grow out of the Dutch Deliverer's, or "Glorious" Revolution? A very pertinent and important questions my friends, and one that it is my duty to answer in the fullest and most satisfactory manner; for this points to the very heart of my subject. We shall, by-and-by, see the American Revolution producing wonderful events; and therefore we must, with the greatest possible care, trace it to its true source; especially as, in all human probability, this nation has yet to receive from that quarter blows far heavier than it has ever yet had to sustain.

397. The "Protestant Deliverer" had, in the first place, brought over a Dutch army for the English nation to support. Next, there were the expenses and bloodshed of a civil war to endure for the sake of the "deliverance from Popery." But these, though they produced suffering enough, were a mere nothing compared to what was to follow; for this was destined to scourge the nation for ages and ages yet to come, and to produce, in the end, effects that the human mind can hardly contemplate with steadiness.

398. King James had, as we have seen, been received in France. Louis XIV. treated him as King of England, Scotland and Ireland. Willam hated Louis for this; and England had to pay for that hatred. All those who had assisted, in a conspicuous manner, to bring in the "deliverer," were now embarked in the same boat with him. They were compelled to humour and to yield to him. They, historians say, wished to give the crown solely to his wife, because, she being James's daughter, there would have been less of revolution in this than in giving the crown to an utter alien. But he flatly told them, that he "would not hold his power by the apron strings;" and, the dispute having continued for some time, he cut the matter short with them by declaring, that if they did not give him the crown, he would go back to Holland, and leave them to their old sovereign! This was enough: they gave him the crown without more hesitation; and they found, that they had got not only a "deliverer," but a master at the same time.

399. The same reasons that induced a submission to this conduct in the "deliverer," induced the same parties to go cordially along with him in his war against France. There was James in France; a great part of his people were still for him; if France were at peace with England, the communication could not be cut off. Therefore, war with France was absolutely necessary to the maintenance of William on the throne; and, if he were driven from the throne, what was to become of those who had obtained from him, as the price of their services in bringing him in, immense grants of Crown lands and various other enormous emoluments, none of which they could expect to retain for a day, if James were restored? Besides this, there was the danger, and very great danger too, to their own estates and their lives; for, though that which they did was, and is, called a "glorious Revolution," it would, if James had been restored, have been called by a very different name; and that name would not have been an empty sound; it would have been applied to very practical purposes; and, the chances are, that very few of the principal actors would have wholly escaped. And there were, moreover, the possessors of the immense property of the Church, founded and endowed by our fathers. The confiscation of this was not yet of so ancient a date as to have been forgotten. Tradition is very long-lived. Many and many, then alive, knew all the story well. They had heard their grandfathers say, that the Catholic Church kept all the poor; that the people were then better off; and, they felt, the whole

of the people felt, that England had lost by the change. Therefore, in case of the restoration of James, the possessors of Church property, whether they were lay or clerical, might reasonably have their fears.

400. Thus, all these deeply interested parties, who were also the most powerful parties in the kingdom, were for a war with France, which they rightly regarded as absolutely necessary to the keeping of William on the throne, and to the quiet enjoyment of their great possessions, if not actually to the safety of their lives. This war ought, therefore, to have been, called, "a war to preserve Church-property, Crown-lands, and other great emoluments, to their present "possessors." But, those who make wars, like those who make confiscations of property belonging to the Church and poor, generally know how to give them a good name; and, accordingly, this was called, and proclaimed, as a war, "to preserve the Protestant Religion, and to keep out Popery and slavery." It was a real "no-popery" war; and, though attended with the most dreadful consequences to the nation, it answered all the purposes of its inventors. The history of this war, as an affair of fighting, is of little con sequence to us. It was, indeed, attended, in this respect, with disgrace enough; but, it answered the great object of its inventors. It did not hurt France; it did not get rid of James and his son; but, it made the English people IDENTIFY their old King and his son with the FOREIGN ENEMIES of England! That was what the inventors of the war wanted; and that they completely got. It was in vain that King James protested, that he meant no harm to England; it was in vain that he reminded the people, that he had been compelled to flee to France; in vain his declarations, that the French only wanted to assist in restoring him to his rights. They saw him in France; they saw the French fighting for him and against England: that was quite sufficient. Men do not reason in such a case; and this the inventors of this war knew very well.

401 . But, though passion muddles the head, though even honest feeling may silence the reasoning faculties, the PURSE is seldom to be quieted so easily: and, this war, though for "the preservation of the Protestant religion, and for keeping out Popery and slavery," soon began to make some most dreadful tugs at this most sensitive part of those accoutrements that almost make part and parcel of the human frame. The expenses of this famous "no-popery" war . . . . Good God! what has this kingdom not suffered for that horrid and hypocritical cry! . . . . The expenses of this famous "no-popery" war were enormous. The taxes were, of course, in proportion to those expenses; and the people, who already paid more than four times as much as they had paid in the time of James, began not only to murmur, but to give no very insignificant, signs of sorrow for having been "delivered!" France was powerful; the French king liberal and zealous; and the state of things was ticklish. Force, as far as law, and the suspension of law, could go, was pretty fairly put in motion; but, a scheme was, at last, hit upon, to get the money, and yet not to tug so very hard at that tender part, the purse.

402. An Act of Parliament was passed, in the year 1694, being the 5th year of William and Mary, chap. 20, the title of which Act is in the following words; words that every man should bear in mind; words fatal to the peace and the happiness of England; words which were the precursor of a scourge greater than ever before afflicted any part of God's creation. -- "An Act for granting to their Majesties several rates and duties upon Tonnage of Ships and Vessels, and upon Beer, Ale, and other Liquors, for securing certain RECOMPENCES and ADVANTAGES in the said Act mentioned, to such persons as shall VOLUNTARILY ADVANCE the sum of fifteen hundred thousand pounds, towards carrying on the war against France." This Act lays

certain duties, sufficient to pay the interest of this sum of 1,500,000*l*. Then it points out the manner of subscribing; the mode of paying the interest, or annuities; and then it provides, that, if so much of the whole sum be subscribed by such a time, the subscribers shall have a charter, under the title of "THE GOVERNOR AND COMPANY OF THE BANK OF ENGLAND"!

403. Thus arose loans, funds, banks, bankers, bank notes, and a NATIONAL DEBT; things that England had never heard or dreamed of, before this war for "preserving" the Protestant religion as by law established; things without Which she had had a long and glorious career of many centuries. and had been the greatest and happiest country in the world; things which she never would, and never could, have heard of, had it not been for what is audaciously called the "REFORMATION," seeing that to lend money at interest; that is to say, for gain; that is to say, to receive money for the use of money; seeing that to do this was contrary, and still is contrary to the principles of the Catholic Church; and, amongst Christians, or professors of Christianity, such a thing was never heard of before that which is impudently called "THE REFORMATION." The Reverend Mr. O'CALLAGHAN, in his excellent little work, which I had the honour to re-publish last winter, and which ought to be read by every man, and especially every young man, in the kingdom, has shown, that the ancient philosophers, the Fathers of the Church, both Testaments, the Canons of the Church, the decisions of POPE and Councils, all agree, all declare, that to take money for the use of money is sinful. Indeed no such thing was ever attempted to be justified, until the savage Henry VIII. had cast off the supremacy of the POPE. JEWS did it; but, then Jews had no civil rights. They existed only by mere sufferance. They could be shut up, or banished, or even sold, at the King's pleasure. They were regarded as a sort of monsters, who professed to be the lineal descendants and to hold the opinions of those who had murdered the SON OF GOD AND OF MEN. They were not permitted to practise their blasphemies openly. If they had synagogues, they were unseen by the people. The horrid wretches them selves were compelled to keep out of public view on Sun days, and on Saints' days, They were not allowed to pollute with their presence the streets or the roads of a Christian country, on days set apart for public devotion. In degraded wretches like these USURY, that is, receiving money for the use of money, was tolerated, just for the same cause that incest is tolerated amongst dogs.

404. How far the base spirit of usury may now have crept in, even amongst Catholics themselves, I know not, nor is it of importance as to the matter immediately before me. It is certain, that, before the "Reformation" there was no such thing known amongst Christians as receiving money, or profit in any shape, merely for the use of money. It would be easy to show, that mischiefs enormous are inseparable from such a practice; but, we shall see enough of those mischiefs in the end. Suffice it, for the present, that this national usury, which was now invented for the first time, arose out of the "Reformation."

405 . This monstrous thing, the usury, or funding system, was not only a Protestant invention; not only arose out of the "Reformation"; not only was established for the express purpose of carrying on a war for the preservation of this Church of England against the efforts of Popery; but, the inventor, BURNET, was the most indefatigable advocate for the "Reformation" that had ever existed. So that the thing was not only invented by Protestants to do injury to Catholics; it was not only intended by them for this purpose; it was not only destined, by the wisdom and justice of God to be a scourge, to be the most terrible of all scourges, to the Protestants themselves; it was

not only destined to make, at last, the "Church by law established" look at the usurers with no very quiet feelings; the thing was not only thus done and thus destined to operate; but, the instrument was the fittest, the very fittest, that could have been found in the whole world,

406. BURNET, whose first name, as the Scotch call it, was GILBERT, was, in the first place, a POLITICAL CHURCH PARSON; next, he was a MONSTROUSLY LYING HISTORIAN; next, he was a SCOTCHMAN; and, lastly, he RECEIVED THE THANKS OF PARLIAMENT for his "History of the Reformation"; that is to say, a mass of the most base falsehoods and misrepresentations that ever were put upon paper. So that, the instrument was the very fittest that could have been found on earth. This man had, at the accession of JAMES II., gone to Holland, where he became a Secretary to WILLIAM (afterwards the "deliverer"); and where he corresponded with, and "aided the Glorious Revolutionisers" in England; and, in 1689, the year after the "deliverance," the "deliverer" made him BISHOP OF SALISBURY, as a reward for his "glorious revolution "services!

407. This was the fittest man in the world to invent that which was destined to be a scourge to England. Though become a Bishop, he was still a most active politician; and, when the difficulty of carrying on the "no-popery" war arose, and when those fears, mentioned in paragraph **401**, began to be powerful this Bishop of the "law-established Church" it was, who invented, who advised, and who, backed by the "deliverer," caused to be adopted the scheme of borrowing, of mortgaging the taxes, and of pawning the property and labour of future generations. Pretty "deliverance"! Besides sparing the purses of the people, and quieting their discontents on account of taxes, this scheme had a further and still more important object in view; namely, to make all those who had money to lend wish to see the new king and new dynasty and all the grants and emoluments of the "glorious revolution" folks upheld! That was the permanent object of this "no-popery" project.

408. The case was this, and we ought clearly to under stand it, seeing that here is the true origin of all our present alarms, dangers and miseries. James II., and his son, had been set aside, because they were Catholics: a "glorious revolution" had been made; the great makers of it had immense possessions, which had been public or church possessions. If James were restored, all these would he taken from them, together with all the titles of nobility, all the bishoprics, and, in short, every thing granted by the "deliverer." And as the "deliverer" was liable to die, it was necessary to these great possessors and "glorious" actors to take care, if possible, that James, or his son should not be the successors of "the deliverer." Acts of Parliament were passed to provide against this danger; but still, experience had shown that Acts of Parliament were in some cases, of but little avail, when the great body of the people, feeling acutely, were opposed to them. Therefore, something was wanted to bind great numbers of the people fast to the new dynasty. The cry of "no-popery" had some power; but it had not power sufficient to weigh down that which, in later times, CASTLEREAGH had the insolence to call, the "ignorant impatience of taxation;" and for which impatience the English were, in former times, always remarkable.

469. The "deliverer," and all those who had brought him in, together with all those who had been fattened or elevated by him, were, as I said before, embarked in the same boat; but the great body of the people were not yet thus embarked. Indeed, very few of them, comparatively, were thus embarked. But, if all, or a great part, of those who had money to lend, could, by the temptation of great gain, he induced to lend

their money on interest to the Government; if they could be induced to do this, it was easy to see that all this description of persons would then be embarked in the same boat, too; and that they, who must necessarily be a class having great influence in the community, would be amongst the most zealous supporters of the "deliverer," and the "glorious" aiders, abettors, and makers of the "revolution" which had just taken place.

410. For these purposes this funding-system was invented. It had the twofold object, of raising money to carry on the "no-popery" war; and, of binding to the "no-popery" Government all those persons who wished to lend money at high interest; and these were, as is always the case, the most greedy, most selfish, least public-spirited, and most base and slavish and unjust part of the people. The scheme, which was quite worthy of the mind of the Protestant Bishop BURNET, answered its purposes: it enabled the "deliverer" to carry on the "no-popery" war; it bound fast to the "deliverer" and his bringers-in all the base and selfish and greedy and unfeeling part of those who had money. The scheme succeeded in effecting its immediate object; but, good God! what a scourge did it provide for future generations! What troubles, what shocks, what sufferings it had in store for a people, whose rulers, in an evil hour, resorted to such means for the purpose of causing to be trampled under foot those whose only crime was that of adhering to the faith of their fathers!

411. The sum at first borrowed was a mere trifle. It deceived by its seeming insignificance. But, it was very far from being intended to stop with that trifle. The inventors knew well what they were about. Their design was to mortgage, by degrees, the whole of the country, all the lands, all the houses, and all other property, and even all labour, to those who would lend their money to the State The thing soon began to swell at a great rate; and before the end of the "glorious" no-popery war, the interest alone of the DEBT, the annual interest, amounted to 1,310,942*l.* a-year, which, observe, was a greater sum than the whole of the taxes had yearly amounted to in the reign of the Catholic James II.! So that here were taxes laid on for ever; mind that: here were, on account of this grand no-popery affair; merely on account of this "glorious revolution," which was expressly made for the purpose of getting rid of a Catholic King: here were additional taxes, laid on for ever, to a greater amount than the whole of the taxes raised by that Catholic King! Thus does the justice of God work! The treatment of the Catholics, at this time, was truly horrible; the main body of the English people either approved of this treatment, or winked at it: this debt-scheme was. invented by a Protestant Bishop for the purpose of utterly extirpating the Catholic religion: and, that religion still lives in the kingdom; nay, there are in the kingdom a greater number of Catholics than there are persons of any one other religion; while the scheme, the crafty, the cunning, the deep scheme, has, from its ominous birth, been breeding swarms of Jews, Quakers, usurers of every description, feeding and fattening on the vitals of the country; till, at last, it has produced what the world never saw before; starvation in the midst of abundance! Yes, verily; this is the picture we now exhibit to the world: the Law-Church Parsons putting up, in all the churches, thanksgiving for a plenteous harvest; and, the main mass of the labouring people fed and clad worse than the felons in the gaols!

412. However, we must not anticipate. We shall, further on, see something of the probable ultimate effects of this dreadful scheme. At present we have to see how it, together with the "glorious revolution," out of which it arose, led to and produced the AMERICAN REVOLUTION, "Reformation" the fourth, by which two things were accomplished; FIRST, the lopping off of a large and valuable part of the dominions of England; SECOND, the creating of a new mercantile and naval power, capable of

disputing with her that dominion of the sea, which has, for so many ages, been her chief glory, and without possessing which she must become a second-rate power in Europe . These were the things which were accomplished by the American Revolution; and, therefore, let us now see what it was that produced that revolution; or, rather, let us see how it grew directly out of the "glorious revolution" and its "no-popery" wars and debts. .

413. BURNET's contrivance did very well for present use: it made the nation deaf to the voice of all those who foreboded mischief from it: made all those who were interested in the funds advocates for taxation; the deep scheme set the rich to live upon the poor, and made the former have no feeling for those who bore the burden of the taxes: in short, it divided the nation into two classes, the tax-payers and the tax-eaters, and these latter had the Government at their back. The great protection of the people of England always had been, that they could not be taxed without their own consent.! This was always, in Catholic times, the great principle of the English Government; and, it is expressly and most explicitly asserted in MAGNA CHARTA, which was the work of a Catholic Archbishop of Canterbury, more than of anybody else. But, how was it to be expected, that this grand principle would be maintained, when a large part of the rich people themselves lived upon the taxes? When a man's next-door neighbour received the taxes paid by that man? When, in short, the community was completely divided, one part having a powerful interest in upholding that which was oppressive and ruinous to the other part?

414. Taxes, of course, went on increasing, and the debt went on in the same way. The Protestant interest demanded more wars, and brought on a couple of civil wars. Taxation marched on with dreadful strides. The people did not like it. At the "glorious revolution" it had been settled and enacted, that there should be a new Parliament called every THREE YEARS at least: and this had been held forth as one of the great gains of the "glorious revolution." Another "great gain" was, that no pensioner and no placeman were to sit in the House of Commons. These things were enacted; they were laws of the land; they were held forth to the people as great things, gained by "Glorious." This last Act was soon repealed; and placemen and pensioners have sitten in the House of Commons ever since! But the other Act, the Act securing the people a fresh choice every three years, at least; that was a vital law. That law was, in the new state of things, a state of taxes and debts; a state of things which demanded new taxes almost every year: in such a state of things frequent and new Parliaments, new choosings at short intervals, were absolutely necessary to give the people a chance, even so much as a chance, of avoiding oppressive taxation, and oppression, indeed, of every sort. It was, in short, the only means of protection that was left to the people.

415. Yet, to uphold the new system it was necessary to demolish even this barrier of liberty and property; and in the year 1715, being the first year of the reign of George 1., chap. xxxviii., this law, this vital law, this solemn compact between the Protestant dynasty and the people, was repealed and for ever abolished; and the THREE YEARS were changed for SEVEN; and that, too, observe, by the very men whom the people had chosen to sit only for THREE YEARS! Yes, men chosen by the people to sit for three years enacted that they would sit for SEVEN; that they themselves would sit for seven; and that those who had chosen them, together with their descendants for ever, should have no choice at all, unless they voted for men who might, at the King's pleasure, sit for seven years.

416. It is useless for us to feel indignation and rage. They can do us no good. We shall do well to keep ourselves cool. But, we ought to bear in mind, that this thing, which has scourged us so famously, was not done by Catholics; that they had no hand in it; nay, that it was not only done under the new Protestant dynasty; but that this thing also; this thing, the like of which the world never had and never has heard of, that this thing also was done from hostility to the religion of our fathers! Good God! What has not this nation suffered, and what has it not yet to suffer, for this hostility! There is hardly one great calamity, or disgrace, that has befallen England during the last three hundred years which we do not clearly trace to this fatal source.

417. But this SEPTENNIAL BILL; this measure, which is perfectly matchless in its nature, and which has led to such dreadful effects; this is a thing which we must have in its original black and white; and we must have every word of it too; for here we have a complete "no-popery" law; and of this law we are tasting the effects to the present hour, and we shall taste them for a long while yet to come. The following are the words, all the words, of this memorable Act.

418. "Whereas in and by an Act of Parliament made in the sixth year of the reign of their late Majesties King William and Queen Mary (of ever blessed memory), intitulated, An Act for the frequent meeting and calling of Parliaments: It was among other things enacted, that from thenceforth, no Parliament whatsoever, that should at any time then after be called, assembled or held, should have any continuance longer than for three years only at the farthest, to be accounted from the day on which by the writ of summons the said Parliament should be appointed to meet: And whereas it has been found by experience, that the said clause hath proved very grievous and burthensome, by occasioning much greater and more continued expense in order to elections of Members to serve in Parliament, and more violent and lasting heats and animosities among the subjects of this realm than were ever known before the said clause was enacted; and the said Provision, if it should continue, may probably at this juncture, WHEN A RESTLESS AND POPISH FACTION ARE DESIGNING and endeavouring to renew the rebellion within this kingdom, and an invasion from abroad be destructive to the peace and security of the Government. Be it enacted by the King's most excellent Majesty, by and with the advice and consent of the Lords Spiritual and Temporal, and Commons, in Parliament assembled, and by the authority of the same, That this present Parliament, and all Parliaments that shall at any time hereafter be called, assembled or held, shall and may respectively have continuance for seven years and no longer, to be accounted from the day on which by the writ of summons this present Parliament hath been, or any future Parliament shall be appointed to meet, unless this present or any such Parliament hereafter to be summoned, shall be sooner dissolved by his Majesty, his heirs, or successors."

419. So, here it is again! The "restless Popish faction" was at work! So that the rights, the most precious rights, of the whole of the people, were to be taken away merely on account of the designs and wishes of a "Popish faction"! What harm could a mere "faction" do at an election? The truth is, these pretences were false: the people, the great body of the people, smarting under the lash of enormous taxation, became disaffected towards the new order of things; they were strongly disposed to revert to their former state: it was suspected, and, indeed, pretty well known, that they would, at the next election, have chosen, almost everywhere, members having the same sentiments: and, therefore, it was resolved, that they should not have the power of doing it. However, the deed was done; we have felt the effects of it from that day to this; and we have now to remember, that even this terrible curtailment of English

liberty we owe to the hostility to the religion of our fathers; that religion, during the dominance of which, there was always a new House of Commons every time the Parliament was assembled: that religion, along with which were bound up the people's civil and political rights; that religion, the followers of which, while it was predominant, never heard of Parliaments for seven years or for three years or even for one year; but who, as often as they saw a Parliament called, saw a Commons' House chosen for that one session, and for no more.

420. After the passing of the Septennial Act, the people would, of course, lose nearly all the control that they had ever had with regard to the laying on of taxes and to the expending of the public money. Accordingly taxes went on increasing prodigiously. The EXCISE-SYSTEM which had had a little beginning in former Protestant reigns, and the very name of which had never been heard of in Catholic times, now assumed somewhat its present form; and the "castles" of Englishmen became thenceforth things to be visited by excisemen. Things went on in this way, until the reign of George III., when, by means of "no-popery" wars, and other measures for "preserving the Protestant Religion as by law established," the debt from 1,500,000*l.* had swelled up to 146,682,844*l.* The yearly interest of it had swelled up to 4,840,821*l.*, which was about four times as much as the whole annual amount of the taxes in the reign of the Popish James II.! And the whole of the yearly taxes had swelled up to 8,744,682*l.* That is to say. about eight times as much as James had raised yearly on this same no-popery" people!

421. Now, though men will do much in the way of talk against "Popery," or against many other things; they are less zealous and active, when it comes to money. The nation most sensibly felt the weight of these burdens; and the burdens received no alleviation from the circumstance of their being most righteously merited. The people looked back with aching hearts to former happy days; and the nobility and gentry began to perceive, with shame and fear, that, already, their estates were beginning to pass quietly from them (as SWIFT had told them they would) into the hands of the Jews, Quakers, and other money-changers, created by the "no-popery" war, and by the scheme of the Scotchman, BURNET. But, it was now too late to look back; and yet, to look forward to this certain, and not very slow, ruin, was dreadful, and especially to men of ancient family and by no means destitute of pride. Fain would they, even at that time, have applied a sponge to the score brought against them by BURNET's tribes. But this desire was effectually counteracted by the same motive which led to the creation of the debt; the necessity of embarking, and of keeping embarked, great masses of the money-owners in the same boat with the Government.

422. in this dilemma, namely, the danger of touching the interest of the debt, and the danger of continuing to pay that interest, a new scheme was resorted to, which, it was hoped, would obviate both these dangers . It was, to tax the American colonies, and to throw a part, first, and, perhaps the whole, in the end, of the "no-popery" debt, upon their shoulders! Now, then, came "Reformation" the fourth, having for cause the measures necessary to affect the "glorious revolution," taking the principles and the manner of that revolution as its example in these respects, beginning with a "CONVENTION," assembled without authority of King, Parliament, or People; proceeding with CHARGES against the king, with making it HIGH TREASON TO ADHERE TO HIM; and ending with setting aside his authority, and extinguishing his rights and those of his family FOR EVER! Ay, but besides all this, bringing the first dawn of relief to the longsuffering Catholics of England, Scotland, and Ireland! What it was that these, our countrymen, had to suffer for the crime of adhering to the

religion of their and our fathers, I shall leave, to state further on; but I now proceed to show how this "Reformation" the fourth commenced. and proceeded.

423. The Septennial gentlemen proceeded, at first, very slowly in their attempts to shift the pressure of the debt from their own shoulders to that of the Americans. They sent out tea to pay a tax; they imposed a stamp duty on certain things in the colonies; but they had a clever, a sharp-sighted, and a most cool and resolute and brave people to deal with. The Americans had seen debts, and funds, and taxation, and abject submission, creep, by slow degrees, over the people of England; and they resolved to resist, at once, the complicated curse. The money people there were not, like those in England, the owners of stock and funds. They were not, as the money people of England were, embarked in the same boat with the government: if they had been, there would have been more hesitation on the subject of resistance; if they had been entangled in BURNET's awful web, the Americans might, at this day, have been hardly known in the world; might have been a parcel of bands of poor devils, doomed to toil for haughty and insolent masters. Happily for them, the Scotch Bishop's deadly trammels had not reached them; and, therefore, they, at once, resolved not to submit to the Septennial commands.

424. It is curious enough that they should, as the "glorious" people had done, call themselves Whigs! But the Septennial people were Whigs too; so that there were now Whigs resisting Whigs. A Whig means, in England, one who approves the setting of JAMES and his heirs aside. A Whig means, in America, one who approves of the setting of GEORGE and his heirs aside. The English Whigs called a convention; so did those of America. The English Whigs published a declaration, containing, as we have seen in paragraph **380**, CHARGES against JAMES: so did those of America against GEORGE. The charges against JAMES were twelve in number. This is a favourite number. with Whigs; for the American Whigs had twelve charges against GEORGE. We have seen, in paragraph **380**, what Protestants accused a Popish King of; and it is but fair for us to see what Protestants and Catholics too accused a Protestant King of. BLACKST0NE, in justifying the "glorious" affair, took good care to say, that the like was never to take place again; and the Septennial gentlemen declared, and, I think, enacted, that the King in future (being, of course, a Protestant) could do no wrong. Now, the Americans seemed to think it hard, that they should thus be positively forbidden to do what was so "glorious" in Englishmen. BLACKSTONE had told them, that, to justify another revolution, all the same circumstances must exist: not a part of them, but the whole of them. The King must not only endeavour to subvert the laws; he must not only commit acts of tyranny; but he must be a Catholic, and must have a design to overthrow the Protestant religion and he must, into the bargain, have abdicated his authority by going out of the kingdom. So that, according to this lawyer, there never could, by any possibility, be a "glorious" revolution again, seeing that two essential circumstances must, in any future case, be wanting, as no Catholic was ever to be king again, and as no king was ever to do wrong any more.

425. But, alas! these American Whigs did not listen to BLACKSTONE, though he had talked so piously about the "dark ages of monkish ignorance and superstition." They thought, nay, they said, that a Protestant King might do wrong, and had done wrong. They thought, or at least, they said, that a king might abdicate his authority, not only without going out of the country, but also without ever having been in it! In short, they drew up, *à la* "glorious," charges against their Protestant King, his late Majesty; and as the charges against James II. are found in an Act of Parliament, so the

charges against George III. are found in an Act of Congress, passed on the memorable 4th of July, 1776. These charges were as follows:

426. "The history of the present King of Great Britain is a history of repeated injuries and usurpations, all having in direct object the establishment of an absolute tyranny over these states. To prove this, let facts be submitted to a candid world.

I. He has refused to pass laws for the accommodation of large districts of people, unless those people would relinquish the right of representation in the Legislature -- a right inestimable to them, and formidable to tyrants only.

II. He has called the legislative bodies at places unusual, uncomfortable, and distant from the repository of their public records, for the sole purpose of fatiguing them into compliance with his measures.

III. He has dissolved representative houses, repeatedly, For opposing with firmness his invasions on the rights of the people.

IV. He has obstructed the administration of justice, by refusing his assent to laws for establishing judiciary powers.

V. He has made judges dependent on his will alone, for the tenure of their offices, and the amount and payment of their salaries.

VI. He has created a multitude of new offices, and sent hither swarms of officers to harass our people, and eat their substance

VII. He has kept among us, in times of peace, standing armies, without the consent of our legislatures.

VIII. He has affected to render the military independent of, and superior to, civil power.

IX. He has combined with others to subject us to a jurisdiction foreign to our constitution, and unacknowledged by our laws; giving his assent to their acts of pretended legislation.

X. He has imposed taxes on us without our consent.

XI. He has deprived us, in many cases, of the benefits of trial by jury.

XII. He has ABDICATED government here, by declaring us out of his protection, and waging war against us. In every stage of these oppressions, we have petitioned for redress in the most humble terms; our repeated petitions have been answered by repeated injury. A prince, whose character is thus marked by every act which defines a tyrant, is unfit to be the ruler of a free people."

427. Now, justice to the memory of the late King demands, that we expressly assert, that here are some most monstrous exaggerations, and especially at the close; but, does not that same justice demand of us, then, to be cautious how we give full credit to the charges made against James II.? However, the question with us, at the present moment, is, not whether the grounds of one of these revolutions were better than those of the other: but, whether the last revolution grew directly out of the former; and, of the affirmative of this question no man, who has read this Letter, can, I think, entertain a doubt.

428. I should now proceed to show, that the French Revolution, or" Reformation" the fifth, grew immediately out of the American Revolution; and then to sum up the consequences; but I am at the end of my paper.

WILLIAM COBBETT

LETTER XV.

AMERICAN "REVOLUTION" BROUGHT RELIEF TO CATHOLICS.
PERSECUTIONS UP TO THE REIGN OF JAMES II..
LAW-CHURCH OPPOSES LIBERTY OF CONSCIENCE.
HORRIBLE PENAL CODE.
SOFTENED, AT LAST, FROM MOTIVES OF FEAR.
FRENCH REVOLUTION, PRODUCES A SECOND SOFTENING OF TUE CODE.
PENAL CODE, AS IT NOW STANDS.
RESULT OF THE "REFORMATION," AS FAR AS RELATES TO RELIGION.

Kensington, 31st Jan., 1826.

MY FRIENDS,

429. WE have now traced the "Reformation," in its deeds, down from the beginning, in the reign of Henry VIII., to the American Revolution; and, all that remains is, to follow it along through the French Revolution, and unto the present day. This is what I propose to do in the present Letter. In the next Letter I shall bring under one view my proofs of this proposition; namely, that, before the event called the" Reformation," England was more powerful and more wealthy, and that the people were more free, more moral, better fed and better clad, than at any time since that, event. And, when I have done that, I shall, in the second volume, give a LIST of all abbeys, priories and other parcels of property, which, according to MAGNA CHARTA, belonged to the Church and the poor, and which were seized on by the Reformation-people. I shall range these under the heads of COUNTIES, and shall give the names of the parties to whom they were granted by the confiscators.

430. The American Revolution, which, as we have seen, grew directly out of those measures which had been adopted in England to crush the Catholics and to extinguish their religion for ever, did, at its very outset, produce good to those same Catholics by inducing the English government to soften, for the sake of its own safety, that PENAL CODE, by which they had so long been scourged. But, now, before we speak of the immediate cause, and of the manner and degree of this softening, we must have a sketch of this HORRIBLE CODE; this monster in legislation, surpassing, in violation of the dictates of humanity and justice, any thing else that the world has ever seen existing under the name of law.

431. We have seen how cruelly the Catholics were treated under "good Queen Bess" and James I.; we have seen how they were fined, mulcted, robbed, pillaged, and punished in body; but, though the penal code against them was then such as to make every just man shudder with horror, we think it, then, gentleness, when we look at its subsequent ferocity. We have seen how Catholics were fined, harassed, hunted, robbed, pillaged, in the reign of "good Bess." We have seen. the same in the reign of her immediate successor, with this addition, that Englishmen were then handed over to be pillaged by Scotchmen. We have seen, that Charles I., for whom they afterwards fought against Cromwell, treated them as cruelly as the two former. We have seen Charles II. most ungratefully abandon them to the persecutions of the Church by law established; and, during this reign we have seen that the Protestants had the baseness, and the King the meanness, to suffer the lying inscription to be put on the MONUMENT on Fish-street Hill, in the city of London, though Lord CLARENDON

- 172 -

(whose name the Law-Church holds in so much honour) , in that work which the University of Oxford publishes at the "Clarendon Press," expressly says (p. 348, continuation), that a Committee of the House of Commons, "who were very diligent and solicitous to make the discovery, never were able to find any probable evidence, that there was any other cause of that woeful fire than the displeasure of Almighty God." What infamy, then, to charge the Catholics with it; what an infamy to put the lying inscription on the pillar; what an act of justice, in James II., to efface it; what a shame to William to suffer it to be restored; and what is it to us, then, who now suffer it to remain, without petitioning for its erasure!

432. But, it was after James II. was set aside that the PENAL CODE grew really horrible. And here it is of the greatest consequence to the cause of truth, that we trace this code to its real authors; namely, the Clergy of the Established Church . This is evident enough throughout the whole of this Church's history; but, until the reign of James II., the sovereign was of the Church religion, so that the persecutions appeared to come from him or her. But now, when the King was for softening the penal code; when the King was for toleration; now the world saw who were the real persecutors: and this is a matter to be fully explained and understood, before we come to a more minute account of the code, and to the causes which finally led to its, in great part, abolition.

433. JAMES II. wished to put an end to the penal code; he wished for general toleration; he issued a proclamation, suspending all penal laws relating to religion; and GRANTING A GENERAL LIBERTY OF CONSCIENCE TO ALL HIS SUBJECTS. This was his OFFENCE . For this he and his family were SET ASIDE FOR EVER! No man can deny this. The clergy of the Church set themselves against him. Six of the bishops presented to him an insolent petition against the exercise of this his prerogative, enjoyed and exercised by all his predecessors. They led the way in that opposition, which produced the "glorious revolution," and they were the most active and most bitter of all the foes of that unfortunate King. , whose only real offence was his wishing to give liberty of conscience to all his subjects, and, by showing respect to whose mortal remains (displaced by the French revolutionists) our present King has done himself very great honour.

434, Now, we are going to see a sketch of this terrible code. It must be a mere sketch; two hundred Letters like this would not contain the WHOLE of it. It went on increasing in bulk and in cruelty, from the Coronation of Elizabeth till nearly twenty years after that of George III., till events came, as we shall see, and broke it up. It consisted, at last, of more than a hundred Acts of Parliament, all made for the express purpose of punishing men, because, and only because, they continued faithfully to adhere to the religion, in which our as well as their fathers had lived and died, during a period of nine hundred years! The code differed, in some respects, in its application with regard to England and Ireland, respectively.

435. In ENGLAND this code -- I. stripped the Peers of their hereditary right to sit in Parliament. --II. It stripped gentlemen of their right to be chosen Members of the Commons' House. -- III. It took from all the right to vote at elections, and, though Magna Charta says, that no man shall be taxed without his own consent, it double-taxed every man who refused to abjure his religion, and thus become an apostate. -- IV. It shut them out from all offices of power and trust, even the most insignificant. -- V. It took from them the right of presenting to livings in the Church, though that right was given to Quakers and Jews. -- VI. It fined them at the rate of 20*l.*, a month for

keeping away from that Church, to go to which they deemed apostacy. --VII. It disabled them from. keeping arms in their houses for their defence, from maintaining suits at law, from being guardians or executors, from practising in law or physic, from travelling five miles from their houses, and all these under heavy penalties in case of disobedience. -- VIII. If a married woman kept away from Church, she forfeited two-thirds of her dower, she could not be executrix to her husband, and might, during her husband's life-time, be imprisoned, unless ransomed by him at 10*l*. a month. -- IX. It enabled any four justices of the peace, in case a man had been convicted of not going to church, to call him before them, to compel him to abjure his religion, or, if he refused, to sentence him to banishment for life (without judge or jury), and, if he returned, he was to suffer death. -- X. It enabled any two justices of the peace to call before them, without any information, any man that they chose, above sixteen years of age, and if such man refused to abjure the Catholic religion, and continued in his refusal for six months, he was rendered incapable of possessing land, and any land, the possession of which might belong to him, came into the possession of the next Protestant heir, who was not obliged to account for any profits. -- XI. It made such man incapable of purchasing lands, and all contracts made by him or for him, were null and void. -- XII. It imposed a fine of 10*l*. a month for employing a Catholic schoolmaster in a private family, and 9*l*., a day on the schoolmaster so employed. -- XIII. It imposed 100*l*.. fine for sending a child to a Catholic foreign school, and the child so sent was disabled from ever inheriting, purchasing, or enjoying lands, or profits, goods, debts, legacies, or sums of money. -- XIV. It punished the saying of mass by a fine of 120*l*., and the hearing of mass with a fine of 60*l*. -- XV. Any Catholic priest, who returned from beyond the seas, and who did not abjure his religion in three days afterwards, and also any person who returned to the Catholic faith, or procured another to return to it, this merciless, this sanguinary code, punished with hanging. ripping out of bowels, and quartering!

436. In IRELAND the code was still more ferocious, more hideously bloody; for, in the first place, all the cruelties of the English code had, as the work of a few hours, a few strokes of the pen, in one single act, been inflicted on unhappy Ireland; and, then, IN ADDITION, the Irish code contained, amongst many other violations of all the laws of justice and humanity, the following twenty most savage punishments. -- I. A Catholic schoolmaster, private or public, or even usher to a Protestant, was punished with imprisonment, banishment, and finally as a felon. -- II. The Catholic clergy were not allowed to be in the country, without being registered and kept as a sort of prisoners at large, and rewards were given (out of the revenue raised in part on the Catholics) for discovering them, 50*l*. for an archbishop, or bishop, 20*l*. for a priest, and 10*l*. for a schoolmaster or usher. -- III. Any two justices of the peace might call before them any Catholic, order him to declare, on oath, where and when he heard mass, who were present, and the name and residence of any priest or schoolmaster that he might know of; and, if he refused to obey this inhuman inquisition, they had power to condemn him. (without judge or jury) to a year's imprisonment in a felon's gaol, or to pay 20*l*. -- IV. No Catholic could purchase any manors, nor even hold under a lease for more than thirty-one years. -- V. Any Protestant, if he suspected any one of holding property in trust for a Catholic, or of being concerned in any sale, lease, mortgage, or other contract, for a Catholic; any Protestant thus suspecting, might file a bill against the suspected trustee, and take the estate, or property, from him. -- VI. Any Protestant seeing a Catholic tenant of a farm, the produce of which farm exceeded the amount of the rent by more than one-third, might dispossess the Catholic, and enter on the lease in his stead. -- VII. Any Protestant seeing a Catholic

with a horse worth more than five pounds, might take the horse away from him upon tendering him five pounds. --VIII. In order to prevent the smallest chance of justice in these and similar cases, none but known Protestants were to be jurymen in the trial of any such cases. -- IX. Horses of Catholics might be seized for the use of the militia; and, beside this, Catholics were compelled to pay double towards the militia. -- X.. Merchants, whose ships and goods might he taken by privateers, during a war with a Catholic Prince, were to be compensated for their losses by a levy on the goods and lands of Catholics only, though, mind, Catholics were at the same time impressed and compelled to shed their blood in the war against that same Catholic Prince. -- XI. Property of a Protestant, whose heirs at law were Catholics, was to go to the nearest Protestant relation, just the same as if the Catholic heirs had been dead, though the property might he entailed on them. -- XII . If there were no Protestant heir; then, in order to break up all Catholic families, the entail and all heirship were set aside, and the property was divided, share and share alike, amongst all the Catholic heirs. -- XIII. If a Protestant had an estate in Ireland, he was forbidden to marry a Catholic, in, or out, of Ireland. -- XIV. All marriages between Protestants and Catholics were annulled, though many children might have proceeded from them -- XV. Every priest, who celebrated a marriage between a Catholic and a Protestant, or between two Protestants, was condemned to he hanged. -- XVI. A Catholic father could not be guardian to, or have the custody of, his own child, if the child, however young, pretended to be a Protestant; but the child was taken from its own father, and put into the custody of a Protestant relation. -- XVII.. If any child of a Catholic became a Protestant, the parent was to be instantly summoned, and to be made to declare, upon oath, the full value of his or her property of all sorts, and then the Chancery was to make such distribution of the property as it thought fit. -- XVIII. "Wives be obedient unto your own husbands," says the great Apostle. "Wives, be disobedient to them," said this horrid code; for, if the wife of a Catholic chose to turn Protestant, it set aside the will of the husband, and made her a participator in all his possessions, in spite of him, however immoral, however bad a wife or bad a mother she might have been -- XIX. Honour thy father and thy mother, that thy days may be long in the land which the Lord, thy God, giveth thee." Dishonour them," said this savage code; for, if any one of the sons of a Catholic father became a Protestant, this son was to possess all the father had, and the father could not sell, could not mortgage, could not leave legacies, or portions out of his estate, by whatever title he might hold it, even though it might have been the fruit of his own toil -- XX. Lastly (of this score, but this is only a part), "the Church, as by law established," was, in her great indulgence, pleased not only to open her doors, but to award (out of the taxes) thirty pounds a year for life to any Catholic priest, who would abjure his religion and declare his belief in hers!

437. Englishmen, Is there a man, a single man, bearing that name, whose blood. will not chill at this recital; who, when he reflects that these barbarities were inflicted on men because, and only because, they adhered with fidelity to the faith of their and our fathers; to the faith of ALFRED, the founder of our nation; to the faith of the authors of Magna Charta, and of all those venerable institutions of which we so justly boast; who, when he thus reflects, and, when he, being as I am, a Protestant of the Church of England, further reflects, that all these cruelties were inflicted for the avowed purpose of giving and preserving predominance to that Church, will not, with me, not only feel deep sorrow and shame for the past, but heartily join me in best endeavours to cause justice to he done to the sufferers for the time to come?

438. As to the injustice, as to the barbarity, as to the flagrant immorality, of the above code, they call for no comment, being condemned by the spontaneous voice of nature herself; but in this shocking assemblage, there are two things which impel us to ask, whether the love of truth, whether a desire to eradicate religious error, could have formed any part, however small, of the motives of these punishers? These two things are, the reward offered to Catholic priests to induce them to come over to our Church; and the terrible means made use of to prevent the intermarriage of Catholics and Protestants, Could these measures ever have suggested themselves to the minds of men, who sincerely believed that the Church religion was supported by arguments more cogent than those by which the Catholic religion was supported? The Law-Church had all the powers, all the honours, all the emoluments, all the natural worldly allurements. These she continually held out to all who were disposed to the clerical order . And if, in addition to all these, she had felt strong in argument, would she have found it necessary to offer, in direct and barefaced words, a specific sum of money to any one who would join her; and that, too, when the pensioned convert, must, as she well knew, break his solemn vow, in order to he entitled to the pay? And, as to intermarriages, why not suffer them, why punish them so severely, why annul them if the Law-Church were sure that the arguments in her favour were the most cogent and convincing? Who has so much power over the mind of woman as her husband? Who over man as his wife? Would one persuade the other to a change of religion? Very likely. One would convert the other in nineteen cases out of twenty. That passion which had subdued religious prejudices, would, in almost every case, make both the parties of the same religion. But, what had the Law-Church to object to this, if she were sure that hers was the true faith; if she were sure that the arguments for her were more clear than those for her opponent; if she were sure that every one who really loved another, who was beloved by that other, and who belonged to her communion, would easily persuade that other to join in that communion? What, in short, had she, if quite sure of all this, to fear from intermarriages? And, if not quite sure of all this, what, I ask you, sensible and just Englishmen, what, had she to plead in justification of the inhuman penal code?

439. Talk of the "fires in Smithfield"! Fires, indeed, which had no justification, and which all Catholics severally condemn; but what, good God! was the death of about two hundred and seventy-seven persons, however cruel and unmerited that death, to the torments above described, inflicted, for more than two hundred years, on millions upon millions of people, to say nothing about the thousands upon thousands of Catholics, who were, during that period, racked to death, killed in prison, hanged, bowelled, and quartered! Besides, let it never be forgotten, that the punishments in Smithfield were for the purpose of reclaiming; for the purpose of making examples of a few, who set at nought the religion of their fathers, and that in which they themselves had been born. And, if these punishments were unjust and cruel as all men agree that they were, what shall we say of, how shall we express sufficient abhorrence of, the above penal-code, which was for the punishment, not of a few, but of millions of people; or the punishment, not of those who had apostatised from the religion of their fathers, but of those who, to their utter worldly ruin, adhered to that religion? If we find no justification, and none, we all say, there was, for the punishments of MARY's reign, inflicted, as all men know they were, on very few persons, and those persons not only apostates from the faith of their fathers, but also, for the most part, either notorious traitors, or felons, and, at the very least, conspirators against, or most audacious insulters of, the royal authority and the person of the Queen; if we find no justification, and we all agree that there was none, for these punishments, inflicted, as

all men know they were, during a few months of furious and unreflecting zeal, just after the quelling of a dangerous rebellion, which had clearly proved that apostate and conspirator were one and the same, and had led to the hasty conclusion, that the apostacy must he extirpated, or that it would destroy the throne: if we find, even under such circumstances, no justification for these punishments, where are we to look for, not a justification, but for a ground of qualification of our abhorrence, of the above-mentioned barbarities of more than two hundred years, inflicted on millions upon millions of people; barbarities premeditated in the absence of all provocation; contrived and adopted in all the calmness of legislative deliberation; executed in cold blood, and persevered in for ages in defiance of the admonitions of conscience; barbarities inflicted, not on apostates, but on those who refused to apostatise; not on felons, conspirators, and. rebels, but on innocent persons, on those who had, under all and every circumstance, even while feeling the cruel lash of persecution, been as faithful to their King as to their God; and, as if we were never to come to the end of the atrocity, all this done, too, with regard to Ireland, in flagrant breach of a solemn treaty with the English King!

440. And, is this the "the tolerant, the mild, the meek Church as by law established"? Have we here the proofs of Protestant faith and good works? Was it thus that St. Austin and St, Patrick introduced, and that St. Swithin and Alfred and William of Wykham inculcated, the religion of Christ? Was it out of works like these, that the cathedrals and the palaces and the universities, and the laws and the courts of justice arose? What! punish men for retaining the faith of their fathers; inflict all sorts of insults and cruelties on them for not having become apostates; put them, because they were Catholics, out of the protection of all the laws that their and our Catholic ancestors had framed for the security of their children; call their religion "idolatrous and damnable," treat them as obstinate idolaters, while your Church-Calendar contains none but saints of that very religion; boast of your venerable institutions, all of Catholic origin, while you insult, pillage, scourge, hunt from the face of the earth, the true and faithful adherents to the faith of the authors of those institutions? "Ay," the persecutors seem to have answered, "and hunt them we will." But why, then, if religion be your motive; if your barbarities arise from a desire to convert men from error; why be so lenient to Quakers and Jews; why not only not punish, but suffer them even to appoint parsons to your churches? Ah! my friends, the Law-Church had taken no tithes and lands, and others had taken no abbeys and the like, from Quakers and Jews! Here was the real foundation of the whole of that insatiable rancour, which went on from 1558 to 1778, producing, to millions of innocent people, torment added to torment, and which, at the end of that long period, seemed to have resolved to be satisfied with nothing short of the total extermination of its victims.

441. But, now, all of a sudden, in 1778, the face of things began to change; the Church, as by law established, was, all at once, thought capable of existing in safety, with a great relaxation of the penal code! And, without even asking it, the Catholics found the code suddenly softened, by divers Acts of Parliament, in both countries, and especially in Ireland! This humanity and generosity will surprise us; we shall wonder whence it came; we shall be ready to believe the souls of the parties to have been softened by a sort of miracle, until we look back to paragraphs **425** and **426**. There we see the real cause of this surprising humanity and generosity; there we see the AMERICANS unfurling the standard of independence, and, having been backed by France, pushing on towards success, and, thereby, setting an example to every oppressed people, in every part of the world, unhappy, trodden down Ireland not

excepted! There was, too, before the end of the war, danger of invasion on the part of France, who was soon joined in the war by Spain and Holland; so that before the close of the contest, the Catholics had obtained leave to breathe the air of their native country in safety; and, though, as an Englishman, I deeply lament, that this cost England her right arm, I most cordially rejoice in contemplating the event. Thus was fear gratified, in a moment, at the very first demand, with a surrender of that, which had, for ages, been refused to the incessant pleadings of justice and humanity; and thus the American Revolution, which, as we have seen, grew immediately out of the "no-popery," or "glorious," revolution in England, which latter was, as we have clearly seen, made for the express purpose of extinguishing the Catholic religion for ever; thus was this very event the cause of the beginning of a cessation of the horrible persecutions of those, who had, with fidelity wholly without a parallel, adhered to that religion!

442. This great event was soon followed by another still greater; namely, the FRENCH REVOLUTION, or "Reformation" the FIFTH. Humiliation greater than the English Government had to endure, in the above event, it is difficult to conceive; but the French Revolution taught the world what "Reformations" can do, when pushed to their full and natural extent. In England the "Reformation" contented itself with plundering the convents and the poor of their all, and the secular clergy in part. But, in France, they took the whole; though we ought to mark well this difference; that, in France, they applied this whole to the use of the public; a bad use, perhaps; but, to public use they applied the whole of the plunder; while, in England, the plunder was scrambled for, and remained divided amongst individuals!

443. Well; but, here was a great triumph for the clergy of the "Church as by law established"? They, above all men, must have hailed with delight the deeds of the French "Reformation"? No: but, on the contrary, were amongst the foremost in calling for war to put down that "Reformation"! What! not like this "Reformation"! Why, here were convents broken up and monks and nuns dispersed; here were abbey-lands confiscated; here was the Catholic religion abolished; here were Catholic priests hunted about and put to death in almost as savage a manner as those of England had been; here were laws, seemingly translated from our own code, against saying or hearing mass, and against priests returning into the kingdom; here was a complete annihilation (as far as legislative provisions could go) of that which our church clergy called "idolatrous and damnable"; here was a new religion "established by law"; and, that no feature might be defective in the likeness, here was a royal family set aside by law for ever, by what they called a "glorious revolution "; and there would have been an abdicating king, but he was, by mere accident, stopped in his flight, brought back, and put to death, not, however, without an example to plead in the deeds of the English double-distilled Protestant "Reformation" people.

444. What! Can it be true, that our church-clergy did not like this French "Reformation "? And that they urged on war against the men who had sacked convents, killed priests, and abolished that which was "idolatrous and damnable"? Can it be true, that they who rose against King James because he wanted to give Catholics liberty of conscience; that they, who upheld the horrid penal code, in order to put down the Catholic religion in England and Ireland; can it be true, that they wanted war, to put down the men, who had put down that religion in France? Ay, ay! But these men had put down all TITHES too! Ay, and all bishoprics, and deaneries, and prebendaries, and all fat benefices and pluralities! And, if they were permitted to do this with impunity, OTHERS might be tempted to do the same! Well, but,

gentlemen of the law-church, though they were wicked fellows for doing this, still this was better than to suffer to remain, that which you always told us was idolatrous and damnable. "Yes, yes; but, then, these men established, by law, ATHEISM, and not Church-of-England Christianity." Now, in the first place, they saw about forty sorts of Protestant religion; they knew that thirty-nine of them must be false; they had seen our rulers make a church by law, just such an one as they pleased; they had seen them alter it by law; and, if there were no standard of faith; no generally acknowledged authority; if English law-makers were to change the sort of religion at their pleasure; why, pray, were not French law-makers to do the same? If English law-makers could take the spiritual supremacy from the successor of Saint Peter, and give it to HENRY-THE-WIFE-KILLER, why might not the French give theirs to LEPEAU? Besides, as to the sort of religion, though ATHEISM is bad enough, could it be WORSE than what you tell us is "idolatrous and damnable"? It might cause people to be damned; but could it cause them to be more than damned? Alas! there remains only the abolition of the TITHES and of the FAT CLERICAL POSTS, as a valid objection, on your part, against "Reformation" the FIFTH; and, I beg the nation to remember, that the war against it has left us to pay, for ever, the interest of a debt, created by that way, of seven hundred millions of pounds sterling, a war which we never should have seen, if we had never seen that which is called a" Reformation."

445. The French Revolution, though it caused numerous horrid deeds to be committed, produced, in its progress and in its end, a great triumph for the Catholics. It put the fidelity of the Catholic priests and the Protestant pastors to the test; and, while not one of the former was ever seen to save his life by giving up his faith, all the latter did it with out hesitation. It showed, at last, the people of a great kingdom returning to the Catholic worship by choice; when they might have been, and may now be, Protestants, without the loss of any one right, immunity, or advantage, civil or military. But the greatest good that it produced fell to the lot of ill-treated Ireland. The revolutionists were powerful, they were daring, they, in 1793, cast their eyes on Ireland; and now, for the second time, a softening of the penal code took place, making a change which no man living ever expected to see! Those who had been considered as almost beneath dogs, were now made capable of being MAGISTRATES; and now amongst many other acts of generosity, we saw established, at the public expense, a COLLEGE for the education of Catholics exclusively, thus doing, by law, that which the law-givers had before made HIGH TREASON! Ah! but, there were the French with an army of four hundred thousand men; and there were the Irish people, who must have been something more, or less, than men, if their breasts did not boil with resentment. Alas! that it should be said of England, that the Irish have never appealed with success but to her fears!

446. And, shall this always be said? Shall it ever be said again? Shall we not now, by sweeping away for ever every vestige of this once horrible and still oppressive code, reconcile ourselves to our long ill-treated brethren and to our own consciences? The code is still a penal code: it is still a just ground of complaint: it has still disqualifications that are greatly injurious, and distinctions that are odious and insulting. I. It still shuts Catholic peers out of those seats in the House of Lords, which are their hereditary right; and Catholic gentlemen out of the House of Commons. II. Then, as if caprice were resolved not to he behind hand with injustice, this code, which allows Catholic freeholders, in Ireland, to vote, at elections, for members of the Parliament of the now "United Kingdom," refuses that right to all Catholics in England! III. It excludes Catholics from all corporations. IV. It excludes them from all

offices under the government, in England, but admits them to inferior offices in Ireland. V. It takes from them the right of presenting to any ecclesiastical benefice, though Quakers and Jews are allowed to enjoy that right! VI. It prevents them from endowing any school, or college; for educating children in the Catholic religion; and this, too, while there is now, by law established, a college, for this very purpose, supported out of the taxes! Here is consistency; and here is, above all things, sincerity! What, maintain, out of the taxes, a college to teach exclusively that religion, which you call "idolatrous and damnable"! VII This code still forbids Catholic priests to appear in their canonical habiliments, except in their chapels, or in private houses; and it forbids the Catholic rites to be performed in any building which has a steeple or bells! What! forbid the use of steeples and bells to that religion, which created all the steeples and all the bells; that built and endowed all the churches, all the magnificent cathedrals, and both the Universities! And, why this insulting, this galling, prohibition? Why so sedulous to keep the symbols of this worship out of the sight of the people? Why, gentle law-church, if your features be so lovely as you say they are, and if those of your rival present, as you say they do, a mass of disgusting deformity; why, if this be the case, are you, who are the most gentle. amiable, and beautiful church that law ever created; why, I say, are you. so anxious to keep your rival out of sight? Nay, and out of hearing too! What! gentle and all-persuasive and only true law-church, whose parsons and bishops are such able preachers, and mostly married men into the bargain, what are you afraid of from the steeples and bells, if used by Catholics? One would think, that the more people went to witness the "idolatrous" exhibitions, the better you would like it. Alas! gentle and lovely law-church, there are not now in the kingdom many men so brutishly ignorant as not to see the real motives for this uncommonly decent prohibition. VIII. It forbids a Catholic priest in Ireland, to be guardian to any child. IX. It forbids Catholic laymen in Ireland, to act in the capacity of guardian to the children, or a child, of any Protestant. X. It forbids every Catholic in Ireland to have arms in his house, unless he have a freehold of ten pounds a year, or 300*l*. in personal property. XI. It disables Irish Catholics from voting at vestries on questions relating to the repair of the church, though they are compelled to pay for those repairs. XII. Lastly, in Ireland, this code still inflicts death, or, at least, a 500*l*. penalty, on the Catholic priest, who celebrates a marriage between two Protestants, or between a Protestant and a Catholic. Some of the judges have decided, that it is death; others, that it is the pecuniary penalty. Death, or money, however, the public papers have recently announced to us, that such a marriage has now been openly celebrated in Dublin, between the pre sent LORD LIEUTENANT OF IRELAND (who must be a Protestant) and a CATHOLIC LADY of the late rebellious American States! So that, all put together, Dublin exhibits, at this moment, a tolerably curious scene: a College established by law, for the teaching of that religion, which our Church regards as "idolatrous and damnable," and to be guilty of teaching which was, only a few years ago, high treason! A Lord Lieutenant of Ireland, who must belong to our Church, and who must have taken an oath protesting against the Catholic supremacy, taking to his arms a Catholic wife, who must adhere to that supremacy! Then comes a Catholic priest marrying this pair, in the face of two unrepealed laws, one of which condemns him to death for the act, and the other of which condemns him to pay a fine of five hundred pounds! And; lastly, comes, as the public prints tell us, a complimentary letter, on the occasion, to the bridegroom, on the part, and in the handwriting of the King!

447. Well, then, is this code, is any fragment of it longer to continue? is it to continue now, when all idea of conversion to Protestantism is avowedly abandoned, and when

it is notorious that the Catholic faith has, in spite of ages of persecution, done more than maintain its ground? Are peers still to be cut off from their hereditary rights and honours; are gentlemen to be shut out of the Commons' House; are lawyers to be stopped in their way to the bench; are freeholders and freemen to be deprived of their franchises; are the whole to lie under a stigma, which it is not in human nature should fail to fill them with resentment; and all this, because they adhere to the religion of their and our fathers, and a religion too, to educate youth in which, exclusively, there is now a college supported out of the taxes? Is all this great body of men, forming one-third part of the whole of the people of this kingdom, containing men of all ranks, from the peer to the labourer, to continue to be thus insulted, thus injured, thus constantly irritated, constantly impelled to wish for distress, danger, defeat, and disgrace to their native country, as affording the only chance of their obtaining justice? And are we, merely to gratify the law-church by upholding her predominance, still to support, in peace, a numerous and most expensive army; still to be exposed, in war, to the danger of seeing concession come too late, and to all those consequences, the nature and extent of which it makes one shudder to think of?

448. Here, then, we are, at the end of three hundred years from the day when Henry VIII. began the work of "Reformation ": here we are, after passing through scenes of plunder and of blood, such as the world never beheld before: here we are, with these awful questions still before us; and here we are, too, with forty sorts of Protestant religion, instead of the one fold, in which our forefathers lived for nine hundred years; here we are, divided and split up into sects each condemning all the rest to eternal flames; here we are, a motley herd of Church people, Methodists, Calvinists, Quakers, and Jews, chopping and changing with every wind; while the faith of St. Austin and St. Patrick still remains what it was when it inspired the heart and sanctified the throne of Alfred.

449. Such, as far as religion is concerned, have been the effects of what is called the "Reformation"; what its effects have been in other respects; how it has enfeebled and impoverished the nation; how it has corrupted and debased the people; and how it has brought barracks, taxing-houses, poor-houses, mad-houses, and gaols, to supply the place of convents, hospitals, guilds, and alms-houses) we shall see in the next letter; and then we shall have before us the whole of the consequences of this great, memorable, and fatal event.

LETTER XVI.

FORMER POPULATION OF ENGLAND AND IRELAND.
FORMER WEALTH.
FORMER POWER.
FORMER FREEDOM.
FORMER PLENTY, EASE, AND HAPPINESS.

Kensington, 31st March, 1826.

MY FRIENDS,

450. This Letter is to conclude my task, which task was to make good this assertion, that the event called the "Reformation" had impoverished and degraded the main body of the people of England and Ireland. In paragraph **4**, I told you that a fair and honest inquiry would teach us, that the word "Reformation" had, in this case, been misapplied; that there was a change, but a change greatly for the worse; that the thing called the "Reformation," "was engendered in beastly lust, brought forth in hypocrisy and perfidy, and cherished and fed by plunder, devastation, and by rivers of innocent English and Irish blood; and that, as to its more remote consequences, they are, some of them, now before us, in that misery, that beggary, that nakedness, that hunger, that everlasting wrangling, and spite, which now stare us in the face and stun our ears at every turn, and which the 'Reformation' has given us in exchange for the ease and happiness and harmony and Christian charity, enjoyed so abundantly, and for so many ages, by our Catholic forefathers."

451. All this has been amply proved in the fifteen foregoing Letters, except that I have not yet shown, in detail, how our Catholic forefathers lived, what sort and what quantity of food and raiment they had, compared with those which we have. This I am now about to do. I have made good my charge of beastly lust, hypocrisy, perfidy, plunder, devastation, and bloodshed; the charge of misery, of beggary, of nakedness and of hunger, remains to be fully established.

452. But, I choose to be better rather than worse than my word; I did not pledge myself to prove anything as to the population, wealth, power, and freedom of the nation; but I will now show not only that the people were better off, better fed and clad, before the "Reformation" than they ever have been since; but, that the nation was more populous, wealthy, powerful and free before, than it ever has been since that event. Read modern romancers, called historians, every one of whom has written for place, or pension; read the statements about the superiority of the present over former times; about our prodigious increase in population, wealth, power, and, above all things, our superior freedom; read the monstrous lies of HUME, who (vol. v, p. 502) unblushingly asserts, "that one good county of England is now capable of making a greater effort than the whole kingdom was in the reign of Henry V., when to maintain the garrison of the small town of Calais, required more than a third of the ordinary revenues;" this is the way in which every Scotchman reasons. He always estimates the wealth of a nation by the money the government squeezes out of it. He forgets, that "a poor government makes a rich people." According to this criterion of HUME, America must now be a wretchedly poor country. This same Henry V. could conquer,

really conquer, France, and that, too, without beggaring England by hiring a million of Prussians, Austrians, Cossacks, and all sorts of hirelings. But writers have, for ages, been so dependant on the government and the aristocracy, and the people have read and believed so, much of what they have said, and especially in praise of the "Reformation" and its effects, that it is no wonder that they should think, that, in Catholic times, England was a poor, beggarly spot, having a very few people on it; and that the "Reformation" and the House of Brunswick and the Whigs, have given us all we possess of wealth, of power, of freedom, and have almost created us, or, at least, if not actually begotten us, caused nine-tenths of us to be born. These are all monstrous lies; but they have succeeded for ages. Few men dared to attempt to refute them; and, if any one made the attempt, he obtained few hearers, and ruin, in some shape or other, was pretty sure to be the reward of his virtuous efforts. Now, however, when we are smarting under the lash of calamity; NOW, when every one says, that no state of things ever was so bad as this; NOW, men may listen to the truth, and, therefore, I wilt lay it before them.

453. POPULOUSNESS is a thing not to be proved by positive facts, because there are no records of the numbers of the people in former times; and because those which we have in our own day are notoriously false; if they be not, the English nation has added a third to its population during the last twenty years! In short, our modern records I have, over and over again, proved to be false, particularly in my Register, No, 2, of Volume 4G. That England was more populous in Catholic times than it is now we must believe, when we know, that in the three first Protestant reigns, thousands of parish churches were pulled down, that parishes were united, in more than two thousand instances, and when we know from the returns now before Parliament, that out of 11,761 parishes, in England and Wales, there are upwards of a thousand which do not contain a hundred persons each, men, women, and children. Then, again, the size of the churches. They were manifestly built, in general, to hold three, four, five or, ten times the number of their present parishioners, including all the sectarians. What should men have built such large churches for? We are told of their "piety and zeal;" yes, but there must have been men to raise the buildings. The Lord might favour the work; but there must have been hands as well as prayers. And, what motive could there have been for putting together such large quantities of stone and mortar, and to make walls four feet thick, and towers and steeples, if there had not been people to fill the buildings? And, how could the labour have been performed? There must have been men to perform the labour; and, can any one believe, that this labour would have been performed, if there had not been a necessity for it? We now see large and most costly ancient churches, and these in great numbers, too, with only a few mud-huts to hold the thirty or a hundred of parishioners. Our forefathers built for ever, little thinking of the devastation that we were to behold! Next come the lands, which they cultivated, and which we do not, amounting to millions of acres. This any one may verify, who will go into Sussex, Hampshire, Dorsetshire, Devonshire and Corn wall. They grew corn on the sides of hills, which we now never attempt to stir. They made the hill into the form of steps of a stairs, in order to plough and sow the flat parts. These flats, or steps, still remain, and are, in some cases still cultivated; but, in nine cases out of ten, they are not. Why should they have performed this prodigious labour, if they had not had mouths to eat the corn? And, how could they have performed such labour without numerous hands? On the high lands of Hampshire and Dorsetshire, there are spots of a thousand acres together, which still bear the uneffaceable marks of the plough, and which now never feel that implement. The modern writings on the subject of ancient population are mere romances; or, they

have been put forth with a view of paying court to the government of the day.
GEORGE CHALMERS, a placeman, a pensioner, and a Scotchman, has been one of
the most conspicuous in this species of deception. He, in what he calls an
"ESTIMATE," states the population of England and Wales, in 1377 , at 2,092,978.
The half of these were, of course, females. The males, then, were, 1,046,486. The
children, the aged, the infirm, the sick, made a half of these; so that there were
523,243 left of able-bodied men, in this whole kingdom! Now, the churches and the
religious houses amounted, at that time, to upwards of 16,000 in number. There was
one priest to every church, and these priests, together with the monks and friars, must
have amounted to about 40,000 able men, leaving 483,243 able men. So that, as there
were more than 14,000 parish churches, there were not quite twelve able-bodied men
to each! HUME says, vol. iii. p. 9, that WAT TYLER had, in 1381 (four years after
Chalmers' date), "a hundred thousand men assembled on BLACKHEATH;" so that, to
say nothing of the numerous bodies of insurgents, assembled, at the same time, "in
"Hertford, Essex, Suffolk, Norfolk, and Lincoln;" to say nothing of "the King's army
of 40,000" (Hume, vol. iii. p. 8); and, to say nothing of all the nobility, gentry, and
rich people, here WAT TYLER had got together, on Blackheath, MORE THAN
ONE-FIFTH of all the able-bodied men in England and Wales! And, he had, too,
collected them together in the space of about six days! Do we want, can we want, any
thing more than this, in answer, in refutation, of these writers on the ancient
population of the country? Let it be observed, that, in these days, there were, as
himself relates, and his authorities relate also, frequently 100,000 pilgrims at a time
assembled at Canterbury, to do penance, or make offerings, at the shrine of THOMAS
À BECKET. There must, then, have been 50,000 men here at once; so that, if we were
to believe this pensioned Scotch writer, we must believe, that more than A TENTH of
all the able-bodied men of England and Wales were frequently assembled, at one and
the same time, in one city, in an extreme corner of the island, to kneel at the tomb of
one single Saint. Monstrous lie! And, yet it has been sucked down by "enlightened
Protestants," as if it had been a part of the Gospel. But, if Canterbury could give
entertainment to 100,000 strangers at a time, what must Canterbury itself have been?
A grand, a noble, a renowned city it was, venerated, and even visited, by no small part
of the Kings, Princes, and Nobles of all Europe. It is now a beggarly, gloomy looking
town, with about 12,000 inhabitants, and, as the published accounts say, with 3,000 of
those inhabitants paupers, and with a part of the site of its ancient and splendid
churches, convents and streets, covered with barracks, the Cathedral only remaining,
for the purpose, as it were, of keeping the people in mind of the height from which
they have fallen. The best criterion of the population is, however, to be found in the
number and size of the churches, and that of the religious houses. There was one
parish church to every four square miles, throughout the kingdom; and one religious
house (including all the kinds) to every thirty square miles. That is to say, one parish
church to every piece of land two miles each way; and one religious house to every
piece of land five miles long and six miles wide. These are facts that nobody can
deny. The geography tells us the number of square miles in the country, and, as to the
number of parishes and religious houses, it is too well known to admit of dispute,
being recorded in books without number. Well, then, if the father of lies himself were
to come, and endeavour to persuade us, that England was not more populous before
the "Reformation" than it is now, he must fail with all but downright idiots. The same
may be said with regard to IRELAND, where there were according to ARCHDALL,
742 religious houses in the reign of Henry VIII.; and, of course, one of these to every
piece of land six miles each way; and where there was a parish church to every piece

of land a little more than two miles and a half each way. Why these churches? What were they built for? By whom were they built? And how were all these religious houses maintained? Alas! Ireland was in those days, a fine, a populous, and a rich country. Her people were not then half-naked and half-starved. There were, then, no projects for relieving the Irish by sending them out of their native land!

454. THE WEALTH of the country is a question easily decided. In the reign of Henry VIII., just before the "Reformation," the whole of the lands in England and Wales, had, according to HUME, been rated, and the annual rental was found to be three millions; and, as to this, HUME (vol. iv. p. 197) quotes undoubted authorities. Now, in order to know what these three millions were worth in our money, we must look at the Act of Parliament, 24th year of Henry VIII., chap. 3, which says that "no person shall "take for beef or pork above a halfpenny, and for mutton or veal above three farthings, a pound, avoirdupois weight, and less in those places were they be now sold for less." This is by retail, mind. It is sale in the butchers' shops. So that, in order to compare the then with the present amount of the rental of the country, we must first see what the annual rental of England and Wales now is, and then we must see what the price of meat now is. I wish to speak here of nothing that I have not unquestionable authority for, and I have no such authority with regard to the amount of the rental as it is just at this moment; but, I have that authority for what the rental was in the year 1804. A return, printed by order of the House of Commons, and dated 10th July, 1804, states, "that the returns to the Tax-office [property tax], prove the rack-rental of England and Wales to be thirty-eight millions a year." Here, then, we have the rental to a certainty; for, what was there that could escape the all-searching, taxing eye, of Pitt and his under-strappers? Old Harry's inexperience must have made him a poor hand, compared with Pitt, at finding out what people got for their land. Pitt's return included the rent of mines, canals, and of every species of real property; and the rental, the rack-rental, of the whole amounted to thirty-eight millions. This, observe, was in time of Bank-restriction; in time of higher prices; in time of monstrously high rents; in time of high price of meat; that very year I gave 18s. a score for fat hogs, taking head, feet, and all together; and, for many years before and after, and including 1804, beef, pork, mutton and veal were, taken on the average, more than tenpence a pound by retail. Now, as Old Harry's Act orders the meat to be sold, in some places, for less than the halfpenny and the three farthings, we may, I think, fairly presume, that the general price was a halfpenny. So that a halfpenny of Old Harry's money was equal in value to tenpence of Pitt's money: and, therefore, the three millions of rental in the time of Harry, ought to have become sixty millions in 1804, and it was, as we have seen, only thirty-eight millions. In 1822, Mr. CURWEN said, the rental had fallen to twenty millions. But, then meat had also fallen in price. It is safer to take 1804, where we have undoubted authority to go on. This proof is of a nature to bid defiance to cavil. No man can dispute any of the facts, and they are conclusive as to the point, that the nation was more wealthy before the "Reformation" than it is now. But, there are two other Acts of Parliament, to which I will refer, as corroborating, in a very striking manner, this fact of the superior general opulence of Catholic times. The Act, 18th year of Henry VI., chap. II, after setting forth the cause for the enactment, provides, that no man shall, under a heavy penalty, act as a justice of the peace, who has not lands and tenements of the clear yearly value of twenty pounds. This was in 1439, about a hundred years before the above mentioned Act, about meat, of Henry VII. The money was of still higher value in the reign of Henry VI. However, taking it as before, at twenty times the value of our money, the justice of the peace must then have had four hundred pounds a year of our money; and we all

know, that we have justices of the peace of one hundred a year. This Act of Henry VI. shows, that the country abounded in gentlemen of good estate; and, indeed, the Act itself says, that the people are not content with having "men of small behaviour set over them." A thousand fellows, calling themselves historians, would never overset such a proof of the superior general opulence and ease and happiness of the country. The other of the Acts, to which I have alluded, is 1st year Richard III. chap. 4., which fixes the qualification of a juror at twenty shillings a year in freehold, or twenty-six and eight-pence copyhold, clear of all charges. That is to say, a clear yearly income from real property of, at least, twenty pounds a year of our money! And yet the Scotch historians would make us believe, that our ancestors were a set of beggars! These things prove beyond all dispute, that England was, in Catholic times, a really wealthy country; that wealth was generally diffused; that every part of the country abounded in men of solid property; and that, of course, there were always great resources at hand in cases of emergency. If we were now to take it into our heads to dislike to have men of "small behaviour set over us"; if we were to take a fancy to justices of the peace of four hundred a year and jurors of twenty pounds a year; if we were, as in the days of good King Henry, to say, that we "would not be governed nor ruled" by men of "small behaviour," how quickly we should see Botany Bay! When CARDINAL POLE landed at Dover, in the reign of Queen Mary, he was met and escorted on his way by two thousand gentlemen, of the country, on horseback. What! 2,000 country gentlemen, in so beggarly a country as Chalmers describes it! Ay, and they must have been found in Kent and Surrey too. Can we find such a troop of country gentlemen there now? In short, everything shows, that England was then a country abounding in men of real wealth, and that it so abounded precisely because the King's revenue was small; yet this is cited by HUME, and the rest of the Scotch historians, as a proof of the nation's poverty! Their notion is, that a people are worth what the government can wring out of them, and not a farthing more. And this is the doctrine which has been acted upon ever since the "Reformation," and which has, at last, brought us into our present wretched condition.

455. As to the POWER of the country, compared with what it is now, what do we want more than the fact, that, for many centuries, before the "Reformation," England held possession of a considerable part of France; that the "Reformation" took, as we have seen, the two towns of Boulogne and Calais from her, leaving her nothing but those little specks in the sea, Jersey and Guernsey? What do we want more than this? France was never a country that had any pretensions to cope with England until the "Reformation" began, Since the "Reformation" she has not only had such pretensions, bat she has shown to all the world that the pretensions are well-founded. She, even at this moment, holds Spain in despite of us, while, in its course, the "Reformation" has wrested from us a large portion of our dominions, and has erected them into a state more formidable than any we have ever before beheld. We have, indeed, great standing armies, arsenals and barracks, of which our Catholic forefathers had none; but, they were always ready for war nevertheless. They had the resources in the hour of necessity. They had arms and men; and those men knew what they were to fight for before they took up arms. It is impossible to look back, to see the respect in which England was held for so many, many ages; to see the deference with which she was treated by all nations, without blushing at the thought of our present state. None but the greatest potentates presumed to think of marriage alliances with England. Her kings and queens had kings and princes in their train. Nothing petty ever thought of approaching her. She was held in such high honour, her power was so universally acknowledged, that she had seldom occasion to assert it by war. And what has she

been for the last hundred and fifty years? Above half the time at war; and, with a Debt, never to be paid, the cost of that war, she now rests her hopes of safety solely on her capacity of persuading her well-known foes, that it is not their interest to assail her. Her warlike exertions have been the effect, not of her resources, but of an anticipation of those resources. She has mortgaged, she has spent before-hand, the resources necessary for future defence. And, there she now is, inviting insult and injury by her well-known weakness, and, in case of attack, her choice lies between foreign victory over her, or internal convulsion. Power is relative. You may have more strength than you had, but if your neighbours have gained strength in a greater degree, you are, in effect, weaker than you were. And, can we look at France and America, and can we con template the inevitable consequences of war, without feeling that we are fast becoming, and, indeed, that we are already become, a low and little nation? Can we look back to the days of our Catholic ancestors, can we think of their lofty tone and of the submission instantly produced by their threats, without sighing, Alas! those days are never to return!

456. And, as to the FREEDOM of the nation, where is the man who can tell me of any one single advantage that the "Reformation" has brought, except it be freedom to have forty religious creeds instead of one? FREEDOM is not an empty sound; it is not an abstract idea; it is not a thing that nobody can feel. It means, and it means nothing else, the full and quiet enjoyment of your own property. If you have not this; if this be not well secured to you, you may call yourself what you will, but you are a slave. Now, our Catholic forefathers took special care upon this cardinal point. They suffered neither kings nor parliaments to touch their property without cause clearly shown. They did not read newspapers, they did not talk about debates, they had no taste for "mental enjoyment"; but they thought hunger and thirst great evils, and they never suffered anybody to put them to board on cold potatoes and water. They looked upon bare bones and rags as indubitable marks of slavery, and they never failed to resist any attempt to affix these marks upon them. You may twist the word freedom as long you please; but, at last, it comes to quiet enjoyment of your property, or it comes to nothing. Why do men want any of those things that are called political rights and privileges? Why do they, for instance, want to vote at elections for members of Parliament? Oh! because they shall then have an influence over the conduct of those members. And of what use is that? Oh! then they will prevent the members from doing wrong. What wrong? Why, imposing taxes that ought not to he paid. That is all; that is the use, and the only use, of any right or privilege that men in general can have. NOW how stand we, in this respect, compared with our Catholic ancestors? They did not, perhaps, all vote at elections. But do we? Do a fiftieth part of us? And have the main body of us any, even the smallest influence in the making of laws and in the imposing of taxes? But the main body of the people had the Church to protect them in Catholic times. The Church had great power; it was naturally the guardian of the common people; neither kings nor parliaments could set its power at defiance; the whole of our history shows, that the Church was invariably on the side of the people, and that, in all the much and justly boasted of triumphs which our forefathers obtained over their kings and nobles, the Church took the lead. It did this, because it was dependant upon neither king nor nobles; because, and only because, it acknowledged another head; but, we have lost the protection of the Church, and have got nothing to supply its place; or rather, whatever there is of its power left, has joined, or has been engrossed by, the other branches of the State, leaving the main body of the people to the mercy of those other branches. "The liberties of England" is a phrase in every mouth; but what are those liberties? The laws which regulate the descent and

possession of property; the safety from arrest, unless by due and settled process; the absence of all punishment without trial before duly authorised and well known judges and magistrates; the trial by jury; the precautions taken by the divers writs and summonses; the open trial; the impartiality in the proceedings. These are the "liberties of England." And had our Catholic forefathers less of these than we have? Do we not owe them all to them? Have we one single law, that gives security to property or to life, which we do not inherit from them? The tread-mill, the law to shut men up in their houses from sun-set to sun-rise, the law to banish us for life if we utter any thing having a tendency to bring our "representatives" into contempt; these, indeed, we do not inherit, but may boast of them, and of many others of much about the same character, as being, unquestionably, of pure Protestant origin.

457. POVERTY, however, is, after all, the great badge, the never-failing badge of slavery. Bare bones and rags are the true marks of the real slave. What is the object of government? To cause men to live happily. They cannot be happy without a sufficiency of food and of raiment. Good government means a state of things in which the main body are well fed and well clothed. It is the chief business of a government to take care, that one part of the people do not cause the other part to lead miserable lives. There can be no morality, no virtue, no sincerity, no honesty, amongst a people continually suffering from want; and, it is cruel, in the last degree, to punish such people for almost any sort of crime, which is, in fact, not crime of the heart, not crime of the perpetrator, but the crime of his all-controlling necessities.

458. To what degree the main body of the people, in England, are now poor and miserable; how deplorably wretched they now are; this we know but too well; and now, we will see what was their state before this vaunted "REFORMATION." I shall be very particular to cite my authorities here. I will infer nothing; I will give no "estimate"; but refer to authorities, such as no man can call in question, such as no man can deny to be proofs more complete than if founded on oaths of credible witnesses, taken before a judge and jury. I shall begin with the account which FORTESCUE gives of the state and manner of living of the English, in the reign of Henry VI.; that is, in the fifteenth century, when the Catholic Church was in the height of its glory. FORTESCUE was Lord Chief Justice of England for nearly twenty years; he was appointed Lord High Chancellor by Henry VI. Being in exile, in France, in consequence of the wars between the Houses of York and Lancaster, and the King's son, Prince Edward, being also in exile with him, the Chancellor wrote a series of Letters, addressed to the Prince, to explain to him the nature and effects of the laws of England, and to induce him to study them and uphold them. This work, which was written in Latin, is called *De Laudibus Legum Angliæ*; or, PRAISE OF THE LAWS OF ENGLAND. This book was, many years ago, translated into English, and it is a book of Law-Authority, quoted frequently in our courts at this day. No man can doubt the truth of facts, related in such a work. It was a work written by a famous lawyer for a Prince; it was intended to be read by other contemporary lawyers, and also by all lawyers in future. The passage that I am about to quote, relating to the state of the English, was purely incidental; it was not intended to answer any temporary purpose. It must have been a true account.

459. The Chancellor, after speaking generally of the nature of the laws of England, and of the difference between them and the laws of France, proceeds to show the difference in their effects, by a description of the state of the French people, and then by a description of the state of the English. His words, words that, as I transcribe them, make my cheeks burn with shame, are as follows: "Besides all this, the

inhabitants of France give every year to their King the fourth part of all their wines, the growth of that year, every vintner gives the fourth penny of what he makes of his wine by sale. And all the towns and boroughs pay to the King yearly great sums of money, when are assessed upon them, for the expenses of his men-at-arms. So that the King's troops, which are always considerable, are subsisted and paid yearly by those common people, who live in the villages, boroughs and cities. Another grievance is, every village constantly finds and maintains two cross-bow-men, at the least; some find more, well arrayed in all their accoutrements, to serve the King in his wars, as often as he pleaseth to call them out, which is frequently done. Without any consideration had of these things, other very heavy taxes are assessed yearly upon every village within the kingdom, for the King's service; neither is there ever any intermission or abatement of taxes. Exposed to these and other calamities, the peasants live in great hardship and misery. Their constant drink is water, neither do they taste, throughout the year, any other liquor, unless upon some extraordinary times, or festival days. Their clothing consists of frocks, or little short jerkins, made of canvas, no better than common sackcloth; they do not wear any woollens, except of the coarsest sort; and that only in the garment under their frocks; nor do they wear any trowse, but from the knees upwards; their legs being exposed and naked, The women go barefoot, except on holidays. They do not eat flesh, except it be the fat of bacon, and that in very small quantities, with which they make a soup. Of other sorts, either boiled or roasted, they do not so much as taste, unless it be of the inwards and offals of sheep and bullocks, and the like, which are killed for the use of the better sort of people, and the merchants; for whom also quails, partridges, hares, and the like, are reserved, upon pain of the gallies; as for their poultry, the soldiers consume them, so that scarce the eggs, slight as they are, are indulged them, by way of a dainty. And if it happen that a man is observed to thrive in the world, and become rich, he is presently assessed to the King's tax, proportionably more than his poorer neighbours, whereby he is soon reduced to a level with the rest." Then comes his description of the ENGLISH, at that same time; those "priest-ridden" English, whom CHALMERS and HUME, and the rest of that tribe, would fain have us believe, were a mere band of wretched beggars. -- "The King of England cannot alter the laws, or make new ones, without the express consent of the whole kingdom in Parliament assembled. Every inhabitant is at his liberty fully to use and enjoy whatever his farm produceth, the fruits of the earth, the increase of his flock, and the like; all the improvement he makes, whether by his own proper industry, or of those he retains in his service, are his own, to use and to enjoy, without the let, interruption or denial of any. If he be in any wise injured, or oppressed, he shall have his amends and satisfactions against the party offending. Hence it is, that the inhabitants are rich in gold, silver, and in all the necessaries and conveniences of life. They drink no water, unless at certain times, upon a religious score, and by way of doing penance. They are fed, in great abundance, with all sorts of flesh and fish, of which they have plenty everywhere; they are clothed throughout in good woollens; their bedding and other furniture in their houses are of wool, and that in great store. They are also well provided with all other sorts of household goods and necessary implements for husbandry. Every one, according to his rank, hath all things which conduce to make life easy and happy."

460. Go, and read this to the poor souls, who are now eating sea-weed in Ireland; who are detected in robbing the pig-troughs in Yorkshire; who are eating horse-flesh and grains (draff) in Lancashire and Cheshire; who are harnessed like horses and drawing gravel in Hampshire and Sussex; who have 3d. a day allowed them by the Magistrates in Norfolk; who are, all over England, worse fed than the felons in the

gaols. Go, and tell them, when they raise their hands from the pig-trough, or from the grains-tub, and, with their dirty tongues, cry "No popery;" go, read to the degraded and deluded wretches, this account of the state of their Catholic forefathers, who lived under what is impudently called "popish superstition and tyranny," and in those times, which we have the audacity to call "the dark ages."

461. Look at the then picture of the French; and, Protestant Englishmen, if you have the capacity of blushing left, blush at the thought of how precisely that picture fits the English now! Look at all the parts of the picture; the food, the raiment, the game! Good God! If any one had told the old Chancellor, that the day would come, when this picture, and even a picture more degrading to human nature, would fit his own boasted country, what would he have said? What would he have said, if he had been told, that the time was to come, when the soldier in England, would have more than twice, nay, more than thrice, the sum allowed to the day-labouring man; when potatoes would be carried to the field as the only food of the ploughman; when soup-shops would be open to feed the English; and when the Judges, sitting on that very bench on which he himself had sitten for twenty years, would (as in the case last year of the complaint against Magistrates at NORTHALLERTON) declare that BREAD AND WATER were the general food of working people in England? What would he have said? Why, if he had been told, that there was to be a "REFORMATION," accompanied by a total devastation of Church and Poor property, upheld by wars, creating an enormous debt and enormous taxes, and requiring a constantly standing army; if he had been told this, he would have foreseen our present state, and would have wept for his country; but, if he had, in addition, been told, that, even in the midst of all this suffering, we should still have the ingratitude and the baseness to cry "No popery," and the injustice and the cruelty to persecute those Englishmen and Irishmen, who adhered to the faith of their pious, moral, brave, free and happy fathers, he would have said, "God's will be done: let them suffer."

462. But, it may be said, that it was not, then, the Catholic Church, but the laws, that made the English so happy; for, the French had that Church as well as the English. Ay! But, in England, the Church was the very basis of the laws. The very first clause of MAGNA CHARTA provided for the stability of its property and rights. A provision for the indigent, an effectual provision, was made by the laws that related to the Church and its property; and this was not the case in France; and never was the case in any country but this: so that the English people lost more by a "Reformation" than any other people could have lost.

463. Fortescue's authority would, of itself, be enough; but, I am not to stop with it. WHITE, the late Rector of SELBOURNE, in Hampshire, gives, in his history of that once famous village, an extract from a record, stating, that, for disorderly conduct, men were punished, by being "compelled to fast a fortnight on bread and beer"! This was about the year 1380, in the reign of RICHARD II. Oh! miserable " dark ages"! This fact must be true. WHITE had no purpose to answer. His mention of the fact, or, rather, his transcript from the record, is purely incidental; and trifling as the fact is, it is conclusive as to the general mode of living in those happy days. Go, tell the harnessed gravel-drawers, in Hampshire, to cry "No popery"; for, that, if the POPE be not put down, he may, in time, compel them to fast on bread and beer, instead of suffering them to continue to regale themselves on nice potatoes and pure water.

464. But, let us come to Acts of Parliament, and, first, to the Act above quoted, in paragraph **454**, which see. That Act fixes the price of meat. After naming the four

sorts of meat, beef, pork, mutton and veal, the preamble has these words: "These being THE FOOD OF THE POORER SORT." This is conclusive. It is an incidental mention of a fact. It is in an Act of Parliament. It must have been true; and, it is a fact that we know well, that even the Judges have declared, from the Bench, that bread alone is now the food of the poorer sort. What do we want more than this to convince us, that the main body of the people have been impoverished by the" Reformation"?

465. But, I will prove, by other Acts of Parliament, this Act of Parliament to have spoken truth. These Acts declare what the wages of workmen shall be, There are several such Acts, but one or two may suffice. The Act of 23rd of EDWARD III. fixes the wages, without food, as follows. There are many other things mentioned, but the following will be enough for our purpose.

	s.	d.
A woman hay-making, or weeding corn, for the day	0	1
A man filling dung-cart	0	3½
A reaper	0	4
Mowing an acre of grass	0	6
Thrashing a quarter of wheat	0	4

the price of shoes, cloth, and of provisions, throughout the time that this law continued in force was as follows

	£	s.	d.
A pair of shoes	0	0	4
Russet broad cloth the yard	0	1	1
A stall-fed ox	1	4	0
A grass-fed ox	0	16	0
A fat sheep unshorn	0	1	8
A fat sheep shorn	0	1	2
A fat hog, two years old	0	3	4
A fat goose	0	0	2
Ale, the gallon, by Proclamation	0	0	1
Wheat, the quarter	0	3	4
White wine, the gallon	0	0	6
Red wine	0	0	4

These prices are taken from the PRECIOSUM of Bishop FLEETWOOD, who took them from the accounts kept by the bursers of convents. All the world knows, that FLEETWOOD's Book is of undoubted authority.

466. We may, then, easily believe, that "beef, pork, mutton and veal," were "the food of the poorer sort," when a dung-cart filler had more than the price of a fat goose and a half for a day's work, and when a woman was allowed, for a day's weeding, the price

of a quart of red wine! Two yards of the cloth made a coat for the shepherd; and, as it cost 2s. 2d., the reaper would earn it in 6½ days; and, the dung-cart man would earn very nearly a pair of shoes every day! This dung-cart filler would earn a fat shorn sheep in four days; he would earn a fat hog, two years old, in twelve days; he would earn a grass-fed ox in twenty days; so that we may easily believe, that "beef, pork, veal and mutton," were "the food of the poorer sort." And, mind, this was "a priest-ridden people"; a people "buried in popish superstition"! In our days of "Protestant light" and of "mental enjoyment" the "poorer sort" are allowed by the Magistrates of Norfolk 3d. a day for a single man able to work. That is to say, a halfpenny less than a Catholic dung-cart man had; and that 3d. will get the "No Popery" gentlemen about six ounces of old ewe mutton, while the popish dung-cart man got, for his day, rather more than the quarter of a fat sheep.

467. But, the popish people might work harder than "enlightened Protestants." They might do more work in a day. This is contrary to all the assertions of the feelosofers; for they insist, that the Catholic religion made people idle. But, to set this matter at rest, let us look at the price of the job-labour; at the mowing by the acre and at the threshing of wheat by the quarter; and let us see how these wages are now, compared with the price of food. I have no parliamentary authority since the year 1821, when a report was printed by order of the House of Commons, containing the evidence of Mr. ELLMAN, of Sussex, as to wages, and of Mr. GEORGE, of Norfolk, as to price of wheat. The report was dated 18th June, 1821 . The accounts are for twenty years, on an average, from 1800 inclusive. We will now proceed to see how the "popish, priest-ridden" Englishman stands in comparison with the "No Popery" Englishman.

	POPISH MAN		NO-POPERY MAN.	
	s.	d.	s.	d.
Mowing an acre of grass	0	6	3	7¾
Threshing a quarter of wheat	0	4	4	0

Here are "waust improvements, Mau'm!" But, now let us look at the relative price of the wheat, which the labourer had to purchase with his wages. We have seen, that the "popish superstition slave" had to give fivepence a bushel for his wheat, and the evidence of Mr. GEORGE states, that the "enlightened Protestant" had to give ten shillings a bushel for his wheat; that is, twenty-four times as much as the "popish fool," who suffered himself to be "priest-ridden." So that the "enlightened" man, in order to make him as well off as the "dark ages" man was, ought to receive twelve shillings, instead of 3s. 7¾d. for mowing an acre of grass; and he, in like manner, ought to receive, for threshing a quarter of wheat, eight shillings, instead of the four shillings which he does receive. If we had the records, we should, doubtless, find, that Ireland was in the same state.

468. There! That settles the matter; and, if the Bible Society and the "Education" and the "Christian-knowledge" gentry would, as they might. cause this little book to be put into the hands of all their millions of pupils, it would, as far as relates to this kingdom, settle the question of religion for ever and ever! I have now proved, that

FORTESCUE's description of the happy life of our Catholic ancestors was correct. There wanted no proof; but I have given it. I could refer to divers other acts of Parliament, passed during several centuries, all confirming the truth of FORTESCUE's account. And there are, in Bishop FLEETWOOD's book, many things that prove that the labouring people were most kindly treated by their superiors, and particularly by the clergy; for instance, he has an item in the expenditure of a convent, "30 pair of autumnal gloves, for the servants." This was sad "superstition." In our "enlightened" and Bible-reading age, who thinks of gloves for the ploughman? We have priests as well as the "dark ages" people had; ours ride as well as theirs; but, theirs fed at the same time; both mount, but theirs seem to have used the rein more, and spur less. It is curious to observe, that the pay of persons in high situations was, as compared with that of the present day, very low when compared with the pay of the working classes. If you calculate the year's pay of the dung-cart man, you will find it, if multiplied by 20 (which brings it to our money), to amount to 91*l.* a year; while the average pay of the JUDGES did not exceed 60*l.* a year of the then money, and, of course, did not exceed 1,200*l.* a year of our money. So that a Judge had not so much pay as fourteen dung-cart fillers. To be sure, Judges had, in those "dark ages," when LITTLETON and FORTESCUE lived and wrote, pretty easy lives; for, FORTESCUE says, that they led lives of great "leisure and contemplation," and that they never sat in court but three hours in a day, from eight to eleven! Alas! if they had lived in this "enlightened age," they would have found little time for their "contemplation"! They would have found plenty of work; they would have found, that theirs was no sinecure, at any rate, and that ten times their pay was not adequate to their enormous labour. Here is another indubitable proof of the great and general happiness and harmony and honesty and innocence that reigned in the country. The Judges had lives of leisure! In that one fact, incidentally stated by a man, who had been twenty years Chief Justice of the King's Bench, we have the true character of the so long calumniated religion of our fathers.

469. As to the bare fact, this most interesting fact, that the main body of the people have been impoverished and degraded since the time of the Catholic sway; as to this fact, there can be no doubt in the mind of any man who has, thus far, read this work. Neither can there, I think, exist, in the mind of such a man, any doubt, that this impoverishment and this degradation have been caused by the event called the "Reformation," seeing that I have, in former Letters, and especially in Letter XIV., clearly traced the debt and the enormous taxes to that event, But, I cannot bring myself to conclude, without tracing the impoverishment in its horrible progress. The well-known fact, that no compulsory collections for the poor, that the disgraceful name of pauper; that these were never heard of in England, in Catholic times; and that they were heard of the moment the "Reformation" had begun; this single fact might be enough, and it is enough; but, we will see the progress of this Protestant impoverishment.

470. The Act, 27 Henry VIII., chap. 25, began the poor laws. The monasteries were not actually seized on till the next year; but, the fabric of the Catholic Church was, in fact, tumbling down; and, instantly the country swarmed with necessitous people, and open begging, which the Government of England had always held in great horror, began to disgrace this so-lately happy land. To put a stop to this, the above Act authorised sheriffs, magistrates and churchwardens to cause voluntary alms to be collected; and, at the same time, it punished the persevering beggar, by slicing off part

of his ears, and, for a second offence, put him to death as a felon! This was the dawn of that "REFORMATION," which we are still called upon to admire and to praise!

471. The "pious young SAINT EDWARD," as Fox, the Martyr-man, most impiously calls him; began his Protestant reign, 1st year Edward VI. chap. 3. by an Act, punishing beggars, by burning with a red-hot iron, and in making them slaves for two years, with power in their masters to make them wear an iron collar, and to feed them upon bread and water and refuse meat! For, even in this case, still there was meat for those who had to labour; the days of cold potatoes and of bread and water alone were yet to come: they were reserved for our "enlightened" and Bible-reading days; our days of "mental enjoyment." And, as to horse-flesh and draff (grains), they appear never to have been even thought of. If the slave ran away, or were disobedient, he was, by this Protestant Act, to be a slave for life. This Act came forth as a sort of precursor of the acts to establish the Church of England! Horrid tyranny! The people had been plundered of the resource, which Magna Charta, which justice, which reason, which the law of nature, gave them, No other resource had been provided; and, they were made actual slaves, branded and chained, because they sought by their prayers to allay the cravings of hunger!

472. Next came "good Queen Bess," who, after trying her hand eight times, without success, to cause the poor to be relieved by alms, passed that compulsory Act, which is in force to the present day. All manner of shifts had been resorted to, in order to avoid this provision fn the poor. During this and the two former reigns, LICENSES TO BEG had been granted. But, at last, the compulsory assessment came, that true mark, that indelible mark, of the Protestant Church as by law established. This assessment was put off to the last possible moment, and it was never relished by those who had got the spoils of the Church and the poor. But, it was a measure of absolute necessity. All the racks, all the law-martial, of this cruel reign could not have kept down the people without this Act, the authors of which seem to have been ashamed to state the grounds of it; for, it has no preamble whatever. The people, so happy in former times; the people described by FORTESCUE, were now become a nation of ragged wretches. DEFOE, in one of his tracts, says that "good Bess," in her progress through the kingdom, upon seeing the miserable looks of the crowds that came to see her, frequently exclaimed, "Pauper ubique jacet;" that is, the poor cover the land. And this was that same country, in which FORTESCUE left a race of people, "having all things which conduce to make life easy and happy"!

473. Things did not mend much during the reigns of the Stuarts, except in as far as the poor-law had effect. This rendered unnecessary the barbarities that had been exercised before the passing of it; and, as long as taxation was light, the paupers were comparatively little numerous. But, when the taxes began to grow heavy, the projectors were soon at work to find out the means of putting down pauperism. Amongst these was one CHILD, a merchant and banker, whose name was JOSIAH, and who had been made a knight or baronet, for he is called Sir JOSIAH. His project, which was quite worthy of his calling, contained a provision, in his proposed Act, to appoint men, to be called, "Fathers of the Poor"; and, one of the provisions relating to these "FATHERS" was to be, "that they may have power to send such poor, as they may think fit, into any of his Majesty's plantations"! That is to say, to transport and make slaves of them! And, gracious God! this was in FORTESCUE's country! This was in the country of Magna Charta! And this monster dared to publish this project! And we cannot learn, that any man had the soul to reprobate the conduct of so hard-hearted a wretch.

474; When the "deliverer" had come, when a "glorious revolution" had taken place, when a war had been carried on and a debt and a bank created, and all for the purpose of putting down Popery for ever, the poor began to increase at such a frightful rate, that the Parliament referred the subject to the Board of Trade, to inquire, and to report a remedy. LOCKE was one of the Commissioners, and a passage in the Report of the Board is truly curious. "The multiplicity of the poor, and the increase of the tax for their maintenance, is so general an observation and complaint, that it cannot be doubted of; nor has it been only since the last war that this evil has come upon us, it has been a growing burden on the kingdom this many years, and the last two reigns felt the increase of it as well as the present. if the causes of this evil be looked into, we humbly conceive it will be found to have proceeded, not from the scarcity of provisions, nor want of employment for the poor; since the goodness of God has blessed these times with plenty no less than the former; and a long peace, during three reigns, gave us as plentiful a trade as ever. The growth of the poor must therefore have some other cause; and it can be nothing else but the relaxation of discipline and corruption; virtue and industry being as constant companions on the one side, as vice and idleness are on the other."

475. So, the fault was in the poor themselves! it does not seem to have occurred to Mr. LOCKE that there must have been a cause for this cause. He knew very well, that there was a time, when there were no paupers at all in England; but, being a fat place-man under the "deliverer," he could hardly think of alluding to that interesting fact. "Relaxation of discipline"! What discipline? What did he mean by discipline? The taking away of the Church and Poor's property, the imposing of heavy taxes, the giving of low wages compared with the price of food and raiment, the drawing away of the earnings of the poor to be given to paper-harpies and other tax-eaters; these were the causes of the hideous and disgraceful evil! this he knew very well, and, therefore, it is no wonder, that his report contained no remedy.

476. After LOCKE, came, in the reign of QUEEN ANNE, DEFOE, who seems to have been the father of the present race of projectors, MALTHUS and LAWYER SCARLET being merely his humble followers. He was for giving no more relief to the poor; he imputed their poverty to their crimes, and not their crimes to their poverty; and their crimes, he imputed to "their luxury, pride and sloth." he said the English labouring people ate and drank three times as much as any foreigners! How different were the notions of this insolent French Protestant from those of the Chancellor FORTESCUE, who looked upon the good living of the people as the best possible proof of good laws, and seems to have delighted in relating that the English were "fed, in great abundance, with all sorts of flesh and fish"!

477. If DEFOE had lived to our "enlightened age," he would, at any rate, have seen "no luxury" amongst the poor, unless he would have grudged them horse-flesh, draff (grains), sea-weed, or the contents of the pig-trough. From his day to the present, there have been a hundred projects, and more than fifty laws, to regulate the affairs of the poor. But still the pauperism remains for the Catholic Church to hold up in the face of the Church of England. "Here," the former may say to the latter, "here, look at this: here is the result of your efforts to extinguish me; here, in this one evil, in this never-ceasing, this degrading curse, I am more than avenged, if vengeance I were allowed to enjoy: urge on the deluded potato-crammed creatures to cry 'No Popery' still, and, when they retire to their straw, take care not to remind them of the cause of their poverty and degradation."

478. HUME, in speaking of the sufferings of the people, in the first Protestant reign, says, that, at last, those sufferings "produced good," for that they "led to our present situation." What, then, be deemed our present situation a better one than that of the days of FORTESCUE! To be sure, HUME wrote fifty years ago; but he wrote long after CHILD, LOCKE, and DEFOE. Surely enough the "Reformation" has led to "our then present and now present situation." it has "at last," produced the bitter fruit of which we are now tasting. Evidence, given, by a Clergyman, too, and published by the House of Commons, in 1824, states the labouring people of Suffolk to be a nest of robbers, too deeply corrupted ever to be reclaimed; evidence of a Sheriff of Wiltshire (in 1821) states the common food of the labourers, in the field, to be cold potatoes; a scale, published by the Magistrates of Norfolk, in 1825, allows 3d . a day to a single labouring man; the Judges of the Court of King's Bench (1825) have declared the general food of the labouring people to be bread and water; intelligence from the northern counties (1826), published upon the spot, informs us, that great numbers of people are nearly starving, and that some are eating horse-flesh and grains while it is well known that the country abounds in food, and while the Clergy have recently put up, from the pulpit, the rubrical thanksgiving for times of plenty; a law recently passed, making it felony to take an apple from a tree, tells the world that our characters and lives are thought nothing worth, or that this nation, once the greatest and most moral in the world, is now a nation of incorrigible thieves; and, in either case, the most impoverished, the most fallen, the most degraded that ever saw the light of the sun.

479. I have now performed my task. I have made good the positions with which I began. Born and bred a Protestant of the Church of England, having a wife and numerous family professing the same faith, having the mains of most dearly beloved parents lying in a Protestant church-yard, and trusting to conjugal or filial piety to place mine by their side, I have, in this undertaking, had no motive, I can have had no motive, but a sincere and disinterested love of truth and justice. It is not for the rich and the powerful of my countrymen that I have spoken; but for the poor, the persecuted, the proscribed. I have not been unmindful of the unpopularity and the prejudice that would attend the enterprise; but, when I considered the long, long triumph of calumny over the religion of those, to whom we owe all that we possess that is great and renowned; when I was convinced that I could do much towards the counteracting of that calumny; when duty so sacred bade me speak, it would have been baseness to hold my tongue, and baseness superlative would it have been, if, having the will as well as the power, I had been restrained by fear of the shafts of falsehood and of folly. To be clear of self-reproach is amongst the greatest of human consolations; and now, amidst all the dreadful perils, with which the event that I have treated of has, at last, surrounded my country, I can, while I pray God to save her from still further devastation and misery, safely say, that, neither expressly nor tacitly, am I guilty of any part of the cause of her ruin.

THE END.

INDEX

[The References apply to the paragraphs, and not to the pages of this work.]

$

GLOSSARY
Of obsolete words, or words used in an obsolete sense

Corrody	A free allowance of meals or food, provided by a monastery to various dependants, or the clients of benefactors.
Swaddler	A Protestant
Impropriated	Of tithes: assigned to some person or body other than the parish clergy.
Bridewell	A prison
Score	Twenty pounds weight
Draff	Spent grains from brewing, used as cheap animal food